THE PSYCHOLOGY OF LEARNING AND MOTIVATION

Advances in Research and Theory

VOLUME 45

THE PSYCHOLOGY OF LEARNING AND MOTIVATION

Advances in Research and Theory

EDITED BY BRIAN H. ROSS

BECKMAN INSTITUTE AND
DEPARTMENT OF PSYCHOLOGY
UNIVERSITY OF ILLINOIS AT URBANA-CHAMPAIGN
URBANA, ILLINOIS

Volume 45

ELSEVIER
ACADEMIC PRESS

AMSTERDAM • BOSTON • HEIDELBERG • LONDON
NEW YORK • OXFORD • PARIS • SAN DIEGO
SAN FRANCISCO • SINGAPORE • SYDNEY • TOKYO

Elsevier Academic Press
525 B Street, Suite 1900, San Diego, California 92101-4495, USA
84 Theobald's Road, London WC1X 8RR, UK

This book is printed on acid-free paper. ♾

For all information on all Academic Press publications visit our Web site at www.academicpress.com

ISBN: 0-12543345-X

PRINTED IN THE UNITED STATES OF AMERICA
04 05 06 07 08 9 8 7 6 5 4 3 2 1

CONTENTS

AGING, METACOGNITION, AND COGNITIVE CONTROL

Christopher Hertzog and John Dunlosky

THE PSYCHOPHARMACOLOGY OF MEMORY AND COGNITION: PROMISES, PITFALLS, AND A METHODOLOGICAL FRAMEWORK

Elliot Hirshman

CONTRIBUTORS

Numbers in parentheses indicate the pages on which the authors' contributions begin.

Rick Dale (87), Department of Psychology, Cornell University, Ithaca, New York 14853

Peter Dixon (143), Department of Psychology, University of Alberta, Edmonton, Alberta, Canada T6G 2E9

John Dunlosky (215), Department of Psychology, University of North Carolina, Greensboro, North Carolina 27402

Scott Glover (143), Department of Psychology, Royal Holloway University of London, Egham, Surrey TW20 0EX, United Kingdom

Christopher Hertzog (215), School of Psychology, Georgia Institute of Technology, Atlanta, Georgia 30332-0170

Elliot Hirshman (253), Department of Psychology, George Washington University, Washington D.C. 20052

Jeffrey P. Lozito (175), Department of Psychology, University of North Carolina, Chapel Hill, North Carolina 27599-3270

Ken McRae (41), Department of Psychology, Social Science Centre, University of Western Ontario, London, Ontario, Canada N6A 5C2

Neil W. Mulligan (175), Department of Psychology, University of North Carolina, Chapel Hill, North Carolina 27599-3270

Michael J. Spivey (87), Department of Psychology, Cornell University, Ithaca, New York 14853

Gert Storms (1), Department of Psychology, University of Leuven, B-3000 Leuven, Belgium

EXEMPLAR MODELS IN THE STUDY OF NATURAL LANGUAGE CONCEPTS

Gert Storms

I. Introduction

Exemplar models have played a prominent role in the category learning literature. Despite this prominence in learning, the exemplar view has been virtually absent in studies of the representation of semantic concepts. In this chapter, I will address why this absence has occurred and outline some research at the University of Leuven that rectifies it. In particular, I elaborate on the major difficulties regarding the application of exemplar models in the context of natural language concepts. I will then continue with an overview of studies that concentrated on structural aspects regarding separability of concepts and within-category structure (i.e., typicality), and on categorization decisions in the context of natural language concepts.

Most psychologists who studied concepts before the 1970s explicitly or implicitly assumed that concepts are mentally represented in terms of definitions. More particularly, they assumed that concepts were defined by singly necessary and jointly sufficient features, much like mathematical concepts, such as triangles or squares, are defined (see, e.g., Hull, 1920; Smoke, 1932). Empirical work in the 1950s and 1960s aimed at studying how people learn such well-defined concepts (e.g., Bruner, Goodnow, & Austin, 1956). However, though the motivation for the research in this area clearly came from natural concepts (e.g., Bruner, 1957), the vast majority of the experiments conducted at the time used artificial categories, like Chinese characters (e.g., Hull, 1920), geometric figures (e.g., Shepard, Hovland, & Jenkins, 1961), and nonword letter combinations (Attneave, 1957). At least part of the reason

0079-7421/04 $35.00

why researchers were driven back on the use of artificial categories was the difficulty in identifying the underlying defining features of natural concepts (see Rosch & Mervis, 1975).

Two publications in the 1970s that later became classics broke with the traditional conceptions of semantic concepts. First, Reed (1972) conducted a series of experiments in which participants were asked to make classifications in situations where categories were defined by sets of exemplars, not by logical rules. He fitted 18 different models, each rigorously mathematically formulated, to the data, and found that a prototype model, based on feature weights that maximally clustered stimuli within a category, explained the data best. Thus, the structure of the categories to be learned differed fundamentally from categories used in previous studies in this area. However, in line with the older studies, Reed also used artificial categories (i.e., schematic faces with four-dimensional features). He motivated the use of such artificial categories by stating that, for natural concepts, "it is often difficult to specify the critical features" (Reed, 1972, p. 383).

The second study was Rosch and Mervis' (1975) seminal paper on family resemblance as the basis of the internal structure of categories. Unlike Reed, Rosch and Mervis studied natural language concepts, like "fruit," "furniture," and "car." In their paper, the focus of attention was not categorization but typicality, that is, a measure of goodness-of-example. They selected a representative set of exemplars of the categories at study. Then, a first group of participants rated the typicality of these exemplars within the category, and a different group of participants was asked to generate features of each of the exemplars. Next, two judges reviewed all pairwise combinations of the exemplars and the generated features (regardless of the exemplar for which the feature was generated) and indicated whether or not the feature was applicable to the exemplar. Using a fully specified formal model, Rosch and Mervis found that the more features an item had in common with other exemplars of the category, the more typical the item was for the category. They also found that the more features an item had in common with exemplars from contrast categories, the less typical the item was for the category.

For the topic of this paper, it is important to look somewhat more closely at the studies of Reed (1972) and Rosch and Mervis (1975). Both studies deviate from the earlier experiments on categorization in that the categories studied were not designed according to simple rules or definitions. In both studies, formal models were used as predictions for category structure: Reed predicted between-category structure by way of categorization decisions, whereas Rosch and Mervis predicted within-category structure by means of typicality ratings. But while Reed used artificial categories with a fixed and limited set of features, Rosch and Mervis studied everyday lexicalized semantic concepts. This difference is important, because both studies can be viewed, in a way, as starting points for two different traditions in the study of categorization.

II. Category Learning Experiments with Artificial Stimuli

The study of Reed (1972) marked the beginning of category learning experiments with artificial categories that are not necessarily structured in a simple way. Category learning experiments with categories that are carefully constructed along a clear set of crucial features allow researchers to differentiate between alternative explanations for the learning process. In such experiments, a wide variety of stimuli has been used, ranging from very abstract stimuli, where a limited set of salient features can be manipulated (e.g., geometrical figures, as in Medin & Schaffer, 1978, or dot patterns, as in Knowlton & Squire, 1993), to categories that were designed to mimic natural categories (e.g., types of teapots, as in Lamberts, 1998, or diseases, as in Ross, 1997).

Many authors who used the latter kind of categories have argued that findings from studies with that type of stimuli can be generalized to natural categories more easily than findings from categorization experiments with the more abstract type of stimuli (Markman & Ross, 2003). Although this is undoubtedly true, others have stressed the differences between category learning experiments per se (regardless of the sort of stimuli used) and the circumstances in which most natural language concepts are acquired. For instance, Malt and Smith (1984) have pointed out that participants in category learning tasks are instructed to encode exemplars in detail in an explicit learning phase, whereas natural language concepts are most often learned erratically and from many different sources.

One important kind of research in the category learning tradition followed up on Reed (1972) in further developing formal models for the prediction of categorization. A particularly influential line of modeling started with Medin and Schaffer's (1978) Context Model. The model states that, in deciding how to categorize a presented stimulus *X*, people do not compare the similarity of *X* to abstract summary representations of the different possible categories. Instead, it is assumed that *X* is compared to memory traces of previously encountered exemplars of the different possible categories. Crucial to the model is that similarity is not evaluated in an additive way, but that information about feature matches and mismatches is combined by multiplication. The model was designed to account for categorization of stimuli with dichotomous feature values (e.g., geometric stimuli that were triangular or square, blue or red, etc.), but it was later adapted to handle dimensional features (e.g., semicircles that vary in size and in angle of orientation of a radial line; Nosofsky, 1985). The continuous dimensions version of the model, developed by Nosofsky (1984, 1986) is called the Generalized Context Model. (Note that the dimensional version is broader in scope and that dichotomous features can be considered special cases where only two values on a particular dimension occur.) Later, a connectionist version of the model was developed by Kruschke (1992). The different models in this tradition are known in the literature as exemplar models.

In the 1980s and 1990s, many studies were published to compare predictions of the original and the generalized version of the context model with formal versions of prototype models (e.g., Medin & Smith, 1984; Nosofsky, 1992; Smith & Minda, 1998), boundary models (e.g., Ashby & Gott, 1989; Nosofsky, Palmeri, & McKinley, 1994), and rule-based models (e.g., Johansen & Palmeri, 2002; Nosofsky, Palmeri, & McKinley, 1994). Furthermore, even though categorization was the dominant dependent variable in these studies, typicality *within* a category has also been investigated and can also be accounted for by the exemplar models, by prototype models, and by boundary models (e.g., Nosofsky, 1986; Smith, 2002). In the majority of the comparison studies, exemplar models were shown to outperform prototype models (e.g., Nosofsky, 1992) and boundary models (e.g., Verguts, Storms, & Tuerlinckx, 2003).

III. Studies of Natural Language Concepts

The study of Rosch and Mervis (1975) was the start of a second line of modeling research, but unlike the studies previously described, this second tradition focused on well-known natural language concepts, such as "*birds*" and "*chairs*."[1] Since such concepts refer to a homogeneous set of stimuli in the real world, it is difficult to manipulate the stimuli, and therefore most of the formal studies on natural language concepts used correlational techniques and concentrated on within-category structure of natural language concepts rather than on categorization decisions (e.g., Hampton, 1979; Malt & Smith, 1984).

Strange enough, despite the success of exemplar models in the category learning literature, prototype-like models have been dominating the formal approaches in the semantic concept literature (Hampton, 1979, 1993; Rosch

[1] Note, however, that Rosch verified her family resemblance theory in experimental studies, using several kinds of artificial categories, namely, letter strings, dot pattern, and stick figures (Rosch & Mervis, 1975; Rosch, Simpson, & Miller, 1976).

& Mervis, 1975), and attempts to implement ideas of the exemplar view have been rare (Heit & Barsalou, 1996; Storms, De Boeck, & Ruts, 2000, 2001).

IV. Two Stumbling Blocks in Applying Exemplar Models to Natural Language Concepts

Applying the ideas expressed by advocates of the exemplar view in the study of natural language concepts is not straightforward (Murphy, 2002). Several authors have pointed at two different problems. The first problem concerns what exactly an exemplar is. The second problem is how to determine the underlying features that guide categorization and other category-related decisions.

A. What Is an Exemplar?

What exactly does the notion "exemplar" mean in the context of natural language concepts? For instance, when studying a category like "vehicles," what are the stored exemplars of this category? Different variants of the exemplar view have been presented in the literature, depending on the assumptions made about the number and nature of the instances stored, about the presence or absence of forgetting, and so on (Barsalou, 1990). At one extreme, exemplar representations may involve no abstraction at all, with representations consisting only of specific memory traces of particular previously encountered instances (e.g., Reed, 1972). At the other extreme, an exemplar representation might be a family resemblance representation that abstracts across different specific instances (Komatsu, 1992). A position in between was proposed by Rosch (1975), assuming that only the most prototypical instances are stored. (Note, however, that this presupposes a mechanism that is able to evaluate the prototypicality of exemplars.)

In the context of category learning experiments with artificial categories, exemplars have usually been equated with presented stimuli during the experimental procedure, and the only question that needed to be solved is whether frequently presented exemplars count as single or multiple exemplars. In other words, are stimuli in an experiment to be treated as types or as tokens? Nosofsky (1988) answered this question in an experiment in which the frequency of presented exemplars was manipulated. Predictions of typicality ratings of a model that viewed every single encounter of the same stimulus as a separate exemplar fitted the data better than predictions of a model that treated the different encounters as the same exemplar. These results suggest that an exemplar is not an actual thing, but rather the encounter with a thing. A similar position has been defended by Barsalou, Huttenlocher, and Lamberts (1998).

Despite these findings, one can doubt whether a theory that assumes no abstraction at all has ever been tested in any of the laboratory studies. In designing these experiments, researchers assume that the representation of the presented stimuli consists of the dimensions that they manipulate (e.g., color, form, size, and position of the stimulus). However, if participants do not abstract these dimensions from other information that may in principle be stored (e.g., the trial number and slight differences in illumination due to uncontrollable events), they might not be able to learn the categories. In this sense, each training exemplar is a sort of a prototype consisting of a set of abstracted features that, in principle, can apply also to other exemplars that differ on some other, irrelevant, features (D. L. Medin, personal communication, May 19, 1997).

There is a second reason to question the assumption that exemplars are simply to be equated to stored memory traces of previous encounters. This question relates to which of all the encountered exemplars are stored and which are activated in category-related decisions. It is intuitively hard to believe that people activate all exemplars of, for instance, "car," every time when they categorize something as a car. We can safely assume that an average adult, who lives in an urbanized area, has encountered thousands of exemplars of cars, if not millions, when counting different experiences involving the same car as different exemplars.

Given the two previously described considerations, it is not clear how to understand the notion of an exemplar in the context of natural language concepts such as "fruit" or "vehicles." Is the notion of an apple an exemplar of the category "fruit?" Or is the notion of a red delicious apple an exemplar? Or is the specific red delicious apple that I bought this morning an exemplar? And when I pick up that same apple tonight to eat it, is that the same or another memory trace that counts as an exemplar?

B. What Are the Relevant Features?

The second problem in applying the ideas of the exemplar view in the study of natural language concepts is how to determine the underlying features that guide categorization and other category-related decisions. As previously explained, in the context of category learning experiments, a limited number of very salient features are manipulated, and it is usually immediately obvious to the participants which features they need to (or are expected to) pay attention to. In the context of natural language concepts, the relevant underlying features are usually not clear, to say the least.

Different procedures have been suggested to derive the relevant features of these concepts. Hampton (1979) interviewed 32 undergraduate students extensively. In a first part of the interview, participants gave free descriptions of the concepts that were studied, and in the second part, Hampton encouraged the participants further to generate as many features as possible by using standard questions. (For instance, he asked why some items only "loosely speaking" belong to the category at study, or why a certain item might be considered a very typical item of the category.) Features that were generated by a minimum percentage of the participants were selected as relevant features. Rosch and Mervis (1975) used a different procedure, in which participants were asked to generate "characteristics and attributes that people feel are common to and characteristic of a series of objects." Every participant generated attributes of one single instantiation of each of the categories that were studied. All attributes generated by the participants (who were given one and a half minute per word) were considered relevant (to a varying degree) for the concept. Thus, the two procedures differ in that Hampton gathered features with the concept name as the stimulus, whereas Rosch and Mervis gathered features with the concept exemplars as the stimuli.

It is important to note, however, that these two procedures have only been used to derive prototype information. They were not applied in the context of exemplar models in any way. In the next section, we will describe similar, but also very different, procedures, which we used in the past few years to apply ideas of the exemplar view in the study of natural language concepts.

V. Attempts to Apply Ideas of the Exemplar View to Natural Language Concepts: Linear Separability, Typicality, and Categorizing Novel Stimuli

As mentioned previously, in the 1980s and 1990s, many studies compared prototype and exemplar models in the context of artificial category-learning experiments. Though most of the results were in favor of exemplar models (e.g., Nosofsky, 1992), some authors questioned the generality of this conclusion (e.g., Blair & Homa, 2001; Minda & Smith, 2001; Smith & Minda, 1998, 2000, 2002). Most remarkable, though, is the virtual absence of exemplar models in the study of natural language concepts. In the past decade, a few such studies have been published. I will describe three different kinds of studies next. First, I will elaborate on tests of the linear separability of natural language concepts. Though a test of linear separability cannot directly produce support or disconfirming evidence for the exemplar view, it can provide indirect evidence against or in favor of particular formal models of category representation, and thus this test can yield evidence in favor of or against particular versions of prototype and exemplar models. Second, I will describe studies where principles of exemplar models have been used to predict intracategorical structure, as measured in typicality ratings and in response times from speeded categorization tasks. Finally, I will describe some studies where prototype and exemplar models have been contrasted in explaining categorization decisions in the context of natural language concepts.

A. Linear Separability

Categorizing stimuli on the basis of similarity to prototypes can be conceived as the summing of evidence (e.g., matching characteristic features) against some criterion. Stimuli are accepted as members of a category if the summed evidence exceeds the criterion; otherwise, they are rejected (Medin & Schwanenflugel, 1981). Categories defined in this way fulfill the constraint of linear separability (Sebestyen, 1962). For a category in isolation, this means that a linear function of attributes must exist that perfectly separates members from nonmembers. Similarly, for any pair of categories within a given domain, there should be a linear function, defined over the set of attributes for the domain, which perfectly separates the two categories. In the case of vague category boundaries, as are commonly found in many natural concepts, then the linear separability constraint simply implies that there exists a linear function of attributes that has a monotonic relation with the relative degree of category membership in each class. Gardenfors (2000) has indeed proposed that a criterion for defining a natural property is that it should form a convex region of a domain in a conceptual space, thus obeying this constraint.

Prototype models are not the only models that incorporate the assumption of linear category separability. Related models, such as the additive-similarity exemplar model (Nosofsky, 1992), the average distance model (Reed, 1972), versions of cue validity and frequency models (Medin & Schaffer, 1978), and some versions of Ashby's decision-boundary model (Ashby & Maddox, 1992), also make the same assumption. The term *independent cue models* refers to a collection of models that all obey linear separability (Franks & Bransford, 1971; Hayes-Roth & Hayes-Roth, 1977). Most exemplar models, such as Medin and Schaffer's (1978) context model or Nosofsky's (1984, 1986) generalized version of that model, do not assume that linear separability constrains category representation. These models are called *relational coding models*. Consequently, finding out whether linear separability constrains natural categories can shed light on the advantages of independent cue models versus multiplicative-similarity exemplar models. If natural categories do *not* obey the constraint of linear separability, then one would have good reason to prefer relational coding models, like Nosofsky's generalized context model, over independent cue models, like most prototype models.

Because linear separability is such an important constraint in formal models of categorization, different studies have investigated linear separability in artificial category-learning experiments. Most of these studies failed to find evidence that linearly separable categories can be learned more rapidly than categories that are not linearly separable (Medin & Schaffer, 1978; Medin & Schwanenflugel, 1981; Wattenmaker, Dewey, Murphy, & Medin, 1986). Recently, however, Smith, Murray, and Minda (1997) and Blair and Homa (2001) reported results in favor of independent cue models when using better differentiated categories with many exemplars and in experiments where participants had to classify stimuli into multiple categories. In conclusion, the results from category learning experiments in which linear separability has been manipulated do not unanimously favor nor argue against independent cue models.

It is surprising how little attention has been paid to the question of whether natural language concepts are themselves linearly separable. The lack of attention is most likely related to the difficulties associated with the selection of the attributes that need to be taken into account when evaluating linear separability in this context. Recently, we investigated linear separability in natural language concepts, both at the superordinate and at the basic level, using multidimensional scaling (MDS; Borg & Groenen, 1997) to derive the underlying features that determine similarity.

1. *Linear Separability in Superordinate-Level Concepts*

In a first study, Ruts, Storms, and Hampton (2004) investigated superordinate natural language concept pairs. Thirteen semantically related contrast pairs of superordinate concepts were studied: eight pairs of natural kinds (insects–fish, insects–birds, insects–mammals, fish–birds, fish–mammals, birds–mammals, trees–flowers, and fruits–vegetables) and five pairs of artifacts (toiletry–sewing gear, kitchen utensils–tableware, cleaning utensils–gardening utensils, vehicles–construction machines, and clothing–accessories).

In a first task, exemplars of all the studied concepts were generated by one group of participants, and (following the procedure of Hampton, 1979, previously described) features were generated by a different group of participants. Note that to provide a strong test of linear separability, it was important to have as complete a sample of category members as possible for each category. Therefore, all exemplars that were generated (regardless of their generation frequency) were included in the linear separability study. All features that were generated by at least 20% of the participants from the feature generation study were selected to calculate pairwise similarities. After removing duplicates (i.e., exemplars and features that were selected for both concepts within a contrast pair), this procedure resulted in sets of 48–85 exemplars and 20–51 features per pair of concepts. Next, participants in a matrix filling task were given a matrix where the rows were labeled with all exemplars of a superordinate concept pair, and where the columns were labeled with the features of the same concept pair. Participants were asked to fill out all entries in the matrix with a 1 or a 0 to indicate whether a feature was considered present in the exemplar corresponding to the row of the entry.

Matrices were summed over participants, resulting in a single exemplar-by-feature matrix for every concept pair. The entries of these matrices are frequencies, corresponding to the number of participants that judged the corresponding feature (column) applicable to the corresponding exemplar (row). The row vectors of feature applicabilities of every exemplar within the concept pair were then pairwise correlated, resulting in an intercorrelation matrix between all possible pairs of exemplars.

Next, geometric configurations of the exemplar sets were obtained using nonmetric MDS, with solutions in two to five dimensions for every concept pair. To evaluate linear separability of the concepts in each pair, a logistic regression procedure was used as follows. First, exemplars were allocated to the category for which they were generated most frequently. The resulting dichotomous variable was used as the criterion variable, and the exemplar coordinates from the MDS solutions functioned as predictors in four separate regressions, corresponding to the MDS solutions with two to five dimensions.

To give an idea of how linear separability can be evaluated based on MDS coordinates, Fig. 1 shows, for the toiletry–sewing gear concept pair, the plotted MDS solution in two dimensions. The solid line, which draws the optimal boundary provided by the logistic regression, divides the group in two categories. The procedure is analogous, but not easily shown in a figure, for solutions in three, four, and five dimensions.

For all pairs of natural kinds, except for fruits–vegetables, category membership could be perfectly predicted in every dimensionality. Fruits were only linearly distinguishable from vegetables in five dimensions. Remarkably, though, none of the artifact categories showed perfect linear separability in any dimensionality up to five. (Note that it doesn't make much sense to investigate higher levels of dimensionality, mainly because of concerns about the reliability of the representations and the increased risk of overfitting the data.)

In a follow-up experiment, using the same general procedure, Ruts, Storms, and Hampton (2004) used another criterion to distinguish the

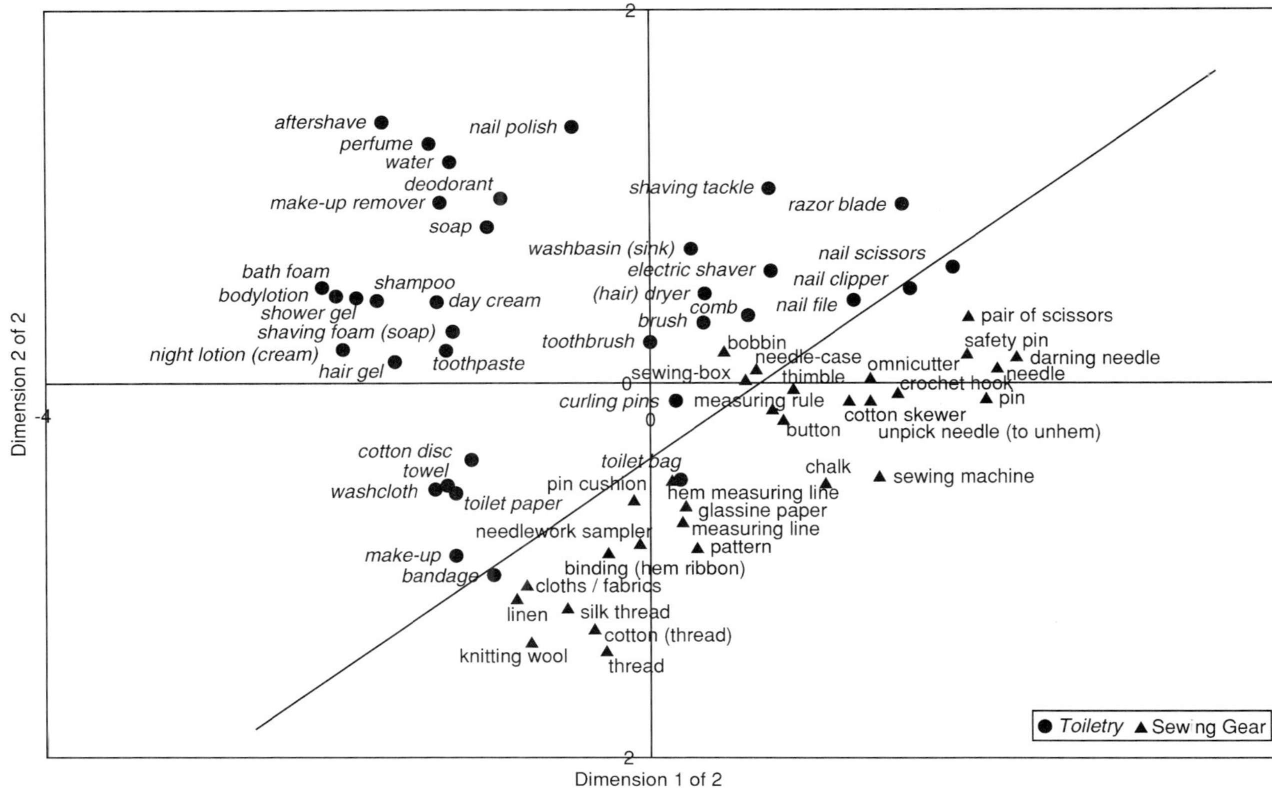

Fig. 1. MDS representation of a two-dimensional solution for the contrast pair "toiletry–sewing gear." The solid line draws the optimal boundary provided by the logistic regression. *Note*. From "Linear Separability in Superordinate Natural Language Concepts," by W. Ruts, G. Storms, and J. A. Hampton, 2004, *Memory & Cognition*. Copyright 2004 by the Psychonomic Society. Reprinted with permission.

exemplars of both categories of a pair. They asked a group of participants to categorize the complete list of exemplars over the two categories of the concept pair. Analyses were carried out for the categorizations of individual subjects and also for categorizations based on the most frequently given classification over subjects. The results of the log linear analysis yielded the same picture as previously described. Again, all "natural kind" concept pairs were perfectly linearly separable, usually even in only two dimensions, whereas "artifact" concept pairs showed several violations, even in up to five dimensions.

In conclusion, Ruts, Storms, and Hampton (2004) showed that the linearly separable pairs of natural kinds are compatible with independent cue models, like most versions of the prototype model. However, the violations in the artifact pairs yield clear evidence against the independent cue models in this semantic domain.

2. *Linear Separability in Basic-Level Concepts*

Recently, Ruts, Van Assche, Storms and Hampton (in preparation) focused on linear separability in basic level concepts. Unlike in superordinate level concepts, basic level concepts cannot be studied by presenting participants with verbal labels of exemplars and then asking to categorize the labels in a set of contrasting basic-level concepts, since many exemplars at that level of abstraction do not have an individualized lexical label.

A different methodology to achieve the same goal is presenting stimuli pictorially. This procedure was earlier used in Malt, Sloman, Gennari, Shi, and Wang (1999), where artifact concepts (like "can," "bottle," "jar," etc.) were studied in different languages. Malt et al. pursued a different goal in their study, but some of their findings are relevant for the linear separability question. Malt et al. used MDS to represent a large and diverse set of containers in a two-dimensional space. The similarities that were used as input were the number of participants in a sorting task who sorted a particular pair of items in the same pile. Malt et al. found that pictured stimuli that were labeled with the same word showed several violations of linear separability in each of the languages they studied. In a second data set, consisting of different kinds of dishes (labeled "plates," "bowls," etc.), the same pattern of clear violations of linear separability was found.

Malt et al.'s conclusions regarding violations of linear separability can be criticized because they only investigated solutions in two dimensions. It is conceivable, though, that a set of stimuli that show clear violations against linear separability in two dimensions are perfectly linearly separable in three or more dimensions. Therefore, further exploration of the issue was called for.

Ruts, Van Assche, Storms, and Hampton (in preparation) investigated linear separability in three different data sets that were gathered independently and for different purposes. First, they reanalyzed the data of Malt et al. (1999), using the modal labeling for each of the stimuli in the bottles and in the dishes set as criterion, and stimulus coordinates in two to five dimensional representations as predictor variables. Only stimuli that were categorized in the three most frequently named categories (e.g., "bowl," "dish," and "plate," for the "dishes" set) were entered in the analyses, and regressions were done for all possible pairs of categories in each of the two stimulus sets. In both sets, and in all dimensionalities, clear violations of linear separability were observed.

It is possible that the earlier described violations are the result of aggregating over subjects. For the data of Malt et al. (1999), however, separate data per individual participant were no longer available. Since more details were available from two different studies that followed up on Malt et al., the results of these studies were analyzed, again using the same procedure.

Ameel, Storms, Malt, and Sloman (2003) replicated Malt et al.'s (1999) study with three sorts of participants: Belgian Flemish monolinguals, Belgian French monolinguals, and Belgian Flemish–French bilinguals. As in Malt et al., two stimulus sets were studied (i.e., "bottles" and "dishes"), but the pictures used were different. Ameel et al.'s main goal was to compare naming patterns in the bilinguals to naming in both monolingual groups, but Ruts et al. (in preparation) investigated their data for linear separability. In the three language groups, and in both stimulus sets, severe violations against linear separability were observed, in two through five dimensions.

Using the same paradigm, Hampton and Kahnam (2003) investigated naming in English and Bengali. They used a bottle and a dish picture set as stimuli. Ruts et al. (preparation) showed that the items that were labeled with the same word were again not linearly separable in two to five dimensions.

In conclusion, the results of these studies show clearly that natural concepts in the artifact domain are not linearly separable at the superordinate level, nor at the basic level. In contrast, superordinate-level natural kind concepts do obey the requirements for linear separability, mostly even in as few as two dimensions. Whether this is also the case for basic level natural kind concepts is an empirical question that has not yet been answered. Though these latter findings do not necessarily favor representations in line of neither exemplar nor prototype models, the violations of linear separability in the artifact domain can be considered direct evidence against the classical (i.e., pure additive similarity) prototype representation for artifact concepts in semantic memory.

B. Within-Category Structure: Typicality

As described earlier, typicality in natural language concepts was explained by Rosch and Mervis (1975) in terms of family resemblance. Hampton (1979) predicted typicality by a different prototype-based measure, which he called a "polymorphous concept predictor." More particularly, participants were asked to generate features of the concepts that were studied. All features that were generated by at least one out of four participants were selected for calculation of the prototype predictor. Later, different participants evaluated the applicability of each of these characteristic features for a representative sample of exemplars that varied widely in typicality. Typicality predictors were calculated by summing over the different features, the number of participants that credited the item with the corresponding feature. Hampton reported correlations ranging from .61 to .78 between the prototype predictors and the typicality ratings in the eight different concepts that he studied. Thus, while Rosch and Mervis (1975) gathered features of the instances of a concept, Hampton elicited features of the concept itself. Both procedures, though, turn out to yield very similar results for the concepts studied by Hampton.

In sharp contrast with prototype predictors as previously described, the ideas expressed in the exemplar view have seldom been related to typicality ratings in natural language concepts. One rare exception is Heit and Barsalou's (1996) instantiation principle, which I will explain in detail. I will continue with follow-up studies on Heit and Barsalou's introduction of the model.

1. Heit and Barsalou's (1996) Instantiation Principle

Though the instantiation principle, presented and tested in the context of typicalities in Heit and Barsalou (1996), can be implemented in a wide class of models, including some abstraction models, the principle fits nicely with the exemplar view and is not compatible with the standard prototype view, nor with the classical view.

Heit and Barsalou assume that people generate instantiations of a category on which to base category-related decisions. More specifically, according to Heit and Barsalou's model, people judge typicality of a subordinate in a superordinate by performing three steps. First, a single instantiation of the subordinate category is retrieved (e.g., *cow* is retrieved to instantiate "mammal"). Second, the instantiation's typicality in the superordinate is evaluated (e.g., the typicality of *cow* in "animal" is judged on a nine-point rating scale, ranging from 1 for very atypical to 9 for very typical). Let us assume that *cow* gets a score of 7 on the typicality scale. Finally, the instantiation's typicality is generalized to the subordinate (e.g., the typicality of *mammal* in "animal" is rated as 7). The only information the model uses to predict performance is a distribution of instantiations of the subordinate (i.e., the frequency distribution over subjects of the first instantiation that is activated given the category label) and the typicalities of these instantiations in the superordinate.

Described formally, the model amounts to

$$P(T(A) = j) = \sum_{i=1}^{n} P(A \text{ is instantiated as } a_i)\, P(T(a_i) = j),$$

where $T(x)$ is the typicality of x within the superordinate category, A is a subordinate category, a_i is an instantiation of A, n is the number of different instantiations of A (that are retrieved as first instantiations given the category label A), and j is an integer on a predefined rating scale. With this model, the distribution of typicality ratings for subordinate categories (e.g., "mammals") within a superordinate category (e.g., "animals") can be simulated using production frequencies of first instantiations of the subordinate categories (e.g., "cow") and the typicalities of these instantiations in the superordinate category that is studied.

Heit and Barsalou (1996) reported three experiments. In the first experiment, they correlated, for seven subordinates of the superordinate category "animal", mean empirically obtained typicalities with mean values of the simulated typicality distribution, and also the standard deviations of the empirically obtained and simulated distributions. The second experiment replicated these findings for nine subordinates of the superordinate category "food." In the third experiment, the instantiation principle was applied to complex categories like "dangerous animals." For the data from Experiment 3, the skewness coefficients of the empirically obtained and the simulated distributions were also correlated. The correlations for the distribution means were high in all three experiments (generally above .90), but the correlations for the distribution standard deviations, though statistically significant, were a bit lower (between .60 and .90). For the skewness (Experiment 3), a correlation of .87 was found. Heit and Barsalou interpreted these results as support for the instantiation principle (i.e., for a process in which subjects judge typicality for members of a category by activating the member's instantiations).

It is important to note that Heit and Barsalou (1996) did not specify how far down the instantiation principle goes in terms of concept hierarchies. The concepts they studied in their experiments ("food," "animals," and the complex concepts from Experiment 3) were situated at the super-superordinate level in the hierarchy described by Rosch, Mervis, Gray, Johnson, and Boyes-Braem (1976). The instantiations of their subordinates are mostly situated at the basic level. However, it is not certain that this is also the level on which participants base their typicalities. More specifically, when participants evaluate the typicality of *cow* within the category "animal," it is possible that they activate specific memory traces of cows they have encountered in the past, or it is conceivable that they activate a (abstract) summary representation at the basic level (i.e., the level of the "cow" category). Nothing in Heit and Barsalou's data gives us a hint as to which of these alternatives comes closest to the actual mental processes involved in the typicality evaluation. As Heit and Barsalou rightfully state, the instantiation principle is therefore still compatible with abstraction processes, but only at a level at least as far down as the basic level.

2. *Further Questioning the Instantiation Principle*

In a follow-up study, De Wilde, Vanoverberghe, Storms and De Boeck (2003) further investigated the instantiation principle. More in particular, they addressed three questions. First, they compared Heit and Barsalou's single-instantiation model with a multiple-instantiation model. Second, they focused on whether the instantiation principle stops at the basic level or whether it goes further down. And third, they evaluated an alternative explanation for Heit and Barsalou's findings.

De Wilde et al. (2003) replicated Heit and Barsalou's typicality rating study for the category "food" with the same nine subordinates ("beverage," "dairy" "produce," "dessert," "fish," "fruit," "meat," "poultry," "seasoning," and "vegetable"). However, they compared typicality predictions of a single-instantiation model (identical to the one proposed by Heit & Barsalou, 1996) with multiple-instantiation models. In the latter models, an increasing number of instantiations were allowed to influence the prediction. More specifically, they conducted an instantiation generation study in which participants wrote down the first five instantiations of each of the nine studied subordinates. Next, participants were simulated according to the frequency distributions for the first up to the fifth instantiation of each of the subordinates (with the restriction that resampling of an instantiation within a single simulated participant was not allowed). Means and standard deviations of the typicalities were calculated for models that assume between one single to five different instantiations. The results showed that the predictions of the multiple-instantiation model for the means were somewhat better than those of the single-instantiation model, but adding more than three exemplars did not improve the prediction. Surprisingly, the results of the single-instantiation model were better than those of the multiple-instantiation model in predicting the standard deviations, but this finding might be due to restriction of range. A second experiment was run for the category "clothes," with a considerably larger number of subordinates ($N = 20$). The results of this replication were virtually identical to those of Experiment 1, with again better predictions of the means and slightly worse predictions of the standard deviations for the multiple instantiation model.

De Wilde et al.'s (2003) Experiment 3 used the same methodology but concentrated on the question of how far down the conceptual hierarchy the instantiation process works. More specifically, the category "fruit," which was one of the subordinates of the category "food" in De Wilde et al.'s and in Heit and Barsalou's experiments, now functioned as the superordinate. Typicalities of seven subordinates ("apple," "berry," "cherry," "grape," "melon," "nut" and "pear") and of their generated instantiations were gathered and used to evaluate the model. In a similar way, another basic-level category ("vehicle" with seven subordinates: "bicycle," "boat," "car," "cart," "plane," "spacecraft" and "truck") and their respective instantiations was studied.

Again, the results showed that the instantiation principle predicted the means and the standard deviations well, even though the subordinates of these categories were defined at the basic level (as defined by Rosch et al., 1976), and thus their instantiations were defined at a level that is lower than the basic level. For "vehicles," the multiple-instantiation model could not outperform single instantiation, since the correlation was already at its maximum for single instantiation, taking into account unreliability in the ratings. For "fruit," calculations based on two instantiations per subordinate were optimal in the prediction of the typicalities.

Note that it is not surprising that the number of activated instantiations decreased as the level of abstraction of the concepts studied decreased: Knowledge of such specific instances is most likely less elaborate than knowledge of basic-level concepts (Rosch et al., 1976). For instance, even though there are many varieties of apples (and people are generally aware of this), their specific knowledge of different varieties is usually rather limited.

Finally, De Wilde et al. (2003) also evaluated an alternative interpretation of the Heit and Barsalou (1996) results. Since the findings were purely correlational, the causal direction was not established in their results. It is very well possible that, in Experiment 3 of De Wilde et al., typicality of the subordinates in the superordinate is generalized to the instantiations instead of the typicality of the instantiations being generalized to the subordinates (as hypothesized by Heit and Barsalou). To make it more concrete, suppose people know that *doyenne* and *braeburn* are sorts of pears, but that they don't know exactly what each sort looks like. In evaluating the typicality of these sorts as "fruit," they may reason in the following way: "Well, I don't know exactly what a *doyenne* looks like, but I know it's a pear and I judge a pear to be a 7 on a 'food' typicality scale. Therefore, I'll indicate a 7 for *doyenne*." A similar argument, though probably less likely intuitively, can be made for all of the previously described experiments in which the instantiation principle was evaluated (including Heit and Barsalou's three experiments).

A consequence of the alternative explanation previously outlined, however, is that there should be no significant differences between the mean typicality ratings of the different instantiations within a subordinate category. For example, there should be no significant differences between the typicality of the different sorts of apples. (Note that the reverse is not true: If there were no significant differences among the instantiations of a subordinate category, the instantiation principle might still apply.) De Wilde et al. (2003) performed, for every subordinate that was used in any of their three experiments, analyses of variance to see whether the typicality ratings for their instantiations differed significantly. In Experiments 1 and 2, where the instantiations were defined at the basic level, significant differences were found for (instantiations of) every single subordinate that was used. In Experiment 3, significant differences were again found for every subordinate of the categories "vehicles" and "fruit," with just one exception: The typicalities of the different sorts of pears did not differ significantly at the .01 level. These findings argue convincingly against the alternative explanation of the results, even at the lower level studied in Experiment 3, and suggest that instantiation goes down at least as low as the level below the basic level. The question whether instantiation goes down as far as the level of memory traces of specifically encountered exemplars cannot be answered based on these results.

3. Comparing Predictions of the Instantiation Principle with Prototype Predictions

The evidence for the instantiation principle that was presented in the studies of Heit and Barsalou (1996) and in De Wilde et al. (2003) consisted of predictions that rejected a null hypothesis. More specifically, they showed that the correlations between the predicted and observed means, standard deviations, and skewness of the typicality ratings for the subordinates within the superordinate was significantly different from zero. No comparison was made with predictions from rivaling models for the same data. A direct comparison of the instantiation-based predictions with two kinds of prototype predictions is reported in Storms, De Boeck, and Ruts (2000).

Storms and his colleagues studied eight different natural language concepts ("fruit," "birds," "vehicles," "sports," "furniture," "fish," "vegetables," and "kitchen utensils"). For every concept, 24 presumed exemplars and 12 nonexemplars that were related to the category were selected. The exemplar set included the most frequently generated exemplars, but also items with presumably varying degrees of typicality. The 12 related nonexemplars were selected from the results of an exemplar generation task, where subjects were asked to write down exemplars of a superordinate of the studied concept, excluding the concept itself (e.g., "food that is not a fruit").

The instantiation predictor was calculated by summing the rated similarity toward the most frequently generated exemplars of the studied concept. Storms et al. (2000) also systematically varied the number of instantiations that were taken into account in the calculation of the instantiation predictor. Actually, for every concept, 25 different instantiation predictors were derived that differed in the number of activated instantiations, which could range from 1–25. For example, the value of the third instantiation predictor for an item *i* was calculated by summing the rated similarity of that item *i* toward the three most frequently generated exemplars of the concept, each weighted for the frequency with which the item was generated.

These instantiation predictors were compared to two kinds of prototype predictors. A first type of prototype prediction was based on the procedure proposed by Hampton (1979). A group of participants indicated for every exemplar and for every related nonexemplar which of the characteristic features gathered by Hampton were applicable. Different prototype predictions were calculated based on the resulting item-by-feature applicability matrix. A first measure used no weighting of the features. Thus, the prediction consisted simply of summing over the different features, the number of subjects that credited the item with the corresponding feature. Three other measures were derived by first weighting the features before summing the applicability features. The weights were based on (1) importance ratings for the features for defining the concept, (2) ratings of how characteristic the defining features are for the concept, and (3) the production frequency of the features. All three weights were taken from Hampton (1979).

The resulting exemplar-based and prototype predictors were used to predict four different dependent variables. First, typicality ratings were gathered for the item set, using a seven-point rating scale. Second, response times from a speeded categorization task were measured. In the task, participants had to indicate whether or not a presented item belongs to the concept. Third, a group of participants were given a list of eight words, one from the item list of each of the eight studied concepts. They were asked to write down for every stimulus word the first category they thought of to which the item belonged. The number of participants that wrote down the label of the studied concept was then counted and used as a dependent variable. Finally, frequencies of the items in an exemplar generation task with the labels of the eight studied concepts as stimuli were taken as the fourth dependent variable.

The prototype and the exemplar-based measures were correlated with all four dependent measures. All correlations were based on the 24 members only (excluding the 12 related nonmembers from the analyses). There were several reasons for this. First, it was problematic for response times to include nonmembers, as fast "yes" responses are observed for typical members and slow "yes" responses are emitted for atypical members, whereas fast "no" responses are observed for totally unrelated nonmembers and slow "no" responses are emitted for related nonmembers (Hampton, 1979). Second, for obvious reasons, the exemplar generation frequencies and the category naming frequencies are almost invariably zero for nonmembers.

Since none of the prototype predictors that used weighting outperformed the no-weighting prototype predictor, only the results of the latter version was relevant in the comparison with the instantiation-based predictors. In Fig. 2, the results are indicated graphically for the four dependent variables and the eight studied concepts. The correlations for the prototype predictor are indicated by the dashed lines on each of the 32 graphs. The typicality ratings were best predicted ($p < .01$ for all eight concepts), and also the response times could be predicted well (again $p < .01$ for all eight concepts). The prototype predictor was less predictive for the generation and for the category naming frequencies (each $p < .05$ for only five of the eight concepts).

Figure 2 also presents the corresponding predictive correlations for the 25 different exemplar measures. The abscise of the diagrams corresponds to the increasing number of best exemplars taken into account in the predictor. The ordinate corresponds to the value of the correlation between the dependent variable and the predictor. (Bear in mind that the values in the second column, corresponding to the response times, are negative.)

The different diagrams are similar in showing that the exemplar predictors improve when taking into account more exemplars, and that the improvement is strong up to seven exemplars. There is almost no improvement in predictive power after adding more than 10 exemplars.

Most of the 32 diagrams show that the exemplar-based measure predicts the dependent variable better or as well as the prototype predictor. The only exceptions were observed for the typicality ratings for "sports," the response times for "kitchen utensils," and category naming frequency for "sports" and "furniture."[2]

[2] One may wonder whether the prototype predictor and the exemplar-based predictor can be differentiated statistically. Averaged over the eight concepts, the exemplar-based and the prototype predictor have 51% of their variance in common, indicating that there is some overlap but that the two predictors are not all indistinguishable.

In a second experiment, Storms et al. (2000) calculated prototype predictions for the same eight concepts in a different way, following the procedure presented by Rosch and Mervis (1975). Attributes were generated by participants for individual exemplars of the concepts. The size of the complete attribute set varied widely over the different concepts from 26–73 in number. Next, different participants filled out the item-by-attribute matrix in an attribute applicability judgment task. Family resemblance scores were calculated in the following way. First, the corresponding cells in the item by attribute applicability matrix were summed over four judges, and then the matrix was again dichotomized according to a majority rule. Next, each attribute received a weight, ranging from 1 to 24, representing the number of items in the category that had been credited with the attribute. Finally, the basic measure of degree of family resemblance for an item was the sum of the weighted scores of each of the attributes that had been credited to that item.

The new family resemblance predictor was correlated with the Hampton-based (1979) prototype predictor, yielding values that varied between .77 and .91 over the eight concepts, with an average value of .81. The average correlation of the family resemblance predictor with an exemplar-based predictor calculated over the 10 best exemplars was somewhat lower: .71. The family resemblance measure predicted the four dependent variables about as well as the prototype measure based on Hampton (1979). Thus, in general, the exemplar-based predictor also outperformed the classic family resemblance measure as proposed by Rosch and Mervis (1975) in predicting the four dependent variables.

In conclusion, the instantiation-based exemplar model yielded better predictions of typicality ratings, response times from a speeded categorization task, exemplar frequencies, and category naming frequencies, than both Hampton's (1979) prototype prediction and Rosch and Mervis' (1975) family resemblance measure. Furthermore, the results show that a multiple instantiation model predicted the dependent measures considerably better than a single-instantiation model as proposed by Heit and Barsalou (1996). More specifically, activation of from 7 to 10 instantiations seems to result in optimal predictions.

Finally, I want to stress that, in the study by Storms et al. (2000), just like in Heit and Barsalou and in De Wilde et al. (2003), no commitment was made to the level of abstraction at which representations are activated. In gathering the dependent variables, as well as in gathering data on which to base the predictions, only verbal stimuli were used. Concepts like "fruit" and "vehicles" were studied using instantiations such as "apples" and "oranges," or "planes" and "boats" (and "trains"). I called these instantiations exemplars, but nothing in the data gives us a hint whether people activate specific

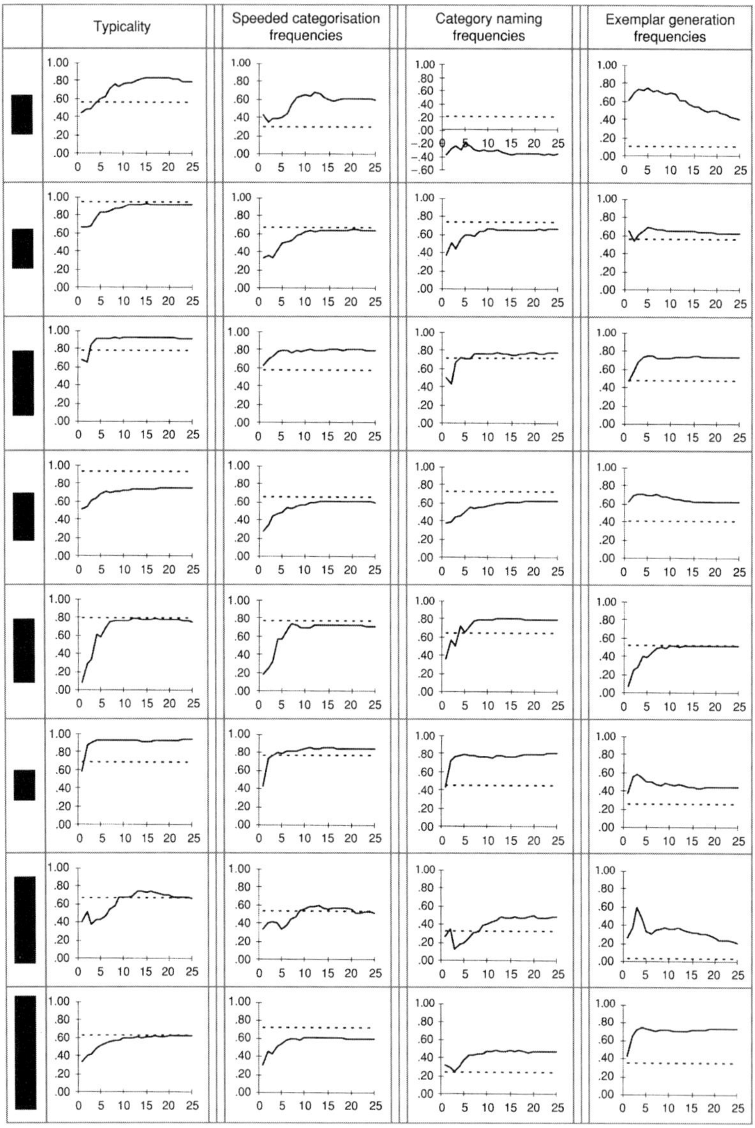

Fig. 2. Correlations of typicality, mean response times, category-naming frequencies, and exemplar-generation frequencies with the sum of 1–25 exemplar-based predictions for the category members only. (The dotted line gives the correlation with the prototype predictions.) *Note.* From "Prototype and Exemplar-Based Information in Natural Language Categories," by G. Storms, P. De Boeck, and W. Ruts, 2000, *Journal of Memory and Language, 42*, 60. Copyright 2000 by Academic Press. Reprinted with permission.

memory traces or abstractions when reading or hearing these labels. The results, though, show that any information activated when the instantiation labels are presented allows us to better predict the dependent variables than do abstract prototype-like summary representations at the level of the concepts studied.

C. Between-Category Structure: Categorizing Novel Stimuli into Well-Known Natural Language Concepts

The main support for exemplar models typically comes from category learning experiments, in which participants learn a pair of categories (say, *C* and *D*) through the repeated presentation of exemplars of both categories (e.g., Medin & Schaffer, 1978; Nosofsky, 1988). Once the participants have mastered the correct labels for all (or the majority) of the items in the learning set, they are presented with a new set of items (called the transfer set) and are asked to classify these new items into one of the learned categories. The two categories are supposed to function as each other's contrast. By manipulating the characteristics of the items in the learning set and in the transfer set, it becomes possible to study the mental representation of the newly learned categories.

Using this methodology, exemplar models have been contrasted with prototype models and with rule-based models. In most comparisons, exemplar models provided the better predictions (e.g., Estes, 1986; Hintzman, 1986; Medin & Schaffer, 1978; Medin & Schwanenflugel, 1981; Medin & Smith, 1981; Medin, Altom, Edelson, & Freko, 1982; Medin, Altom, & Murphy, 1984; for an overview, see Nosofsky, 1992). Recently, though, the generality of this conclusion has been contested, and evidence has been presented that both exemplar-based and rule-based representations may be guiding categorization choices (Erickson & Kruschke, 1998; Palmeri & Nosofsky, 1995).

Generalizing the findings from such artificial category-learning experiments to situations where natural language concepts are learned and used is not straightforward because of the complexity of the latter kind of concepts. Nevertheless, in everyday life, people often come across situations that strongly resemble the categorization experiments. New and unfamiliar stimuli often have to be classified into one of several well-known categorizations. For example, new products bought in the supermarket are spontaneously labeled as "a bottle" or "a jar" (Malt et al., 1999). In such situations, people use their knowledge of categories that were learned much earlier, mostly in childhood. These categorizations resemble the transfer phase of category learning experiments.

In a series of studies, we explored to what extent exemplar-based and prototype models can be applied to categorization in natural language concepts. For these studies, we selected two natural language categories that are presumed to function as each other's contrast category and that are embedded in the same concept hierarchy and at the same hierarchical level. Furthermore, we wanted to choose two concepts for which stimuli could be gathered that were novel to the participants and that could easily be believed to belong to one or the other category. On the basis of these criteria, "fruits" and "vegetables" were chosen. Intuitively, both these categories seem to function as each other's contrast category, and they reside under a more abstract category consisting of edible natural foods. Equally important, there exists a rich variety of exotic foods with which our participants were unfamiliar and that could be used as stimuli to be categorized in either one of these concepts.

1. Instantiation-Based Exemplar Prediction of Categorization Choices

In a first study (Storms et al., 2001), an instantiation version of the exemplar model was compared with a prototype model as computed in Hampton (1979). The instantiation predictor was calculated as follows. Participants rated the similarity of 30 unknown (mostly tropical) kinds of natural food (which were presented on a plate) toward the eight most frequently generated instantiations of the category "fruit" and toward the eight most frequently generated exemplars of the category "vegetables." (Eight was considered a large enough exemplar set, given the results from Storms et al., 2000, where the predictive value of an instantiation-based exemplar predictor was shown to increase as a function of the number of "best" exemplars taken into account, but only up to approximately seven.) Instantiation predictors were calculated for "fruit" and for "vegetables" by simply summing the similarity ratings over the eight exemplars of the corresponding category. (Different weightings were tried out, based on generation frequencies and rank order information in an exemplar generation task, but none of these weightings improved the prediction.)

Two prototype predictors were calculated as follows. First, for every unknown food item, the applicability frequency of the item to the 10 most frequently generated features of the category "fruit" (taken from a feature generation task with different participants) were summed. The applicability frequencies were weighted on the basis of generation frequency, since this turned out to yield the best predictor from a set where different kinds of weightings were tried out. Next, a prototype predictor for the category "vegetables" was calculated in an analogous way, based on the applicability frequency of the item to the 10 most frequently generated features of the category "vegetables."

A group of 20 participants categorized each of the 30 unknown food items (again presented on a plate) as either belonging to the category "fruit" or the category "vegetables." The resulting categorization proportions were predicted in a number of regression analyses. When the two prototype predictors functioned as the predictor variables, 73% of the variance in the categorization choices was accounted for, with both predictors entering in the model significantly ($p < .01$). Note that the two prototype predictors correlated $-.45$ ($p < .05$). The model with the two instantiation-based exemplar predictors accounted for a slightly larger proportion of the variance (76%). Again, the two predictors entered in significantly ($p < .01$). The correlation between both exemplar predictors was also significant (–48, $p < .01$). The difference between the proportion of the variance accounted for by the prototype and by the exemplar-based predictors, however, was not significant.

When predicting the categorization choices from the two exemplar and the two prototype predictors together, a significant improvement in prediction was obtained (87%). The two prototype predictors and the exemplar predictor for "fruit" reached significance ($p < .05$), but the "vegetable" exemplar predictor was only marginally significant ($p = .07$).

The results thus showed that there was predictive information in the prototype predictors that was not contained in the exemplar predictors. This finding was shown not to be the result of different strategies across participants. Extending the exemplar set taken into account in the exemplar predictors from 8–13 for "vegetables" and 8–14 for "fruit" resulted in an increase in prediction. Combining the extended exemplar predictors with the prototype predictors showed that there was still additional information in the "fruit" prototype predictors that was not contained in the exemplar predictors. Further analysis revealed that three of the features of the "fruit" category (i.e., "is sweet," "is/looks tasty," and "can get rotten") correlated significantly with the residuals of a regression analysis, with the extended exemplar measures as predictors. The bottom line was thus that the instantiation-based exemplar predictors yielded significantly better predictors than the prototype model, but that some of the features used in the prototype predictors were not captured well enough by the rated similarities toward the best exemplars to render the prototype predictor useless.

2. *Applying the Generalized Context Model (GCM)*

Though the instantiation approach (De Wilde et al., 2003; Heit & Barsalou, 1996; Storms et al., 2000, 2001) fits nicely in the study of natural language concepts, it is somewhat remote from the exemplar models presented in the category learning literature. The most dominant framework in that area is that of the Context Model (Medin & Schaffer, 1978), which was later generalized by Nosofsky (1984, 1986). (For a connectionist version of the model, see Kruschke, 1992.)

In a second fruit and vegetable study, we used the same paradigm previously described but compared a different version of the prototype model with Nosofsky's GCM (Smits, Storms, Rosseel, & De Boeck, 2002). Since the prototype version in this study was also heavily based on the GCM, we will briefly recapitulate the main ideas of that model first.

The GCM assumes that subjects' classifications of a new stimulus are based on its similarity to stored category exemplars. The GCM situates stimuli along continuous dimensions, usually after applying a multidimensional scaling procedure (Borg & Groenen, 1997). The model is based on Shepard's similarity choice model (Shepard, 1958). Formally, for the case of two categories A and B, the probability that a given stimulus X is classified in category A is given by

$$P(A|X) = \frac{\beta_A \eta_{XA}^{\alpha}}{\beta_A \eta_{XA}^{\alpha} + (1 - \beta_A)\eta_{XB}^{\alpha}}$$

where β_A is a response bias toward category A and η_{XA}, and η_{XB} are similarity measures of stimulus X toward all stored exemplars of categories A and B, respectively. The parameter α was first introduced into the GCM by Ashby and Maddox (1993) and represents a response-scaling parameter. When $\alpha = 1.0$, observers respond by "probability matching" to the relative summed similarities. When α grows larger than 1.0, observers respond more deterministically with the category that yields the largest summed similarity (McKinley & Nosofsky, 1995; Nosofsky & Johansen, 2000). If α is less than 1.0, observers respond less deterministically than "probability matching." The similarity measures are summed similarities of the stimulus X toward all these stored exemplars. Formally,

$$\eta_{XA} = \sum_{j \in A} \exp\left\{ - \left[c \left(\sum_{k=1}^{D} w_k |y_{xk} - y_{jk}|^r \right)^{1/r} \right]^q \right\}$$

where c is an overall scaling parameter, y_{xk} and y_{jk} are the coordinates of the stimulus X and the j-th stored exemplar on dimension k, respectively, and w_k is the weight of dimension k. The weights of the different dimensions are restricted to sum to 1.0. The Minkowski r-metric usually takes values between 1 and 2, where $r = 1$ results in the city-block metric and $r = 2$ results in Euclidean distances. Finally, the parameter q determines the shape of the similarity function, with $q = 1$ resulting in a similarity function with exponential decay and $q = 2$ resulting in a Gaussian decay.

To predict categorization, the GCM requires that all stored exemplars are taken into account. Though it is impossible to find out exactly which fruits and vegetables a participant knows, one can assume that a large set of approximately the 40 best-known exemplars of both categories approaches the complete set of individual participants well. (Actually, 34 fruits and 45 vegetables were selected based on the results of an exemplar generation task.)

To obtain the MDS solution, usually pairwise similarity ratings are gathered. However, collecting pairwise ratings for 79 well-known and 30 unknown natural food items is virtually impossible, since it would amount to gathering $109 \times 108/2 = 5886$ pairwise ratings. Therefore, the following procedure was used to gather similarities. First, features for both concepts were taken from a feature generation task (described in Storms, De Boeck, Van Mechelen, & Ruts, 1996). Next, an applicability matrix of the 109 items by 17 features was gathered from 10 different participants, and these matrices were summed over the 10 participants. Then a 109-by-109 similarity matrix was derived by correlating the feature vectors of all pairs of stimuli. Finally, the similarity matrix was analyzed using the MDS program ALSCAL (Takane, Young, & De Leeuw, 1977). Based on the goodness of fit, the three-dimensional solution was selected for further analyses.

Different models were fitted, using the maximum likelihood criterion, to the categorization proportions of three stimulus sets: (1) only the unknown items (30 in number), (2) only the well-known items (79 in number), and (3) the complete set of well-known and unknown items together (109 in number). Euclidean distances fitted the data better than the city block metric, indicating that the underlying dimensions can be considered integral dimensions (Nosofsky, 1986; Shepard, 1964). Likewise, the results of the exponential decay similarity function ($q = 1$) were clearly better than the results of the Gaussian decay function ($q = 2$).

A version of the GCM with five free parameters (α, c, a bias parameter β, and two dimension weights) was compared to a prototype model. The latter model was identical to the GCM in terms of its assumptions regarding similarity, selective attention, and response-ratio rule, but unlike the GCM, the prototype version used only two stored exemplars—that is, the prototypes of "fruits" and the prototype of "vegetables." The coordinates of these prototypes were calculated by averaging the coordinates for each dimension over all well-known exemplars within each category. This prototype model used only four free parameters instead of five, because the values of α and of c cannot be estimated separately in this model. (For details, see Smits et al., 2002.) When q equals 1, this version of the prototype model amounts to a multiplicative similarity prototype model, which was described previously by Minda and Smith (2001), Nosofsky (1987), and Smith and Minda (1998).

The GCM predicted the categorization proportions of the novel, unknown items better than the prototype version. The correlation between the predicted and the observed categorization proportions was .92 and .88, for the exemplar and for the prototype model, respectively. Akaike's Information Criterion (AIC; Akaike, 1974), a fit measure directly based on the likelihood of the data that penalizes for the use of free parameters, also favored the exemplar model over the prototype model.

In a second analysis, where the categorization proportions of only the well-known items were taken into account, the GCM clearly outperformed the prototype model, both in terms of the correlation between predicted and observed categorization proportions (.98 vs. .90) as in terms of the AIC.

Finally, in a third analysis, the categorization data of the complete item set (novel as well as well-known items) were analyzed. Again, the GCM was favored in terms of correlations (.93 vs. .90) and in terms of the AIC value.

Since the stimulus set of the novel stimuli used in Storms et al. (2001) and in Smits et al. (2002) were exactly the same, the predictions of the GCM, of the multiplicative-similarity prototype model, and of the (extended) instantiation-based exemplar predictions could be directly compared on categorizations of these novel stimuli (For details, see Smits et al., 2002). Both in terms of the correlation between predicted and observed categorization proportions and in terms of the AIC value, the GCM fitted the data somewhat better than the extended instantiation-based model. The slight superiority of the GCM is possibly caused by the similarity-scaling transformations of the GCM. The instantiation-based model was also shown to yield better fits than the multiplicative-similarity prototype model.

3. *Exploring the Effect of Alternative Similarity Representations on Categorization Prediction*

As previously explained, the GCM is a formal model for categorization that starts from a multidimensional representational of the stimuli. The representation is based on similarity data. In the cognitive literature, however, the use of spatial representations to represent similarity has been criticized strongly (e.g., Gati & Tversky, 1982, 1984, 1987; Tversky, 1977), and alternative conceptions of similarity have been proposed. The seminal paper of Tversky (1977), on similarity as a function of discrete feature sets, was the starting point of the development of alternative similarity representations, such as additive clustering (Shepard & Arabie, 1979) and additive trees (Corter, 1982; Sattath & Tversky, 1977).

Recently, the effect of such alternative similarity representations on categorization predictions (Lee & Navarro, 2002) and on recognition predictions (Nosofsky & Zaki, 2003) has been explored in the context of artificial (perceptual) stimuli. There are, however, reasons to believe that an exploration of alternative similarity representations is warranted, especially in the context of categorizing semantic concepts. A hint in that direction comes from Pruzansky, Tversky, and Carroll (1982), who showed that tree representations (like additive clustering) in general fitted similarity data for conceptual stimuli better than MDS representations, whereas MDS yielded better fits than tree representations for analyses of perceptual stimuli.

In a recent study, Verbeemen, Storms, and Verguts (2003) compared four different models for the fruit and vegetable data described earlier. The four models resulted from a combination of two different similarity representations, the geometric (MDS) model and a featural (tree) model, with two different representation models, the exemplar model and the prototype model. The geometric exemplar and prototype models were the common GCM and the multiplicative-similarity prototype models, as used in Smits et al. (2002). For the two featural models, a similarity representation of ADDTREE (Corter, 1982; Sattath & Tversky, 1977) was used as a starting point. ADDTREE produces a classification structure in the form of a tree. An example of what an ADDTREE solution may look like is presented in Fig. 3, for a fictive data set of mammals and birds. In the model, distances between objects are defined by summing the weights of the features that are distinctive, which corresponds in the figure to adding the lengths of the horizontal segments on the shortest path between two stimuli.[3] Thus, horizontal segments correspond to features that characterize all objects that are connected with the segment to the right side in the tree structure. As an illustration, Table I shows the feature structure that corresponds to the tree presented in Fig. 3.

Since the position of the root does not change distances between objects, the root indeterminacy has no effect at all on exemplar models. For prototype models, however, the particular feature structure does have an effect. Moreover, for the prototype model to be effective, it is required that the root should be chosen such that it maximizes the number of stored different-category

[3] ADDTREE does not distinguish between different feature structures of the same classification family (Sattath & Tversky, 1987): if a feature adds to the distance of a pair of objects, it may either belong to one object or the other. This indeterminacy is reflected in indeterminacy in placing the root of the tree. Once the root is chosen, it is conventionally placed at the far left of the tree structure. In the example in Fig. 3, the root is placed on the segment that adds to the difference between members of the different categories (birds vs. mammals), but not to the distance between members within the same category.

TABLE I

INDICATOR MATRIX FOR THE FEATURES IN FIGURE 1A, FOR ALL STIMULI AND FOR THE PROTOTYPES OF CATEGORY A AND B

	1	2	3	4	5	6	7	8	9	10	11	12	13	14	15	16	17	18
Category A																		
Dog	1	1	0	0	0	0	0	0	1	0	0	0	0	0	0	0	0	0
Rat	1	1	0	0	0	0	0	0	0	1	0	0	0	0	0	0	0	0
Donkey	1	0	1	1	1	0	0	0	0	0	1	0	0	0	0	0	0	0
Cow	1	0	1	1	1	0	0	0	0	0	0	1	0	0	0	0	0	0
Pig	1	0	1	1	0	0	0	0	0	0	0	0	1	0	0	0	0	0
Elephant	1	0	1	0	0	0	0	0	0	0	0	0	0	1	0	0	0	0
Category B																		
Eagle	0	0	0	0	0	1	1	0	0	0	0	0	0	0	1	0	0	0
Chicken	0	0	0	0	0	1	1	0	0	0	0	0	0	0	0	1	0	0
Sparrow	0	0	0	0	0	1	0	1	0	0	0	0	0	0	0	0	1	0
Robin	0	0	0	0	0	1	0	1	0	0	0	0	0	0	0	0	0	1
FPT																		
Cat A	1	1	1	1	1	0	0	0	1	1	1	1	1	1	0	0	0	0
Cat B	0	0	0	0	0	1	1	1	0	0	0	0	0	0	1	1	1	1

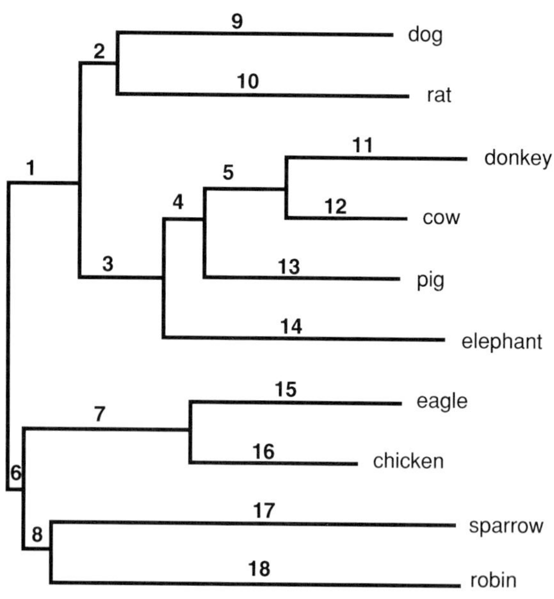

Fig. 3. Plausible classification structure of an example of mammals (Category A) and birds (Category B). The numbering of the branches corresponds to the features in Table I.

pairs that fall under different branches (starting from the root) and the number of stored within-category pairs that fall under the same branch.

Once the root has been fixed according to that criterion, the formulation of the featural exemplar model is straightforward:

$$\eta_{XA} = \sum_{j \in A} \exp - \left[c \left(\sum_{k=1}^{D} w_k \left(y_{xk}(1 - y_{jk}) + y_{jk}(1 - y_{xk}) \right) \right) \right],$$

where $y_{jk} = 1$ if stimulus j has feature k, and $y_{jk} = 0$ otherwise. Thus, the term y_{xk} $(1 - y_{jk})$ is 1 if and only if the target stimulus x possesses the feature and the "reference" stimulus j does not, and vice versa for y_{jk} $(1 - y_{xk})$.

Note that one can either reestimate the feature weights to fit the ADDTREE-based categorization models, or one can use the original weights of the ADDTREE solution, which were calculated to fit the similarity data. Because of the nature of a tree structure, an ADDTREE solution has $2n - 3$ free parameters (corresponding to the number of segments, i.e., feature weights), where n denotes the number of objects in the stimulus set. Due to the large number of stimuli in the fruits and vegetables study, adding free parameters for all $(2 \times 109 - 3 =)$ 215 different features in the tree would make the estimation of the model practically impossible. Therefore, the feature weights were fixed at the values based on the similarity analysis. This implies that the featural exemplar model used two free parameters less than the GCM (i.e., corresponding to the free parameters for the dimension weights) and that the featural prototype model likewise used two parameters less than the MDS-based prototype model.

Analogous to the two MDS-based models, the featural prototype model is formally similar to the featural exemplar model, with the prototype treated as a pseudo-exemplar. In fact, different versions of the featural prototype model can be constructed, depending on what the pseudo-exemplar prototype looks like. A first model is the *no cutoff, weighted frequency model*, which assumes that if a member has a particular feature, then the category prototype has it as well. "No cutoff" refers to the fact that only one exemplar that has a feature is enough to attribute the feature to the prototype. The distance function then amounts to

$$\eta_{XA} = \exp - \left[c \left(\sum_{k=1}^{F} w_k \left(y_{pk}(1 - y_{pk}) + freq_{bk} y_{bk}(1 - y_{xk}) \right) \right) \right]$$

where y_{pk} equals 1 if the prototype A has the feature, and 0 otherwise. The frequency weighting term corresponds to the relative frequency or proportion with which the feature occurs within A. This formalizes the idea that the impact of the features in the prototype depends on the prevalence of those features in the category. As a consequence, the impact of *not* having a feature that belongs to the prototype decreases with decreasing frequency, an idea that is also present in Rosch and Mervis' (1975) family resemblance notion.

A second model is the *core prototype model* (Malt & Johnson, 1992), where the prototype only possesses the most frequent "feature" that is shared by most exemplars of the category and by few members of the contrast category. Although in this model the prototype just has one single feature in the formal sense, it may very well correspond to a larger set of features in the interpretative sense of the word.

An ADDTREE analysis of the same similarity data used in Smits et al. (2002) explained 84% of the variance. Compared to 96% for the three-dimensional MDS solution, the fit of the tree solution is a bit worse, but the MDS model used many more free parameters to fit the similarity data (321 vs. 215). More important, a better representation for the similarity data need not imply a better fit for the categorization data.

All models were fitted by maximizing the likelihood of the data, and the fit was always evaluated using the BIC statistic (Schwarz, 1978), which penalizes for the number of free parameters as a function of the number of data points. The featural exemplar model was fitted with the exponential decay function ($q = 1$), whereas the featural prototype models were fitted with the Gaussian decay function ($q = 2$), as this resulted in the best fit values.

In the analysis of the novel (i.e., unknown) stimuli only, all ADDTREE-based models performed worse than the geometric models save for the core prototype model: The classical (MDS-based) GCM and the core prototype model[4] yielded the best (and equal) fit values. In the comparison of the two versions of the feature-based prototype models, the core model showed a clearly better fit than the no cutoff prototype model.

In the analysis of the 79 well-known stimuli, the opposite was true: the ADDTREE-based models outperformed the geometric models, and the ADDTREE-based prototype model was the best fitting model. The no cutoff model was also clearly better fitting than the core prototype model. Finally, when analyzing both novel and well-known items together, the results were similar to those of the well-known items separately.

[4] It is important to keep in mind that the core prototype model is in fact formally equivalent to a one-dimensional geometric prototype model: Because the two prototypes are the two branches that fall under the root, all distances to these two points can be represented on one dimension. The difference with a one-dimensional geometric prototype lies in the fact that the prototypes here are abstracted from a different similarity algorithm and with a different procedure, so they need in no way be identical. It is striking, though, that both best fitting models share low dimensionality as a trait.

In conclusion, these data suggest a complex interaction of stimulus type, underlying similarity representation, and conceptual representation. Categorization of well-known stimuli is best accounted for by a featural (tree-based) prototype model, which assumes a very detailed notion of the concept that is stored at the category level, rather than at the level of individual instances. Indeed, a tree structure, although formally sparser than a three-dimensional spatial representation, implies that participants have extensive knowledge of categories. For novel stimuli, this detailed information may be inadequate, as indicated by the improving fit when reducing the amount of category information that is stored in the prototype. When someone is confronted with novel, unknown stimuli that are perceptually presented, the common GCM, based on a three-dimensional similarity representation, predicts the categorization results best.

This finding is also in agreement with Pruzansky, Tversky, and Carroll (1982), who found that conceptual stimuli were better represented by a tree structure (ADDTREE), whereas perceptual stimuli are better represented by a limited number of continuous properties. Because the novel stimuli were unknown to the participants, it is unlikely that they were judged on more than a few basic perceptual characteristics. It would make little sense to use the detailed information about well-known stimuli as a means of deciding about category membership in the case of novel stimuli.

The conclusions formulated above are based on the study of categorization in just one single pair of natural concepts. A replication in other concepts is definitely called for. However, it is very hard to find two categories that fulfill the necessary requirements for applying the same research paradigm. More specifically, it is difficult to find two categories (1) that can be considered each contrast category and that exhaust a well-defined group of entities, (2) for which there exists a large enough set of stimuli that are novel to the participants but that can be categorized in one of the two categories, and (3) for which the better known exemplars of the categories can be (more or less) delineated and can be lexicalized. The fact that such concepts are hard to find does not mean that the studies by Storms et al. (2001), Smits et al. (2002), and Verbeemen et al. (2003) are unimportant because they deal with exceptional categories. It only means that similar categorization situations, which occur quite often in everyday life, cannot be studied *using the same procedure*.

VI. Some Final Remarks

In this chapter, I reviewed a series of studies in which ideas of the exemplar view were used to predict between-category and within-category structure in natural language concepts. These studies proved that it is possible to overcome the two major stumbling blocks associated with applying exemplar models to natural language concepts.

First, there is no need to specify exactly what an exemplar is. In line with arguments formulated by Heit and Barsalou (1996), it suffices to assume that the relevant activated information is stored at a level that is hierarchically lower than the level at which the concept under study is defined. For instance, when studying superordinate level concepts, like "furniture," "birds," or "fruit," one can use verbal labels of their exemplars, like "chairs," "robins," and "apples," respectively, to gather information needed for calculating exemplar-based predictor variables. Indeed, the representation that is activated to provide the necessary information can be situated either at the level of abstract summary representations of "chair," "robins," and so forth, or at the level of specific memory traces of previously encountered exemplars, or at any other level of abstraction in between these two extremes. Moreover, the empirical data offer us no clue at all to determine which of these possible representations is the most adequate. However, if the exemplar-based predictors turn out to be better than the prototype predictors, as was shown to be true in most of the reviewed studies, then this is evidence against abstraction at the level of the studied concepts.

Second, we also showed that several strategies can be used to circumvent the difficulties of specifying the underlying concept features. In De Wilde et al. (2003), Heit and Barsalou (1996), and Storms et al. (2000, 2001), direct ratings were used to derive instantiation-based predictors. Thus, in these studies there was no need to specify the underlying features of dimensions. In Ruts et al. (2004), Smits et al. (2002), and Verbeemen et al. (2003), generated features at the concept level (gathered similarly, as in the seminal paper by Rosch and Mervis, 1975) were shown to be adequate to calculate similarities between exemplars. These similarities were then analyzed by statistical techniques such as MDS and ADDTREE.[5] The dimensions or features extracted by these techniques were then plugged into the formal GCM-based categorization models. The very good fits of these models to the data prove

[5] Note that MDS is used somewhat differently in this context than the way the same technique has been used in the category-learning literature (e.g., Ashby and Maddux, 1992; Nosofsky, 1985). In the context of artificial categories, the experimenter knows exactly which dimensions are manipulated. MDS is then used only as a psychophysical tool, that is, to obtain psychological scale values along the manipulated dimensions. In the studies on linear separability (Ruts et al., 2004) and on categorization of novel stimuli into well-known categories (Smits et al., 2002; Verbeemen et al., 2003), MDS, and also ADDTREE, are used mainly as data-reduction techniques, in which a large number of features are used to calculate similarities, which then are used to obtain a limited number of dimensions or features that are assumed to underlie the input similarities.

that these dimensions or features at least approach the "true" attributes of the psychological representations well.

The different studies reviewed in this chapter also showed that the exemplar-based models succeeded in explaining a wide varicty of dependent measures, ranging from typicality, over response times, to categorization decisions. Moreover, Storms et al. (2000) showed that in predicting typicality, an instantiation-based exemplar predictor is superior to the family resemblance predictor of Rosch and Mervis (1975), which can be called a classic in this context, and to Hampton's (1979) prototype predictor. Within the framework of the instantiation principle, the results also clearly argued for the activation of multiple instantiations, since multiple-instantiation predictors outperformed single-instantiation predictors. Furthermore, a GCM predictor (which also assumes activation of multiple exemplars, or even the complete set of stored exemplars) was shown to even yield better predictions than the instantiation-based predictor in fitting categorization data from the fruit and vegetable task (Smits et al., 2002; Verbeemen et al., 2003).

Finally, we have shown that new types of exemplar models, based on other similarity representation models than the classical spatial representation, can be developed and tested in the context of natural language concepts (Verbeemen et al., 2003).

Acknowledgments

The research summarized in this chapter was supported by Grant G.0266.02 from the Belgian National Science Foundation (Fundamental Human Sciences), and Grants OT/01/15 and IDO/02/004 of the Leuven University Research Council to G. Storms. The research would not have been possible without the help of my collaborators and students, who helped in several stages of the diverse research projects: Eef Ameel, Paul De Boeck, Simon De Deyne, Els De Wilde, Yves Rosseel, Wim Ruts, Tim Smits, Veerle Vanoverberghe, Timothy Verbeemen, and Tom Verguts I also thank Brian Ross for his useful comments on an earlier version of this chapter.

References

Akaike, H. (1974). A new look at statistical model identification. *IEEE Transactions on Automatic Control, 19*, 716–723.

Ameel, E., Storms, G., Malt, B. C., & Sloman, S. A. (2003). Linguistic diversity and object naming by Dutch-speaking, French-speaking, and biligual Belgians. *Poster presented at the 44th annual meeting of the Psychonomic Society, Vancouver, British Columbia, Canada.*

Ashby, F. G., & Gott, R. (1988). Decision rules in the perception and categorization of multidimensional stimuli. *Journal of Experimental Psychology: Learning, Memory, & Cognition, 14*, 33–53.

Ashby, F. G., & Maddox, W. T. (1992). Complex decision rules in categorization: Contrasting novice and experienced performance. *Journal of Experimental Psychology: Human Perception & Performance, 18*, 50–71.

Ashby, F. G., & Maddox, W. T. (1993). Relations between prototype, exemplar, and decision bound models of categorization. *Journal of Mathematical Psychology, 37*, 372–400.

Attneave, F. (1957). Transfer of experience with a class-schema to identification-learning of patterns and shapes. *Journal of Experimental Psychology, 54*, 81–88.

Barsalou, L. W. (1990). On the indistinguishability of exemplar memory and abstraction in category representation. In T. K. Srull and R. S. Wyer (Eds.), *Advances in social cognition: Content and process specificity in the effects of prior experiences* (Vol. 3, pp. 61–88). Erlbaum: Hillsdale, NJ.

Barsalou, L. W., Huttenlocher, J., & Lamberts, K. (1998). Basing categorization on individuals and events. *Cognitive Psychology, 36*, 203–272.

Blair, M., & Homa, D. (2001). Expanding the search for a linear separability constraint on category learning. *Memory and Cognition, 29*, 1153–1164.

Borg, I., & Groenen, P. J. F. (1997). *Modern multidimensional scaling*. New York: Springer.

Bruner, J. S. (1957). On perceptual readiness. *Psychological Review, 64*, 123–152.

Bruner, J. S., Goodnow, J. J., & Austin, G. A. (1956). *A study of thinking*. New York: Wiley.

Corter, J. E. (1982). ADDTREE/P: A PASCAL program for fitting additive trees based on Sattath & Tversky's ADDTREE algorithm. *Behavior Research Methods & Instrumentation, 14*, 353–354.

De Wilde, E., Vanoverberghe, V., Storms, G., & De Boeck, P. (2003). The instantiation principle re-evaluated. *Memory, 11*, 533–548.

Erickson, M. A., & Kruschke, J. K. (1998). Rules and exemplars in category learning. *Journal of Experimental Psychology: General, 127*, 107–140.

Estes, W. K. (1986). Memory storage and retrieval processes in category learning. *Journal of Experimental Psychology: General, 115*, 155–175.

Franks, J. J., & Bransford, J. D. (1971). Abstraction of visual patterns. *Journal of Experimental Psychology, 90*, 65–74.

Gardenfors, P. (2000). *Conceptual spaces: The geometry of thought*. Cambridge, MA: MIT Press.

Gati, I., & Tversky, A. (1982). Representations of qualitative and quantitative dimensions. *Journal of Experimental Psychology: Human Perception and Performance, 8*, 325–340.

Gati, I., & Tversky, A. (1984). Weighting common and distinctive features in perceptual and conceptual judgments. *Cognitive Psychology, 16*, 341–370.

Gati, I., & Tversky, A. (1987). Recall of common and distinctive features of verbal and pictorial stimuli. *Memory and Cognition, 15*, 97–100.

Hampton, J. A. (1979). Polymorphous concepts in semantic memory. *Journal of Verbal Learning and Verbal Behavior, 18*, 441–461.

Hampton, J. A. (1993). Prototype models of concept representations. In I. Van Mechelen, J. A. Hampton, R. S. Michalski, and P. Theuns (Eds.), *Categories and concepts: Theoretical views and inductive data analysis* (pp. 67–95). London: Academic Press.

Hampton, J. A., & Kahnam, Z. (2003). *Perceived similarity and the linguistic categorization of artifacts by English, Bengali, and bilingual speakers.* [Internal report]. London: City University.

Hayes-Roth, B., & Hayes-Roth, F. (1977). Concept learning and the recognition and classification of exemplars. *Journal of Verbal Learning and Verbal Behavior, 16*, 321–338.

Heit, E., & Barsalou, L. W. (1996). The instantiation principle in natural language categories. *Memory, 4*, 413–451.

Hintzman, D. L. (1986). "Schema abstraction" in a multiple-trace memory model. *Psychological Review, 93*, 411–428.

Hull, C. L. (1920). Quantitative aspects of the evolution of concepts. *Psychological Monographs, 28*.

Johansen, M. K., & Palmeri, T. J. (2002). Are there representational shifts during category learning? *Cognitive Psychology, 45*, 482–553.

Knowlton, B. J., & Squire, L. R. (1993). The learning of categories: Parallel brain systems for item memory and category knowledge. *Science, 262*, 1747–1749.

Komatsu, L. K. (1992). Recent views of conceptual structure. *Psychological Bulletin, 112*, 500–526.

Kruschke, J. K. (1992). ALCOVE: An exemplar-based connectionist model of category learning. *Psychological Review, 99*, 22–44.

Lamberts, K. (1998). The time course of categorization. *Journal of Experimental Psychology: Learning, Memory, and Cognition, 24*, 695–711.

Lee, M. D., & Navarro, D. J. (2002). Extending the ALCOVE model of category learning to featural stimulus domains. *Psychonomic Bulletin and Review, 9*, 43–58.

Malt, B. C., & Johnson, E. C. (1992). Do artifact concepts have cores? *Journal of Memory and Language, 31*, 195–217.

Malt, B. C., Sloman, S. A., Gennari, S., Shi, M., & Wang, Y. (1999). Knowing versus naming: Similarity and the linguistic categorization of artifacts. *Journal of Memory and Language, 40*, 230–262.

Malt, B. C., & Smith, E. E. (1984). Correlated properties in natural categories. *Journal of Verbal Learning and Verbal Behavior, 23*, 250–269.

Markman, A. B., & Ross, B. H. (2003). Category use and category learning. *Psychological Bulletin, 129*, 592–613.

McKinley, S. C., & Nosofsky, R. M. (1995). Investigation of exemplar and decision-bound models in large-size, ill-defined category structures. *Journal of Experimental Psychology: Human Perception & Performance, 21*, 128–148.

Medin, D. L., Altom, M. W., Edelson, S. M., & Freko, D. (1982). Correlated symptoms and simulated medical classification. *Journal of Experimental Psychology: Learning, Memory, & Cognition, 8*, 37–50.

Medin, D. L., Altom, M. W., & Murphy, T. D. (1984). Given versus induced category representations: Use of prototype and exemplar information in classification. *Journal of Experimental Psychology: Learning, Memory, & Cognition, 10*, 333–352.

Medin, D. M., & Schaffer, M. M. (1978). Context theory of classification learning. *Psychological Review, 85*, 207–238.

Medin, D. L., & Schwanenflugel, P. J. (1981). Linear separability in classification learning. *Journal of Experimental Psychology: Human Learning and Memory, 5*, 355–368.

Medin, D. L., & Smith, E. E. (1981). Strategies and classification learning. *Journal of Experimental Psychology: Learning, Memory, & Cognition, 7*, 241–253.

Medin, D. L., & Smith, E. E. (1984). Concepts and concept formation. *Annual Review of Psychology, 35*, 113–138.

Minda, J. P., & Smith, J. D. (2001). Prototypes in category learning: The effects of category size, category structure, and stimulus complexity. *Journal of Experimental Psychology: Learning, Memory and Cognition, 27*, 775–799.

Murphy, G. L. (2002). *The big book of concepts*. Cambridge, MA: MIT Press.

Nosofsky, R. M. (1984). Choice, similarity, and the context model of classification. *Journal of Experimental Psychology: Learning, Memory, and Cognition, 10*, 104–114.

Nosofsky, R. N. (1985). Luce's choice model and Thurstone's categorical judgment model compared: Kornbrot's data revisited. *Perception & Psychophysics, 37*, 89–91.

Nosofsky, R. M. (1986). Attention, similarity, and the identification-categorization relationship. *Journal of Experimental Psychology: General, 115*, 39–57.

Nosofsky, R. M. (1987). Attention and learning processes in the identification and categorization of integral stimuli. *Journal of Experimental Psychology: Learning, Memory, & Cognition, 13*, 87–108.

Nosofsky, R. M. (1988). Similarity, frequency, and category representation. *Journal of Experimental Psychology: Learning, Memory, and Cognition, 14*, 54–65.

Nosofsky, R. M. (1992). Exemplars, prototypes, and similarity rules. In A. F. Healy, S. M. Kosslyn, and R. M. Shiffrin (Eds.), *From learning theory to connectionist theory: Essays in honor of William K. Estes* (Vol. 1, pp. 149–167). Hillsdale, NJ: Erlbaum.

Nosofsky, R. M. (1998). Selective attention and the formation of linear decision boundaries: A reply to Maddox and Ashby. *Journal of Experimental Psychology: Human Perception and Performance, 24*, 322–339.

Nosofsky, R. M., & Johansen, M. K. (2000). Exemplar-based accounts of "multiple-system" phenomena in perceptual categorization. *Psychonomic Bulletin & Review, 7*, 375–402.

Nosofsky, R. M., Palmeri, T. J., & McKinley, S. C. (1994). Rule-plus-exception model of classification learning. *Psychological Review, 101*, 53–79.

Nosofsky, R. M., & Zaki, S. R., (2003) A hybrid-similarity exemplar model for predicting distinctiveness effects in perceptual old-new recognition. *Journal of Experimental Psychology: Learning, Memory, & Cognition, 29*, 1194–1209.

Palmeri, T. J., & Nosofsky, R. M. (1995). Recognition memory for exceptions to the category rule. *Journal of Experimental Psychology: Learning, Memory, & Cognition, 21*, 548–568.

Pruzansky, S., Tversky, A., & Carroll, J. D. (1982). Spatial versus tree representations of proximity data. *Psychometrika, 47*, 3–24.

Reed, S. K. (1972). Pattern recognition and categorization. *Cognitive Psychology, 3*, 382–407.

Rosch, E. (1975). Cognitive representations of semantic categories. *Journal of Experimental Psychology, 104*, 192–233.

Rosch, E., & Mervis, C. B. (1975). Family resemblances: Studies in the internal structure of categories. *Cognitive Psychology, 7*, 573–605.

Rosch, E., Mervis, C. B., Gray, W. D., Johnson, D. M., & Boyes-Braem, P. (1976). Basic objects in natural categories. *Cognitive Psychology, 8*, 382–439.

Rosch, E., Simpson, C., & Miller, R. S. (1976). Structural bases of typicality effects. *Journal of Experimental Psychology: Human Perception and Performance, 2*, 491–502.

Ross, B. H. (1997). The use of categories affects classification. *Journal of Memory and Language, 37*, 240–267.

Ruts, W., Storms, G., & Hampton, J. A., (2004). Linear separability in superordinate natural language concepts. *Memory & Cognition, 32*, 83–95.

Ruts, W., Van Assche, F., Storms, G., & Hampton, J. A. (2004). *Linear separability in basic level artifacts.* Unpublished manuscript.

Ruts, W., Van Assche, F., Storms, G., & Hampton, J. A., (in preparation). *Linear separability in basic level concepts.*

Sattath, S., & Tversky, A. (1977). Additive similarity trees. *Psychometrika, 42*, 319–345.

Sattath, S., & Tversky, A. (1987). On the relation between common and distinctive feature models. *Psychological Review, 94*, 16–22.

Schwarz, G. (1978). Estimating the dimension of a model. *The Annals of Statistics, 6*, 461–464.

Sebestyen, G. S. (1962). *Decision-making processes in pattern recognition.* New York: Macmillan.

Shepard, R. N. (1964). Attention and the metric structure of the stimulus space. *Journal of Mathematical Psychology, 1*, 54–87.

Shepard, R. N., & Arabie, P. (1979). Additive clustering: Representation of similarities as combinations of discrete overlapping properties. *Psychological Review, 86*, 87–123.

Shepard, R. N., Hovland, C. I., & Jenkins, H. M. (1961). Learning and memorization of classifications. *Psychological Monographs: General and Applied, 75*, 1–42.

Smith, J. D. (2002). Exemplar theory's predicted typicality gradient can be tested and disconfirmed. *Psychological Science, 13*, 437–442.

Smith, J. D., & Minda, J. P. (1998). Prototypes in the mist: The early epochs of category learning. *Journal of Experimental Psychology: Learning, Memory, and Cognition, 24*, 1411–1436.

Smith, J. D., & Minda, J. P. (2000). Thirty categorization results in search of a model. *Journal of Experimental Psychology: Learning, Memory, and Cognition, 26*, 3–27.

Smith, J. D., & Minda, J. P. (2002). Distinguishing prototype-based and exemplar-based processes in dot-pattern category learning. *Journal of Experimental Psychology: Learning, Memory and Cognition, 28*, 800–811.

Smith, J. D., Murray, M. J., & Minda, J. P. (1997). Straight talk about linear separability. *Journal of Experimental Psychology: Learning, Memory, and Cognition, 23*, 659–680.

Smits, T., Storms, G., Rosseel, Y., & De Boeck, P. (2002). Fruits and vegetables categorized: An application of the generalized context model. *Psychonomic Bulletin and Review, 9*, 836–844.

Smoke, K. L. (1932). An objective study of concept formation. *Psychological Monographs, 42.*

Storms, G., De Boeck, P., & Ruts, W. (2000). Prototype and exemplar-based information in natural language categories. *Journal of Memory and Language, 42*, 51–73.

Storms, G., De Boeck, P., & Ruts, W. (2001). Categorization of novel stimuli in well-known natural concepts: A case study. *Psychonomic Bulletin & Review, 8*, 377–384.

Storms, G., De Boeck, P., Van Mechelen, I., & Ruts, W. (1996). The dominance effect in concept conjunctions: Generality and interaction aspects. *Journal of Experimental Psychology: Learning, Memory, & Cognition, 22*, 1–15.

Takane, Y., Young, F. W., & De Leeuw, J. (1977). Nonmetric individual differences multidimensional scaling: An alternating least squares method with optimal scaling features. *Psychometrika, 42*, 7–67.

Tversky, A. (1977). Features of similarity. *Psychological Review, 84*, 327–352.

Verbeemen, T., Storms, G., & Verguts, T. (2003). *Planes, trees, and categories: A comparison of categorization models in natural language concepts.* Manuscript submitted for publication.

Verguts, T., Storms, G., & Tuerlinckx, F. (2003). Decision-bound theory and the influence of familiarity. *Psychonomic Bulletin & Review, 10*, 141–148.

Wattenmaker, W. D., Dewey, G. I., Murphy, T. D., & Medin, D. L. (1986). Linear Separability and concept learning: Context, relational properties, and concept naturalness. *Cognitive Psychology, 18*, 158–194.

SEMANTIC MEMORY: SOME INSIGHTS FROM FEATURE-BASED CONNECTIONIST ATTRACTOR NETWORKS

Ken McRae

I. Introduction

Making our way around the world during our daily lives depends on a great deal of knowledge about events and the entities and things that are part of those events. This knowledge includes information regarding how entities behave on their own and how we use things to perform the functions that are necessary for daily living, like driving a car, putting on our clothes, preparing food, eating our fruits and vegetables, listening to music, and understanding the behaviors of the creatures that cohabit the earth with us. This knowledge builds across the developmental life span, seems to be computed naturally and effortlessly during adulthood, and can, unfortunately, break down due to neural impairments of various sorts.

Central to our ability to deal with all of these aspects of our daily lives is the knowledge that is subsumed under the umbrella of semantic memory. I use the term *semantic memory* to refer to people's memory for word meaning, where word meaning is construed broadly. Thus, semantic memory includes the various types of conceptual information that are tied to specific words. This subset of people's knowledge is central to accomplishing tasks such as recognizing and naming objects or pictures, computing the meaning of spoken and written words, and reasoning about possible identities, functions, and behaviors of objects or entities when presented with partial information. In this chapter, I focus on people's knowledge of concrete noun concepts, that is, lexical concepts corresponding to living

0079-7421/04 $35.00

and nonliving things such as *chair* and *robin*.[1] The meaning of these types of words consists of the confluence of multiple knowledge types, including visual knowledge of various sorts (e.g., parts, shape, size, color, characteristic motion), knowledge associated with the other senses (the sounds things produce and how they smell, taste, and feel), typical behaviors of creatures, and multiple types of situation knowledge, such as knowledge about how, where, when, by whom, and for what purpose things tend to be used. Semantic memory, of course, also includes verb (event) concepts such as *telling* and *running,* abstract concepts such as *love* and *justice,* and concepts corresponding to adjectives and adverbs. However, a great deal can be and has been learned from the study of concrete nouns.

For quite a while now, among researchers who study semantic memory, spreading activation networks (Collins & Loftus, 1975; Collins & Quillian, 1969) have been the bases for the majority of theorizing and empirical investigation. In fact, arguably, in terms of overall popularity, they may still be the approach on which most researchers base their work. Without question, spreading activation networks have played a huge role in propelling the field forward.

The game is changing, however, in large part due to two developments. One is the rise to prominence of connectionist models of semantic memory, particularly in the form of attractor networks (which can be viewed as computational updates and extensions of feature list models, such as those espoused by E. E. Smith, Shoben, & Rips, 1974). This includes important work by Farah and McClelland (1991), Hinton and Shallice (1991), Masson (1995), and Plaut (1995; Plaut & Shallice, 1993). Attractor networks offer principles and metaphors that are extremely useful for understanding various phenomena in this domain. The second development is the excitement generated by the conjunction of research on patients with semantic impairments (Forde & Humphreys, 1999; Martin & Caramazza, 2003) and the imaging of semantic memory (Martin & Chao, 2001). These two developments are central to the story presented herein.

In this chapter, I describe some research that has been conducted in our lab over the past 8 years or so that focuses on predictions and insights derived from a connectionist feature-based approach to studying semantic computations. The methodological basis of our research has been semantic feature production norms that provide an empirically derived representation of people's semantic knowledge. Features are verbal proxies for packets of knowledge, such as <has a handle> or <swims>. Almost all models of semantic memory and concepts and categorization are based at least in part

[1] Throughout the chapter, concept names and experimental items are presented in italics, and feature names are presented in angled brackets, such as <has fur>.

on the notion of semantic features, although they may be instantiated in various architectures (Collins & Loftus, 1975; Kruschke, 1992; Love, Medin, & Gureckis, 2004; Medin & Shaffer, 1978; Rehder & Murphy, 2003; Sloman, Love, & Ahn, 1998).

Connectionist attractor networks serve as the theoretical basis for our semantic memory research and the testing ground of our theories. There are two key aspects of attractor networks on which I focus in this chapter. The first is the fact that these models naturally encode and use the distributional statistics of patterns to which they are exposed. This serves as a straightforward prediction that humans do as well. The second aspect concerns the temporal dynamics of computations in these networks. Conducting simulations using models that gradually compute representations over time leads to intriguing insights and predictions that would not be possible otherwise (as compared to, for example, feed-forward back-propagation networks or static computations of similarity). These two aspects of attractor networks are interdependent because the manner in which concepts are computed over time depends on the distributional statistics that are stored in a network's weights. Predictions derived from the principles underlying these models and concrete simulations of human experiments can be used to test the validity of this approach. Thus, the goal of this chapter is to present evidence that a view inspired by feature-based attractor networks provides insight into behavioral phenomena regarding significant aspects of semantic knowledge and computations.

The outline of this chapter is as follows. Section II briefly describes our large set of feature norms and outlines how I view them, including some of their strengths and limitations. Section III presents some arguments concerning the reasons why attractor networks are a useful tool for studying semantic memory and conceptual computations. Section IV focuses on people's knowledge of implicit statistically based feature correlations and explicit theory-based feature relations. I emphasize a careful consideration of the character of each of these types of knowledge with respect to analyses of various tasks that might be used to test for their influence. In short, I illustrate that the influence of both types of knowledge is apparent in appropriate tasks. Section V focuses on the dynamics of concept similarity, in particular how the computational dynamics of attractor networks cohere seemingly inconsistent results regarding priming between basic-level concepts (*truck–van*) versus priming from superordinate to basic-level exemplar concepts (*vehicle–truck*). Section VI presents insights into the organization of semantic memory in the mind and brain that were inspired by connectionist principles and neural imaging. This investigation uses data regarding category-specific semantic deficits as the target phenomena to be explained. I conclude in Section VII.

II. Why Feature Norms?

We use semantic feature production norms to construct empirically derived conceptual representations for testing theories of semantic representation and computation. In a feature norming task, subjects typically are provided with the name of a concept (in our norms, a basic-level concept such as *dog* or *cherry*) and are asked to list features of various types that are relevant to that concept. In our norming task, subjects were given 10 lines on which to write down features. For cherry, for example, subjects listed features such as <a fruit>, <has a stem>, <has a pit>, <is round>, <is small>, <is red>, <grows on trees>, <eaten in pies>, <tastes sweet>, and <is delicious>. Our current set of norms consists of 541 living and nonliving things, although much of the research reported in the chapter was based on our original set of 190 concepts (described in McRae, de Sa, & Seidenberg, 1997). Each conceptual representation is constructed by summing across 30 subjects' responses (and each subject listed features for either 20 or 24 concepts). A complete description of the norms is presented in McRae, Cree, Seidenberg, and McNorgan (in press).

Semantic feature production norms have been used for 30 years as the basis for studies of semantic memory and concepts and categorization. For example, Rosch and Mervis (1975) collected feature norms and used them to calculate family-resemblance scores for a set of categories, where family resemblance is a measure of the degree to which a concept's features overlap with those of other concepts in a category. They showed that family resemblance predicts typicality ratings (people's ratings of how typical an exemplar is with respect to a specific category; e.g., a robin is a highly typical bird, but a penguin is not). Since then, featural representations derived from norms have been the basis of accounts of numerous empirical phenomena such as semantic similarity priming (Cree, McRae, & McNorgan, 1999; McRae et al., 1997; Vigliocco, Vinson, Lewis, & Garrett, 2004), feature verification (Ashcraft, 1978; McRae, Cree, Westmacott, & de Sa, 1999; Solomon & Barsalou, 2001), categorization (Hampton, 1979; E. E. Smith, Shoben, & Rips, 1974), and conceptual combination (Hampton, 1997; E. E. Smith, Osherson, Rips, & Keane, 1988).

Representations derived from feature norms are also a useful tool for any type of modeling that requires vector representations because such representations can be derived easily from norms. Cree et al. (1999) argued for basing models on empirically derived representations, rather than either algorithmically generated pseudo-random representations or representations based on experimenters' intuitions. The primary reason is that empirically derived representations substantially reduce degrees of freedom in modeling. A second factor is that feature norms lead to representations that incorporate valid distributional statistics of the patterns that a network learns. Simulating human behavior on relevant tasks benefits from training a model on representations that approximate the actual distributional statistics present in the world. In contrast, models based on pseudo-representations may capture broad generalities of the underlying distributional statistics, or they may miss them entirely. This point is exemplified in Daugherty and Seidenberg's (1992) past-tense verb modeling in which simulations were successful only when the model was trained on patterns that incorporated proper distributional information.

Feature norms provide valid information about lexical concepts not because they offer a literal record of people's semantic representations (i.e., they are not a verbatim readout), but rather because those representations are used systematically when people generate features (Barsalou, in press). Note that we do not believe that semantic knowledge is represented in the brain literally as a list of verbalizable features. Instead, we believe that when subjects produce features, they exploit representations that have developed through repeated multisensory exposure to, and interactions with, exemplars of the target category. Barsalou uses his framework of perceptual symbol systems to account for processes underlying feature production. In his view, subjects generate features by constructing a holistic simulation of a category, followed by interpreting that representation and translating it into verbalizable feature names. Thus, feature norms are not a measure of a category's underlying static memory abstraction (which we agree does not exist), but instead correspond to a temporary abstraction constructed online for the purpose of producing verbal features. Because there is substantial variability both across and within participants due to the dynamic nature of feature listing, multiple participants are asked to list features for each concept (30 subjects in our norms). Responses are then amalgamated to produce an averaged representation. Thus, feature norms provide a window into critical aspects of word meaning without necessarily being definitive (Medin, 1989).

Because feature listing requires subjects to convey their conceptual knowledge through a linguistic filter, information varies in how clearly it is transmitted. Knowledge types such as parts (<has a handle>), color (<is red>), what an object typically is used for (<used for cutting>), who typically uses it (<used by children>), where an object or entity typically is located (<found in kitchens>), and characteristic behaviors of animals (<barks>) are relatively easily verbalizable. However, some knowledge types are omitted to a large extent in verbal feature norms, particularly when subjects list features as short written descriptors. For example, knowledge of spatial and size relations among parts is important to recognizing objects and entities. Because they are difficult to verbalize, they simply are missing from the norms (see Cree & McRae, 2003, for further discussion).

III. Why Attractor Networks?

Forster (1994) stated that connectionist networks are inappropriate for modeling semantic processing because the mappings from spelling or sound to meaning are largely arbitrary, whereas connectionist networks are best suited for learning pseudo-regular mappings. For example, Seidenberg and McClelland's (1989) feed-forward back-propagation model of computing phonology from orthography was successful to a large degree because the mapping between those two domains in English is pseudo-regular (i.e., there exist regularities of various strengths between letters and sounds, or groups of letters and sounds, but there are numerous exceptions to those regularities as well. For example, "int" is pronounced as in *mint* most of the time, but it is also pronounced as in *pint*. Feed-forward back-propagation models are well suited for learning this type of pseudo-regular between-domain structure. In contrast, there do not exist subword regularities between word form (spelling or sound) and word meaning; that is, for monomorphemic words at least, there is little if any word form to meaning between-domain structure. For example, the letter *c* or the letters *int* do not reliably indicate any component of meaning; *lint, mint*, and *tint* are not similar in meaning.

When Forster made his statement, he presumably considered only between-domain structure and only feed-forward back-propagation networks. However, it is crucial to consider within-domain structure and other types of connectionist models. There is a great deal of structure within spelling, sound, and meaning. In spelling or sound, some pairs of letters or phonemes co-occur much more often than do others (e.g., *st* vs. *sl* vs. *kt*). The regularities that exist in terms of how letters (or phonemes) co-occur within words in languages such as English have been well documented and studied (Solso & Juel, 1980; Westbury & Buchanan, 2002). Most important for our purposes, precisely the type of semantic regularities that can easily be exploited by recurrent connectionist attractor networks exists in terms of how features co-occur across basic-level concepts. That is, there is a great deal of within-domain semantic structure because there are numerous pairs of correlated features in the world, with some pairs of features co-occurring much more often than others (<has a beak> and <has feathers> vs. <has a beak> and <swims>; McRae et al., 1997). Attractor networks (but not standard feed-forward networks) naturally pick up on these within-domain semantic regularities, and the weights in which these regularities are encoded play a major role in driving processing, as is outlined in detail below in Section IV. In summary, although Forster was correct to claim that standard feed-forward networks are probably not a great way to simulate semantic processing, the key point here is that attractor networks are particularly well suited for modeling semantic computations.

Our research borrows heavily from attractor networks of semantic memory and word pronunciation that have been conducted by researchers such as Farah and McClelland (1991), Hinton and Shallice (1991), Masson (1995), and Plaut (1995; Plaut & Booth, 2000; Plaut, McClelland, Seidenberg, & Patterson, 1996; Plaut & Shallice, 1993). For example, Farah and McClelland (1991) used a network that divided semantic knowledge into sensory and functional information to account for a number of the primary behavioral phenomena that were known at that time regarding category-specific semantic deficits patients. The network proposed in Section VI is an extension of their model. Hinton and Shallice and Plaut and Shallice used attractor networks to account for the intriguing phenomena regarding deep dyslexics. In doing so, they shed a great deal of light on how attractor networks work, and how the notion of attractor landscapes, both before and after damage to a network, can be used to understand these phenomena. Finally, Masson, Plaut, and Plaut and Booth have all used attractor networks to provide mechanistic explanations of semantic priming effects in adults and children.

We have used various instantiations of attractor networks of semantic processing, depending on the specific principles being highlighted (see Fig. 1). Unlike the models cited in the previous paragraph that used either random vectors, variants from idealized prototypes, or experimenter-generated featural representations, all of our models have used semantic representations in which each semantic unit corresponds to a feature from our norms. In addition, we have used random patterns to represent word forms (either spelling or sound). Thus, our previous networks did not actually encode within-domain word form regularities; basically, all the important action happens within semantics. Because the monomorphemic words on which we have focused do not exhibit regularities in their form-meaning mapping, we have avoided introducing systematicity into the mapping. McRae et al. (1997, 1999) used a modified Hopfield (1982, 1984) network with fully interconnected semantic units (Fig. 1a). This allows the network to encode semantic structure; that is, the pseudoregularities that exist between (or among) semantic features. Because our Hopfield network contained feature–feature connections, semantic structure was in the form of correlations between pairs of features across basic-level concepts (such as the fact that things in the world that have fur also tend to have four legs). Sets of feature–feature connections also allow these networks to learn clusters of intercorrelated features (such as <has wings>, <has a beak>, <has feathers>, and <lays eggs> across the set of birds on which they were trained).

We have also used two variants of back-propagation through time networks with continuous time units in which unit activations change gradually over time. The use of algorithms based on back-propagation overcomes the

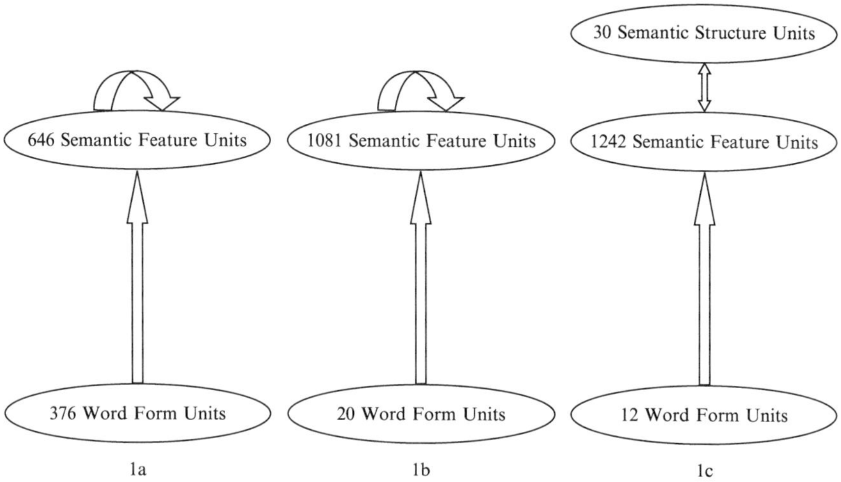

Fig. 1. Depictions of the attractor networks used in McRae et al. (1997, 1999; Fig. 1a), Cree and McRae (1999; Fig. 1b), and Cree et al. (1999; Fig. 1c).

limited capacity storage problems inherent to Hopfield networks that are due to the simplicity of the Hebb (1949); learning rule (Hertz, Krogh, & Palmer, 1991; Hopfield, 1982, 1984). In one network discussed later (Cree & McRae, 1999; Fig. 1b), the semantic feature units were fully interconnected, as in the Hopfield network. In the other (Cree et al., 1999, Fig. 1c), semantic structure hidden units were used to encode how features co-occur, although they do so in a more opaque manner than direct feature–feature weights. This type of network was introduced by Hinton and Shallice (1991), who called the semantic structure units "clean-up units."

The architecture of an attractor network must contain some sort of recurrent connections. Due to recurrence, units can be updated over multiple time cycles (ticks), and units change their activation over time in response to changes in other units' activations. Therefore, a network changes state not only in response to new input, but also due to its own evolving state while the input is held constant. We have implemented recurrence in semantics using either direct feature-to-feature connections (Fig. 1a and b) or indirect connections accomplished by having feature units feed activation to a set of hidden units (called semantic structure units in Fig. 1c to highlight their function), which in turn feed activation back to the feature units.

In our attractor networks, an input (e.g., a concept name such as *dog*) is presented constantly over multiple time ticks (this is called hard-clamping the input). During these time ticks, the state of the trained network changes slowly until it settles into the activation state corresponding to the learned concept (e.g., the features of *dog* are turned on, with all other feature units turned off). In the back-propagation through time networks shown in Fig. 1b and 1c, the net input function is constructed to promote gradual settling. This is accomplished by having the net input to a unit depend on both the net input at the current time tick and the net input at the previous time tick (called time-averaged inputs; Plaut et al., 1996). In our networks, a feature unit's net input is .8 times its net input at the previous tick, plus .2 times its net input at the current tick. In this manner, net input to a unit, and thus activation of a unit, changes gradually over time. Time-averaged inputs keep units from jumping to their correct end-state activation immediately.

We also implement back-propagation through time learning in such a way as to promote gradual settling by back-propagating error over only certain time ticks. We typically have provided the target pattern for error-driven learning for only the final half of the ticks for each pattern. We have trained our networks using 20 ticks per concept and back-propagate error over only the final 10. In this manner, the network essentially is given 10 ticks for feature unit activations to gradually change in order to reach the target activations. Thus, the network is not forced to compute the target immediately.

In an attractor network, learned patterns can be thought of as stable states in a multidimensional state space. For example, a lexical concept can be considered as a point (or a location) in a space that is defined by the various types of visual, other sensory, functional, and other features that exist for the entire set of concepts on which a model is trained. Thus, in a model such as that presented in Fig. 1c that was based on our original set of 190 concepts, each concept is a point in a 1242-dimensional space (the total number of features required to represent all 190 concepts). A learned concept is referred to as a stable state because when a network arrives at this state, it will remain there until it is perturbed by new input. That is, a stable state is a state of equilibrium (low energy) for the network. Surrounding each of these attractor points is what is called a basin of attraction. An attractor basin can be thought of as a valley in the set of possible network states. When a trained network is in a state corresponding to being within an attractor basin (corresponding to one of the learned patterns), unless new input intervenes, it will settle down to the stable attractor point (the lowest point in the valley), which represents a concept, in our case. Therefore, a major characteristic of attractor networks is that they perform pattern completion; given a partial pattern of a learned concept, they settle to a state representing that concept.

In many of our simulations, when we input a representation of a concept's name (the word's form), the network initially computes a representation that approximates the concept to some degree; it is a messy representation that is, however, close enough that it resides within the correct concept's attractor basin. Therefore, to learn a set of patterns, one task for the network is to partition the state space so that the initial pattern of activation from an input lies somewhere within the correct basin of attraction. From this initial point in semantic space, the speed with which the network settles to the stable attractor point is determined by encoded clusters of features comprising the concept (i.e., within-domain semantic structure), plus further input from the concepts' name (word form).

In the ensuing sections, I focus on predictions derived from the factors that influence the speed with which a network settles to an attractor once it is in the appropriate attractor basin, the distance between attractors, the ease with which a network can move from one attractor to another, and the factors that influence the probability of getting to the correct attractor in the first place, particularly following damage to the system.

IV. Feature Correlations and Relations

Semantic/conceptual representations serve as the basis for many types of computations. These include the computations underlying tasks such as computing word meaning, object recognition, categorization, rating typicality, predicting how one should interact with something, and making inferences about novel exemplars. These conceptual tasks span a range from speeded online judgments to slower, more problem-solving-type tasks, both in the real world and in the laboratory. Therefore, it is reasonable to assume that the knowledge and/or computations underlying these tasks also span a range, from statistically based knowledge that can be considered more implicit, to complex theory-based knowledge and computations that can be considered more explicit (Holyoak & Spellman, 1993; Lin & Murphy, 1997). In this section, I focus on how carefully considering the degree of correspondence between type of knowledge and type of task is essential to understanding and illuminating the types of knowledge that people learn and use. That is, it seems reasonable to expect that these types of knowledge and computations would show more or less of an influence on various tasks, depending on the degree to which they match task demands (Jones & L. B. Smith, 1993).

In this section, I focus on two types of knowledge. The first is statistically based knowledge of feature correlations that is highlighted in statistical learning approaches, such as attractor networks that naturally encode how features co-occur. The term *feature correlations* in this chapter refers to the fact that two features are correlated if they tend to occur in the same basic-level concepts. For example, <has fur> and <has four legs> are correlated because things like dogs, cats, cows, and chipmunks that have fur on their bodies also have four legs. Correlation is a matter of degree, of course; some pairs of features are much more strongly correlated than others. Attractor networks of the types that we have used not only encode that a dog <has four legs>, <has fur>, <barks>, and so forth, but also encode the degree to which certain pairs of features co-occur across concepts. The network's knowledge of feature correlations that is encoded in either feature–feature weights or through semantic structure units influences its settling dynamics and is the primary determinant of its semantically based pattern completion abilities (Cree et al., 1999; McRae et al., 1997, 1999). Although this type of knowledge is portrayed in terms of statistics, if asked, people typically are able to report that feature pairs such as these do indeed tend to co-occur (e.g., they will likely concur that things that have fur also tend to have four legs). However, it appears that for most feature pairs of this sort, people have rarely explicitly thought about their co-occurrence, nor do they necessarily possess a theory about why these features tend to go together.

The second type of knowledge is theory-based relations between features, which is highlighted in knowledge-based theories of concepts and categorization (Ahn, Marsh, Luhmann, & Lee, 2002; Murphy & Medin, 1985). In this chapter, I refer to this type of knowledge as *feature relations*. Explicit theory-based feature relations are often explicated in terms of causal theories that link two features, such as the fact that <has wings> is causally related to <flies>, or that <has a blade> is causally related to <used for cutting>. Of course, these pairs of features also do co-occur statistically across basic-level concepts, presumably relatively strongly. It is central to explicit theory-based feature relation accounts that people can both report that the features co-occur and that people possess a coherent (typically causal) theory regarding why they do so.

A central issue that has been raised in the literature concerns the extent to which either or both of feature correlations and relations are part of people's conceptual knowledge. Ahn et al. (2002) recently conducted a series of studies to address this issue. They directly asked people for their knowledge of feature relations and found that subjects could reliably report both the direction and strength of such relations for a subset of correlated features. They also found evidence that subjects possess a causal theory for some pairs (although not all theories were causal). Unfortunately, they did not compare a statistical measure of correlational strength for feature pairs that were related in this way versus those that were not. Therefore, the relationship between statistical and causal strength is unknown for their items. Ahn et al. collected offline categorization judgments and typicality ratings for artificial concepts consisting of small sets of features. They contrasted feature sets in which feature relations versus correlations were either preserved or violated. Subjects' performance on these tasks was influenced by feature relations, and thus Ahn et al. concluded that causally based knowledge regarding why certain pairs of features co-occur across basic-level concepts is represented in people's minds. Ahn et al. took this as evidence for knowledge-based theories of conceptual representation. We agree with these conclusions.

However, Ahn et al. (2002) also concluded that "correlations that are present in our representations of real-world concept are the ones with explanatory relations" (p. 115). They went on to state that people "do not encode all conjunctions of features" because "there are too many conjunctions of features to keep track of" (p. 115). This view has been expressed in various other articles as well (Malt & Smith, 1984; Medin & Coley, 1998; Murphy & Medin, 1985), and it is one with which we strongly disagree. In this view, the task of learning feature correlations consists of both explicitly noticing that two features co-occur (kind of an "aha" phenomenon), and then constructing a link between them in a model such as a spreading activation network, or a prototype-style feature list. Because the sets of entity and object parts, sounds, functions, characteristic behaviors, and so forth is large, and therefore because the set of feature pairs is even larger, this is viewed as a computationally intractable problem. The core problem here is that there is a mismatch between type of knowledge (implicit statistically based) and type of learning (explicit noticing).

In stark contrast, if these issues are approached from either a cognitive neuroscience or a statistical-learning point of view, it would be somewhat shocking if people failed to learn feature correlations in natural observational-learning settings. Many psychologists and neuroscientists would argue that correlational learning is a major aspect of what the brain does; it appears that sets of neurons are particularly proficient at learning correlations. For example, developmental research in language learning shows that infants are adept at picking up on phonotactic regularities (Saffran, Aslin, & Newport, 1996), prosodic structure (Jusczyk, Cutler, & Redanz, 1993), and regularities among visual features of novel animals (Younger & Cohen, 1983, 1986). Attractor networks of cognitive processing, being neurally inspired models, are particularly adept at learning exactly this type of structure, and thus our models of semantic processing naturally encode feature correlations. (Note that I certainly do not wish to be too literal about the correspondence between the types of networks that we have used and actual neural processing. However, they presumably do correspond in terms of encoding environmental structure that then influences computational dynamics.) Therefore, this change in viewpoint shifts the focus from intentional, explicit learning of structure to incidental, observational, implicit learning of structure, suggesting that learning feature correlations is a natural part of learning object concepts and that this knowledge influences online semantic computations.

A. Tasks, Computations, and Types of Knowledge

Given the contrasting natures of feature correlations versus feature relations, they should influence online and offline tasks to different degrees. As Ahn et al. (2002) showed, the influence of feature relations should be most apparent in offline tasks such as category judgments and typicality ratings (see also Murphy & Ross, 1994). In contrast, given that feature correlations play a role in the temporal dynamics of attractor networks, their influence should be most apparent in online speeded tasks. Note that studies such as Ahn et al. and Malt and Smith (1984), who failed to find effects of feature correlations, used offline tasks only.

In accord with these predictions, we have demonstrated influences of feature correlations in online tasks in two articles (McRae et al., 1997, 1999). Here, I focus on the speeded feature verification studies and associated simulations of McRae et al. (1999). We began by calculating the Pearson correlation between all pairs of features that occurred in at least 3 of the 190 concepts on which this research was based (correlations involving features occurring in only 1 or 2 concepts were treated as spurious). Each feature was represented as a 190-unit vector (one element for each concept) in which each vector element corresponded to the number of subjects in the norming study who listed that feature for the specific concept. For example, 17 of 30 subjects listed <has four legs> for *zebra*, so the <has four legs>-*zebra* unit had a value of 17. Feature pairs varied greatly in their proportion of shared variance, ranging from <chirps> <eats seeds> sharing 96% of their variance, to pairs such as <has drawers> <is heavy> which resided at $p < .01$ cutoff of 6.5%. The fact that these feature vectors tended to be quite sparse also has some important ramifications. Mainly, the absence of a feature in a particular concept carries little information in a sparse representation. This presumably is true for humans as well; the fact that a chair does not fly is uninformative; there are numerous features that do not apply to chairs. Therefore, feature correlations are dominated by features present in objects, and negative correlations are extremely rare.

We used percentage-shared variance between significantly correlated feature pairs to define a measure called intercorrelational strength. Intercorrelational strength measures the degree to which a specific feature is correlated with the other features of a concept; it is the sum of the percentage shared variance between a target feature and the other features of a specific concept. One example used in McRae et al. (1999) is that of <hunted by people> as a target feature. According to the norms, this feature is strongly intercorrelated with the other features of *deer* (intercorrelational strength = 326), but weakly intercorrelated with the other features of *duck* (intercorrelational strength = 61). This occurs because, in general, things that people hunt have antlers, hooves, fur, four legs, and live in the woods, all of which are features of *deer* but not of *duck*.

McRae et al. (1999) conducted two feature verification experiments in which we manipulated intercorrelational strength. In Experiment 1, a concept name such as *deer* was presented for either 300 or 2000 ms, and then a target feature name such as <hunted by people> was presented below the concept name until the subject responded ("Is the feature reasonably true of the concept?"). Nine possible confounding variables were equated (something that was possible due to distributional statistics calculated from the feature norms, plus other norms that we collected, such as familiarity ratings for concepts). In addition, all variables associated with the feature itself were equated because two concepts were paired with one feature, the feature was presented second, and verification latency was measured from feature name onset.

This experiment was simulated using the attractor network of McRae et al. (1997; Fig. 1a). The concept word form was presented to the network, and the target feature's activation was tracked over time. The activation of the target feature increased more quickly when the semantic representation of the concept from the strongly intercorrelated group was computed. This was due to mutual reinforcement among co-occurring features that resulted because feature correlations were encoded in the network relatively transparently in the feature–feature weights. Therefore, as the features of *deer* become activated, they strongly coactivate the <hunted by people> unit via their strong positive weights to that feature. In addition, "hunted by people" in turn activates those other features; it is part of a cluster of intercorrelated features that boost each other's activations. The features of *duck* also tend to share positive weights with <hunted by people> because these features do co-occur with it, at least in that concept, but to an overall lesser degree than in the case of *deer*. The simulation further predicted an intercorrelational strength by SOA interaction with a larger difference between the strongly and weakly intercorrelated groups at the shorter SOA. This interaction was predicted because the target feature was included in both concepts, so that its activation differed only marginally at later time ticks for the strongly and weakly intercorrelated concepts (it was close to the ceiling of 1.0 for both). The human data corresponded nicely with the network's predictions. There was an intercorrelational strength by SOA interaction due to an 83 ms effect for the 300 ms SOA versus a 37 ms effect for the 2000 ms SOA, with both effects of feature correlations being significant.

In McRae et al.'s (1999) Experiment 2, the presentation order was reversed such that a target feature name such as <has wheels> was presented first, followed by a concept name such as *van*. Because the concept name was presented second, this design calls for pairing each concept with two features, so that all variables associated with the concepts themselves are equated because decision latency is measured from the onset of the concept name. Therefore, each concept, such as *van* was paired with both a feature that was highly intercorrelated with its other features, <has wheels>, and one that was weakly intercorrelated with its other features, <has doors>. Eight potentially confounding variables were equated. In addition, all variables associated with the concept itself were equated because the same concept was used in both groups, the concept name was presented second, and decision latency was measured from its onset (either 300 or 2000 ms after the onset of the feature name).

The reversed presentation order required a different simulation. We assumed that feature verification latency in this case is at least partly and monotonically determined by the time it takes to move from a semantic state corresponding to the target feature's meaning to the state corresponding to the basic-level concept. Therefore, we highly activated the semantic unit representing the target feature and let the model iterate (with the word form to semantic units disabled). Hopfield networks are pattern completion devices; given part of a learned pattern, such a network settles to a state representing the entire pattern. Of course, in this instance, only a single feature unit was activated, and this feature was shared by multiple concepts (on average, 10 for the strongly intercorrelated features and 9 for the weakly intercorrelated ones), so a stable state representing a specific concept was not achieved. However, a single feature will activate the units of features that are correlated with it, and they will in turn mutually activate one another through shared positive weights. As the network iterated, we counted the number of features of the target concept that were activated at each time tick.

The network again predicted an intercorrelational strength by SOA interaction, but this time the interaction was opposite to the one predicted when the concept name was presented first (i.e., a stronger effect of feature correlations as time went on). This interaction occurred because the feature that was strongly intercorrelated with the other features of the target concept (as in <has wheels> *van*) mutually reinforced those features, so that a number of features of the target concept remained activated over time. Because it was part of a cluster of intercorrelated features, the number of features of the target concept that were turned on by the strongly intercorrelated target feature remained relatively stable over time. In contrast, features that were weakly intercorrelated with the target concept's other features (as in <has doors> *van*) either mutually reinforced a cluster of features that were not in that concept or failed to activate any cluster of intercorrelated features at all (so that activation basically dispersed throughout the network). Therefore, the difference between the two conditions increased over time. The human data also showed this interaction; there was a significant 37 ms effect of intercorrelational strength at the 300 ms SOA, and a much larger 76 ms effect when the SOA was 2000 ms. In summary, an attractor network successfully predicted contrasting intercorrelational strength by SOA interactions on feature verification latency that were obtained with human subjects.

Given an attractor network viewpoint, it is completely natural and understandable that people would (implicitly) pick up on statistical correlations among features and that these correlations would influence online conceptual computations. The notion that people learn feature correlations present in real-world stimuli that possess a great deal of semantic structure is consistent with research using incidental concept learning (Billman & Knutson, 1996; Clapper & Bower, 1991; Wattenmaker, 1993; Younger & Cohen, 1983, 1986). Billman and Heit (1988) have shown that a greater degree of structure makes learning feature correlations easier rather than harder, in that learning a specific correlation is easier if it is part of a system exhibiting coherent structure, as in the case of real-world object concepts. Finally, it appears that people do not possess theory-based relations for the vast majority of the correlated feature pairs that were part of the calculation of intercorrelational strength (Ahn et al., 2002; McRae & McNorgan, 2003), discussed in more detail later. It is certainly difficult to imagine how theory-based relations might account for the contrasting intercorrelational strength by SOA interactions found by McRae et al. (1999).

Neither Ahn et al. (2002) nor McRae et al. (1999) directly compared speeded versus untimed tasks. However, McRae et al. (1997) did do so, in that we directly compared the influence of feature correlations in two yoked pairs of online versus offline tasks, short SOA priming versus similarity ratings, and speeded feature verification versus untimed feature typicality ratings. McRae et al. (1997) found that feature correlations influenced priming in that concept similarity calculated over correlated feature pairs predicted short SOA priming effects for living things, but not for nonliving things (priming was predicted by similarity calculated over individual features). We attributed the living–nonliving difference to the fact that living things tend to possess a greater number of correlated feature pairs, and thus there was an increased opportunity to detect their effects. In contrast, offline similarity ratings for both living and nonliving things were accounted for by similarity calculated over individual features. McRae et al. (1997) obtained an analogous result when comparing online speeded feature verification versus offline feature typicality ratings ("How typical is feature *X* of concept *Y*?"). Intercorrelational strength (as previously described) predicted feature verification latencies but not feature typicality ratings.

In summary, taking into account the results of McRae et al. (1997, 1999), Ahn et al. (2002), and Malt and Smith (1984), it appears that type of knowledge lines up rather nicely with type of task. Theory-based knowledge concerning the manner in which pairs of features are related influences performance on slower offline tasks, whereas statistically based knowledge of feature correlations influences performance on speeded online tasks.

Given that the task/type of knowledge correspondence has been established, it is interesting to ask whether, under the right conditions, it might be possible to observe influences of feature correlations in an offline task or feature relations in a speeded task. McRae and McNorgan (2003) investigated whether it might be possible to observe an influence of feature correlations in an offline task. The most likely candidate would be a task that directly taps knowledge of feature pairs (in contrast to, e.g., categorization judgments or typicality ratings). Therefore, we chose 65 pairs of features that spanned a wide range of degree of percentage of shared variance. For each pair, subjects were asked to "Please indicate the degree to which the following feature pairs are related, that is, the extent to which the two features tend to go together." A nine-point scale ranged from "not at all related" (1) through "moderately related" (5) to "extremely highly related" (9). The percentage of shared variance between pairs of features as measured by the norms, and as is encoded in an attractor network, predicted subjects' relatedness ratings ($r = .42$, $p < .001$).

McRae and McNorgan (2003) also used the 65 feature pairs as stimuli in an interview study. For each pair, we asked subjects questions such as whether they had ever noticed that these features occur together in things, and whether they had a theory about why these features go together. We also asked subjects to describe their theory, and then whether they had generated this theory during the interview, or whether they had thought of it prior to that day. From this task, we took the liberal measure of the number of subjects who attested to having a theory at all (whether or not they invented it at that moment) and used it to predict feature relatedness ratings, which it did ($r = .57$, $p < .001$).

McRae and McNorgan (2003) then used a stepwise regression analysis to investigate whether effects of both feature correlations (percentage shared variance) and feature relations (likelihood of having a theory, whether invented at that moment or not) would be apparent in the prediction of feature relatedness ratings. Both variables entered the equation and predicted 37% of the variance in total. In terms of unique variation accounted for by each variable, the feature relation measure was a somewhat stronger unique predictor ($r = .49, p < .001$) than was the feature correlation measure ($r = .27, p < .05$). Thus, in this offline task that directly taps knowledge about feature co-occurrence, the influence of theory-based feature relations, at least as measured in this liberal manner, is somewhat stronger than that of feature correlations.

The remaining question concerns whether the influence of feature relations might be detected in speeded tasks. Contrary to this notion, Sloman, Love, and Ahn (1998) stated that "we propose that early access to concepts ignores the contents of relations; only slower processing makes use of it. One cognitive activity that involves such slow processing is the explicit application of naive or scientific theories to categorization" (p. 204). Two studies have investigated whether background theory-based knowledge of some sort can affect speeded tasks.

Palmeri and Blalock (2000) asked subjects to learn to categorize cartoon drawings of people. One group of subjects were told that the people in one category had been drawn by creative children, whereas the others were drawn by noncreative children. Using a response deadline of 500 ms, they found differences between these two conditions in speeded categorization. One conclusion from these results might be that the background theory-based knowledge was computed and brought to bear extremely quickly during the decision process. However, Palmeri and Blalock favored the conclusion that their manipulation fostered a gestaltlike holistic response strategy for the subjects given the creativity cover story. They concluded that subjects were able to respond quickly on the basis of global differences between the two sets of drawings, such as the fact that the creative drawings generally were more detailed. Thus, they concluded that background theory-based knowledge was not being computed and used quickly in this task, per se.

Lin and Murphy (1997) conducted a set of studies that is more closely related to the issue of feature relations and correlations. Two sets of subjects were given novel line drawings to learn, and each was provided with cover stories regarding the function of the objects, and relations between that function and specific parts. In this clever design, a part was either essential or nonessential to the object's function (e.g., a loop of rope at the end of the instrument was used to catch a small animal in one cover story, versus being used to hang up a pesticide spraying device in the other). Lin and Murphy found strong effects of these part–function relations in offline percent categorization and typicality measures (Experiment 1). They also found effects in timed percent categorization and verification latencies in their Experiment 2, although the latencies were quite long, ranging from about 2100–2900 ms on average by condition (in contrast, the feature verification latencies in McRae et al., 1999, were about 700–900 ms, depending on the presentation order and SOA). Lin and Murphy also found influences of feature relations when using a 1-second response deadline, although they reported the percentage correct, but not latencies (Experiment 4). When the pictures were presented for only 50 ms followed by a mask, effects were found for percentage category verification decisions, but no effects were found in the response latency measure (Experiment 6). The same basic pattern of results obtained for part detection tasks ("Are all parts of the object present?"; Experiments 3, 5, and 7).

Lin and Murphy (1997) concluded that background theory-based knowledge concerning the relations between function and parts influences speeded online processing. There are two main possible mechanistic accounts. The first is that explicit theory-based knowledge regarding the relations between each part and its function is computed and used extremely quickly when people make categorization or part-detection decisions. The second, as Lin and Murphy stated, "is that background knowledge primarily influences the salience or weight of the critical parts encoded in subjects' representations of the categories during learning.... On this account then, the locus of knowledge effects is at the stage of acquiring the concept" (p. 1167). This appears to be the most likely account of the data. Basically, the background knowledge acts to direct attention differentially to various parts of an object during learning, thus altering people's conceptual representations. The influence of feature salience is then observed in speeded tasks (see also Murphy, 2002). Certainly, it seems likely that background knowledge of feature relations influences learning, and thus influences encoded statistics. Likewise, the strength of statistical feature correlations likely influences the probability that people would be motivated to generate a theory to explain a co-occurrence. In these ways, the two types of knowledge seem certain to be intertwined.

Finally, further effects of statistically based feature correlations have been highlighted in recent simulations by Rehder and Murphy (2003). They implemented an attractor network of categorization (using contrastive Hebbian learning) to illustrate that background knowledge influences people's ability to learn novel categories. Interestingly, one of the two types of background knowledge was feature correlations, which our modeling and human studies illustrate that people naturally learn and use. Although Rehder and Murphy sometimes refer to the knowledge as feature intercorrelations and sometimes as feature relations, they implement this background knowledge by setting feature–feature weights by hand (although they do not code for strength of correlation and they include strong negative correlations, which we do not find). Given that the weights in their model are bidirectional and symmetrical, this presumably cannot represent causally based feature relations, which are by definition directional (e.g., wings cause flying but not the other way around). Thus, by showing an influence of hand-coded feature correlations on learning novel categories, Rehder and Murphy provide further evidence for the use of statistically based feature correlations in conceptual processing.

In summary, conceptual representations are multifaceted and serve as the basis for numerous types of computations. Various types of knowledge/computations show more or less influence on various types of tasks, depending on the degree of correspondence between knowledge/computation and task. Using a variety of conceptual tasks, one can see that both feature relations highlighted in knowledge-based accounts, and statistically based feature correlations highlighted in attractor network accounts, are learned and influence conceptual computations.

V. The Dynamics of Similarity

Similarity effects are ubiquitous in perception and cognition. In line with this, concept similarity has played a role in numerous accounts of semantic processing and categorization, and its influence has been studied in a variety of ways. For example, researchers have investigated the factors underlying how people explicitly rate similarity between pairs of concepts (Tversky, 1977) and how people align multiple concepts to facilitate similarity or same–different judgments (Markman & Gentner, 1993). Similarity has also played a role in most accounts of how people rate the typicality of exemplars such as *jeep* and *tricycle* with respect to superordinate categories like *vehicle* (although not for ad hoc categories, e.g., "things to take out of the house if it's on fire"; Barsalou, 1985). Online tasks such as word–picture interference in picture naming and short SOA semantic priming have also been used to uncover the influence of similarity between basic-level concepts like *van* and *truck* (McRae & Boisvert, 1998; Vigliocco et al., 2004). Priming has also been used to test whether superordinate concepts (e.g., *vehicle*) prime high typicality exemplars (*jeep*) versus lower typicality exemplars (*tricycle*); Schwanenflugel & Rey, 1986). This section focuses on understanding two pairs of results that appear to be mutually inconsistent. On the one hand, similarity ratings between pairs of basic-level exemplars align nicely with the magnitude of exemplar–exemplar semantic priming effects. On the other hand, however, typicality ratings of basic-level exemplars with respect to superordinate categories do not align with the magnitude of superordinate–exemplar priming effects. This research highlights an advantage of using attractor networks to simulate such tasks, in that these results that seem inconsistent when viewing similarity as a static measure can be explained when we consider the temporal dynamics of the influences of similarity.

A. A Network that Learns Superordinates

Empirical phenomena such as rating the typicality of exemplars or verifying their membership in a particular category have often been explained by positing a literally hierarchical organization of concepts in people's minds (Collins & Quillian, 1969). An intriguing issue is whether it is possible to capture such empirical phenomena without using an explicitly hierarchical model. Although it is not the focus of the points being made here, I describe an attractor network that learns to compute representations of superordinate concepts without employing a hierarchical structure. The focus here however, is on processing dynamics, rather than issues regarding hierarchical representations per se (and far from all of them are addressed by our model). It just so happens that comparing phenomena involving exemplar–exemplar versus superordinate–exemplar relationships highlights insights provided by a distributed attractor model that settles over time.

Cree and McRae (1999) trained a network (Fig. 1b) to compute representations of basic-level exemplar concepts and superordinate concepts, such as *jeep* and *vehicle*, respectively. The superordinate categories such as *vehicle* and *fruit* and their exemplars were established using the superordinate features provided by subjects in the feature norming study. Norming subjects routinely list the category (or categories) in which an exemplar resides when providing features (e.g., *jeep* <is a vehicle>). Note that this research was conducted when the norms included only 190 concepts, and for this simulation we excluded 9 concepts because of unfamiliarity or ambiguity (e.g., *emu, crane*). Each superordinate category consisted of all exemplars for which at least one subject produced the superordinate as a feature. The only exceptions to this were a few obvious outright errors (e.g., one subject stated that a *lime* <is a vegetable>). This resulted in 13 superordinates that each contained a minimum of 10 exemplars. The network, as shown in Fig. 1b, included 1081 fully interconnected semantic feature units and 20 word-form units that were unidirectionally connected to the semantic units. Thus, there is no way in which it could be claimed that the architecture of this network is hierarchical (which is the major reason why we used this architecture rather than one including semantic structure units that could be perceived by some researchers as having the appearance of being at a "higher" level than the semantic feature units). The network was trained to compute a semantic representation from a word's form for the 181 exemplars and 13 superordinates.

There were two major assumptions underlying the training procedure. We assumed that learning the meaning of superordinate terms such as *vehicle* can be accomplished by a mechanism that encodes semantic structure, such as a distributed attractor network. Second, we assumed that people at least partly learn the meaning of superordinate terms by experiencing a superordinate label paired with an exemplar of that category. Although exemplars are most often labeled by basic-level terms (Rosch, Mervis, Gray, Johnson, & Boyes-Braem, 1976), they are sometimes labeled using superordinate terms. This can happen when an exemplar physically is present in the environment (e.g., "What's that animal doing in here?" or "Hand me that tool, would you?") or via anaphora in speech or text ("She jumped into her car and jammed it into gear. She pulled her vehicle out onto the busy street"). Based on a corpus analysis, Wisniewski and Murphy (1989) estimated that basic-level terms are used 90% of the time, and superordinate terms 10% of the time.

As in our other models, basic-level exemplars such as *cow* and *desk* were trained in a one-to-one manner, with each label paired with its feature-based representation. These exemplars were trained on 90% of the trials. On the remaining 10%, a superordinate label (e.g., *vehicle*) was paired with the semantic representation of one of its exemplars. For example, the word form *vehicle* might be trained in conjunction with the features of *jeep* on one learning trial, *bus* on another, and *truck* on another. Thus, for superordinates, the mapping from word form-to-semantics was one-to-many. Within a superordinate category, all exemplar semantic representations were paired equally often with the superordinate label. We considered a number of schemes to compute differential probabilities for pairing exemplar semantic representations with superordinate word forms during training, but decided that training them with equal probability within a category was the most theory-neutral manner of doing so. The important point here is that using equal probabilities ensured that typicality was in no way built into the network's training regime.

The model was trained until it accurately computed the basic-level exemplar semantic representations. Because the superordinates were trained using a one-to-many mapping, there is no single "correct" output for them. That is, the network never was told what the ultimate semantics of *vehicle* should be; it was free to develop them from its experience with all of the vehicles. On each learning trial, however, weights were updated based on the specific exemplar semantic representation that was paired with the superordinate word form on that trial. Therefore, a consequence of this training regime is that the model learned about individual features and how they co-occur in basic-level concepts on every training trial because the semantic representation of some exemplar was always presented. Following training, the network was presented with a superordinate word form representation, allowed to settle, and its output was recorded. The model produced reasonable semantic representations for the superordinates. For example, Table I presents all of the semantic feature units that were activated greater than .2 for

TABLE I

THE FEATURES OF TOOL ACTIVATED GREATER THAN .2 IN THE MODEL

Feature	Activation
Made of wood	.72
Has a handle	.66
Used for carpentry	.62
Has a blade	.44
Is sharp	.42
Made of metal	.40
Is loud	.34
Found in toolboxes	.33
Used for construction	.32
Has a wooden handle	.32
Used for war	.27
Has a head	.24
Used for tightening	.22
Used by turning	.21
Is heavy	.21
Used for loosening	.20

tool. Note that the activations range from .2–.68 (activations can range from 0–1). In contrast, after this amount of training, for the same number of processing cycles for each basic-level exemplar, all features were very close to being turned completely on or off.

In summary, the network learned to compute both basic-level and superordinate concepts without implementing an explicitly hierarchical architecture. Because learning the superordinates depended on both the number of exemplars in which a feature occurred and the correlations among features across the exemplars of a superordinate category, coherent superordinate representations were learned.

B. Priming Between Similar Basic-Level Exemplars

When comparing exemplar–exemplar priming versus superordinate-exemplar priming, and considering the influence of concept similarity in the two cases, the results appear to be inconsistent. First consider priming between pairs of similar basic-level exemplars, such as *truck* and *van*, or *eagle* and *hawk*. Researchers have treated short SOA priming as reflecting the organization of semantic memory because it is considered to be influenced minimally by any sort of strategic processing (de Groot, 1984; den Heyer, Briand, & Dannenbring, 1983). Semantic memory models based on distributed representations predict that similar concepts should prime one another. Short SOA priming in attractor networks is simulated by presenting the prime's word form for some number of processing cycles and then presenting the target's word form with the computed semantic representation of the prime left initially active. Thus, prime-target similarity is reflected in the number of semantic features of the target that are correctly (and incorrectly) preactivated when the prime's meaning is computed. The greater the featural overlap between the prime and target, the less time it should take to compute the meaning of the target. In this way, distributed attractor networks appear to predict clearly that concept similarity should strongly influence priming.

In contrast to this prediction, some human studies have shown null short SOA priming effects for prime–target pairs that the researchers assumed were semantically similar (Moss, Ostrin, Tyler, & Marslen-Wilson, 1995; Shelton & Martin, 1992). However, McRae and Boisvert (1998) used similarity ratings to compare the prime–target pairs of those two studies with a set of items that we constructed (such as *truck–van*). Our pairs were significantly more similar than those of Moss et al., whose items were in turn more similar than Shelton and Martin's. Using these highly similar exemplar pairs, McRae and Boisvert found significant semantic similarity priming effects using short SOA paired presentation with both lexical decision and concreteness decision tasks ("Does the word refer to something that is concrete, i.e., touchable?"). We also found significant priming using the single-presentation technique with both decision tasks. We then compared priming effects for targets paired with highly similar primes (*goose–turkey*) and less similar primes (*robin–turkey*). McRae and Boisvert found that the magnitude of priming effects depends on concept similarity. Short SOA priming occurred only for the highly similar pairs. Although longer SOA priming occurred for both, it was much larger for the highly similar pairs. These results make sense on a strictly similarity-based account. Furthermore, Cree et al. (1999) simulated these differential priming effects using the model shown in Fig. 1c. Because the human behavioral studies and the simulations were based on items from the feature norms, the simulations used the same items as were used in the McRae and Boisvert study. In summary, the degree of priming between similar basic-level concepts depends directly on concept similarity in both humans and in the model.

C. Typicality Effects and Superordinate–Exemplar Priming

A number of studies have investigated priming effects from superordinate to exemplar concepts. The majority of these are long SOA studies specifically designed to investigate explicit expectancy generation, but one study compared short SOA priming effects for exemplars of varying typicality. Schwanenflugel and Rey (1986) found no systematic differences in degree of priming from superordinates to high, medium, and low typicality exemplars. These results are curious and unexpected because typicality effects generally are explained in terms of the similarity between superordinate and exemplar concepts. That is, *hammer* is rated as a more typical tool than is *shovel* because *hammer* is more similar to *tool* than is *shovel*. If concept similarity underlies both exemplar–exemplar priming and typicality effects, why does it not influence superordinate–exemplar priming in the same manner?

Because these results are difficult to explain, Cree and McRae (1999) began by replicating the superordinate–exemplar priming results. We constructed a set of 24 high-typicality (*tool–hammer*) and 24 medium-typicality (*tool–shovel*) superordinate–exemplar pairs. The superordinate prime was presented for 200 ms, followed by a 50 ms mask, and then the target was presented until subjects decided whether or not it referred to a concrete object. Table II shows that significant priming obtained for both high- and medium-typicality exemplars, with similar magnitudes of priming in each case. Thus, the results of Schwanenflugel and Rey (1986) were replicated.

Cree and McRae (1999) also conducted a typicality rating task for all of the exemplars in the 13 superordinate categories. We then used the network to simulate typicality effects and superordinate–exemplar priming. The network accounted for typicality effects because the two factors most responsible for the formation of superordinate concepts were the number of a category's exemplars possessing a specific feature and the correlations among features across exemplars, akin to Rosch (1978). The assumption underlying our simulation of untimed typicality ratings is that subjects compute the superordinate concept, compute the exemplar concept, and then compare them. Therefore, to simulate typicality, we presented the network with the superordinate's word form and allowed it to compute its

TABLE II

SUPERORDINATE–EXEMPLAR PRIMING EFFECTS FOR HIGH AND MEDIUM TYPICALITY EXEMPLARS

	High typicality	Medium typicality
Unrelated	661	694
Related	633	655
Facilitation	28*	39*

*Significant by subjects and items.

semantic representation, which was then stored. We then presented the network with the exemplar's word form and allowed it to compute its semantic representation. The cosine between the two vector representations was used as the prediction for mean typicality rating across subjects. Table III shows that the model successfully predicts typicality ratings, except for the superordinates of *mammal* and *animal*, which have been problematic in previous accounts of typicality.[2] Thus, using an offline measure of representational similarity, the network accounts for typicality ratings.

Cree and McRae (1999) then simulated superordinate–exemplar priming using the identical method that Cree et al. (1999) used to simulate exemplar–exemplar priming effects. The superordinate's word form was presented to the network, which was then allowed to settle for the same number of processing cycles as in Cree et al.'s priming simulations (15 in this case, the specific number being determined by a combination of the number of processing cycles used during training, which was 20 in both cases, and the fact that the SOA was 250 ms). The relevant exemplar's word form was then presented with the superordinate's semantic representation left initially active. One issue that arises when simulating decision latency is that it is unclear when subjects initiate a response when making a speeded decision such as "does the word refer to a concrete object." Therefore, Cree and McRae compared the number of processing cycles required to reach various error criteria (as was done in Cree et al.) when the target was preceded by a related superordinate (*tool–hammer*) versus an unrelated one (*fruit–hammer*). The simulation results are presented in Fig. 2. As in the human data, the model produces significant priming effects of similar magnitude for the high and medium typicality exemplars. That is, across the range of error values, the network requires fewer processing cycles to reach the specified error value when the target exemplar is preceded by a related versus unrelated superordinate.

To this point, we have seen that priming between basic-level exemplars is modulated strongly by similarity both in humans and in the model. In addition, typicality ratings are accounted for by the degree of superordinate–exemplar similarity both in humans and in the model. However, degree of superordinate–exemplar similarity is not apparent in short SOA priming, either in humans or in the model. How can this be? The answer lies in the combination of the differences between superordinate and basic-level

[2] The major reason that the model failed to account for the typicality ratings for animals is that the numerous birds for which at least one participant listed "is an animal" skewed the representation of the animal superordinate representation toward birds. However, the birds received lower typicality ratings on average than did four-legged mammals like "dog" or "horse."

TABLE III

PREDICTING TYPICALITY RATINGS USING THE MODEL

Domain	Category	N	r
All		260	.6
Nonliving things		122	.7
	Weapon	28	.9
	Vehicle	17	.9
	Utensil	11	.8
	Furniture	12	.8
	Appliance	10	.7
	Clothing	18	.6
	Tool	26	.5
Living things		138	.3
	Fruits	22	.7
	Vegetables	18	.6
	Bird	16	.6
	Pet	12	.4
	Mammal	19	.3
	Animal	35	−.5

exemplar representations, and the processing dynamics of the model (and presumably of humans as well). Because exemplars are well learned, when an exemplar was computed in the network, all semantic feature units tend to be activated quite close to 1 if they represent a feature of that concept, or 0 if they do not (see Fig. 3). That is, net input to each unit tends to be strongly positive or negative so that when an exemplar prime is computed, all units are either on the basically flat portions of the sigmoidal activation function or extremely close to them.

When an exemplar target word form is presented to the network, the units shared between the prime and target are already turned on, and must remain on. Furthermore, the feature units that are off for the prime and should be off for the target need to remain deactivated. In addition, the network must activate the target concept's features that are not included in the prime and turn off the features that the prime activates but are not part of the target's semantic representation. The necessary change to such a unit's net input, and thus to its activation, can take some time, particularly if the prime preserves a feature correlation that the target violates. Because the network must change the activation of the units that are fully activated or turned off, processing is particularly sensitive to similarity in terms of shared and distinct features.

In contrast, Table I shows that when superordinate representations are computed in the model, because they were trained in a one-to-many fashion,

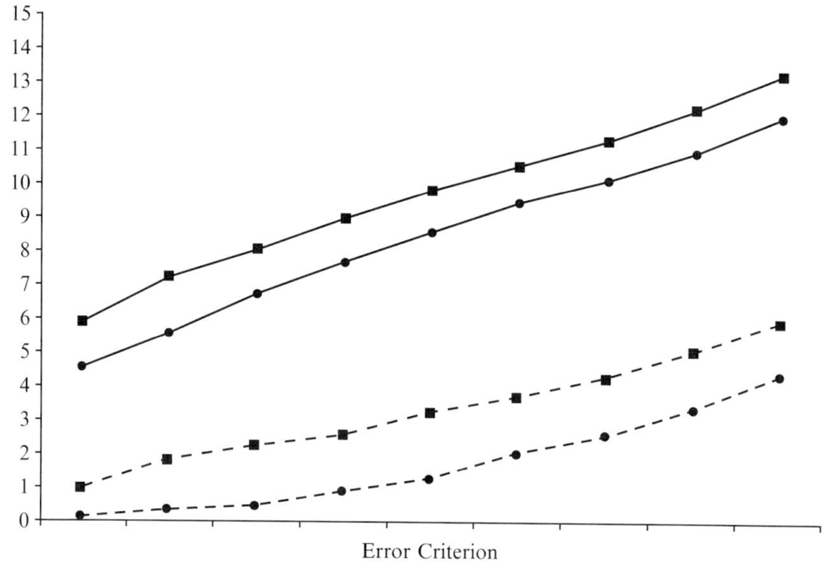

Fig. 2. Simulated priming effects from superordinates to high and medium typicality exemplars.

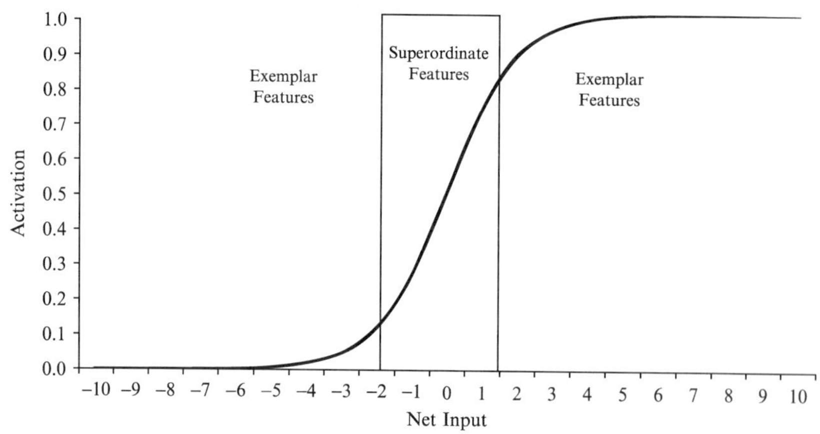

Fig. 3. The sigmoidal activation function and exemplar versus superordinate features.

semantic feature units tend not to be activated close to 0 or 1. Rather, the feature activations tend to fall on the steeper part of the sigmoidal function (with the net input to these units being closer to 0 than for the basic-level exemplars). Therefore, it is easier for the network to change this net input over time to fully activate the feature units that are part of the exemplar's semantic representation and to turn off the ones that are not. The upshot is that the dynamics of computing exemplar meaning when beginning in a state representing a superordinate are not as sensitive to the degree of semantic similarity as they are when it starts in a state corresponding to an exemplar. Note that the network's dynamics definitely are influenced by semantic similarity because there is priming for high and medium typicality exemplars versus when they are preceded by an unrelated superordinate; it is simply a matter of degree.

In summary, the network's temporal computational dynamics provide insights into a set of empirical results that seem, on the face of it, to be inconsistent. These insights would be difficult to obtain without an implemented model, and in fact, we were somewhat initially surprised when the network simulated the equivalent priming effects from superordinates to high versus medium typicality exemplars. In other words, the temporal dynamics of a fully interacting nonlinear computational system can sometimes be intuited but often produce counterintuitive results that can then be understood by analyzing the network's behavior under the relevant circumstances.

VI. Category-Specific Semantic Deficits

In previous sections, I focused on insights provided by two principles inherent to connectionist attractor networks; they naturally encode and use the distributional statistics of the environment, and they settle over time, thus presenting an opportunity to derive and test accounts based on the temporal dynamics of their computations. Specific simulations and associated human data were used as concrete examples.

In this section, I again focus on an account of human data that is inspired by the fact that models are sensitive to multiple distributional statistics inherent to the concepts on which they are trained. The target data for the research described in this section are the patterns of performance exhibited by patients with neural impairments who present with differential loss of knowledge of various types of concepts (e.g., types of creatures vs. fruits and vegetables vs. nonliving things), that is, patients with category-specific semantic deficits. Because reaction time data seldom are collected from these patients, the temporal dynamics of semantic computations are not a central issue at the moment (although further research and modeling might point to ways in which they are). However, because many patients exhibiting category-specific semantic deficits have brain lesions that are at least relatively focal, the ways in which semantic knowledge is distributed throughout the brain is a primary issue. In this section, I outline an account of these patients' data that is inspired by distributed attractor models of semantic memory. In our view, patterns of performance of patients with category-specific deficits can be explained by the manner in which types of knowledge (e.g., visual form, sound, smell, taste, touch, and motor knowledge) and multiple distributional statistics (e.g., feature distinctiveness, visual complexity, and concept familiarity) vary systematically across types of concepts. Thus, in addition to principles of attractor networks, our account is inspired by recent insights from research in cognitive neuroscience regarding how semantic memory is organized in the brain.

The models shown in Fig. 1 that we have used so far in our research have not differentiated between the types of knowledge denoted by various features. Rather, in these models, a feature is a feature, regardless of the type of knowledge to which it refers. Recent evidence from cognitive neuroscience suggests that the brain, at least to some degree, segregates knowledge based on type of information. For example, multiple researchers have provided evidence, typically using fMRI, that information regarding visual knowledge of objects and knowledge of how humans use objects are computed in modality-specific semantic processing channels in the brain (see Martin & Chao, 2001, for a recent review). Furthermore, using speeded feature verification without imaging, Solomon and Barsalou (2001) and Pecher, Zeelenberg, and Barsalou (2003) have illustrated modality-specific aspects of lexical concepts. This research suggests that types of knowledge such as visual, auditory, tactile, smell, taste, and motor information are stored in somewhat distinct brain regions. There also appears to be evidence for some degree of segregation for a few types of visual information, for example, parts and shape versus color versus perceived motion of entities and objects. In other words, this evidence suggests that a concept is computed in the brain as a highly distributed pattern over multiple types of knowledge.

A reasonable assumption is that not all types of information are equally salient for various types of concepts. For example, visual information might be more salient than motor information for creatures because visual information is important for identifying creatures, but people have few established motor patterns associated with them (other than, e.g., petting some types of domesticated animals). In contrast, various aspects of motor and functional information are crucial for our concepts of nonliving things such as tools, whereas visual information might (or might not) be less important (Farah & McClelland, 1991; Martin & Chao, 2001; Warrington & Shallice,

1984). Fruits and vegetables presumably differ from both creatures and nonliving things because taste information is particularly salient for them. In addition, it has been shown that color information is particularly critical for recognizing fruits and vegetables because they tend to have few parts, and many have the same basic shape (Humphrey, Goodale, Jacobson, & Servos, 1994). In other words, it seems reasonable to assume that distributional statistics regarding the differential salience of knowledge types might vary systematically across types of concepts and that this could have important consequences for conceptual representation and computations.

Although we have yet to implement a model that incorporates these insights, we envision implementing such a network. This model will incorporate knowledge types based on data from cognitive neuroscience. That is, there will be multiple pools of units, each corresponding to one of the nine knowledge types described in Section VI.B. These pools of knowledge types units will be connected via either separate sets of hidden units or one large pool of hidden units. These hidden units would therefore correspond to a computational implementation of Damasio's (1989) convergence zones (see Simmons & Barsalou, 2003, for a proposal similar in spirit to this).

This type of model would naturally pick up on multiple types of distributional statistics, and they would influence both its attractor dynamics and the probability of loss of specific concepts following damage to the system. For example, a number of distributional statistics regarding concept–feature and concept–concept relations can be viewed as influencing the distance between an attractor and neighboring attractors, and thus the likelihood of attractor overlap following damage (see Hinton & Shallice, 1991, for a discussion of how attractor basins might change following damage so that ones close in space become overlapped, thus producing confusions). Semantic confusability refers to the degree to which a concept potentially is confusable with other similar concepts and thus can be indexed by a concept's overlap with other concepts. Semantic confusability can be measured in a number of ways: the degree to which a concept's features are distinguishing, feature distinctiveness, the related measure of feature cue validity that has existed in the concepts literature for quite some time, and the degree of overall semantic similarity between a concept and the ones that are closest to it. Finally, visual similarity, a measure that has played a significant role in accounts of category-specific deficits, also is an index of confusability, but has its primary influence on the visual component of the overall attractor landscape. Visual similarity might be particularly relevant to category-specific deficit data because many of the tasks used to establish deficits demand that patients recognize or name pictures of objects.

Factors that index how well people learn a concept and its name may also partly determine the probability of getting an item correct following damage.

Concept familiarity is a measure of the degree to which semantic patterns are learned, or entrenched in the weights. This factor is related to the probability that an attractor is perturbed following damage. That is, better learned attractors are more resistant to damage, on average. Word frequency is related to concept familiarity, but it is specifically a measure of people's experience with the word itself. More frequent words have stronger connections to conceptual information. Furthermore, if a word and its meaning are viewed as a distributed stable state in a space defined over conceptual, orthographic, and phonological information, then more frequent and thus well-learned orthographic and phonological patterns will be more resistant to damage. This should show itself in performance on tasks such as picture naming, word–picture matching, naming given verbally presented features, and providing features given a concept name, which form the primary set of tasks used to establish category-specific semantic deficits.

In summary, the representations and computations of a model such as this would be influenced by all of these distributional statistics. These ideas inspired our recent account of data from patients who present with category-specific semantic deficits. Our feature norms (plus other norms) enabled us to test these hypotheses in more detailed ways than had been done previously.

A. Hypothesis

Patients with category-specific semantic deficits typically are characterized as having a differential impairment in their knowledge of living things like dogs and bananas, versus nonliving things like wrenches and shirts. These impairments are found in patients with neural damage following herpes simplex viral encephalitis, stroke, closed head injury, or Alzheimer's dementia. Category-specific impairments are usually established empirically using one or more of picture naming, word-picture matching, providing a featural definition given a concept name, providing a concept name given a featural definition, or feature verification. Patients with these deficits are far from isolated; over 100 cases have been reported thus far (see Forde & Humphreys, 1999, for a review).

One observation that stands out when reviewing the category-specific deficits literature is the degree of variation in both patients' neurological damage and the ways in which various patients have been tested. For example, there is variability in the etiology of patient's damage, the area of the brain that is damaged, the size of the damaged area, and even whether damage is relatively focal or nonfocal. In addition, there is variability in the tasks used to assess patients' performance and tremendous variability in the categories, exemplars, and features used to probe patients' knowledge.

Despite this variability, there are relatively stable patterns of performance across patients, and these are somewhat more subtle than the broad living–nonliving dichotomy that is used often as a characterization. For example, there is the tripartite distinction among the domains of creatures, fruits–vegetables, and nonliving things on which Caramazza has focused (Caramazza & Shelton, 1998; Mahon & Caramazza, 2001). That is, each of these three domains can be selectively impaired, and categories within each domain tend to move together in terms of whether they are relatively impaired or preserved. In addition, fruits–vegetables sometimes pattern with the creatures in terms of whether they are impaired or not in specific patients, and sometimes with the nonliving things. There are also two reasonably well-studied exception categories. Musical instruments, curiously enough, are often impaired along with living-thing categories. Nonliving foods such as *bread* and *pie* can be impaired along with living things. The final pattern of performance regards the prevalence of types of deficits: Patients presenting with living things deficits (often tested as a mixture of creatures and fruits–vegetables) are much more frequent than those presenting with nonliving things deficits.

Cree and McRae's (2003) main hypothesis was that given the variability in patients and the ways in which they are tested, combined with the relatively consistent probabilistic trends in the patient data, there must be multiple factors that probabilistically converge to produce those trends. This type of prediction is typical for researchers who use distributed connectionist models as their theoretical basis (in essence, a constraint-satisfaction view with multiple probabilistic constraints). Because there exist multiple probabilistic factors that could play a role in producing these behavioral trends, it is not necessary for any single component of semantic representations and computations to account for all aspects of the data. In fact, given the complexity of the data, it is highly unlikely that any single factor would suffice. Rather, we claim that multiple factors, all of which may produce reasonable but not precise solutions on their own, combine to provide a solution. In terms of category-specific semantic deficits patients, note that the patient data themselves are definitely probabilistic in nature and are a matter of degree; they are not clean in the sense that no patient has lost all knowledge of one type of concept with all knowledge of other types of concepts being perfectly spared.

To test this hypothesis, Cree and McRae (2003) investigated virtually every factor that has been implicated in accounts of category-specific deficits. The challenge of evaluating the various distributional factors that might underlie category-specific semantic deficits requires having reasonably valid quantitative estimates of each of the underlying variables. Subsets of these factors had been investigated using small sets of lexical concepts (60 or fewer; Farah &

McClelland, 1991; Garrard, Lambon-Ralph, Hodges, & Patterson, 2001; Gonnerman, Anderson, Devlin, Kempler, & Seidenberg, 1997). However, because we had collected feature production norms for 541 living and nonliving things that span a broad range, we could investigate hypotheses in a manner that was more in-depth than had previously been possible.

As in the superordinate modeling that was described in Section V, we used subjects' responses from the norms to construct superordinate categories and their exemplars (34 categories, in this case). This included 12 creature categories such as *fish* and *mammal*, 16 nonliving thing categories such as *tool* and *clothing*, four fruit and vegetable categories such as *fruits* and *vegetables* themselves, as well as *musical instruments* and *foods*. The 34 categories varied widely in their number of exemplars, and some exemplars were in multiple categories.

B. Knowledge Types

The first factor that Cree and McRae (2003) investigated combines insights from cognitive neuroscience with the fact that distributed attractor networks naturally are sensitive to variations in the saliency of representational components. The sensory–functional hypothesis has been an influential account of category-specific deficits (Farah & McClelland, 1991; Martin & Chao, 2001; Warrington & Shallice, 1984). The basic notion is that sensory (or sometimes just visual) versus functional knowledge are stored in separate brain areas. Because sensory information is disproportionately important for the representation of living things, damage to sensory cortex produces a living-things deficit. In contrast, because functional or motor information is disproportionately important for the representation of nonliving things, damage to motor cortex produces a nonliving things deficit. Caramazza and colleagues (Caramazza & Shelton, 1998; Mahon & Caramazza, 2001) have argued strenuously against the sensory–functional dichotomy as an account of performance underlying category-specific deficit patients. Their primary argument is that this binary distinction simply has too few degrees of freedom to account for the behavioral trends outlined earlier, specifically the tripartite distinction among creatures, fruits–vegetables, and nonliving things. Therefore, they have concluded that an account based on knowledge types is not useful.

Rather than concluding that knowledge types provide no insight into the data, Cree and McRae (2003) asked whether the appropriate behavioral predictions might emerge if multiple types of information are stored in somewhat distinct brain regions so that relatively focal lesions could differentially damage those regions. Thus, we extended the sensory–functional hypothesis in a manner that had been discussed previously but had never been implemented (Allport, 1985). We developed what we called a "brain region taxonomy" that included nine types of knowledge: visual form and surface, <has a handle>; color, <is red>, visual motion <swims>; auditory, <moos>; taste, <is spicy>; smell, <smells bad>; tactile, <is smooth>; function, <used by turning>; and finally, encyclopedic information, such as <lives in Africa> that did not fit into any of the other classes of knowledge. There exists evidence that these types of knowledge (with perhaps the exception of encyclopedic knowledge) are stored in somewhat distinct brain regions (see Cree & McRae for an extended discussion).

Cree and McRae (2003) classified every feature in our norms according to the brain region taxonomy. We then derived a nine-dimensional representation to estimate the salience of each knowledge type for each of the 34 categories. For each category, we counted the number of features of each knowledge type for the category's exemplars. For example, because there were 133 function features across the 33 tools in the norms, the tool–function cell in this representation was given a value of 133. Thus, this representation abstracts away from the individual features and instead provides a representation of the importance of each knowledge type to a category. We then conducted a cluster analysis on the resulting category by knowledge type matrix to investigate how the categories grouped in terms of the relative salience of each knowledge type. The results are shown in Fig. 4. In this cluster analysis, the distance from the category names (terminal nodes) at which two categories or clusters of categories are joined is an index of their similarity in the nine-dimensional knowledge-type salience space, that is, similarity in terms of their distributions of knowledge types (rather than their precise features per se). There are three major clusters in Fig. 4, each corresponding basically to one of the domains in the tripartite distinction. The 12 creature categories are at the top, the 16 nonliving-thing categories in the middle, and the 4 fruit–vegetable categories at the bottom. Thus, distributional statistics regarding the relative salience of knowledge types can indeed account for the tripartite distinction found in the patient data. Furthermore, although the category of musical instruments did not cluster with the creatures or fruits–vegetables, it was an outlier with respect to the other nonliving thing categories, basically forming a cluster unto itself. Nonliving foods, which have been found to sometimes pattern with living things (tested typically as a mixture of creatures and fruits–vegetables), clustered late with the fruits–vegetables (rather than the creatures or nonliving things, as seems entirely reasonable).

Cree and McRae (2003) describe in detail why these results were obtained, basing their explanation on the relative salience of each knowledge type. I briefly outline their description here. The tripartite distinction among creatures, fruits–vegetables (along with foods), and nonliving things occurred for

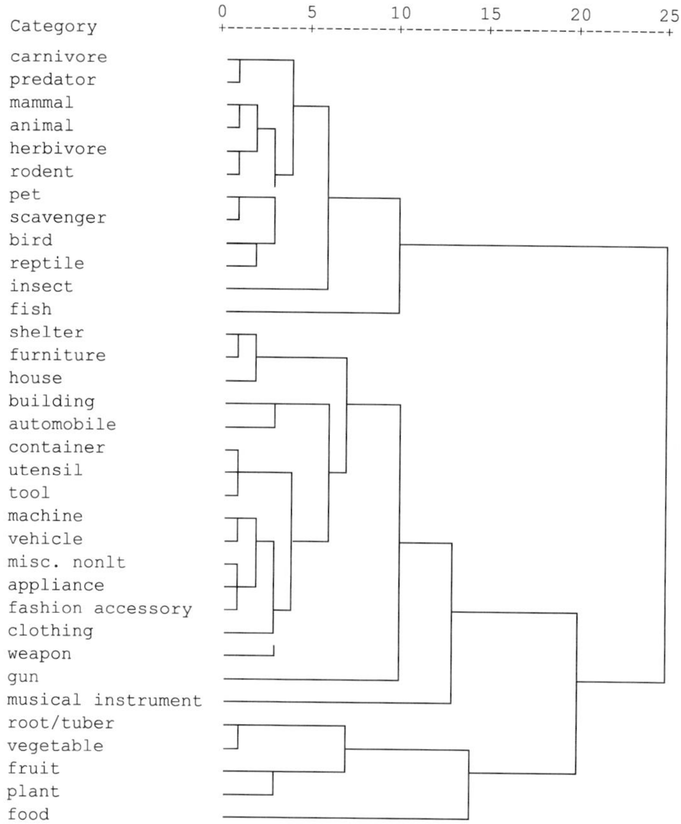

Fig. 4. Dendogram produced by the brain region feature types hierarchical cluster analysis. The category vectors entered into the analysis were nine-dimensional representations of the salience of each feature type for those categories.

a number of interrelated reasons. Visual parts and surface features are highly salient for creatures (e.g., dogs have lots of interesting parts), midsalient for nonliving things (wrenches have some parts, but fewer than creatures), and are not very salient for fruits–vegetables and foods (apples and pies have few parts). Visual motion is important for creatures (dogs move about on their own), much less so for nonliving things (only vehicles might be thought of as moving about on their own), and almost nonexistent for fruits–vegetables and foods. Taste and smell are extremely salient for fruits–vegetables and foods but not for creatures or nonliving things. Functional information regarding how humans use things is not at all important for creatures but is salient for the other categories. Finally, color information is highly salient for fruits–vegetables but less so for the other types of concepts. Musical instruments differ from other nonliving things in terms of sound being highly salient, greater salience of visual parts and surface features and color, and lower salience in terms of functional, tactile, and visual motion information.

We concluded from these analyses that concrete noun concepts are indeed organized in the mind and brain by knowledge type, but it is more complex than the sensory–functional dichotomy suggests. Combinations of all of the knowledge types contributed to how the sets of categories patterned in the cluster analysis. Furthermore, to account for the behavioral trends, it is necessary to separate various types of sensory information; seven of the nine knowledge types were sensory in nature.

It appears, however, that a complete account of category-specific deficits must involve more than knowledge types. For example, although musical instruments often pattern with living things in the patient data (typically they are impaired along with them), musical instruments clustered late with the nonliving things rather than the creatures or fruits–vegetables. Furthermore, it is unclear how knowledge types could be used to account for the fact that about 90% of category-specific deficit patients present with living-things deficits (seemingly due to poor performance on creatures). Finally, patients with Alzheimer's dementia also sometimes present with category-specific deficits (almost always living-things deficits), and Alzheimer's, at least in the latter stages, is associated with relatively diffuse nonfocal damage, so damage to a single knowledge type, or small subset of knowledge types, seems unlikely. There do exist, however, a number of what Cree and McRae (2003) called susceptibility factors—distributional statistics that may provide insight into why some types of concepts are more susceptible than others to damage.

C. Susceptibility Factors

Four of the distributional statistics that Cree and McRae (2003) investigated can be considered as indexes of the extent to which a concept is confusable with other similar concepts. Confusability can, in general, be considered the distance between attractor points (and between their surrounding basins) in a multidimensional semantic state space. The degree to which a concept's attractor basin is off by itself in state space, or near to other attractor basins, determines its potential confusability with other concepts. This appears to be an important factor in accounting for the performance of patients with category-specific deficits. Take a picture-naming task, for example. If a patient is shown a picture of a zebra and responds *horse*, that is counted as part of their deficit. In general, most of the tests used for establishing deficits hinge on discriminating among basic-level concepts. Cree and McRae defined multiple measures of confusability and then sorted the 34 categories on each measure.

The first measure was distinguishing features. Distinguishing features are those such as <moos> that enable discriminating among similar concepts (it gets you directly to *cow*), versus features such as <eats> or <made of metal>, which are applicable to multiple entities or objects. We operationalized distinguishing features as those that occur in only one or two of the 541 normed concepts. The hypothesis is that the greater the number of a concept's features that can be used to distinguish it, the less confusable it is, and thus the greater the probability of performing correctly on that item following brain damage. Cree and McRae calculated the percentage of distinguishing features for each of the 541 concepts, and then calculated the mean for each of the 34 categories. We then sorted the categories from the least susceptible to most susceptible to impairment. Fifteen of the 16 nonliving thing categories were the least susceptible (with *gun* being the exception, as it and weapon were in many of the analyses). The fruit–vegetable categories were in the middle in terms of susceptibility, and the creature categories were most susceptible to damage. Musical instruments showed up as more susceptible than the nonliving things, being embedded near the top of the creature categories. Nonliving foods were the third least susceptible category overall. Cree and McRae conducted the same type of analyses for feature distinctiveness, which is a continuous measure of the degree to which a feature distinguishes a concept from other concepts (one divided by the number of concepts in which a feature occurs). The results were almost identical to the distinguishing feature analysis.

We also measured the degree to which a concept is similar to its nearest neighbors by calculating the mean similarity of each concept with its four nearest neighbors. This concept similarity measure did not sort the categories as cleanly as did the previous two but still produced the same basic results. Finally, an analysis based on similarity in terms of visual features did not produce a clean sort (although other researchers' analyses using picture-based visual similarity measures have provided insight, as in Tranel, Logan, Frank, & Damasio, 1997). In summary, the sets of categories were ordered appropriately in terms of susceptibility to impairment using distributional statistics regarding the degree to which a concept is confusable with its neighbors, which presumably is related to the probability that it can be discriminated from its neighbors following damage. All of these measures would naturally influence processing in both an intact and damaged attractor network of the sort described in this section.

A measure that is not correlated with the confusability measures but provides insights into category-specific deficits is visual complexity (Dixon,

Bub, & Arguin, 1997; Forde & Humphreys, 1999; Tranel et al., 1997). Visual complexity is an index of the ability to parse a visually presented object or depiction of that object into its constituent parts. Research has shown that visual complexity is related to object recognition and naming in normal adults (Ellis & Morrison, 1998). For category-specific deficits patients, the basic notion is that the greater the complexity of an object's appearance, the more difficult it is to parse that object, and the higher the probability of an error given a brain that has been perturbed by damage. To derive a measure of visual complexity based on the norms, we calculated the number of external parts and surface features per concept (this was one knowledge type in the brain region taxonomy). Cree and McRae (2003) then calculated the mean number of external parts per concept in each of the 34 categories. With the exception of the category of fish, this measure discriminated the 16 nonliving thing categories from the 12 creature categories. The fruits–vegetables were again middling but were embedded in the nonliving things rather than in the creatures. Of the nine susceptibility analyses that we conducted, this was the only one in which musical instruments patterned with the nonliving things rather than the creatures. Finally, nonliving foods like *bread* and *pie* have few external parts and surface features, and thus showed up as the least susceptible to damage.

The final two distributional measures were concept familiarity and word frequency, which are estimates of people's experience with concepts and their names. In terms of people's familiarity with the actual concept, the typical notion is that the more often an object or entity is encountered, the better learned is the concept. In a model, concept familiarity would be reflected in a network's training regime and would result in better defined attractor points and basins (ones that are more firmly entrenched in the weights). Cree and McRae (2003) collected familiarity ratings for all of the relevant concepts and sorted the 34 categories in terms of mean concept familiarity. The creature categories were the most susceptible to damage (least familiar). The fruits–vegetables resided with the nonliving things, with foods also being highly familiar. Finally, musical instruments, being low in familiarity and thus relatively highly susceptible to damage, again resembled the creatures.

Word frequency is an estimate of people's familiarity with a word, in this case, a concept's name. Although it is related to concept familiarity, it differs to a measurable degree (they were correlated only at .45 across the concepts). Word frequency should influence category-specific deficits data because the tasks used to establish deficits are language based. In a model, the degree to which a concept name has been learned in and of itself, and the degree to which it has been learned as part of a multidimensional lexico-conceptual representation, should influence its resistance to damage. Sorting the 34 categories based on concept name frequency produced fairly clean results similar to concept familiarity. The major exception was that fruits–vegetables are much more familiar in terms of their concepts than in terms of their names. This is interesting because studies that have uncovered specific fruits–vegetables deficits have determined that they are due to naming, rather than conceptual, deficits (Farah & Wallace, 1992; Hart, Berndt, & Caramazza, 1985).

Across all of the susceptibility distributional statistics, the correct predictions resulted regarding patterns of performance of category-specific deficits patients. The least susceptible set of categories were the nonliving things, along with nonliving foods. Fruits–vegetables were middling in susceptibility. Musical instruments were next, with creatures being the most susceptible.

In summary, a distributed attractor network account, combined with insights from cognitive neuroscience, provides an extremely useful framework for understanding data underlying patients presenting with category-specific semantic deficits, and thus understanding the factors that influence semantic representations and computations. Distributional statistics in terms of the salience of various knowledge types showed that knowledge types can indeed differentiate among sets of concepts in ways that match the patient data. Analyses of multiple distributional statistics that do not necessarily depend on knowledge types illustrated that they converge on a solution in a manner that also matches the patient data quite well. However, Cree and McRae (2003) analyzed each factor separately. We did so in an attempt to understand the utility of each factor individually. In reality, many or all of these factors would interact in a fully interactive nonlinear dynamical system such as the brain, or the model outlined herein. A distributed attractor network would be sensitive to all of these factors, but simulations are necessary to determine precisely how various patterns of performance would arise when these factors interact.

VII. Summary

Lexical-conceptual knowledge regarding concrete concepts is multifaceted. It includes perceptual information associated with each of the senses. It also includes situational–event-based knowledge regarding where things typically are found, what they are typically used for, how they are used, who uses them, and so on. In this chapter, I have presented evidence that a feature-based attractor network approach provides multiple central insights into how semantic memory is organized, as well as the computations underlying people's knowledge and use of lexical concepts.

Sections II and III briefly described the feature norms on which our research has been based and the attractor networks that have served as the theoretical guide for our work. In Section IV, I presented evidence that people learn and use both feature correlations and relations. The discussion focused on careful consideration of the nature of the knowledge, how it is learned, and the type of task used to tap into that knowledge, with particular emphasis on matching task and knowledge to maximize the probability of observing an influence of both feature correlations and relations. The influence of statistically based feature correlations was predicted by attractor network simulations of speeded tasks and found in corresponding human studies. Furthermore, feature correlations influenced an offline task that directly asked people about relationships between pairs of features. At present, there is no evidence that theory-based knowledge is computed quickly enough to influence speeded tasks, although theories can influence lower-level learning, which in turn affects performance on speeded tasks.

Section V focused on another example of insights provided by the computational dynamics of attractor networks. I described a network that learned both basic-level and superordinate semantic representations. Seemingly inconsistent results regarding the role of similarity in exemplar–exemplar versus superordinate–exemplar priming were understandable when the dynamics of the influence of similarity in such a network were explicated.

Section VI used a theoretical perspective inspired by attractor networks, combined with insights from cognitive neuroscience, to account for data regarding patients presenting with category-specific semantic deficits. The analyses highlight the importance of the salience of various types of knowledge, in conjunction with the influence of multiple distributional statistics to which attractor networks are sensitive. It was shown that multiple probabilistic constraints regarding the organization and computation of concrete noun concepts converge to provide a solution that maps nicely onto the patterns of performance found in category-specific semantic deficits patients.

In conclusion, a full understanding of semantic memory will benefit maximally by striving to combine research on language use, concepts and categorization, object recognition, patient research, imaging research, and implemented computational models. The work described in this chapter is one aspect of that research program.

Acknowledgments

This work was supported by a Natural Sciences and Engineering Research Council grant OGP0155704 and NIH grants R01-DC0418 and R01-MH60517. Correspondence concerning this article should be addressed to Ken McRae, Department of Psychology, Social Science Centre, University of Western Ontario, London, Ontario, Canada, N6A 5C2. E-mail: mcrae@uwo.ca.

References

Ahn, W. K., Marsh, J. K., Luhmann, C. C., & Lee, K. (2002). Effect of theory-based feature correlations on typicality judgments. *Memory & Cognition, 30*, 107–118.

Allport, D. A. (1985). Distributed memory, modular systems and dysphasia. In S. K. Newman & R. Epstein (Eds.), *Current perspectives in dysphasia* (pp. 32–60). Edinburgh, Scotland: Churchill Livingstone.

Ashcraft, M. H. (1978). Feature dominance and typicality effects in feature statement verification. *Journal of Verbal Learning and Verbal Behavior, 17*, 155–164.

Barsalou, L. W. (1985). Ideals, central tendency, and frequency of instantiation as determinants of graded structure in categories. *Journal of Experimental Psychology: Learning, Memory & Cognition, 11*, 629–654.

Barsalou, L. W. (in press). Abstraction in perceptual symbol systems. *Philosophical Transactions of the Royal Society of London: Biological Systems.*

Billman, D., & Heit, E. (1988). Observational learning from internal feedback: A simulation of an adaptive learning method. *Cognitive Science, 12*, 587–625.

Billman, D., & Knutson, J. (1996). Unsupervised concept learning and value systematicity: A complex whole aids learning the parts. *Journal of Experimental Psychology: Learning, Memory, and Cognition, 22*, 458–475.

Caramazza, A., & Shelton, J. R. (1998). Domain specific knowledge systems in the brain: The animate-inanimate distinction. *Journal of Cognitive Neuroscience, 10*, 1–34.

Clapper, J. P., & Bower, G. H. (1991). Learning and applying category knowledge in unsupervised domains. In G. H. Bower (Ed.), *The psychology of learning and motivation: Advances in research and theory*. (Vol. 27, pp. 65–108). Toronto, Canada: Academic Press.

Collins, A. M., & Loftus, E. F. (1975). A spreading-activation theory of semantic processing. *Psychological Review, 82*, 407–428.

Collins, A. M., & Quillian, M. R. (1969). Retrieval time from semantic memory. *Journal of Verbal Learning and Verbal Behavior, 8*, 240–247.

Cree, G. S., & McRae, K. (2003). Analyzing the factors underlying the structure and computation of the meaning of chipmunk, cherry, chisel, cheese, and cello (and many other such concrete nouns). *Journal of Experimental Psychology: General, 132*, 163–201.

Cree, G. S., & McRae, K. (1999, November). *Instantiating hierarchical semantic relationships in a connectionist model of semantic memory*. Paper presented at the Fortieth Annual Meeting of the Psychonomic Society, Los Angeles, CA.

Cree, G. S., McRae, K., & McNorgan, C. (1999). An attractor model of lexical conceptual processing: Simulating semantic priming. *Cognitive Science, 23*, 371–414.

Damasio, A. R. (1989). Time-locked multiregional retroactivation: A systems-level proposal for the neural substrates of recall and recognition. *Cognition, 33*, 25–62.

Daugherty, K., & Seidenberg, M. S. (1992). Rules or connections? The past tense revisited. *Proceedings of the 14th Annual Meeting of the Cognitive Science Society*. Hillsdale, NJ: Erlbaum.

De Groot, A. M. B. (1984). Primed lexical decision: Combined effects of the proportion of related prime-target pairs and the stimulus-onset asynchrony of prime and target. *The Quarterly Journal of Experimental Psychology, 36A*, 253–280.

Den Heyer, K., Briand, K., & Dannenbring, G. L. (1983). Strategic factors in a lexical-decision task: Evidence for automatic and attention-driven processes. *Memory & Cognition, 11*, 374–381.

Dixon, M. J., Bub, D. N., & Arguin, M. (1997). The interaction of object form and object meaning in the identification performance of a patient with category-specific visual agnosia. *Cognitive Neuropsychology, 14*, 1085–1130.

Ellis, A. W., & Morrison, C. M. (1998). Real age of acquisition effects in object naming. *Journal of Experimental Psychology: Learning, Memory, and Cognition, 24*, 515–523.

Farah, M. J., & McClelland, J. L. (1991). A computational model of semantic memory impairment: Modality specificity and emergent category specificity. *Journal of Experimental Psychology: General, 120*, 339–357.

Farah, M. J., & Wallace, M. A. (1992). Semantically-bounded anomia: Implications for the neural implementation of naming. *Neuropsychologia, 30*, 609–621.

Forde, E. M. E., & Humphreys, G. W. (1999). Category-specific recognition impairments: A review of important case studies and influential theories. *Aphasiology, 13*, 169–193.

Forster, K. I. (1994). Computational modeling and elementary process analysis in visual word recognition. *Journal of Experimental Psychology: Human Perception and Performance, 20*, 1292–1310.

Garrard, P., Lambon-Ralph, M. A., Hodges, J. R., & Patterson, K. (2001). Prototypicality, distinctiveness, and intercorrelation: Analyses of the semantic attributes of living and nonliving concepts. *Cognitive Neuropsychology, 18*, 125–174.

Gonnerman, L. M., Anderson, E. S., Devlin, J. T., Kempler, D., & Seidenberg, M. S. (1997). Double dissociation of semantic categories in Alzheimer's disease. *Brain and Language, 57*, 254–279.

Hampton, J. A. (1979). Polymorphous concepts in semantic memory. *Journal of Verbal Learning and Verbal Behavior, 18*, 441–461.

Hampton, J. A. (1997). Conceptual combination: Conjunction and negation of natural concepts. *Memory & Cognition, 25*, 888–909.

Hart, J., Berndt, R. S., & Caramazza, A. (1985). Category-specific naming deficit following cerebral infarction. *Nature, 316*, 439–440.

Hebb, D. O. (1949). *The organization of behavior*. New York: Wiley.

Hertz, J., Krogh, A., & Palmer, R. G. (1991). *Introduction to the theory of neural computation. Santa Fe Institute Studies in the Sciences of Complexity lecture notes, (Vol. 1)*. Workingham, England: Addison-Wesley.

Hinton, G. E., & Shallice, T. (1991). Lesioning an attractor network: Investigations of acquired dyslexia. *Psychological Review, 98*, 74–95.

Holyoak, K. J., & Spellman, B. A. (1993). Thinking. *Annual Review of Psychology, 44*, 265–315.

Hopfield, J. J. (1982). Neural networks and physical systems with emergent collective computational abilities. *Proceedings of the National Academy of Science, 79*, 2254–2558.

Hopfield, J. J. (1984). Neurons with graded response have collective computational features like those of two-state neurons. *Proceedings of the National Academy of Science, 81*, 3088–3092.

Humphrey, G. K., Goodale, M. A., Jacobson, L. S., & Servos, P. (1994). The role of surface information in object recognition: Studies of a visual form agnosic and normal subjects. *Perception, 23*, 1457–1481.

Humphreys, G. W., & Forde, E. M. E. (2001). Hierarchies, similarity and interactivity in object recognition: "Category-specific" neuropsychological deficits. *Behavioral and Brain Sciences, 24*, 453–509.

Jones, S. S., & Smith, L. B. (1993). The place of perception in children's concepts. *Cognitive Development, 8*, 113–139.

Jusczyk, P. W., Cutler, A., & Redanz, N. J. (1993). Infants' preference for the predominant stress patterns of English words. *Child Development, 64*, 675–687.

Kruschke, J. K. (1992). ALCOVE: An exemplar-based connectionist model of category learning. *Psychological Review, 99*, 22–44.

Lin, E. L., & Murphy, G. L. (1997). Effects of background knowledge on object categorization and part detection. *Journal of Experimental Psychology: Human Perception and Performance, 23*, 1153–1169.

Love, B. C., Medin, D. L., & Gureckis, T. M. (2004). SUSTAIN: A network model of category learning. *Psychological Review, 111*, 309–332.

Mahon, B., & Caramazza, A. (2001). The sensory/functional assumption or the data: Which do we keep? Commentary on G. W. Humphreys & E. M. E. Forde, Hierarchies, similarity and interactivity in object recognition: "Category-specific" neuropsychological deficits. *Behavioral and Brain Sciences, 24*, 488–489.

Malt, B., & Smith, E. E. (1984). Correlated properties in natural categories. *Journal of Verbal Learning and Verbal Behavior, 23*, 250–269.

Markman, A. B., & Gentner, D. (1993). Splitting the differences: A structural alignment view of similarity. *Journal of Memory and Language, 32*, 517–535.

Martin, A., & Caramazza, A. (2003). The organization of conceptual knowledge in the brain: Neuropsychological and neuroimaging perspectives [Special issue]. *Cognitive Neuropsychology, 20*, 195–592.

Martin, A., & Chao, L. L. (2001). Semantic memory and the brain: structure and processes. *Current Opinion in Neurobiology, 11*, 194–201.

Masson, M. E. J. (1995). A distributed memory model of semantic priming. *Journal of Experimental Psychology: Learning, Memory, and Cognition, 21*, 3–23.

McRae, K., & Boisvert, S. (1998). Automatic semantic similarity priming. *Journal of Experimental Psychology: Learning, Memory and Cognition, 24*, 558–572.

McRae, K., Cree, G. S., Seidenberg, M. S., & McNorgan, C. (in press). Semantic feature production norms for a large set of living and nonliving things. *Behavioral Research Methods, Instrumentation, & Computers.*

McRae, K., Cree, G. S., Westmacott, R., & de Sa, V. R. (1999). Further evidence for feature correlations in semantic memory. *Canadian Journal of Experimental Psychology, 53*, 360–373.

McRae, K., de Sa, V. R., & Seidenberg, M. S. (1997). On the nature and scope of featural representations of word meaning. *Journal of Experimental Psychology: General, 126*, 99–130.

McRae, K., & McNorgan, C. (2003, November). *Statistical feature correlations and explicit feature relations: Both matter.* Paper presented at the Forty-Forth Annual Meeting of the Psychonomic Society. Canada: Vancouver.

Medin, D. L. (1989). Concepts and conceptual structure. *American Psychologist, 44*, 1469–1481.

Medin, D. L., & Coley, J. D. (1998). Concepts and categorization. In J. Hochberg (Ed.), *Perception and cognition at century's end. Handbook of perception and cognition* (pp. 403–439). San Diego, CA: Academic Press.

Medin, D. L., & Schaffer, M. M. (1978). Context theory of classification learning. *Psychological Review, 85*, 207–238.

Moss, H. E., Ostrin, R. K., Tyler, L. K., & Marslen-Wilson, W. D. (1995). Accessing different types of lexical semantic information: Evidence from priming. *Journal of Experimental Psychology: Learning, Memory and Cognition, 21*, 863–883.

Murphy, G. L. (2002). *The big book of concepts.* Cambridge, MA: MIT Press.

Murphy, G. L., & Medin, D. L. (1985). The role of theories in conceptual coherence. *Psychological Review, 92*, 289–316.

Murphy, G. L., & Ross, B. H. (1994). Predictions from uncertain categorizations. *Cognitive Psychology, 27*, 148–193.

Palmeri, T. J., & Blalock, C. (2000). The role of background knowledge in speeded categorization. *Cognition, 77*, B45–B57.

Pecher, D., Zeelenberg, R., & Barsalou, L. W. (2003). Verifying conceptual properties in different modalities produces switching costs. *Psychological Science, 14*, 119–124.

Plaut, D. C. (1995). Semantic and associative priming in a distributed attractor network. In *Proceedings of the Seventeenth Annual Conference of the Cognitive Science Society*. (Vol. 17, pp. 37–42).

Plaut, D. C., & Booth, J. R. (2000). Individual and developmental differences in semantic priming: Empirical and computational support for a single-mechanism account of lexical processing. *Psychological Review, 107*, 786–823.

Plaut, D. C., McClelland, J. L., Seidenberg, M. S., & Patterson, K. E. (1996). Understanding normal and impaired word reading: Computational principles in quasi-regular domains. *Psychological Review, 103*, 56–115.

Plaut, D. C., & Shallice, T. (1993). Deep dyslexia: A case study of connectionist neuropsychology. *Cognitive Neuropsychology, 10*, 377–500.

Rehder, B., & Murphy, G. L. (2003). A knowledge-resonance (KRES) model of category learning. *Psychonomic Bulletin & Review, 10*, 759–784.

Rosch, E. (1978). Principles of categorization. In E. Rosch & B. B. Lloyd (Eds.), *Cognition and categorization* (pp. 27–48). Hillsdale, NJ: Erlbaum.

Rosch, E., & Mervis, C. B. (1975). Family resemblances: Studies in the internal structure of categories. *Cognitive Psychology, 7*, 573–695.

Rosch, E., Mervis, C. B., Gray, W. D., Johnson, D. M., & Boyes-Braem, P. (1976). Basic objects in natural categories. *Cognitive Psychology, 8*, 382–439.

Saffran, J. R., Aslin, R. N., & Newport, E. L. (1996). Statistical learning by 8-month-old infants. *Science, 274*, 1926–1928.

Schwanenflugel, P. J., & Rey, M. (1986). Interlingual semantic facilitation: Evidence for a common representational system in the bilingual lexicon. *Journal of Memory and Language, 25*, 605–618.

Seidenberg, M. S., & McClelland, J. L. (1989). A distributed, developmental model of word recognition and naming. *Psychological Review, 96*, 523–568.

Shelton, J. R., & Martin, R. C. (1992). How semantic is automatic semantic priming? *Journal of Experimental Psychology: Learning, Memory and Cognition, 18*, 1191–1210.

Simmons, W. K., & Barsalou, L. W. (2003). The similarity-in-topography principle: Reconciling theories of conceptual deficits. *Cognitive Neuropsychology, 20*, 451–486.

Sloman, S. A., Love, B. C., & Ahn, W. K. (1998). Feature centrality and conceptual coherence. *Cognitive Science, 22*, 189–228.

Smith, E. E., Osherson, D. N., Rips, L. J., & Keane, M. (1988). Combining prototypes: A selective modification model. *Cognitive Science, 12*, 485–527.

Smith, E. E., Shoben, E. J., & Rips, L. J. (1974). Structure and process in semantic memory: A feature model for semantic decisions. *Psychological Review, 81*, 214–241.

Solomon, K. O., & Barsalou, L. W. (2001). Representing properties locally. *Cognitive Psychology, 43*, 129–169.

Solso, R. L., & Juel, C. L. (1980). Positional frequency and versatility of bigrams for two- through nine-letter English words. *Behavioral Research Methods and Instrumentation, 12*, 297–343.

Tranel, D., Logan, C. G., Frank, R. J., & Damasio, A. R. (1997). Explaining category-related effects in the retrieval of conceptual and lexical knowledge for concrete entities: Operationalization and analysis of factors. *Neuropsychologia, 35*, 1329–1339.

Tversky, A. (1977). Features of similarity. *Psychological Review, 84*, 327–352.

Vigliocco, G., Vinson, D. P., Lewis, W., & Garrett, M. F. (2004). Representing the meanings of object and action words: The featural and unitary semantic space hypothesis. *Cognitive Psychology, 48*, 422–488.

Warrington, E. K., & Shallice, T. (1984). Category specific semantic impairments. *Brain, 107*, 829–854.

Wattenmaker, W. D. (1993). Incidental concept learning, feature frequency, and correlated properties. *Journal of Experimental Psychology: Learning, Memory, and Cognition, 17*, 908–923.

Westbury, C., & Buchanan, L. (2002). The probability of the least likely non-length-controlled bigram affects lexical decision RTs. *Brain and Language, 81*, 66–78.

Wisniewski, E. J., & Murphy, G. L. (1989). Superordinate and basic category names in discourse: A textual analysis. *Discourse Processes, 12*, 245–261.

Younger, B. A., & Cohen, L. B. (1983). Infant perception of correlations among attributes. *Child Development, 54*, 858–867.

Younger, B. A., & Cohen, L. B. (1986). Developmental change in infants' perception of correlations among attributes. *Child Development, 57*, 803–815.

ON THE CONTINUITY OF MIND: TOWARD A DYNAMICAL ACCOUNT OF COGNITION

Michael J. Spivey and Rick Dale

It should be obvious by now that this minute inflow of stimulus energy does not consist of discrete inputs—that stimulation does not consist of stimuli. The flow is continuous. There are, of course, episodes in the flow, but these are nested within one another and cannot be cut up into elementary units. Stimulation is not momentary. (J. J. Gibson, 1979).

I. Introduction

In 1960, J. J. Gibson reviewed technical uses of the term *stimulus* and found that it did not have a consistent agreed-upon definition, but instead connoted several different conceptions of "stimulating" an organism. Most of those conceptions did, however, have a property also found in the word's original uses: A stimulus is a temporally discrete, momentary happening in the life of an organism. Challenging this intuition, Gibson's ecological psychology assumes at its foundation the continuity of the stimulation in the surrounding environment. What this means is that the "flowing array of stimulus energy," as Gibson called it, is never presegmented into easily defined independent chunks, or "stimuli,"— even though we feel as though we perceive it that way.

Before Gibson, Dewey (1896) famously made a similar point in his influential critique of the reflex arc concept. The reflex arc concept was a relatively new idea, framing the questions of psychology in terms of causal arcs among stimulus, mental event, and response. Essentially, studying the causal arcs between just the former two, or the latter two, was considered a legitimate scientific enterprise in and of itself. In contrast, treating the

0079-7421/04 $35.00

progression of the three components as one continuous process, which naturally loops back on itself, was what Dewey influentially encouraged (Leahey, 1994). From his perspective, actions take place over time and they continuously alter the stimulus environment, which in turn continuously alters mental activity, which is continuously expressing and revising its inclinations to action. One of the most famous reactions to Dewey's criticism, behaviorism, found a long-standing solution by eliminating the second (mental) stage. But Dewey's critique still stands: Segmenting the natural life of an organism into discretely identifiable stimuli and responses is artificial and potentially misleading.

Although originally aimed predominantly at behaviorism, Gibson and Dewey's critiques echo into modern cognitive psychology. Essentially, cognitive psychology replaced behaviorism's emphasis on "stimulus and response" with an emphasis on "stimulus and interpretation"—not really addressing the continuity problem. But if the environmental stimulation impinging on our sensory systems is almost always partially overlapping in space and continuous through time, why would our minds work in the staccato fashion of a digital computer, momentarily entertaining one discrete stable non-overlapping representational state, and then instantaneously flipping to entertain another one?

The goal of this chapter is to challenge the notion of discrete representational states. The mind, like Gibson's stimulation, exists in continuity, moving gradually between mental states, never standing still in time. Indeed, these "mental states" themselves are not really static states at all, but rather graded regions in mental state-space that are more or less interpretable than others and are briefly visited (or perhaps merely "flirted" with) by the mind during its continuous motion through this state-space. We offer the "continuity of mind" as a rubric for a psychological framework in which internal perceptual-cognitive processing exhibits continuous change in the salience of multiple simultaneously active representations. This framework forces one to rethink many representational and architectural assumptions that have persisted in cognitive psychology and poses as an "intervention" procedure to wean the cognitive sciences from their obsession with formal logical descriptions of mental representation. The continuity of mind attempts to replace the overidealized notion of discrete symbolic mental states, borrowed from antiquated artificial intelligence research, with distributed patterns of neural activation that are always partially consistent with multiple mental states. Most important, this framework focuses on the continuous temporal dynamics of these patterns of neural activation and the resulting consequences for descriptions of various perceptual-cognitive processes.

Of course, there exist several important precedents to this line of thinking. Kelso (1995), for example, explored how dynamic patterns in several perceptual and motor processes can be accounted for by the concepts of coordination and self-organization imported from synergetics (Haken, 1983). Port and Van Gelder (1995) offered a foundational collection of papers exploring a wide range of topics in which dynamical architectures and equations account for a wide variety of behavior. Thelen and Smith (1994) marshaled these dynamic-systems concepts in the service of explaining and predicting patterns in behavioral development. Even further back, Gregson (1983) offered a discussion of time series and recommended a radical reconceptualization of psychological explanation by invoking time as a crucial concern.

The proposal herein pushes in some of the same directions as these preexisting dynamical theses but takes an important, different overall route. We will focus on processes at a specific time scale, perception and behavior on the order of hundreds of milliseconds, and how these processes importantly exemplify the continuity of mind. Mental activity at this time scale has been a battlefield of dispute between frameworks in cognitive science. For example, one possible modern target for Dewey's critique is the computer metaphor of the mind. This metaphor sees stages of cognitive processing as temporally discrete representational states (Dietrich & Markman, 2003). Not only does the approach recommend an analysis of the human mind in terms of temporally discrete representation, but supposes as an ontological matter that the mind entertains discrete representations and states. The processes at the time scale considered here have often involved heated debate between this and other explanatory frameworks. For years this traditional computational perspective has enjoyed a firm grip over the time scale, offering explanations for different processes in language and perception. The success of this paradigm permitted the computer metaphor to even trickle down into explorations of the properties of neural processes. For example, in the early years of cognitive science, there were a few who were inspired both by digital computing theory and by the physical processes of the human brain. These researchers invested quite a bit of intellectual stock in the idea that populations of spiking neurons would behave more or less the same as populations of digital bits (e.g., McCulloch, 1965; Von Neumann, 1958; Wickelgren, 1977; see also Barlow, 1972; Lettvin, 1995; Rose, 1996).

However, what we know now about real neurophysiological processes seems to suggest instead great promise for the continuity of mind rather than the digital computer metaphor. A great deal more has been learned in the past few decades about how populations of neurons work (e.g., Georgopoulos, Kalaska, Caminiti, & Massey, 1982; Pouget, Dayan, & Zemel, 2000; Sparks, Holland, & Guthrie, 1976; Tanaka, 1997; Young & Yamane, 1992), and it is nothing at all like the instantaneous binary flip-flopping from one discrete state to another that characterizes information processing in digital computers. In neuroscience, the closest thing to a classical mental representation is the population code. A population code is a sparse distributed representation comprised of a group of neurons that cooperate and resonate in response to a familiar perceptual input. Importantly, the individual neurons that make up a population code do not appear to update their states in lockstep to the beat of a single global clock. Population codes spend a substantial amount of their time in partially coherent patterns of activity. And thus the brain's state is often dynamically traversing intermediate regions of a state-space that contains what could be described as many meta-stable attractors.

Whether these population codes end up approximating discrete representations is an important question open to debate. The distant and tenuous connection between digital symbolic computation and distributed neural processing is nevertheless an attractive idea to some (cf. Marcus, 2001). According to this perspective, the activity of populations of neurons is sufficiently approximated by models that use rule-based operations on logical symbols, despite the fact that real neural hardware does not quite work that way.

There are two key properties of the representations instantiated by neural populations that we argue separate them from computer-like symbolic representations: (1) continuity in time and (2) continuity in space. Continuity in space has been dealt with elsewhere in roughly two different ways: (1) a contiguous high-dimensional state-space where proximity serves as similarity and prototypical representations exist as partially overlapping attractor basins (e.g., Aleksander, 1973; Edelman, 1999; Elman, 1991; Lund & Burgess, 1996; Pasupathy & Connor, 2002) and (2) a two-dimensional space based on sensory surfaces, in which the shape and layout of internal representations are roughly homologous to actual physical patterns of stimulation (e.g., Barsalou, 1999; Farah, 1985; Johnson-Laird, 1998; Kosslyn, Thompson, Kim, & Alpert, 1995; Langacker, 1990; Spivey, Richardson, & Gonzalez-Marquez, in press; Talmy, 1983). Continuity in time has also been dealt with elsewhere in two (at least superficially) different ways: (1) the continuous temporal dynamics of the neural connectivity patterns that constitute knowledge and intelligence changing over developmental time (e.g., Elman, Bates, Karmiloff-Smith, Parisi, & Plunkett, 1996; Spencer & Schöner, 2003; Thelen & Smith, 1994), and (2) the continuous temporal dynamics of representation and behavior in real-time processing (e.g., Kelso, 1995; Port & Van Gelder, 1995; Spivey, in preparation). This latter emphasis on continuous temporal dynamics in real-time processing is where this chapter will focus its arguments against digital-computational accounts of cognition.

By describing demonstrations, in psycholinguistics and in visual perception, of representations that are analog (rather than digital), partially overlapping, and change gradually over the course of hundreds of milliseconds, we hope to convince some readers that symbolic accounts of cognition that do not accommodate such continuous temporal dynamics are missing a crucial aspect of an accurate description of the mind. Such graded mental states appear to be more than just temporary transitions between discrete mental representations but instead may be the modus operandi of the mind. Therefore, we suggest that approximating patterns of neural activation, and the continuous temporal dynamics of these patterns, with a metaphor of discrete symbolic computation, is not merely a stretched analogy, but in fact a misleading one. Although the conversion of a continuous trajectory through a high-dimensional state-space into a string of emitted symbols is a powerful mathematical concept, it faces statistical problems with regard to the exact placement of symbolic partitions (Bollt, Stanford, Lai, & Zyczkowski, 2000), it faces representational problems with regard to how a discrete perfectly repeatable logical symbol is implemented by an inherently noisy and distributed neural system, and it faces architectural problems with regard to an unrealistic degree of modularity required of the systems to and from which these symbol strings are being sent. Instead of pretending to be able to chop time into chunks that are associated with individual nonoverlapping symbolic representations, we argue that patterns of brain and behavior inevitably exhibit temporal and representational continuity and that adopting this perspective can help predict and explain a considerable database in the study of cognition.

II. Continuously Changing Graded Representations

A. Probabilistic Versus Pure Mental States

Before evaluating support for continuity in language and vision, we present some simple illustrations that may help further limn our perspective. First, consider a very simple demonstration of how we might visualize continuous change in neural population codes. Readers familiar with dynamical metaphors will doubtless find this example highly simplistic. Nevertheless, it will help solidify the predictions about temporal dynamics that are made by the continuity of mind thesis.

Imagine you've taken over a sturdy stool at the bar of your favorite pub, awaiting a close friend. Call him Ken. He's late. After a couple beers, you continue to keep your eye out for him, noting various faces as they enter the pub. Imagine catching glimpses of someone you think might be Ken among an entering crowd. In that brief period of time, before being certain of this person's identity, your brain will exhibit patterns of activity that are partially consistent with a number of alternative people. Figure 1A is a cartoon illustration of a 100-ms time slice of that brain state—that uncertain, fuzzy state—if one were measuring a mere 14 of your cortical neurons (out of about a billion).

In the idealized brain state in Fig. 1A, a few neurons are excited near their maximum firing rate, several neurons are moderately above their resting level of activation, and several neurons are conspicuously inhibited below their resting level. (As these are firing rates and not action potentials, this "state" is obviously an average over the 100-ms time slice.) Although this pattern of neural activation can be treated as a discrete location in the space of possible brain states, it does not correspond to a discrete, pure, mental state. That is, we have devised this demonstration such that the pattern of neural activity in Fig. 1A corresponds to a brain state that is partially consistent with two different identifiable mental states (Fig. 1B and C; the surface similarity in the two names here is irrelevant for our purposes).

Imagine we had the capacity to record previous moments in which you perceived Ken and another friend Kevin, and could establish which specific set of neurons corresponded to this identification, averaged over many instances. Figures 1B and C depict the pattern of neural activity that would emerge in the situations, "I see Ken" and "I see Kevin," respectively. In Fig. 1B, one can see that neurons 1, 3, 6, 7, and 9 compose the population code of "I see Ken." Partially overlapping with this, in Fig. 1C, it becomes clear that neurons 1, 4, 6, 7, and 10 compose the population code "I see Kevin." Due to the complexity of multiple sensory inputs, the nonlinear dynamics in neural processing, and noise in neural activity, these "pure" ideals of interpretation (Fig. 1B and C) are practically unattainable, but they are regularly approximated by the brain's actual pattern of activity.

Let us simplify further and assume that each neuron in these population codes is encoding some small feature about Ken and Kevin. Figure 2 shows the same pattern of neural activity as in Fig. 1A, but with pretend interpretations for what each neuron represents. Of course, individual neurons probably encode far finer details than those depicted in Fig. 2. The term *microfeatures* has been used to refer to the properties of the sensory input to which individual neurons respond (Hinton, 1981). Often times, these individual microfeatures are not easily deciphered, either in artificial neural networks or in biological neural networks.

By comparing the actual neural pattern of microfeatures in Fig. 2 to various "pure" population codes (such as those in Fig. 1B and C), we can calculate the actual neural pattern's Euclidian proximity to these "pure" population codes, normalize those proximity values so that they sum to 1.0,

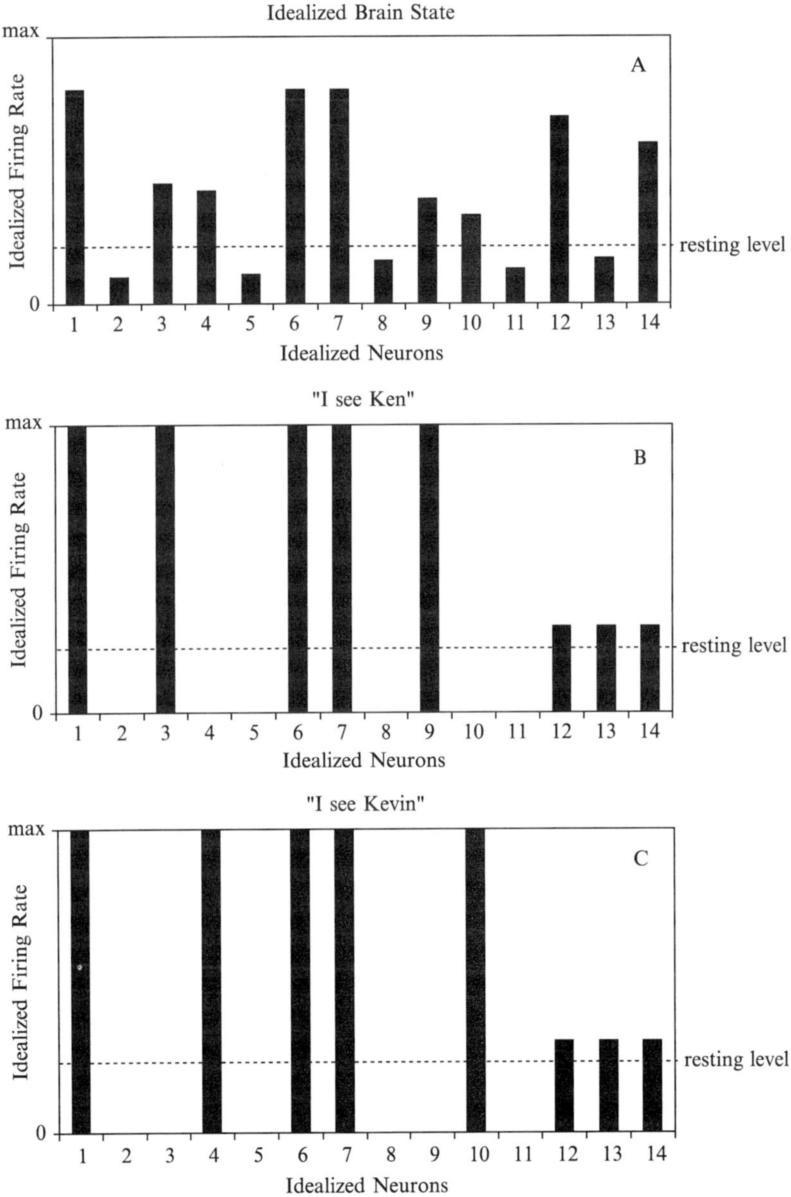

Fig. 1. Idealized neural patterns that correspond to a graded brain state (A), and two example "pure" states (B & C).

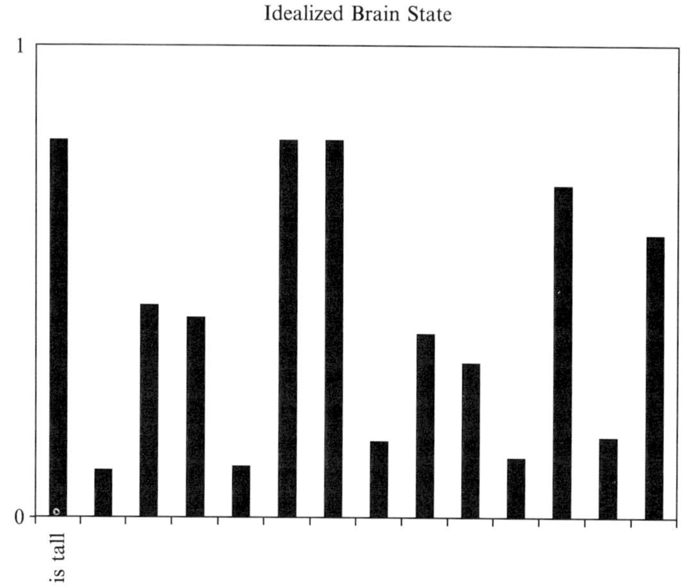

Fig. 2. Idealized labels for each neuron in the graded brain state.

and thus generate a rough probability distribution over possible interpretations of the person who is entering the pub. See Fig. 3. In this way, a neural pattern can be seen as a probabilistic mental state, represented in the form of its proximity to idealized pure (discretely interpretable) mental states, instead of mere activity levels of individual neurons. In contrast, a supposed pure mental state refers to an ideal precise pattern of neural activation that—due to the complex and noisy dynamics of a brain with billions of neurons and trillions of synapses—is never actually perfectly instantiated. In this framework, a pure discrete (i.e., symbolic) mental state is an abstract concept. It is a useful construct for theory development, but we argue that an actual physical instantiation of a symbolic mental state never comes into being. Rather, a fuzzy region of state-space broadly encompassing the specific coordinates that correspond to a "pure" mental state (i.e., the basin of attraction that surrounds an individual attractor point), is what gets briefly visited by the trajectory defining the system's state as a function of time. The precise set of coordinates corresponding to that "pure" mental state (i.e., the idealized identifiable population code) is never quite reached. Nonetheless, the labels attached to these "pure" mental states are extremely helpful in understanding the probabilistic mental states (cf. Barber, Clark, & Anderson, 2003; Zemel, Dayan, & Pouget, 1998). Without the descriptive

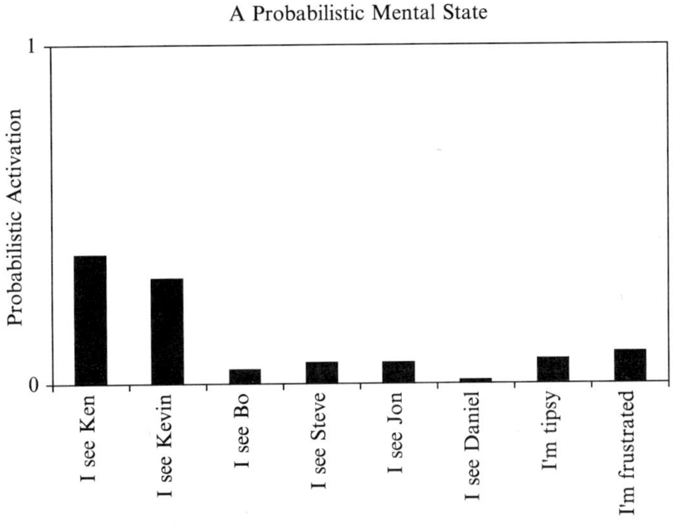

Fig. 3. An idealized pattern of normalized proximities (treated as probabilities) to various "pure" states in the space of possible mental states.

conveniences of the labels along the abscissa in Fig. 3, a probabilistic mental state would be essentially uninterpretable.

Our talk of "states" could imply that this specific pattern of activation is stable for a certain period of time. The continuity of mind suggests, however, that it would be continuously moving toward some interpretable population codes and away from others. When the activations of these neural patterns are tracked over time, they change gradually and nonlinearly. In Fig. 4, a time course plot of probabilities of different interpretable population codes is illustrated. In the particular settling algorithm used here, it is guaranteed that the probability value that starts out higher will be the eventual winner, but this will not be true with all settling algorithms.

Although this scenario quaintly displays the multifarious character of graded mental states changing over time, its simplicity reveals theoretical flaws in the form of what might be called "edge effects" in time. Figure 4 assumes that this process occurred in a contextual vacuum, involving no new informative events while it was settling, and involved no action. It simply gravitated to a stable corner (attractor basin) in its state-space. In real life, no such event is free of some context, new information is constantly arriving, and we are often producing continuous motor actions during perception. Thus, by the time your brain state has approached a location in state-space that is roughly consistent with only one pure population code, such as .8

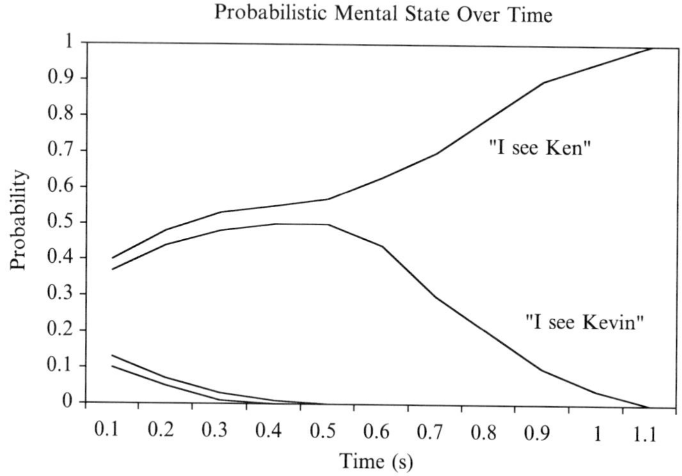

Fig. 4. An idealized evolution of these probabilistic activations (or normalized proximities) depicting a dynamic graded mental state over the course of several hundred milliseconds.

activation for "I see Ken," changes in the environment and your own behavior will alter the brain state such that it travels back into "unlabeled" regions in state-space, preparing for another near settling event where it gets just close enough to another pure mental state to elicit appropriate action and perhaps then veers off once again. This more ecologically valid perspective of continuous change in natural behavior gives considerable bite to the continuity of mind proposal: It means that the vast majority of the mind's time is spent in between identifiable mental states rather than in them.

It is perhaps tempting to think of achieving one briefly relatively stable state for one temporal portion of sensory stimulation (such as that in the later time period of Fig. 4) as producing a symbol-like representation that could somehow persist in some mental arena, and that when the system then gravitates to other attractors in state-space this mental arena could somehow accumulate accurate renditions of these symbol-like representations that are visited in the continuous state-space (but cf. Bollt et al., 2000). This perspective has much in common with the way a digital computer might shunt one symbol into a working memory buffer and then shunt another and another, thus giving the system several complete representational entities to work with at the same time. In fact, there are hybrid theoretical frameworks for cognition and language that implement this kind of temporally dynamic accrual of activation for competing representations in a first stage, with the winning symbolic representation then becoming part of a discrete rule-driven computational system in a second stage (e.g., Anderson &

Lebiere, 1998; Budiu & Anderson, 2004; Stevenson, 1994; see also Hummel, 2001; Marcus, 2001; Pinker & Ullman, 2002). Such frameworks hypothesize a rather drastic schism between one part of the mind that functions in ways that are consistent with the temporally continuous ebb and flow of neuronal population codes and another part of the mind that functions in ways that are substantially inconsistent with the neurophysiology.

This tempting notion of "accumulating symbols" after their attractors are visited necessarily requires this problematic schism. Where else could those accumulated symbols be stored but in a separate additional system? If one accepts that this neural state-space can pose as a description of the activation of every neuron in the brain, then such a description would have no room for an additional separate system in the brain that could be a repository for such an accumulation of symbols. The only sense in which these semistable population codes—which may act something like fuzzy (nondiscrete) symbols—could accumulate, in this account, is if they continue to reverberate their coherent activation pattern while new population codes also become coherently active. Note, however, that this still requires the coordinates describing the state of the system in this space to move away from their original location near that first attractor and now find a location that is roughly equidistant from the previous attractor and the new one. Thus, if one endeavors to describe the entire state of mind as a system with one state-space (and not as a collection of independent noninteractive systems with separate state-spaces), then one cannot accumulate complete unchanged symbols as the state of the system travels from one attractor to another. Hence, dealing with the fast and complex temporal sequence of sensory stimulation that occurs in normal everyday circumstances (although not necessarily in the cognitive psychologist's laboratory), and the spatiotemporally contiguous movement in state-space that this instigates, forces the behavior of the system to be best described by its continuous trajectory (spending much of its time in intermediate unlabeled regions of state-space) rather than by an enumerated list of the interpretable attractors it visits.

B. Continuity in Categorization?

To offer a more substantive demonstration, we further exemplify this continuity by considering a particular realm of research in cognitive psychology. The study of categorization has been at the core of psychology, and especially cognitive psychology, for many decades (cf. Harnad, 1987). A continuity account, similar to that cartooned in Fig. 4, would naturally predict that categorization tasks often show quite different results from speeded responses than from nonspeeded responses (e.g., Lamberts, 1995, 1998, 2000; Lin & Murphy, 1997; Nosofsky & Alfonso-Reese, 1999; see also Brownell & Caramazza, 1978; Medin & Smith, 1981). This prediction derives from the idea that a speeded response forces an unsettled trajectory to select among multiple nearby attractors in an unsystematic fashion (e.g., perhaps stochastically). The results can allow one to infer partial activation of multiple competing "interpretations" of the stimulus array. Unfortunately, as noted by Lamberts (2000), it is still somewhat new and unusual for categorization studies to give consideration to temporal dynamics. The bulk of the literature over the past few decades has focused almost exclusively on the outcome of categorization rather than the process. This tradition may miss the fact that by examining the continuous time course of online categorization, one can tease apart various theoretical accounts that would never have been rigorously tested by outcome-based offline experimental measures.

For example, one theoretical account of the process of categorization, which is generally consistent with Lamberts' (2000) information accumulation theory, can be idealistically demonstrated by a very simple neural network architecture called normalized recurrence (McRae, Spivey-Knowlton, & Tanenhaus, 1998; Spivey, Fitneva, Tabor, & Ajmani, 2002a; Spivey & Tanenhaus, 1998; Tanenhaus, Spivey-Knowlton, & Hanna, 2000). Normalized recurrence simulates the temporal dynamics of the competition that emerges when multiple information sources weigh in on alternative interpretations of a stimulus array. Like the probabilistic activations of idealized population codes (see Fig. 3), the architecture simply generates a probability distribution over possible categories in order to track their evolution over time (usually corresponding to hundreds of milliseconds of real-time cognitive processing).[1] Figure 5 shows the diagram of a very simple normalized recurrence architecture used to approximate the changing patterns of activation during the categorization of different animals into their respective classes (fish, mammal, bird, and reptile). As the normalized recurrence competition algorithm works, these five feature vectors (framed circles) are normalized to sum to 1 and are then combined at the integration layer (framed ovals), replacing its previous activation pattern. In this simulation, there are no differential weights for the five feature vectors; they simply sum together at the integration vector. The integration layer then divides each of its nodes' activation by the vector's sum activation, thus making the integration vector simply an average of the five feature vectors. Cumulative feedback is then sent by adding to each feature node the product of itself and its corresponding integration node. The next time step begins

[1] The distributed population codes of the network are simplified as localist nodes for features and classes, as in our first example. However, this competition algorithm does not address what the localist representations are made of, nor how they developed. Despite these idealizations, the architecture allows for rather sophisticated modeling of temporal processes of interpretation and categorization.

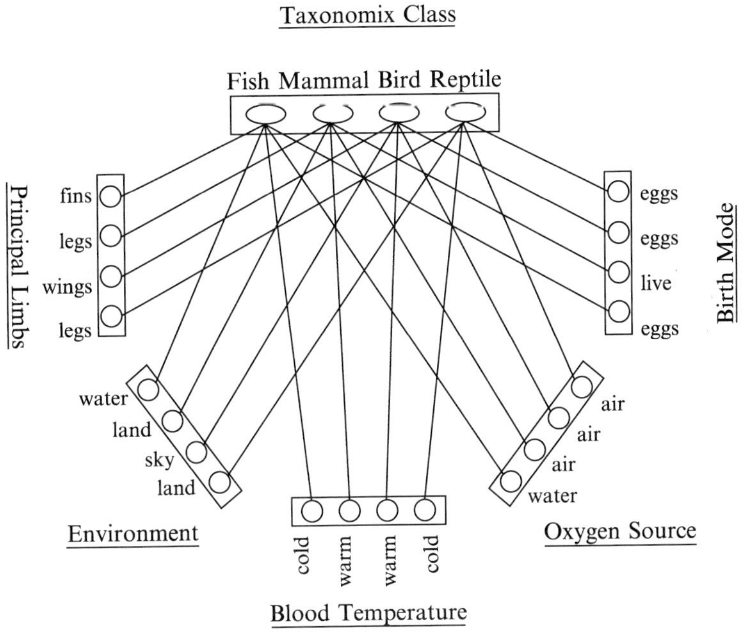

Fig. 5. Schematic diagram of a normalized recurrence simulation of the temporal dynamics of categorization. The repeated node labels in some of the feature vectors (circles) are necessary because each integration node (ovals) must have its own unique feature node. This allows the feature vectors to function as probability distributions in their support for the appropriate taxonomic class. For example, after the initial feature vector normalization step, the birth mode vector for a live-birth animal would pass 1.0 activation to the Mammal node and 0 activation to the other taxonomic class nodes, whereas for an egg-laying animal the birth mode vector would send .333 activation to the Fish, Bird, and Reptile nodes, and 0 activation to the Mammal node.

with the feature nodes normalizing themselves again (dividing each node by the vector's sum), and the integration, normalization, and feedback take place again. These four calculations are computed within each time step, and the network continues until a criterion activation (often .95) is reached by an integration node. The cyclic recurrent flow of activation between the integration vector and the feature vectors allows strong and selective biases within certain feature vectors to coerce weak and uncertain biases in others, until the system gradually settles into a stable state.

This localist attractor network, inspired significantly by McClelland and Rumelhart's (1981) Interactive Activation model, and Anderson, Silverstein, Ritz, and Jones's (1977) Brain-State-in-a-Box model (see also Grainger & Jacobs, 1998; Zemel & Mozer, 2001); easily categorizes animals that are typical exemplars of their taxonomic class, such as "toucan," "goldfish," and "cat" (see Fig. 6). However, with animals that are unusual members of their class, the network undergoes a long, drawn-out competition due to the animal's partial match with multiple taxonomic classes.[2] The gradual activation curves are similar to those produced by Lamberts' (2000) information accumulation model, and the overall typicality effects coincide with theories of graded category structure (e.g., Rosch & Mervis, 1975; Smith, Shoben, & Rips, 1974). Note how, in Fig. 6, the simulations for "seal," "whale," "penguin," "turtle" and "platypus" exhibit slow rises to criterion for the correct classification, and even then their asymptotes are substantially below 1.0. In the end, the model concludes that a whale is .6 a mammal and .4 a fish. And, in fact, during its first few time steps of processing, the model briefly conceives of a whale as slightly more a fish than a mammal. A similar crossing of curves is seen with a turtle.

This simulation serves as a simple existence proof of how graded temporal dynamics can be realized in a system of neural population codes. Admittedly, even if the model's predictions were to fit human data perfectly, we would not contend that the mechanism matches the brain's own. But could these curves really be anything at all like what a human mind does when it categorizes animals? During the early moments of settling on a categorization for an animal, do people simultaneously partially consider multiple categories? And do those partially active representations compete over time in order for a cognitive trajectory to settle into eliciting a unique motor output?

Using the method of eye tracking, Nederhouser and Spivey (2004) conducted a pilot experiment that supports this speculation. Although, as described, comparing speeded instinctive responses to slow contemplative responses (e.g., Lin & Murphy, 1997) is a good start for measuring this kind of time course question, a semicontinuous measure may be more revealing by demonstrating accruing activation that supports different interpretations. Because eye movements occur about 2–3 times per second and are largely unaffected by deliberative strategies, they can provide a stream of multiple honest "proto-actions" over the course of the few seconds required to produce a single overt verbal or manual action.

In the pilot study, the eye movements of 17 participants were recorded while they categorized small plastic toy animals (about 2″ × 3″) into either of

[2] In fact, in this rather small and oversimplified simulation, since the Principal Limbs and Environment feature vectors for "bat" uniquely support the "bird" category, and only the Birth Mode feature vector uniquely supports the mammal category, there actually winds up being more overall support for incorrectly categorizing a bat as a bird (asymptote at .8) than as a mammal (asymptote at .2). Expansion of the model to include more features, more classes, and perhaps differential weights for the feature vectors would be necessary to eradicate errors like this.

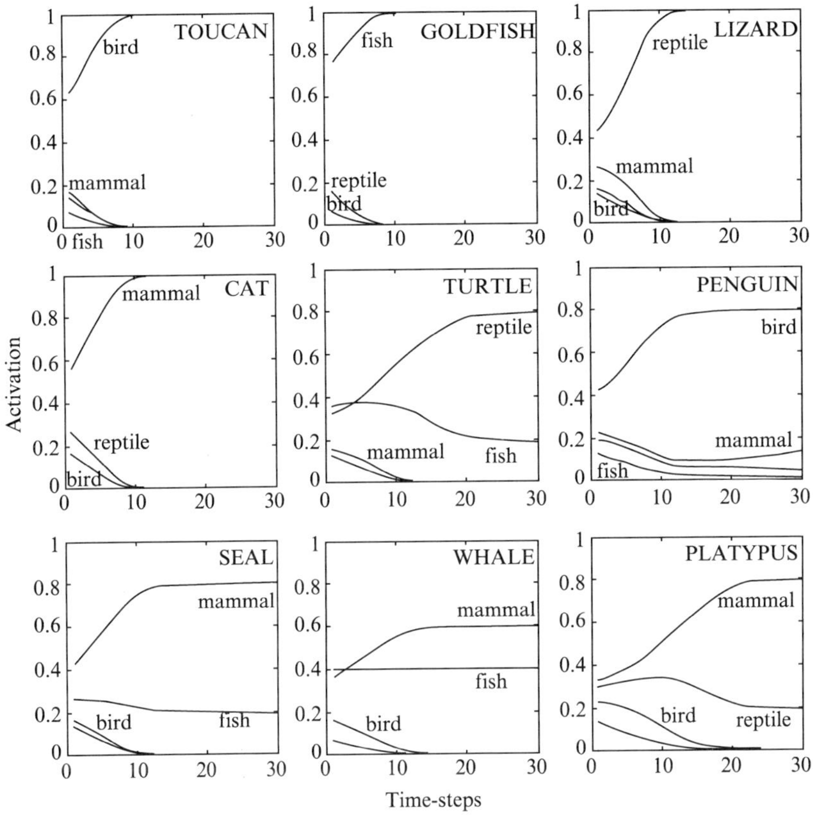

Fig. 6. Activation curves from the simulation of the temporal dynamics of categorization. Feature nodes that received 1.0 activation at start, for the five input vectors, were the following: CAT (legs, land, warm, air, live), SEAL (fins, water, warm, air, live), WHALE (fins, water, warm, air, live), TOUCAN (wings, sky, warm, air, eggs), DUCK (wings–legs, water–land–sky, warm, air, eggs), PENGUIN (wings, land–water, warm, air, eggs), LIZARD (legs, land, cold, air, eggs), GOLDFISH (fins, water, cold, water, eggs), EEL (all limbs, water, cold, water, eggs), TURTLE (legs, water, cold, air, eggs), WATERSNAKE (all limbs, land–water, cold, air, eggs), and PLATYPUS (legs, land–water, warm, air, eggs).

two bins. Participants were first shown a set of animals (half from one taxonomic class, half from another), and then were presented each animal one at a time. It was observed that animals that are atypical members of their taxonomic classes, like turtles, penguins, seals, and whales, took longer to categorize than more typical animals (cf. Glass & Meany, 1978; Rips, Shoben, & Smith, 1973), and they also elicited quite a bit of vacillation in eye movements between the two category bins. When participants categorized an atypical member of a category, they often fixated both bins multiple times before settling on the correct bin and dropping the animal into it. Crucially, when one looks again at the records of eye position over time, one can plot fixation curves based on the proportion of fixations at each time slice (Fig. 6) that resemble somewhat the activation curves from the network simulations (Fig. 7). The curves in Fig. 6 show, for each 33-ms time slice, the proportion of trials in which the subjects were fixating the correct category bin or the incorrect category bin, following their first saccade away from the toy animal that was placed in front of them. Note how, in the case of penguins, seals, and whales, some subjects continued to fixate the incorrect bin for the full 2 s shown; in some cases, they even placed the whale in the fish bin.

This comparison of pilot simulation and pilot data provides a glimpse into the beginning stages of how we might better understand the temporal dynamics of real-time categorization. The demonstration is intended to illustrate how one can begin to visualize the fuzzy and graded representations that change over time during categorization, both in a localist attractor network and in a semicontinuous record of cognitive processing. And perhaps some of the more static, formal approaches to concepts and categorization might have trouble accommodating such evidence that, during a categorization event, the mind spends so much of its time in graded, rather than discrete, mental states.

The important point to be made here is that these very specific locations in state-space that seem to have easily labeled identities, these pure mental states of "I see Ken" or "I see a mammal" can only be approximated by the actual neural system for which this state-space is an abstracted mathematical description. That is not to say those pure mental states are irrelevant or nonexistent. They do exist, as possible locations in the neural system's state-space. The neural population codes get sufficiently activated (i.e., the system approaches close enough to a frequently visited and identifiable attractor basin) to convince one phenomenologically that these pure mental states have been perfectly instantiated. We would argue instead that they have an infinitesimally small likelihood of ever happening.

With these simple examples to help guide our path, we now discuss language and vision, and the rather impressive support each brings to this perspective that cognition inherently consists of continuity.

III. Continuity in Language Processing

Here we consider language comprehension in real time as a particularly evocative example of continuous sensory input producing continuous cognitive processing—in spite of our clumsy metalinguistic introspection that we perceive one word and then silence and then another word. We argue that

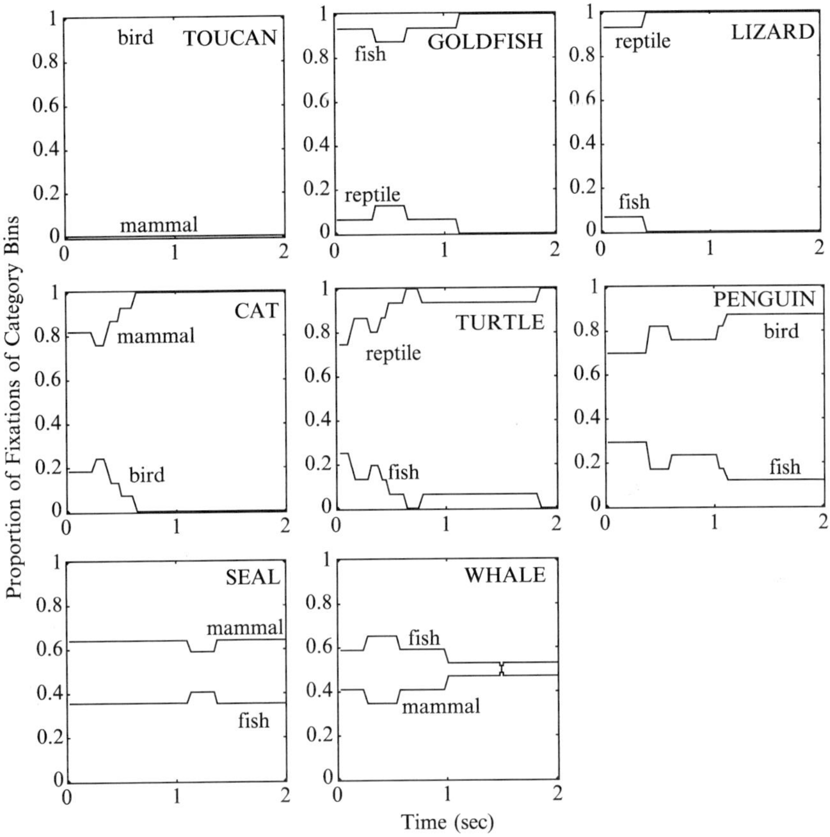

Fig. 7. Eye-fixation curves from Nederhouser and Spivey (2004). Animals that are atypical examples of their taxonomic class elicited considerable vacillation in eye movements during the early moments of categorization.

this process, at its various levels of complexity, is driven by graded and partially active information. We present these processes at increasing time scales, beginning with speech perception (hundredths of seconds), word recognition (tenths of seconds), and concluding with sentence processing (seconds). Despite these different time scales, each exhibits the continuity of mind.

A. Speech Perception

Humans are wont to carve up their world into seemingly very discrete categories. These categories are often imposed even within variation among the things being categorized. Categorical perception describes the general tendency to cut a fine line along a gradient of variation; any inputs that fall to the left or right of this line will be part of one or the other category. Despite its name, "categorical" perception of speech sounds can be made consistent with more temporally dynamic approaches to categorization (e.g., Anderson et al., 1977; Dailey, Cottrell, Padget, & Adolphs, 2002; Lamberts, 2000; Pisoni & Tash, 1974; Tuller, Case, Ding & Kelso, 1994; see also Cree, McRae, & McNorgan, 1999). Indeed, the previous sections would suggest that categorical speech perception does not just consist in graded patterns of neural activation, but might exhibit such gradation in behavior when we use continuous-time measures to investigate its finer temporal structure (rather than simply observe explicit identification of a speech sound).

In pursuit of this, McMurray and Spivey (1999) tracked participants' eye movements while they performed the standard categorical identification task. This task involves categorizing different versions of "pah" and "bah" sounds, lying along the voice-onset time (VOT) dimension that distinguishes them, by clicking /ba/ and /pa/ icons on a computer screen. Thus, in addition to recording the participants' explicit choice, there was also a semicontinuous record of how the eyes tended toward one or the other response icon during categorization. With "pah" or "bah" sounds near their categorical boundary, eye movements clearly exhibited conspicuous vacillation between the /ba/ and /pa/ icons. Figure 8 shows two typical eye-fixation-over-time plots during the speech categorization process for a clear "pah" stimulus (panel A) and for a sound that was near the category boundary but was nonetheless identified (by mouse click) as /pa/ 95% of the time (panel B). The eye position records depicted here came only from trials in which the /pa/ icon was indeed clicked at the end of the trial. Despite the identification outcome being identical in this subset of trials (all categorized as /pa/), the pattern of eye movements reveals substantially more time spent fixating the / ba/ icon (dashed area in panel B) when the speech stimulus was near the VOT category boundary, thus indicating a clear effect of perceptual gradations in speech sounds.

In fact, these temporary phonemic ambiguities, as tested with VOT continua and eye movement records, exhibit their effects not just in phoneme identification tasks but also in spoken word recognition tasks (McMurray, Tanenhaus, & Aslin, 2002; McMurray, Tanenhaus, Aslin, & Spivey, 2003). For example, within-category variation of VOT does not affect the final outcome of recognizing *bear* versus *pear*; however, it does affect the eye movement records of participants looking at and clicking the corresponding images on the computer screen (McMurray et al., 2002). A particularly compelling way to visualize these eye movement data for the phoneme identification task is to convert them into identification functions for early, intermediate, and late periods of time during the identification process.

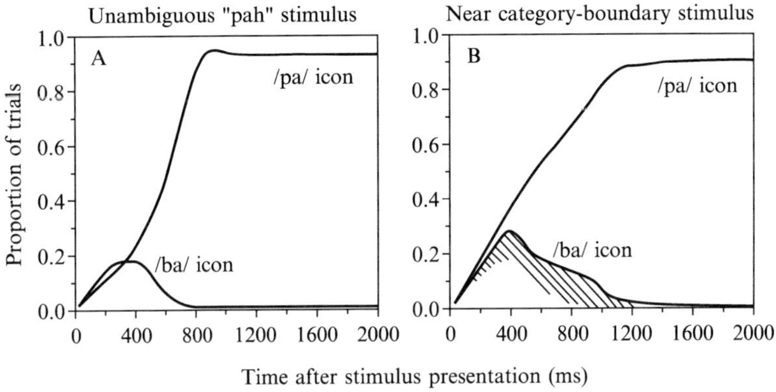

Fig. 8. Proportion of trials in which participants were fixating the /ba/ or the /pa/ icons, time slice by time slice, after hearing an unmistakable "pah" from the VOT continuum (panel A) and after hearing a speech sound near the category boundary (panel B). The hatched region in the panel B indicates the degree to which within-category variation (in contrast to panel A) affected eye movements to the competitor icon /ba/, even for just those trials that were identified as /pa/ (adapted from McMurray et al., 2003).

Figure 9 shows an example of the proportion of time the eyes spent fixating the /pa/ icon as a function of VOT. The later period of the identification process (1201–1500 ms) reveals an eye movement identification function that looks just like the typical discrete categorical identification function produced by button press responses. However, the earlier periods of the identification process (i.e., 0–300 ms, 301–600 ms, and even 601–900 ms) look significantly more probabilistic and are graded in a way that reveals some sensitivity to the continuous variation in VOT.

As done in the previous exploration of categorization, it can be illuminating to simulate the graded temporal dynamics of "categorical" speech perception with a localist attractor network. This practice helps to visualize the continuous changes taking place in the patterns of activation corresponding to competing "graded category" states. Figure 10 illustrates the architecture of a normalized recurrence simulation that integrates a speech vector (that pits "bah"-like sounds against "pah"-like sounds) and a visual vector (that compares fixation probabilities to a /ba/ icon, a /pa/ icon, and the central fixation dot). The speech vector is given a pattern of input corresponding to a speech sound somewhere along the VOT continuum. For example, a rather unambiguous "pah" sound might get a starting activation of (.1 0 .9) for those three nodes, whereas a borderline "bah" sound might get (.6 0 .4). The visual vector always starts at (.33 .33 .33), treating each visual object as equally worthy of attracting an eye movement.

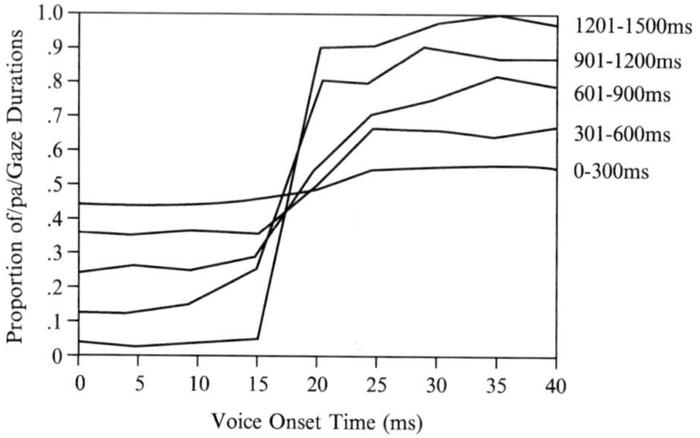

Fig. 9. When proportion of eye movements to /ba/ and /pa/ are treated like an identification response across the stimuli of the VOT continuum, the later periods of time after presentation (1201–1500 ms) exhibit the typical step-function of categorical perception, but the early periods of time (301–600 ms) exhibit a substantially more graded transition between "ba"-like states and "pa"-like states (adapted from McMurray & Spivey, 1999).

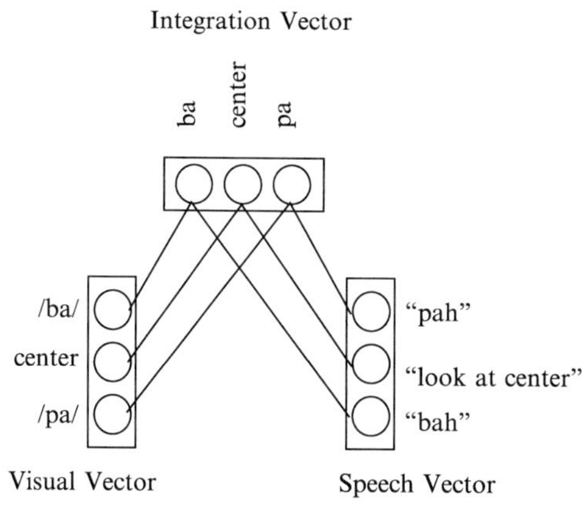

Fig. 10. A simple normalized recurrence localist attractor simulation of speech input from a VOT continuum and visual input from a set of response icons. See text for details.

As in the previous section, these two vectors simply sum at the integration layer, which then normalizes itself and sends feedback to the feature vectors.

In this simulation, we can sample the proportion of fixations from the visual vector, and thus watch the simulated eye movement patterns move away from fixating the central dot and toward one or the other response icon. Figure 11 shows the activation curves over time for the /pa/ visual node and the /ba/ visual node. Panel A plots these curves for a rather clear "pah" speech input (.2 0 .8), and panel B plots these curves for a "pah" speech input that is near the category boundary (.4 0 .6). These activation curves from the visual vector mimic the proportion of fixations at each time slice (Fig. 8) in the results of McMurray and Spivey (1999); and McMurray et al. (2002, 2003).

When this simulation is run for all 11 speech tokens along the VOT continuum, it is possible to calculate the proportion of time the model spends "fixating" the /pa/ icon versus the /ba/ icon, and thus plot a categorical identification function. Crucially, this can be done for early periods of time during the network's settling process, as well as for intermediate and late periods of time—just as was done in Fig. 9. The resulting graph is shown in Fig. 12.

In both the normalized recurrence and human cases, the identification function starts out rather unbiased and gradually approaches the classic step-function profile by continuously increasing one-half of the curve and decreasing the other half of the curve over time. Thus, if the identification function is to be interpreted as a kind of signature of the internal pattern of activation favoring the perception of "bah" or "pah," then this signature at those early moments in time looks decidedly more continuous than the legendary step function that motivated the aphorism, "speech is special" (cf. Liberman, 1982).

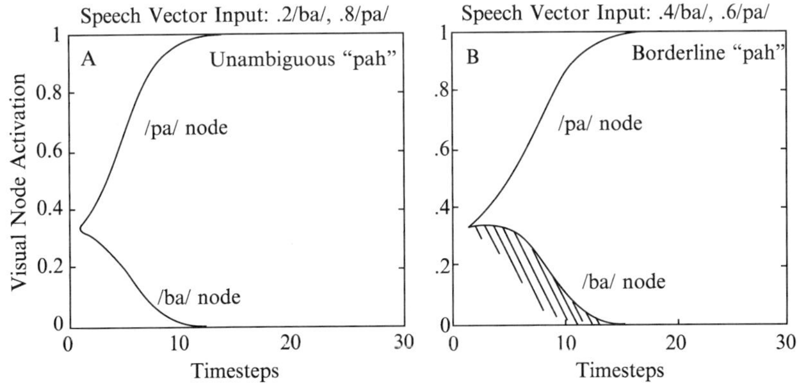

Fig. 11. Activation over time of the /ba/ and /pa/ visual nodes after an unmistakable "pah" (panel A) and after a speech sound near the category boundary (panel B). The hatched region in panel B shows portion of /ba/ node activation over and above that in panel A. (Compare to Fig. 8.)

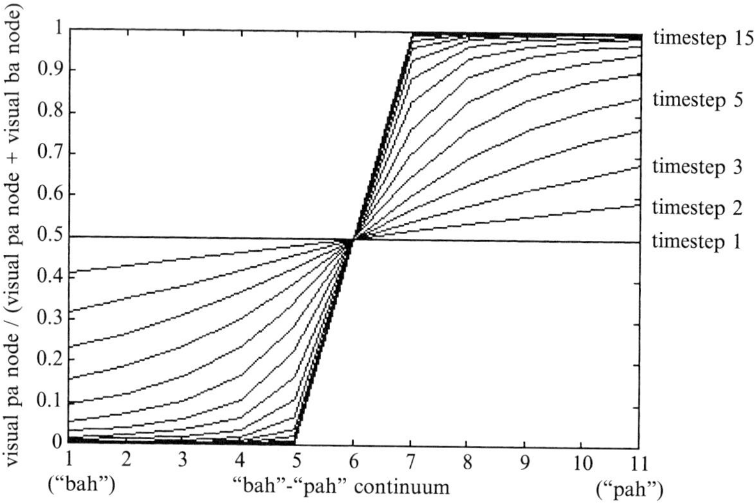

Fig. 12. Relative proportion of the /ba/ and /pa/ visual node activations (excluding "center" node) across different stimulus gradations between "ba" and "pa" at different cycles of competition in normalized recurrence.

B. Spoken Word Recognition

Even those readers wary of the continuity of mind must admit that the speech signal for word recognition is continuous. Individual phonemes do not occur discretely, as categorical perception described might suggest; instead, individual sounds, so to speak, smoothly blend into each other in natural speech. Speech is indeed quite exemplary of Gibson's continuous "flowing array of stimulus energy."

In a classic set of experiments, Marslen-Wilson and colleagues demonstrated that, to a first approximation, complete recognition of a word occurs shortly after the auditory input uniquely specifies a lexical candidate (for review, see Marslen-Wilson, 1987). For words of many syllables, this can occur prior to the end of the word. For example, the word *elephant* would be recognized shortly after the sound /f/. Prior to that, the auditory input would be consistent with the beginnings of several words, including *elephant, elegant, eloquent*, and *elevator*. Thus, recognition of a spoken word is strongly influenced by the words to which it is phonetically similar, especially those words that share initial phonemes. Marslen-Wilson referred to the set of lexical candidates that is activated in the same phonetic environment as a "cohort."

Evidence from several experimental paradigms indicates that these candidates are partially activated as a word is being processed (not unlike the partial activations over time for the mental states in Fig. 4). For example, cross-modal lexical priming experiments demonstrate that semantic information associated with cohort members is temporarily activated as a word unfolds (Zwitserlood, 1989). The prior context of the utterance and subsequent input provide evidence that is used to evaluate the competing alternatives. While current models differ in how they account for these data, nearly all models incorporate the idea that the time it takes to recognize a word depends on a set of potential lexical candidates (see Cutler, 1995, for a review).

Providing concrete evidence for the activation of multiple alternative lexical items during recognition of a spoken word, Spivey-Knowlton, Sedivy, Eberhard, and Tanenhaus (1994) reported cohort effects in eye movement patterns by having subjects follow instructions to manipulate real objects. Participants sat in front of a table containing a central fixation cross and various objects around it (e.g., a fork, a mug, a candle). In some trials, objects whose names had similar initial phonemes were present on the table, available for manipulation (e.g., a bag of candy and a candle). For this "cohort competitor present" condition, Fig. 13 shows the proportion of trials, at each time slice, in which the participants' eyes were fixating each of the various objects. The probability of looking at the cohort object, (e.g., the candy, when instructed to "Pick up the candle"), rose just as quickly as

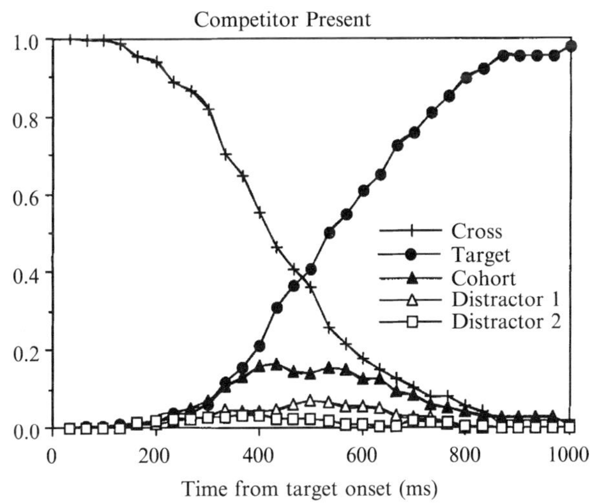

Fig. 13. Proportion of fixations of various objects across time as the target word unfolds (e.g., about 300 ms for the word *candle*). Note the conspicuous rise of eye movements to the cohort competitor object (filled triangles; from Spivey-Knowlton & Allopenna, 1997).

the probability of looking at the target object, for a period of about 200 ms around the tail end of the spoken word. And even when the two curves diverge, the proportion of fixations of the cohort object still persists for a few hundred milliseconds. This salience of the cohort object conspicuously attracting eye movements is indicative of the competing lexical representation being partially active during, and perhaps shortly after, delivery of the spoken word.

Headband-mounted eye-tracking studies like this have demonstrated this real-time lexical competition using computer-displayed objects (Allopenna, Magnuson, & Tanenhaus, 1998), using artificial lexicons (Magnuson, Tanenhaus, Aslin, & Dahan, 2003), with young children (Fernald, Swingley, & Pinto, 2001), and even across two languages in bilingual participants (Marian & Spivey, 2003; Spivey & Marian, 1999).

Marslen-Wilson's (1987) cohort theory naturally predicts findings like these, and McClelland and Elman's (1986) TRACE model can quantitatively simulate them. In the TRACE model of word recognition, activation is passed forward and backward between a layer of phonetic feature nodes, a layer of phoneme nodes, and a layer of word nodes. As the network receives phonetic feature activation corresponding to early speech information, it gradually settles toward a state of exhibiting activation for only the words that are consistent with the current speech input. In this way, TRACE can explicitly implement the cohort effect described in the Marslen-Wilson's cohort theory. In fact, by integrating TRACE with the normalized recurrence architecture previously described, to impose the visual constraints on which objects and lexical items accrue significant activation, quite accurate predictions about eye movement dynamics can be made (Spivey, in preparation).

The TRACE network also makes a prediction that diverges from Marslen-Wilson's cohort theory. Since TRACE has only positive connections *between* layers (and only inhibitory connections *within* layers), it does not prevent, and will in fact induce, the activation of lexical items that rhyme with the word being spoken. Therefore, TRACE predicts that when instructed to "Pick up the candle," a person should conspicuously fixate a handle in the display, whereas the standard version of the cohort theory would not predict this. Indeed, TRACE's prediction holds true. Listeners will briefly look at an object whose name rhymes with the spoken word more so than unrelated control objects (Allopenna et al., 1998). Allopenna et al., showed that the activations of the lexical nodes in TRACE (once scaled by an exponential and normalized) closely mimic the probability-of-fixation functions from these eye-tracking experiments (compare Figs. 13 & 14).

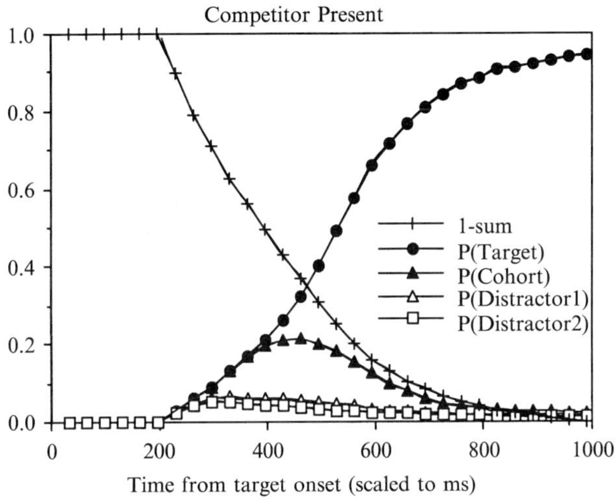

Fig. 14. Activations of the lexical nodes in McClelland and Elman's (1986) TRACE model of speech processing, scaled by an exponent and normalized (from Spivey-Knowlton & Allopenna, 1997). (Compare to Fig. 13.)

C. Sentence Processing

In the 1970s, a "clausal processing theory" emerged in psycholinguistics, arguing that most of the syntactic and semantic processing of a sentence took place at the ends of its clauses rather than continuously throughout the sentence (e.g., Bever & Hurtig, 1975). The impetus for this theory largely derived from two sources. One was to maintain some level of consonance between psycholinguistic investigation and linguistic theories that incorporated a unique syntactic level of processing. The second, interestingly, was largely induced by Marslen-Wilson's famous shadowing experiments (Marslen-Wilson, 1973). In these experiments, participants verbally followed a spoken passage played to them and tried to repeat it out loud as quickly as possible. This close speech-shadowing task revealed that mistakes made by participants were largely grammatically and semantically appropriate amidst their previous and subsequent repetition. This suggested that syntax and semantics are in fact being processed together continuously during sentence processing. Clausal processing theory aimed to counter these results and bring psycholinguistics closer to contemporary syntactic theories in linguistics.

Subsequent theories of sentence processing often urged the continuous nature of syntactic and semantic computations on linguistic input, but assailed the interactive aspect of Marslen-Wilson's (1973; Tyler & Marslen-Wilson, 1977) framework. Frazier and Fodor (1978) proposed a set of syntactic structuring heuristics for real-time sentence processing that offered an account of certain errors and hence misunderstandings in parsing a sentence. Frazier and colleagues argued that a syntactic parsing module in the mind automatically attaches each new incoming word in such a way that minimizes the number of branches in a syntactic tree structure. With sentences like that in (1), taken from Bever (1970), which contain temporary syntactic ambiguities, the particular tree-structuring format that Frazier employed posited fewer branching nodes if the verb "raced" was integrated as part of the sentence's main verb rather than as a relative clause describing "horse." This "minimal attachment" hypothesis predicted that a reader or listener will build the syntactic structure consistent with the horse doing the racing (rather than being raced by someone), and this would essentially lead comprehension "down a garden path" that will not work with the subsequent words. The result is that by the end of the sentence, the verb *fell* has nowhere to attach and thus cannot easily be grammatically integrated into the sentence.

(1) The horse raced past the barn fell.

Throughout the 1980s, Frazier and colleagues recorded eye movements during reading tasks and concluded that sentence processing did not involve real-time interaction between syntax and meaning because semantic and discourse context did not appear to prevent the all-important syntactic heuristics from generating garden path effects (e.g., Ferreira & Clifton, 1986; Rayner, Carlson, & Frazier, 1983). In addition, in opposition to clausal processing theory, they argued that sentence processing involved continuous flow of information (or at least word-by-word incremental flow) because the effects of the syntactic heuristics are detectable in the eye movement data (as increases in reading times) the moment the reader fixates the critical word disambiguating the sentence, regardless of where any clauses begin or end (Frazier, 1998; Frazier & Clifton, 1989; Frazier & Rayner, 1982). This work constituted more than a decade of research characterizing comprehension as an incremental word-by-word (not clause-by-clause) process in which syntax alone was processed in an early stage of the system, and then semantics and other contextual constraints were consulted in a later stage of the system, in the event of anomalies like garden path effects.

There remains ongoing debate about the interactive nature of sentence processing. To illustrate, consider sentence (2) (from Tanenhaus & Trueswell, 1995). It has exactly the same structure as (1) but does not induce a garden path effect.

(2) The land mine buried in the sand exploded.

If syntax were sovereign in this situation, it should be equally difficult to process sentences (1) and (2). The semantic constraints imposed by the lexical items in (2), "landmine" and "buried," seem to steer the reader away from the garden path, implicating a more interactive perspective on sentence processing. MacDonald, Pearlmutter, and Seidenberg (1994) argued that examples like these illustrate that structural biases during parsing emerge out of the interaction of both syntactic and semantic constraints. They report extensive experimental evidence in support of this perspective. The theoretical upshot from MacDonald et al. was to propose that multiple constraints are marshaled in the service of sentence processing. These constraints (lexical, semantic, pragmatic) act simultaneously to influence online interpretation of sentences. Indeed, when these various factors are controlled for their relative contribution, the accumulating evidence overwhelmingly supports an interactive perspective on sentence processing (e.g., Altmann, Garnham & Dennis, 1992; Altmann & Steedman, 1988; Farrar & Kawamoto, 1993; Pearlmutter & MacDonald, 1995; McRae et al., 1998; Spivey & Tanenhuas, 1998; Spivey-Knowlton & Sedivy, 1995; Trueswell & Kim, 1998; Trueswell, Tanenhaus, & Garnsey, 1994; van Berkum, Brown, & Hagoort, 1999).[3]

One way of demonstrating the power of these contextual effects is through the semicontinuous record of eye movements during spoken sentence comprehension. For example, when presented with a real 3-D display containing an apple on a towel, another towel, and an empty box, and then instructed to "Put the apple on the towel in the box," participants often look briefly at the irrelevant lone towel near the end of the spoken instruction before returning their gaze to the apple, grasping it, and then placing it inside the box (Spivey, Tanenhaus, Eberhard, & Sedivy, 2002b; Tanenhaus, Spivey-Knowlton, Eberhard, & Sedivy, 1995). (With unambiguous control sentences, such as "Put the apple that's on the towel in the box," they almost never look at the irrelevant lone towel). In this case, the syntax is ambiguous as to whether the prepositional phrase *on the towel* is attached to the verb *put* (as a movement destination) or to the noun *apple* (as a modifier). Given the actions afforded by the display, the latter syntactic structure is the correct one. However, people tend to have a bias toward interpreting an ambiguous prepositional phrase as attached to the verb (Rayner, Carlson, & Frazier, 1983), at least

[3] In fact, at this point in the literature, the debate has largely shifted to determining how the syntactic alternatives of an ambiguity, supported by their various constraints, are adjudicated; with some researchers advocating a temporally dynamic competition process (e.g., McRae et al., 1998; Spivey & Tanenhaus, 1998; Spivey, Fitneva, Tabor & Ajmani, 2002a; Stevenson, 1994; Tabor & Tanenhaus, 1999; Tanenhaus et al., 2000) and others describing an immediate winner-take-all framework (e.g., Jurafsky, 1996; van Gompel, Pickering, & Traxler, 2001).

when it is an action verb like *put* (cf. Spivey-Knowlton & Sedivy, 1995). Thus, the brief fixation of the irrelevant lone towel indicates a temporary partially activated incorrect parse of the sentence. To demonstrate the influence of visual context on this syntactic ambiguity resolution process, the display was slightly altered to include a second apple (resting on a napkin). In this case, the visual copresence (in Herb Clark's, 1992, words) of the two potential referents for the phrase *the apple* should encourage the listener to interpret the ambiguous prepositional phrase *on the towel* as a modifier (in order to determine which apple is being referred to) rather than as a movement destination (cf. Altmann & Steedman, 1988; Crain & Steedman, 1985; Spivey & Tanenhaus, 1998). And, indeed, with this display, participants rarely fixated the irrelevant lone towel, indicating that visual context had exerted an immediate influence on the incremental syntactic parsing of the spoken sentence (Spivey et al., 2002b; Tanenhaus et al., 1995; see also Knoeferle, Crocker, Scheepers, & Pickering, 2003).

The current state of affairs in the field of sentence processing is at a consensus with regard to the continuity of information flow and has been gradually approaching consensus with regard to the rapid integration of syntax, semantics, and pragmatic context. Just as the processing of speech sounds, at the scale of tens of milliseconds, appears to be characterized by multiple partially active phonemic representations competing over time (McMurray et al., 2002, 2003), and the comprehension of spoken words, at the scale of hundreds of milliseconds, appears to be characterized by multiple partially active lexical representations competing over time (Allopenna et al., 1998; Marslen-Wilson, 1987; McClelland & Elman, 1986), so does the resolution of syntactic ambiguity, at the scale of seconds, appear to be characterized by multiple partially active syntactic representations competing over time (MacDonald et al., 1994; Spivey & Tanenhaus, 1998; Stevenson, 1994; Tabor & Tanenhaus, 1999).

IV. Continuity in Visual Perception

As speech enters the sensory system through time, it is perhaps an obvious case where continuous temporal dynamics would be prominent in the resulting perceptual-cognitive processing. Visual input, however, is often delivered to the sensory system in an instantaneous fashion (in the laboratory, at least). Does the internal processing of an instantaneously presented visual stimulus exhibit any interesting temporal dynamics? In this section, we describe a number of findings and demonstrations of continuous accrual of activation during visual processing.

A. Object and Face Recognition

As vision is a modality in which we share much in common with nonhuman primates, it has been studied in depth with neurophysiologically invasive real-time measures that, indeed, quite richly illustrate the temporal dynamics of the resulting perceptual-cognitive processing. Vision research is replete with examples of temporal continuity in real-time perception. The gradual settling (or pattern completion) of a neuronal population code, over the course of hundreds of milliseconds, is a common way to think about how the visual system recognizes objects and faces. Compelling visualizations of the continuous manner in which sensory input gradually produces a percept can easily be found in visual neuroscience. For example, Rolls and Tovee (1995) recorded from multiple neurons in the inferotemporal cortex of the macaque monkey and found that it takes a few hundred milliseconds for the right population of cells to achieve their appropriate firing rates for fully identifying a fixated object or face. The cumulative information (in bits) provided by an inferotemporal neuron in the service of recognizing a face or object accrues continuously (though nonlinearly) over the course of about 350 ms (see Fig. 15). About 80 ms after the presentation of the visual stimulus, these cells begin firing, and during the first 70 ms of firing, about 50% of the total information to be encoded is already accumulated. Thus, very quickly, the inferotemporal network is able to project itself into the correct "neighborhood" in its state-space. (This allows some coarse gistlike visual discriminations to actually be made with 100 ms or less of stimulus presentation time; e.g., Potter, 1976, 1993; Van Rullen & Thorpe, 2001.) However, over the next 200 ms or so, the process of object or face recognition is still in progress, during which the remaining 50% of the information to be represented by the distributed population code is gradually accumulated.

Perrett, Oram, and Ashbridge (1998) report further patterns of gradual accumulation of neuronal evidence for face recognition. When an object or face is partly rotated away from a canonical or frontal view, recognition or matching will generally take longer as a function of how far it is rotated (e.g., Cooper & Shepard, 1973; Jolicoeur, 1985; Shepard & Metzler, 1971; see also Georgopoulos, Lurito, Petrides, Schwartz, & Massey, 1989). Perrett et al. (1998) describe recordings from cells in the monkey temporal cortex during viewing of frontal, three-fourth profile, profile, and one-fourth profile schematic faces. When the accumulated action potentials are plotted over time, these curves rise at different rates as a function of how canonical the face orientation is. Figure 16 depicts the continuous nonlinear rise in accumulated neuronal spikes over the course of several hundred milliseconds as recognition takes place. As these curves plot accumulated spikes, rather than

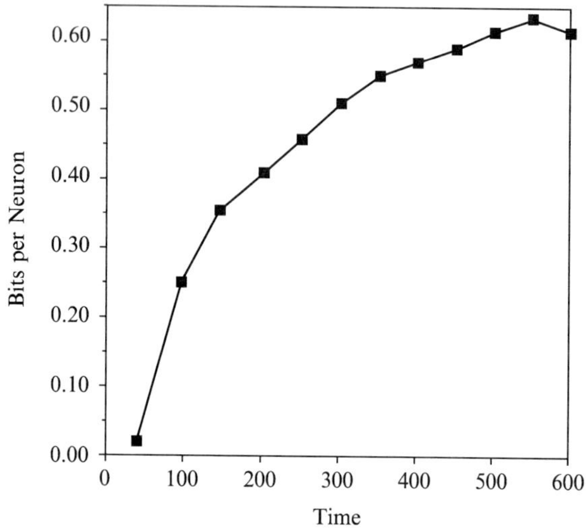

Fig. 15. Average cumulative information accrued over milliseconds by inferotemporal cells representing objects and faces (adapted from Rolls & Tovee, 1995).

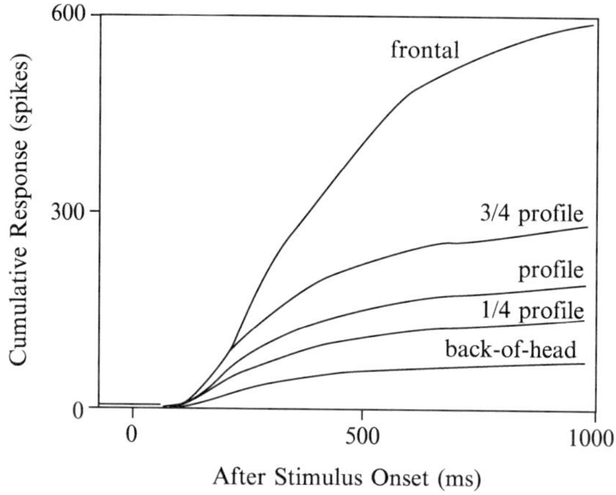

Fig. 16. The accumulation over time of neuronal spikes (over and above the baseline spike rate) from cells responding to faces at various rotations around the vertical axis (adapted from Perrett et al., 1998).

information-theoretic bits per neuron, they asymptote somewhat later in time than the curve in Fig. 15. Note again how these curves reach their half height relatively early on, yet still spend several hundred milliseconds gradually approaching their respective asymptotes (except for the back-of-head view, which asymptotes rather low within a few hundred milliseconds).

A few (or even several) hundred milliseconds for a population code to be "in transit" on the way toward achieving its potentially stable asymptotic state might initially seem like a rather small amount of time to get excited about. Are these transition periods perhaps just interesting curiosities, while the important observation is that a stable state is eventually reached, and is it *that* on which discrete mental computations might be performed? We think not. It is our hypothesis that in more complex visual (as well as auditory, somatosensory, etc.) environments, the proportion of time spent in these unstable regions of state-space—that is, in the process of traveling toward an attractor basin, but not in one yet—is actually much greater than the proportion of time spent in relatively stable regions of state-space.

This gradual accrual of the information comprising a population code (Figs. 15 and 16) has powerful consequences for how we conceptualize what the brain is doing when we go about our business of naturally perceiving the world around us. Consider how your eyes move around a complex scene like the one in front of you right now. Your eyes rest, with the two foveas fixating on a particular location in the visual field, for about 300–400 ms on average (cf. Rayner, 1998). They then make a fast, ballistic, jump (lasting a few dozen milliseconds or so) away from that location to fixate on another location in the visual field. After resting there for another 300–400 ms, they jump yet again to another location. Each new fixation brings a new word, object, or object part into the high-resolution view of your foveas for little more than one-third of a second. Now, if it takes almost half a second for the appropriate population code to get fully settled in recognizing a fixated object (Figs. 15 & 16), but your eyes normally move to a new object every one-third of a second, how can the brain possibly achieve a genuinely stable asymptotic state (or temporally discrete representation) for any object recognition event?

B. Visual Search

The same kind of gradual accumulation of perceptual evidence can be observed when multiple objects are competing for attention during visual search. The field of visual search has generally been driven by two opposing treatments of attention. The serial-processing perspective holds that the observer allocates attentional resources wholly and discretely to individual objects, one at a time (e.g., Treisman, 1988; Treisman & Gelade, 1980). The parallel-processing perspective holds that attention is best characterized as comprised of partially active representations of objects simultaneously competing for probabilistic mappings onto motor output (e.g., Desimone & Duncan, 1995; Reynolds & Desimone, 2001).

In a conjunction search task, the target object is defined by a conjunction of features, and reaction time increases linearly with the number of distractors, often in the range of 15–25 ms per item (Duncan & Humphreys, 1989; Treisman & Gelade, 1980; Wolfe, 1994). These linearly increasing reaction times as a function of set size were originally interpreted as evidence for serial processing of the objects in the display and contrasted with the near flat function of reaction time by set size observed with feature search displays, where a single feature is sufficient to identify the target object. It was argued that the early stages of the visual system process individual features independently and in parallel (Livingstone & Hubel, 1988), allowing the target object to "pop out" in the display if it is discriminable by a single feature, but requiring application of an attentional window to the individual objects, one at a time, if the target object is discriminable only by a conjunction of features (Treisman & Gelade, 1980).

However, several studies have discovered particular conjunctions of features that do not produce steeply sloped reaction-time functions by set size (McLeod, Driver & Crisp, 1988; Nakayama & Silverman, 1986; Theeuwes & Kooi, 1994). Moreover, it has been argued that steeply sloped reaction-time functions may not reflect serial processing of objects in the display, but rather noise in the human visual system (Eckstein, 1998; Palmer, Verghese, & Pavel, 2000; see also McElree & Carrasco, 1999). Overall, a wide range of studies have suggested that the distinction between putatively "serial" and "parallel" search functions is continuous rather than discrete and should be considered extremes on a continuum of search difficulty (Duncan & Humphreys, 1989; Nakayama & Joseph, 1998; Olds, Cowan, & Joliceur, 2000; Wolfe, 1998; see also Spivey, Tyler, Eberhard, & Tanenhaus, 2001).

Desimone and Duncan (1995; see also Reynolds & Desimone, 2001) describe a theory of "biased competition" in which multiple representations of objects are simultaneously partially active and compete for the privilege of driving motor output (e.g., pressing the "target present" button, reaching to grasp the attended object, or turning to shoot the computer-generated avatar of your opponent in a video game). Experimenter instructions, goal-oriented plans, and contextual constraints also provide some of the "bias" for this competition process.

The following normalized recurrence simulation serves as a kind of abstract implementation of a "biased competition" account of visual search (see Humphreys & Müller, 1993; Phaf, Van der Heijden, & Hudson, 1990, for somewhat similar models). In this simulation, one feature vector represents the likelihood of each object being the target based solely on it exhibiting the target property of *redness*, and the other feature vector represents the likelihood of each object being the target based solely on it exhibiting the target property of *verticalness*. The integration vector serves as a measure of each object's overall likelihood of being the target. Figure 17 shows a schematic diagram of this normalized recurrence network with input values corresponding to a target-present conjunction search for a red vertical bar with a set size of seven (i.e., one red vertical, three red nonverticals, and three nonred verticals).

Within each cycle of competition, the two feature vectors are normalized, then averaged at the integration layer,[4] and the integration vector then sends pointwise multiplicative cumulative feedback to those feature vectors. As cycles of competition continue, the integration node corresponding to the target object (exhibiting both redness and verticalness) increases in activation while the other nodes decrease in activation. Competition continues until an integration node exceeds a .95 activation criterion.

This normalized recurrence competition algorithm produces a nearly perfectly linear slope of settling time as a function of set size; $r^2 = .995$[5] (see Fig. 18). This basic result out of such a simple localist attractor network is noteworthy. One of the field's landmark findings that has traditionally been taken as evidence for a serial fixed-duration template-matching of each object one at a time, that is linear search functions, is exactly mimicked by a parallel competitive architecture where the only "capacity limitations" are that its representations share a probability density function.

Initially, it is not necessarily obvious why normalized recurrence should produce this linear increase in search time as a function of set size. As set size increases linearly, the initial activation of the target object's integration node decreases nonlinearly. In addition, as competition takes place within a given trial, that target integration node's activation value increases nonlinearly over time. In fact, this nonlinear increase over time exactly compensates for the nonlinear differences in starting activation across set size. For example, as shown in Fig. 19, competition increases the target integration node's activation with an asymmetric sigmoid function over time. Thus, although the initial activation values vary nonlinearly with set size (i.e., .415, .225, .155, .118, .095, for set sizes 4, 8, 12, 16, and 20), their nonlinear rise over

[4] The Bayesian approach to this feedforward integration process would be to multiply these probabilities and then normalize them, but with binary feature vectors that would of course eliminate any temporal dynamics, as the target integration node would achieve 1.0 activation on the first time step.

[5] Moreover, it is clearly not simply operating within a linear portion of an otherwise nonlinear function. All the way to a set size of 300, in steps of 10, the slope function produced by normalized recurrence is perfectly linear, $r^2 = 1.0$.

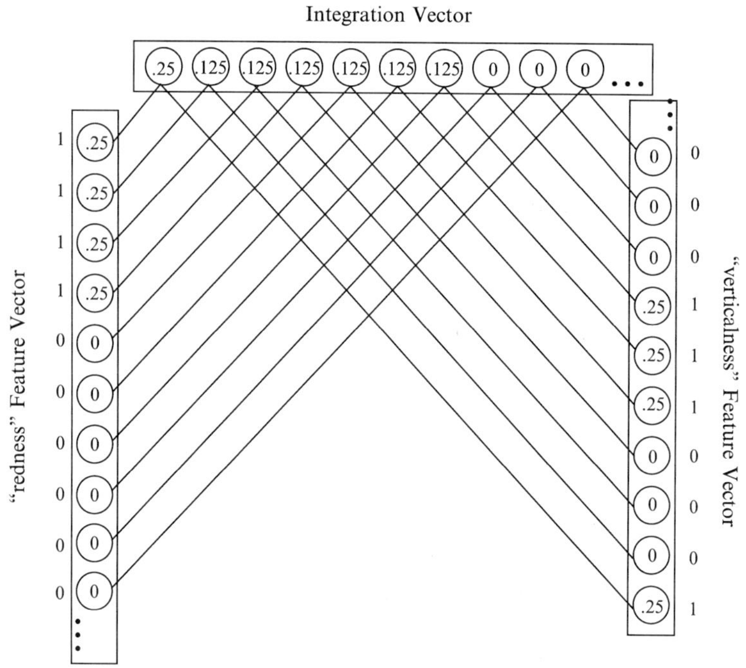

Fig. 17. Schematic diagram of a normalized recurrence simulation of visual conjunction search.

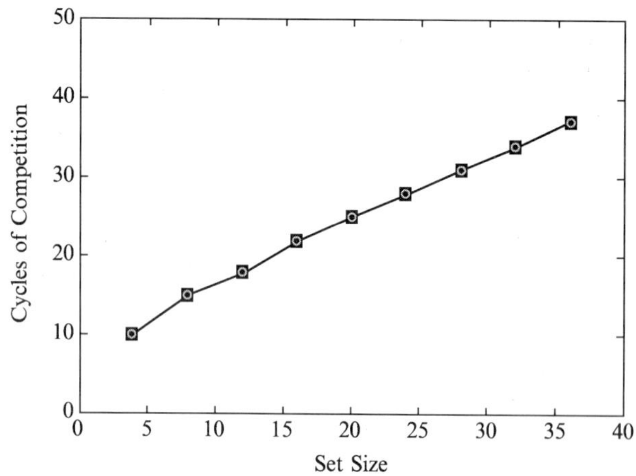

Fig. 18. Settling times for normalized recurrence during a conjunction search with different set sizes.

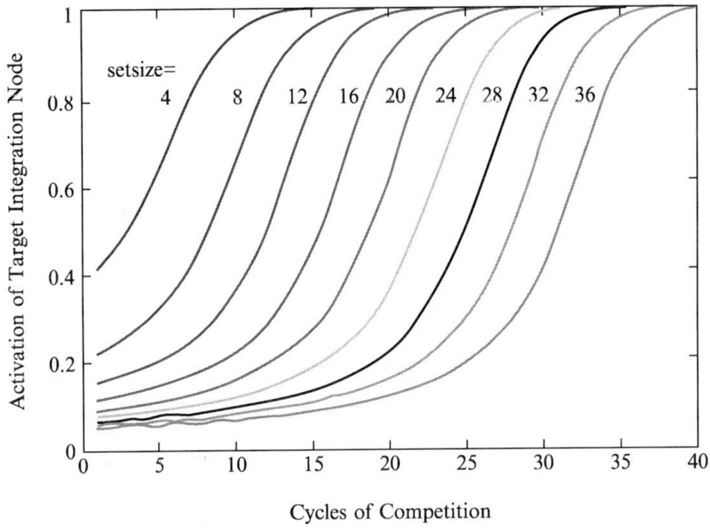

Fig. 19. In normalized recurrence, the winning node's activation rises with a sigmoid function, but this curve shifts linearly in time as set size increases.

time causes them to achieve a criterion of activation at approximately linear intervals in time (Spivey-Knowlton, 1996). In a sense, two nonlinearities make a linearity.

A key observation from this little simulation is the fact that the representations of the various objects are all processed simultaneously, their activations updated in tandem. Despite this parallel processing of all object representations, the network produces linearly increasing settling times, as a function of set size, which were previously interpreted as evidence for serial processing. Thus, the simulation stands as an existence proof that linear functions can come out of a system in which multiple partially active representations are competing simultaneously, and an object's "targethood" gradually emerges over the course of hundreds of milliseconds during visual search.

C. Perceptual Decisions

Our final example of continuous temporal dynamics in visual processing comes from work by Gold and Shadlen (2000) examining decision processes in the frontal eye field (FEF) of the macaque. A common task in visual psychophysics involves presenting a display of quasi-randomly moving dots. As the experimenter increases the proportion of dots that move in a roughly consistent direction, the perception of a coherent direction of flow amidst the dots becomes more apparent (Britten, Shadlen, Newsome, & Movshon, 1992). Gold and Shadlen presented such displays foveally to monkeys and trained them to indicate the perceived direction of dot flow, upon offset of the stimulus, by making an eye movement to one peripheral location or an opposite one. Then they found a region of FEF in which electrical microstimulation produced an involuntary saccade that was perpendicular to the two voluntary response saccades. On some of the direction-of-flow judgment trials, this region of FEF was microstimulated immediately after the moving dot display disappeared, that is, exactly when the monkey was supposed to produce a voluntary eye movement that would indicate his response regarding the perceived direction of flow of the dots.

Perhaps not surprisingly, the evoked involuntary saccade was executed first, and a corrective saccade typically redirected the eyes to the voluntarily chosen response location. However, the evoked saccade was not bereft of influence from the burgeoning perceptual decision. In fact, when the percentage of coherent motion was greater and (more importantly, for our argument) when viewing time was longer, more perceptual evidence apparently accrued to induce greater deviation of that initial involuntary saccade in the direction of the voluntary response.

Essentially, by incrementally increasing viewing time, the experimenters could observe the gradual increase in "strength" or "confidence" of the perceptual decision over time, as indicated by the degree to which that voluntary decision "leaked into" the execution of the FEF-microstimulated evoked saccade. Thus, the population of cells that—once some of them were microstimulated—produced the *evoked* saccade were already somewhere in the process of settling on a pattern of activation that would produce the *voluntary* response saccade. If the microstimulation took place early on in this decision process, rather little effect of the voluntary response would be apparent in the evoked saccade, but if the microstimulation took place later on in the decision process, a significant amount of the voluntary response would be apparent in the evoked saccade. These results suggest that decision processes themselves may be coextensive with the gradual settling of partially active and competing neural representations in motor areas of cortex (Gold & Shadlen, 2001; Schall, 2000; see also Georgopoulos, 1995).

Overall, this brief selection of observations in visual processing is consistent with a general view of perception, cognition, and action in which partially active mental representations compete over time until one (or in some cases an amalgam of more than one) wins the privilege to execute its associated motor output. Whether the visual system is recognizing a face, searching among a cluttered array for a "target" object, or deciding on what oculomotor signal to send to the eye muscles, the population code corresponding to the representation that will get to drive behavior (or even just constitute an internal monolog) spends a considerable amount of time approaching that status, and (in natural complex real-time interactive environments) rather little time enjoying it.

V. Continuity in Complexity

We have so far argued that our cognitive system consists of partially active and gradually emerging information, the "states" of which are more or less interpretable regions of the state-space in which a system lives. As described in many previous studies, this continuity "resides" in the neural substrate of the brain—vast arrays of networks blending into each other, sometimes moderately functionally specific (Zeki, 1993), and other times highly redundant across regions (Haxby et al., 2001). We would argue that continuity is itself a consequence of this inevitable complexity of the brain. Patterns of activity emerge gradually through local interaction of individual neurons, themselves composing more global connectivity. There is, therefore, organization within the system at varying time scales, from local neural influences to larger and larger organization, within regions and across them. Several theorists in the past 20 years have suggested that such a state of affairs admits of particular dynamics, regardless of the specific subject matter. For example, dynamic analyses of earthquakes (Bak & Tang, 1989), radioactive decay (Prestwich, Kenneth, & Pepper, 1986), and even traffic flow (Choi & Lee, 1995) suggest that complex systems of this kind exhibit certain global patterns (for an excellent review of this and related phenomena, see Ward, 2002).

If human cognition is indeed a complex dynamic system of the kind we are arguing, then similar patterns should be observable in this domain. In this section, we offer a review showing that behavior related to the previous sections, language and vision, also exhibits dynamic properties of complex systems.

A. Pink Noise

Among these properties, pink noise has perhaps invited the most investigation and speculation (Ward, 2002). Indeed, it is its apparent violation of a basic intuition about experimental procedures and inferential statistics that has likely engendered such interest (Gilden, 2001). According to this traditional intuition, pure experimental error should generate a random noise signal. When such a noisy signal is subjected to a fast-Fourier transform, it exhibits equal energy across its component frequencies (Press, Teukolsky,

Vetterling, & Flannery, 1992). Pink noise, instead, is error or noise that is correlated with the frequency components contributing to it. The most common kind of model to describe correlated noise is that of colored noise:

$$Power(freq) \propto \frac{1}{freq^{\alpha}}$$

Pink noise is usually referred to as a pattern of noise whose power spectrum has a value of approximately 1 for α, also known as 1/f noise (see Fig. 20). Vast ranges of natural phenomena exhibit this kind of noise. Another form of colored noise, *brown noise*, is often illustrated using Brownian motion and is generated by a random walk process (i.e., a small random process that cumulatively adds or subtracts from a moving scalar time series). Brown noise has a power spectrum $1/f^2$. Pink noise is the most thoroughly investigated in psychological data and generally considered more interesting in other physical systems as well.

Gilden, Thornton, and Mallon (1995) sparked the recent spate of interest in pink noise in human brain and behavior. By the time these authors published their well-known results, others had already investigated pink noise in other areas (e.g., Voss and Clarke, 1975, offer a now-famous

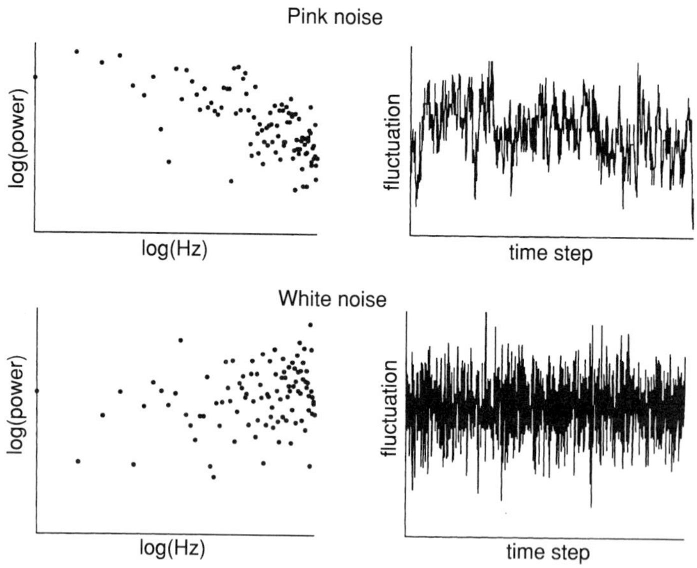

Fig. 20. Top row: the power spectrum (left panel) for pink noise (right panel) is correlated negatively with frequency. Bottom row: white noise has a power spectrum that is not correlated with frequency.

demonstration in musical structure and speech). Gilden et al.'s results demonstrate that certain human behaviors also exhibit this general property of complex systems. Their experiments primarily demonstrate that judgments, such as of time or space, have error in time that reveals a pink power spectrum. However, in an experiment involving reaction time to a simple discriminative stimulus, no such pink noise was found. The authors speculate that 1/f noise emerges as a consequence of mental judgments. Clayton and Frey (1997) soon after demonstrated that pink noise can emerge in reaction time measurements in experiments with a memory load. Three different response-time tasks were presented to subjects. In the easiest, subjects responded to a stimulus immediately. In another task of intermediate difficulty, they responded to the sameness of two subsequent stimuli; in the most difficult, subjects pressed a key if the stimulus was the same as presented two trials back in the experiment. All conditions produced colored noise in time series analyses of the reaction times, indicating that reaction times also display pink noise. In fact, the authors demonstrated that the harder the task, the more whitened the power spectrum becomes.

In an extensive series of experiments, Gilden (1997) demonstrated pink noise in a wide variety of decision tasks. In reaction times for both mental rotation and lexical decision, pink noise was observed in the time course of fluctuations from the mean. More recently, further evidence has surfaced that the visual system also reveals these patterns. Aks and Sprott (2003) revealed that perspective shifts in Necker cube interpretation exhibit pink noise effects. In an earlier paper, Aks, Zelinsky, and Sprott (2002) demonstrated that visual search performance shows both pink and brown noise. Variation in absolute eye position exhibits $1/f^2$ noise, resembling the random walk pattern of brown noise. However, variation in saccade amplitude generates a highly pink signal, indicating that long-term correlations emerge out of differences in eye position.

Several simple mathematical models can be devised to generate a pink signal (for a review, see Ward, 2002). Also, theories about coordinated time scales across brain regions have been offered (e.g., Chen, Ding, & Kelso, 1997; Ding, Chen, & Kelso, 2002; Gilden, 2001; Gilden et al., 1995; Ward, 2002). Most recently, Van Orden, Holden, and Turvey (2003) lament the concoction of these relatively simplistic models, sometimes just to capture data from a few experiments. The authors offer experiments demonstrating that relatively automatic processes (e.g., word naming) can generate pink noise, despite the suggestion by some that this should not happen in such automatic processes (e.g., Gilden, 2001). Given their results and extensive theoretical discussion, Van Orden et al. suggest that pink noise "is not the product of a particular component of the mind or body. It appears to illustrate something general about human behavior" (p. 345). To Van Orden et al., pink noise may be a by-product of interaction-dominant dynamics, dynamics dependent upon the activity of large numbers of interactive components (see also Usher, Stemmler, & Olami, 1995). Indeed, this perspective is highly consonant with our own. As discussed, such neural complexity begetting 1/f noise would also be responsible for the temporal continuity of cognitive processes.

B. Stochastic Resonance

Stochastic resonance is a phenomenon of nonlinear systems in which a weak periodic signal is amplified by "optimal" noise. As mentioned in the previous section, noise is generally considered troublesome from a traditional perspective, yet the discovery of stochastic resonance in the 1980s has resulted in entire conferences and textbooks on the topic, from statistical theory to applications (e.g., Ando & Graziani, 2000). The simplest way of picturing stochastic resonance, as it is traditionally introduced (Gammaitoni, Haenggi, Jung, & Marchesoni, 1998), is a bistable symmetric nonlinear system: a double-well potential. With the addition of noise, if past a certain threshold of average amplitude, the system will "hop" between the two states. Consider then subjecting this double-well potential to a weak sinusoidal, periodic signal that can bias or shift the probability distribution in the system wherein one potential becomes a favored absolute minimum for the system by having the hopping synchronize with the weak signal. The hopping will result in a stable state while this resonating of noise

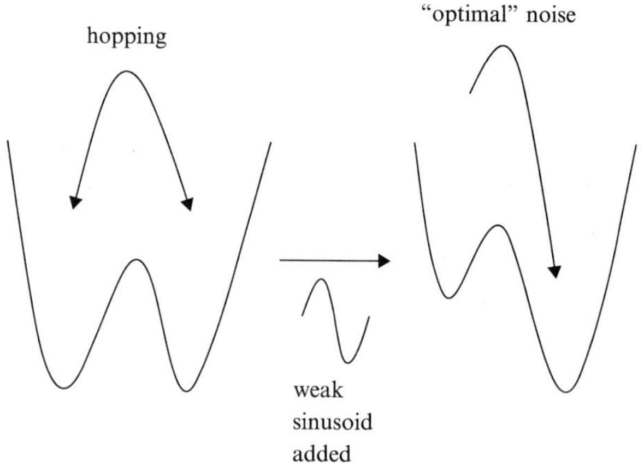

Fig. 21. When a weak sinusoid is added to an equibiased stochastic process, resonance can produce a significantly biased stochastic process.

and sinusoid occurs (see Fig. 21). Stochastic resonance was initially proposed as the explanation for the ice ages due to synchronization between the "weak signal" of climate change due to orbital situation of the earth, and a "Gaussian" noise signal from smaller-scale temperature fluctuations (Benzi, Sutera, & Vulpiani, 1981; Nicolis, 1982). It was then experimentally demonstrated in simple devices, such as electronic logic gates and lasers.

Ward (2002) paints an interesting portrait of the relevance of stochastic resonance by describing the life of a crayfish. Its "watery world of a rippling brook" (p. 183) is terribly dangerous. The crayfish is preyed upon by other creatures, such as larger fish, that can quickly spring upon this species, if it were not for stochastic resonance in uniquely tuned hair cells on the crayfish. These cells can detect the specific frequency of the crayfish's predators, helping the animal escape. It functions highly efficiently in its "watery world" due to the ambient noise in the watery environment and having that noise amplify the weak signal generated by an oncoming predator. Douglass, Wilkens, Pantazelou, and Moss (1993) demonstrated this experimentally in the crayfish by generating the relevant noise and weak predatory signal in an experimental chamber.

This is one of the simplest demonstrations of the potential biological benefit of cells that can take advantage of this statistical effect. It has also been demonstrated, for example, in the visual system of the cat. Noisy jitter induced by micro-ocular tremor may actually enhance visual acuity to a stimulus. By generating noise in a visual stimulus by producing motion jitter of different amplitudes, Hennig, Kerscher, Funke, and Woergoetter (2002) demonstrated that certain cells in cortical areas 17 and 18 of the cat increase responding to a moving oriented bar at intermediate levels of noise. Other animals may make use of stochastic resonance as well, including crickets, toads, and rats (see Ward, 2002, for a review).

In humans, Simonotto and colleagues (Simonotto, Riani, Seife, Roberts, Twitty, & Moss, 1997; Simonotto et al., 1999) have demonstrated the role of stochastic resonance in both human psychophysical and neuro-physiological recordings. Simonotto et al. (1997) exposed subjects to contrast gratings of variable spatial frequency under different noise conditions and asked them to report where their sensitivity to spatial frequency ceased. An intermediate amount of noise reduced perceptive threshold considerably lower than when the stimulus was noise-free. Simonotto et al. (1999) extended these results to the human brain through imaging. Results of fMRI demonstrated that visual regions of the brain contained more activity by volume under optimal noise conditions. These kinds of experiments have been extended to audition (Ward, Moss, Desai, & Rootman, 2001; Zeng, Fu, & Morse, 2000) and tactile stimulation (Richardson, Imhoff, Grigg, & Collins, 1998).

As with pink noise, very simple systems can also be devised to model stochastic resonance. For example, as mentioned, a simple double-well potential can exhibit it. Also, it can be modeled with a relatively simple threshold mechanism (Ward, 2002). However, much as we discussed in the context of pink noise, these simplistic models may belie the interactive complexity through which stochastic resonance emerges in the human brain. Though these simple models may serve as useful mathematical predictors, the means by which the human brain shows stochastic resonance may be considerably more complex. In a sophisticated neural model, Stemmler, Usher, and Neibur (1995) simulated lateral neural interaction in V1 that can benefit from internal noise. A large 20,000-node artificial neural network, consisting of half excitatory neurons and half inhibitory neurons, served to model receptive fields (with these receptive fields having varied sensitivities organized in a spatially distributed manner across the large network). Connections among these neurons served to model spatial excitatory and inhibitory input: Inhibitory inputs were sparsely distributed, coming from throughout the visual cortex, and excitatory input more closely packed. The model actually enhances a weak signal to a receptive field by having noise-induced input from inhibitory surround neurons. The model illustrates that patterns of stochastic resonance (among other patterns the model can fit, such as visual search pop-out), can emerge from the interaction of large numbers of small units.

C. Recurrence in Time

Recurrence quantification analysis (RQA) is a novel method of investigating the time course of complex systems (Webber & Zbilut, 1994; Zbilut & Webber, 1992). RQA permits its users to establish both global and local measures of regularity or even randomness in a system. RQA exemplifies the benefit of these dynamical analyses, showing how human brain and behavior are highly amenable to analysis of the global properties of very complex systems.

RQA is the quantification of a recurrence plot (RP), introduced by Eckmann, Kamphorst, and Ruelle (1987), and related to the correlation integral of dynamic systems mathematics (Takens, 1985). An RP is produced by measuring at regular intervals some scalar quantity generated by a system. For example, one might measure the temperature in a certain region or error generated by a neural network. *Any* scalar quantity in any kind of system will do, provided the measurements are at regular intervals. This time series is then embedded in multiple dimensions by overlaying the time series with temporally staggered versions of itself. Figure 22 illustrates this process. Roughly, the columns of this embedded time series have a time index

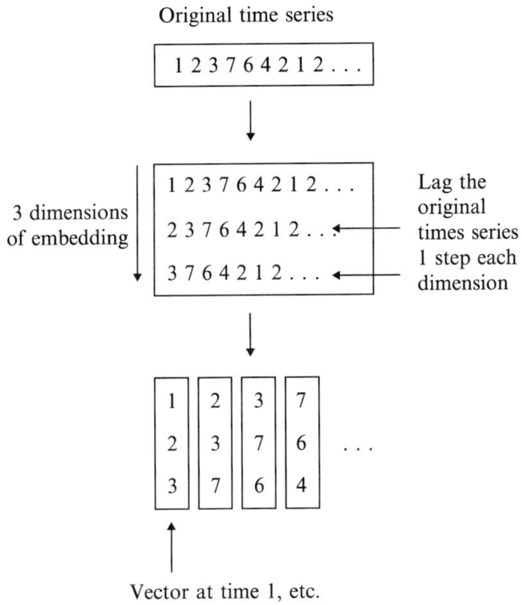

Fig. 22. An example of embedding a time series using, for example, three dimensions and a lag of 1. (See text for details.)

themselves and can be compared to column vectors of other time indices. When two such columns are compared, we can compute the distance between them. For any two vectors, at index i and j, say, we draw a point on the RP (i, j) if their distance satisfies a certain threshold. In this way, periodicities in the system result in undulating streaks of points in the RP (see Fig. 23). RQA directly quantifies the pattern of points on the RP (for a clear and concise introduction, see Riley, Balasubramaniam, & Turvey, 1999).

A particularly fruitful area in which RQA has been applied is the study of postural control. The studies of Riley, Balasubramaniam, and Turvey (1999) and Balasubramaniam, Riley, and Turvey (2000) primarily used RQA to study the variables controlling minor adjustments in our center of pressure (COP) during standstill (see also Riley & Clark, 2003). Riley et al. had subjects look at depth gratings while standing on a device that could monitor minor changes in their postural control (along the two axes of control, antero-posterior, [AP] and medio-lateral [ML]). Subjects performed trials in different conditions, including eyes—open versus closed, and looking straight-on versus looking to the right. The time series generated by recording postural control, generally regarded as nonstationary and fluctuating,

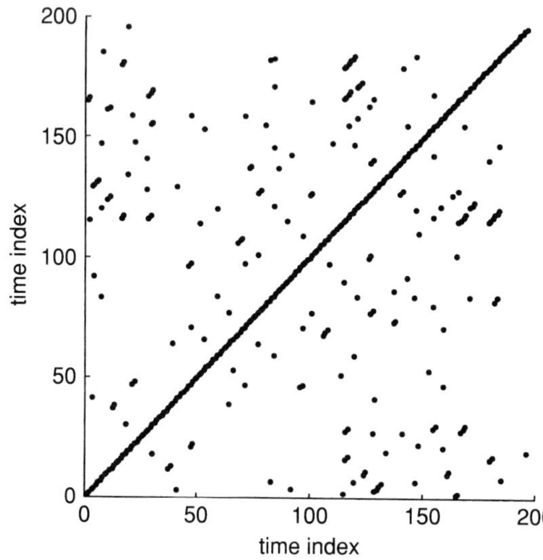

Fig. 23. In this very simple example of a recurrence plot, a series of sine values with some noise added was subjected to embedding. The diagonal is the line of identity, where $i = j$, and one can observe further diagonal structure emerging at other time indices, indicating some periodicity in the noisy sinusoidal time series.

permitted the authors to make the tentative observation that COP dynamics are more "complex" when the eyes are closed. Also, postural sway was not entirely random in that the RQA measure of determinism was fairly high for the various COP time series. However, nonstationarity obviously present in the RP analysis indicated that postural control may be a coupled dynamic between stochastic processes and more deterministic controlled processes (e.g., closing the eyes resulted in more deterministic, controlled patterns in the RP).

In an interesting pair of experiments, Balasubramaniam et al. (2000) used RQA to explore the conditions of fluctuation of COP in a precision task: maintaining a laser pointer on a target at a certain distance. Once again, measurements along the same two axes were compared. They used RQA to measure, for example, determinism, recurrence, entropy, and trend in the time series of these axes (these are values RQA generates from the RP; see Balasubramaniam et al., 2000). The authors demonstrated that the axis relevant to the task, such as the ML axis for holding the laser straight on (for accuracy), and the AP axis for across your body to the side toward the target, exhibited higher values of these measures, especially as task difficulty increased. The overall analyses indicate that there is a level of independence between these two sources of postural sway.

In a similar application, Shockley, Santana, and Fowler (2003) used RP and RQA to analyze postural shifts during conversational interaction. Participants engaged in discussion about cartoon images in different conditions, depending on whether they were conversing with each other or confederates outside the experimental area and whether they were facing each other or away from each other during interaction. The authors measured postural shifts by measuring changes in the location of the head and waist during conversation. Participants talking to each other, rather than a silent confederate, always exhibited more recurrence (a simple RQA measure) in a cross-recurrence plot of their postural sway (i.e., an RP generated by comparing two separate, embedded time series). Current related work is showing that cross-recurrence in eye movements of a speaker and a listener predicts accuracy on comprehension questions (Richardson & Dale, 2004) and that recurrence of linguistic forms in novel contexts characterizes the acquisition of various syntactic categories in children's language learning (Dale & Spivey, submitted).

Importantly, as related to our above discussion, the crucial aspect of RP and RQA is that they visualize processes that change in time, whether stationary or nonstationary, highly periodic or random. The fact that human behavior—such as visual–postural interaction, postural control during conversation, and eye movements during instruction and comprehension—is amenable to this analysis at least indirectly supports the perspective of continuity (see also Marwan & Meinke, 2004, for an application of RQA to event-related potentials). In summary, all the previous phenomena, especially when taken together, suggest that cognition is based in a complex system composed of interaction-dominant subcomponents blending at multiple time scales, thus generating continuity in behavioral outcomes. Indeed, all these properties of complexity substantiate our highlighted time scale (of hundreds of milliseconds), since both noise and recurrence seem implicated in real-time visual and linguistic processes.

VI. Conclusion

In this chapter, we have strolled briskly through a number of different examples of using continuous (or semicontinuous) measures of perceptual-cognitive processing to reveal various mental phenomena as composed of multiple partially active representations that compete over time. However, it can sometimes seem that whenever a mental process is shown to exhibit such continuous temporal dynamics (or to rely on distributed representations), then the process in question is relegated to "part of perception, not cognition," where analog processing is not surprising. In Sections I–V, we touched on evidence for, and simulations of, the temporal continuity of representational dynamics in categorization, speech perception, spoken word recognition, sentence processing, object and face recognition, visual attention, and perceptual decisions, as well as correlational cross-talk between rather different time scales of task performance. If all of these mental phenomena were to be expunged from the domain of cognition on the grounds that they do not rely on discrete temporally static symbolic representations, then scant little would remain in that vaunted realm—perhaps only problem solving and reasoning. (And, just to warn you, the movement has its eyes on those processes as well; cf. Townsend & Busemeyer, 1995).

Rather than imputing to cognitive processes the unrealistic property of functioning in a discretely symbolic way that real biological neural hardware is incapable of implementing, perhaps we can instead welcome a smooth merging of perception, cognition, and action as encouraged by Dewey (1896). Environmental stimulation continuously flows into perceptual areas of the brain, but since those areas receive some degree of feedback from more cognitive areas of the brain, they're really processing a combination of afferent sensory patterns of activation and reentrant cognitive patterns of activation. These blended patterns of activation cascade to "higher" areas of the brain where the relative concentrations of cognitive-like versus perceptual-like components in the patterns may shift toward the cognitive end. And soon, as these patterns of activation continuously travel toward motor areas of the brain, in preparation for influencing behavior, the distributed patterns begin to exhibit a significant degree of actionlike components as well. For example, action representations themselves may be predominantly defined in terms of their anticipated perceptual outcomes (cf. Prinz & Hommel, 2002, for an excellent collection of reviews). And don't forget Dewey and Gibson's reminder that relatively continuous motor output dramatically alters the patterns of continuous sensory stimulation, thus looping the entire system back onto itself. There simply does not appear to be, nor should there actually need to be, an internal stage in which the graded, distributed patterns of activation are converted into single unitary symbols with logical truth values. After all, they would only have to be reconverted right back into the graded, distributed patterns of activation that we know occur in the motor cortices (e.g., Georgopoulos, 1995).

Although it is comforting to think of cognition in terms of multiple different easily labeled interpretations of individuated stimuli having non-overlapping symbolic descriptions (e.g., Dietrich & Markman, 2003; Fodor & Pylyshyn, 1988), the fact of the matter is that the brain spends most of its time in regions of state-space that do not allow discrete symbolic descriptions. Thus, rather than being the digital computational intermediary between analog perception and action, whose job is to collapse the probabilistic distributions into discrete symbols, cognition is perhaps just as analog and graded as the sensory and motor systems themselves. And the much awaited collapsing of those distributed multifarious representational patterns does not actually take place until motor movement is executed (and even then it sometimes comes out as an amalgam of two motor programs, e.g, Gold & Shadlen, 2001).

Finally, we should acknowledge that, in our effort to speak to the traditional cognitive psychologist, it is possible that we have focused too much on the dynamics of internal cognitive processing and not enough on the dynamics of larger systems such as that of a human coupled with its environment (e.g., A. Clark, 2003; Gibson, 1979; O'Regan & Nöe, 2001; Spivey, Richardson, & Fitneva, 2004; Turvey & Carello, 1981) or multiple humans interacting with one another (e.g., Knoblich & Jordan, 2003; Schmidt, Carello, & Turvey, 1990; Sebanz, Knoblich, & Prinz, 2003; Shockley, Santana, & Fowler, 2003). However, in describing and supporting the continuity of mind for an audience of cognitive psychologists, showing how internal perceptual-cognitive processing exhibits continuous change in the salience of multiple simultaneously active representations is perhaps the crucial first step in steering the field away from its digital computer metaphor for cognition. By first replacing the concept of discrete representations in the mind with multifarious patterns of neural activation that change continuously over time, we can set the stage for exploring a reconsideration of exactly how "representation-like" these continuous trajectories in state-space really are (regardless of whether we're talking about a neural state-space or an organism-environment state-space). In this way, we hope that the cognitive sciences can eventually find a responsible and coherent integration of the useful, lasting insights that came from cognitive psychology and from connectionism, and those that are coming from neuroscience, ecological psychology, and dynamic systems theory.

Acknowledgments

We are grateful to Brian Ross for extremely helpful comments on a previous version of this manuscript, and to Paul Allopenna, Catharine Carlin, Eric Dietrich, Shimon Edelman, Günther Knoblich, Ken Kurtz, Art Markman, Bob McMurray, Ulric Neisser, Daniel Richardson, Mike Tanenhaus, Michael Turvey, Melinda Tyler, and Guy Van Orden for helpful discussions of these topics. The first author's work on this chapter was supported by NIMH grant R01-63961.

References

Aks, D. J., & Sprott, J. C. (2003). The role of depth and 1/f dynamics in perceiving reversible figures. *Nonlinear Dynamics, Psychology, and Life Sciences, 7*, 161–180.

Aks, D. J., Zelinsky, G. J., & Sprott, J. C. (2002). Memory across eye-movements: 1/f dynamic in visual search. *Nonlinear Dynamics, Psychology, and Life Sciences, 6*, 1–25.

Aleksander, I. (1973). Random logic nets: Stability and adaptation. *International Journal of Man Machine Studies, 5*, 115–131.

Allopenna, P. D., Magnuson, J. S., & Tanenhaus, M. K. (1998). Tracking the time course of spoken word recognition using eye movements: Evidence for continuous mapping models. *Journal of Memory and Language, 38*, 419–439.

Altmann, G., Garnham, A., & Dennis, Y. (1992). Avoiding the garden-path: Eye movements in context. *Journal of Memory and Language, 31*, 685–712.

Altmann, G., & Steedman, M. (1988). Interaction with context during human sentence processing. *Cognition, 30*, 191–238.

Anderson, J. A., Silverstein, J. W., Ritz, S. A., & Jones, R. S. (1977). Distinctive features, categorical perception, and probability learning: Some applications of a neural model. *Psychological Review, 84*, 413–451.

Anderson, J. R., & Lebiere, C. (1998). *The atomic components of thought*. Mahwah, NJ: Erlbaum.

Ando, B., & Graziani, S. (2000). *Stochastic resonance: Theory and applications*. Boston: Kluwer.

Bak, P., & Tang, C. (1989). Earthquakes as a self-organized critical. *Geophysics Research—Solar. Earth Planet, 94*, 15635–15637.

Balasubramaniam, R., Riley, M. A., & Turvey, M. T. (2000). Specificity of postural sway to the demands of a precision task. *Gait and Posture, 11*, 12–24.

Barber, M., Clark, J., & Anderson, C. (2003). Neural representation of probabilistic information. *Neural Computation, 15*, 1843–1846.

Barlow, H. (1972). Single units and sensation: A neuron doctrine for perceptual psychology. *Perception, 1*, 371–394.

Barsalou, L. W. (1999). Perceptual symbol systems. *Behavioral and Brain Sciences, 22*, 577–660.

Benzi, R., Sutera, A., & Vulpiani, A. (1981). The mechanism of stochastic resonance. *Journal of Physics A: Mathematical and General, 14*, 453.

Bever, T. (1970). The cognitive basis for linguistic structures. In J. Hayes (Ed.), *Cognition and the Development of Language*. New York: Wiley.

Bever, T. G., & Hurtig, R. R. (1975). Detection of a nonlinguistic stimulus is poorest at the end of a clause. *Journal of Psycholinguistic Research, 4*, 1–7.

Bollt, E., Stanford, T., Lai, Y., & Zyczkowski, K. (2000). Validity of threshold crossing analysis of symbolic dynamics from chaotic time series. *Physical Review Letters, 85*, 3524–3527.

Britten, K., Shadlen, M., Newsome, W., & Movshon, J. (1992). The analysis of visual motion: A comparison of neuronal and psychophysical performance. *Journal of Neuroscience, 12*, 4745–4767.

Brownell, H. H., & Caramazza, A. (1978). Categorizing with overlapping categories. *Memory and Cognition, 6*, 481–490.

Budiu, R., & Anderson, J. R. (2004). Interpretation-based processing: A unified theory of semantic sentence comprehension. *Cognitive Science, 28*, 1–44.

Chen, Y., Ding, M., & Kelso, J. A. S. (1997). Long memory processes (1/f type) in human coordination. *Physical Review Letters, 79*, 4501–4504.

Choi, M. Y., & Lee, H. Y. (1995). Traffic flow and 1/f fluctuations. *Physical Review E, 52*, 5979–5984.

Clark, A. (2003). *Natural-born cyborgs*. London: Oxford University Press.

Clark, H. (1992). *Arenas of language use*. Chicago: University of Chicago Press.

Clayton, K., & Frey, B. B. (1997). Studies of mental "noise." *Nonlinear Dynamics, Psychology, and Life Sciences, 1*, 173–181.

Cooper, L. A., & Shepard, R. N. (1973). The time required to prepare for a rotated stimulus. *Memory and Cognition, 1*, 246–250.

Crain, S., & Steedman, M. (1985). On not being led up the garden path. In D. Dowty, L. Kartunnen, and A. Zwicky (Eds.), *Natural language parsing* (pp. 320–358). Cambridge, MA: Cambridge University Press.

Cree, G. S., McRae, K., & McNorgan, C. (1999). An attractor model of lexical conceptual processing: Simulating semantic priming. *Cognitive Science, 23*, 371–414.

Cutler, A. (1995) Spoken word recognition and production. In J. L. Miller and P. D. Eimas (Eds.), *Speech, language, and communication. Handbook of perception and cognition* (2nd ed., Vol. 11, pp. 97–136). San Diego, CA: Academic Press.

Dailey, M. N., Cottrell, G. W., Padgett, C., & Adolphs, R. (2002). EMPATH: A neural network that categorizes facial expressions. *Journal of Cognitive Neuroscience, 14*, 1158–1173.

Dale, R., & Spivey, M.J. (submitted). *Data visualization of complex behavioral structure across time*. Manuscript submitted for publication.

Desimone, R., & Duncan, J. (1995). Neural mechanisms of selective visual attention. *Annual Review of Neuroscience, 18*, 193–222.

Dewey, J. (1896). The reflex arc concept in psychology. *Psychological Review, 3*, 357–370.

Dietrich, E., & Markman, A. B. (2003). Discrete thoughts: Why cognition must use discrete representations. *Mind and Language, 18*, 95–119.

Ding, M., Chen, Y., & Kelso, J. A. S. (2002). Statistical analysis of timing errors. *Brain and Cognition, 48*, 98–106.

Douglass, J. K., Wilkens, L., Pantazelou, E., & Moss, F. (1993). Noise enhancement of the information transfer in crayfish mechanoreceptors by stochastic resonance. *Nature, 365*, 337–340.

Duncan, J., & Humphreys, G. (1989). Visual search and stimulus similarity. *Psychological Review, 96*, 433–458.

Eckmann, J.-P., Kamphorst, S. O., & Ruelle, D. (1987). Recurrence lots of dynamical systems. *Europhysics Letters, 5*, 973–977.

Eckstein, M. P. (1998). The lower visual search efficiency for conjunctions is due to noise and not serial attentional processing. *Psychological Science, 9*, 111–118.

Edelman, S. (1999). *Representation and recognition in vision*. Cambridge, MA: MIT Press.

Elman, J. L. (1991). Distributed representations, simple recurrent networks, and grammatical structure. *Machine Learning, 7*, 195–224.

Elman, J. L., Bates, E. A., Johnson, M. H., Karmiloff-Smith, A., Parisi, D., & Plunkett, K. (1996). *Rethinking innateness: A connectionist perspective on development*. Cambridge, MA: MIT Press.

Farah, M. J. (1985). Psychophysical evidence for a shared representational medium for mental images and percepts. *Journal of Experimental Psychology, 114*, 91–103.

Farrar, W. T., & Kawamoto, A. H. (1993). The return of "visiting relatives": Pragmatic effects in sentence processing. *Quarterly Journal of Experimental Psychology: Human Experimental Psychology, 46A*, 463–487.

Fernald, A., Swingley, D., & Pinto, J. P. (2001). When half a word is enough: Infants can recognize spoken words using partial phonetic information. *Child Development, 72*, 1003–1015.

Ferreira, F., & Clifton, C. (1986). The independence of syntactic processing. *Journal of Memory and Language, 25*, 348–368.

Fodor, J. A., & Pylyshyn, Z. W. (1988). Connectionism and cognitive architecture: A critical analysis. *Cognition, 28*, 3–71.

Frazier, L., & Clifton, C. (1989). Successive cyclicity in the grammar and the parser. *Language and Cognitive Processes, 4*, 93–126.

Frazier, L. (1998). Getting there (slowly). *Journal of Psycholinguistic Research, 27*, 123–146.

Frazier, L., & Fodor, J. D. (1978). The sausage machine: A new two-stage parsing model. *Cognition, 6*, 291–325.

Frazier, L., & Rayner, K. (1982). Making and correcting errors during sentence comprehension: Eye movements in the analysis of structurally ambiguous sentences. *Cognitive Psychology, 14*, 178–210.

Gammaitoni, L., Haenggi, P., Jung, P., & Marchesoni, F. (1998). Stochastic resonance. *Reviews of Modern Physics, 70*, 223–287.

Georgopoulos, A. (1995). Motor cortex and cognitive processing. In M. Gazzaniga (Ed.), *The cognitive neurosciences* (pp. 507–517). Cambridge, MA: MIT Press.

Georgopoulos, A. P., Kalaska, J. F., Caminiti, R., & Massey, J. T. (1982). On the relations between the direction of two dimensional arm movements and cell discharge in primate motor cortex. *Journal of Neuroscience, 2*, 1527–1537.

Georgopoulos, A. P., Lurito, J. T., Petrides, M., Schwartz, A. B., & Massey, J. T. (1989). Mental rotation of the neuronal population vector. *Science, 243*, 234–236.

Gibson, J. J. (1979). *The ecological approach to visual perception*. Boston: Houghton Mifflin.

Gilden, D. L. (1997). Fluctuations in the time required for elementary decisions. *Psychological Science, 8*, 296–301.

Gilden, D. L. (2001). Cognitive emissions of 1/f noise. *Psychological Review, 108*, 33–56.

Gilden, D. L., Thornton, T., & Mallon, M. W. (1995). 1/f noise in human cognition. *Science, 267*, 1837–1839.

Glass, A. L., & Meany, P. J. (1978). Evidence for two kinds of low-typical instances in a categorization task. *Memory and Cognition, 6*, 622–628.

Gold, J. I., & Shadlen, M. N. (2000). Representation of a perceptual decision in developing oculomotor commands. *Nature, 404*, 390–394.

Gold, J. I., & Shadlen, M. N. (2001). Neural computations that underlie decisions about sensory stimuli. *Trends in Cognitive Sciences, 5*, 10–16.

Grainger, J. and Jacobs, A (Eds.). *Localist connectionist approaches to human cognition*. Mahwah, NJ: Erlbaum.

Gregson, R. A. M. (Ed.), *Time series in psychology*. Hillsdale, NJ: Erlbaum.

Haken, H. (Ed.), *Synergetics: An introduction*. Berlin: Springer-Verlag.

Harnad, S. (Ed.), *Categorical perception: The groundwork of cognition*. New York: Cambridge University Press.

Haxby, J. V., Gobbini, M. I., Furey, M. L., Ishai, A., Schouten, J. L., & Pietrini, P. (2001). Distributed and overlapping representations of faces and objects in ventral temporal cortex. *Science, 293*, 2425–2430.

Hennig, M. H., Kerscher, N. J., Funke, K., & Woergoetter, F. (2002). Stochastic resonance in visual cortical neurons: Does the eye-tremor actually improve visual acuity? *Neurocomputing, 44–46*, 115–120.

Hinton, G. (1981). Implementing semantic networks in parallel hardware. In G. Hinton and J. Anderson (Eds.), *Parallel models of associative memory* (pp. 191–217). Hillsdale, NJ: Erlbaum.

Hummel, J. E. (2001). Complementary solutions to the binding problem in vision: Implications for shape perception and object recognition. *Visual Cognition, 8*, 489–517.

Humphreys, G., & Müller, H. (1993). SEarch via Recursive Rejection (SERR): A connectionist model of visual search. *Cognitive Psychology, 25*, 43–110.

Johnson-Laird, P. N. (1998). Imagery, visualization, and thinking. In J. Hochberg (Ed.), *Perception and cognition at century's end. Handbook of perception and cognition* (2nd ed., pp. 441–467). San Diego, CA: Academic Press.

Jolicoeur, P. (1985). The time to name disoriented natural objects. *Memory and Cognition, 13*, 289–303.

Jurafsky, D. (1996). A probabilistic model of lexical and syntactic access and disambiguation. *Cognitive Science, 20*, 137–194.

Kelso, J. A. S. (1995). *Dynamic patterns: The self organization of brain and behavior*. Cambridge, MA: MIT Press.

Knoblich, G., & Jordan, J. S. (2003). Action coordination in groups and individuals: Learning anticipatory control. *Journal of Experimental Psychology: Learning, Memory, and Cognition, 29*, 1006–1016.

Knoeferle, P., Crocker, M., Scheepers, C., & Pickering, M. (2003). Actions and roles: Using depicted events for disambiguation and reinterpretation in German and English. *Proceedings of the 25th Annual Meeting of the Cognitive Science Society*. Boston: Cognitive Science Society.

Kosslyn, S. M., Thompson, W. L., Kim, I. J., & Alpert, N. M. (1995). Topographical representations of mental images in primary visual cortex. *Nature, 378*, 496–498.

Lamberts, K. (1995). Categorization under time pressure. *Journal of Experimental Psychology: General, 124*, 161–180.

Lamberts, K. (1998). The time course of categorization. *Journal of Experimental Psychology: Learning, Memory, and Cognition, 24*, 695–711.

Lamberts, K. (2000). Information-accumulation theory of speeded categorization. *Psychological Review, 107*, 227–260.

Langacker, R. W. (1990). Foundations of cognitive grammar. *Descriptive Applications Prerequisites, 2*, Stanford, CA: Stanford University Press.

Leahey, T. H. (1994). *A history of modern psychology* (2nd ed.). Upper Saddle River, NJ: Prentice Hall.

Lettvin, J. Y. (1995). J. Y. Lettvin on grandmother cells. In M. Gazzaniga (Ed.), *The cognitive neurosciences* (pp. 434–435). Cambridge, MA: MIT Press.

Liberman, A. (1982). On finding that speech is special. *American Psychologist, 37*, 148–167.

Lin, E., & Murphy, G. L. (1997). Effects of background knowledge on object categorization and part detection. *Journal of Experimental Psychology: Human Perception and Performance, 23*, 1153–1169.

Livingstone, M., & Hubel, D. (1988). Segregation of form, color, movement, and depth: Anatomy, physiology, and perception. *Science, 240*, 740–749.

Lund, K., & Burgess, C. (1996). Producing high dimensional semantic spaces from lexical co-occurrence. *Behavior Research Methods, Instruments and Computers, 28*, 203–208.

MacDonald, M., Pearlmutter, N., & Seidenberg, M. (1994). The lexical nature of syntactic ambiguity resolution. *Psychological Review, 101*, 676–703.

Magnuson, J. S., Tanenhaus, M. K., Aslin, R. N., & Dahan, D. (2003). The time course of spoken word learning and recognition: Studies with artificial lexicons. *Journal of Experimental Psychology: General, 132*, 202–227.

Marcus, G. F. (2001). *The algebraic mind: Integrating connectionism and cognitive science*. Cambridge, MA: MIT Press.

Marian, V., & Spivey, M. (2003). Bilingual and monolingual processing of competing lexical items. *Applied Psycholinguistics, 24*, 173–193.

Marslen-Wilson, W. (1973). Linguistic structure and speech shadowing at very short latencies. *Nature, 244*, 522–523.

Marslen-Wilson, W. (1987). Functional parallelism in spoken word recognition. *Cognition, 25*, 71–102.

Marwan, N., & Meinke, A. (2004). Extended recurrence plot analysis and its application to ERP data. *International Journal of Bifurcation and Chaos, 14*, 761–771.

McClelland, J., & Elman, J. (1986). The TRACE model of speech perception. *Cognitive Psychology, 18*, 1–86.

McClelland, J., & Rumelhart, D. (1981). An interactive activation model of context effects in letter perception: Part 1. An account of basic findings. *Psychological Review, 88*, 375–407.
McCulloch, W. (1965). *Embodiments of mind.* Cambridge, MA: MIT Press.
McElree, B., & Carrasco, M. (1999). The temporal dynamics of visual search: Evidence for parallel processing in feature and conjunction searches. *Journal of Experimental Psychology: Human Perception and Performance, 25*, 1517–1539.
McLeod, P., Driver, J., & Crisp, J. (1988). Visual search for conjunctions of movement in visual search. *Nature, 332*, 154–155.
McMurray, R., & Spivey, M. (1999). The categorical perception of consonants: The interaction of learning and processing. *In Proceedings of the Chicago Linguistic Society* (pp. 205–219).
McMurray, B., Tanenhaus, M. K., & Aslin, R. N. (2002). Gradient effects of within-category phonetic variation on lexical access. *Cognition, 86*, B33–B42.
McMurray, B., Tanenhaus, M. K., Aslin, R. N., & Spivey, M. J. (2003). Probabilistic constraint satisfaction at the lexical/phonetic interface: Evidence for gradient effects of within category VOT on lexical access. *Journal of Psycholinguistic Research, 32*, 77–97.
McRae, K., Spivey-Knowlton, M., & Tanenhaus, M. (1998). Modeling the effects of thematic fit (and other constraints) in on-line sentence comprehension. *Journal of Memory and Language, 37*, 283–312.
Medin, D. L., & Smith, E. E. (1981). Strategies and classification learning. *Journal of Experimental Psychology: Human Learning and Memory, 7*, 241–253.
Nakayama, K., & Joseph, J. (1998). Attention, pattern recognition, and pop-out in visual search. In R. Parasuraman (Ed.), *The attentive brain* (pp. 279–298). Cambridge, MA: MIT Press.
Nakayama, K., & Silverman, G. (1986). Serial and parallel processing of visual feature conjunctions. *Nature, 320*, 264–265.
Nederhouser, M., & Spivey, M. (2004). Eye-tracking and simulating the temporal dynamics of categorization. *Proceedings of the 26th Annual Meeting of the Cognitive Science Society.* Chicago: Cognitive Science Society.
Nicolis, C. (1982). Stochastic aspects of climatic transitions—response to a periodic forcing. *Tellus, 34*, 1.
Nosofsky, R. M., & Alfonso-Reese, L. A. (1999). Effects of similarity and practice on speeded classification response times and accuracies: Further tests of an exemplar-retrieval model. *Memory and Cognition, 27*, 78–93.
O'Regan, J. K., & Noe, A. (2001). A sensorimotor account of vision and visual consciousness. *Behavioral and Brain Sciences, 24*, 939–1031.
Olds, E. S., Cowan, W., & Jolicoeur, P. (2000). The time-course of pop-out search. *Vision Research, 40*, 891–912.
Palmer, J., Verghese, P., & Pavel, M. (2000). The psychophysics of visual search. *Vision Research, 40*, 1227–1268.
Pasupathy, A., & Connor, C. E. (2002). Population coding of shape in area V4. *Nature Neuroscience, 5*, 1332–1338.
Pearlmutter, N. J., & MacDonald, M. C. (1995). Individual differences and probabilistic constraints in syntactic ambiguity resolution. *Journal of Memory and Language, 34*, 521–542.
Perrett, D. I., Oram, M. W., & Ashbridge, E. (1998). Evidence accumulation in cell populations responsive to faces: An account of generalisation of recognition without mental transformations. *Cognition, 67*, 111–145.
Phaf, R. H., Van der Heijden, A. H., & Hudson, P. T. (1990). SLAM: A connectionist model for attention in visual selection tasks. *Cognitive Psychology, 22*, 273–341.

Pinker, S., & Ullman, M. T. (2002). The past and future of the past tense. *Trends in Cognitive Sciences, 6*, 456–463.

Pisoni, D. B., & Tash, J. (1974). Reaction times to comparisons within and across phonetic categories. *Perception and Psychophysics, 15*, 285–290.

Port, R. F. and van Gelder, T. (Eds.), *Mind as motion: Explorations in the dynamics of cognition.* Cambridge, MA: MIT Press.

Potter, M. C. (1976). Short-term conceptual memory for pictures. *Journal of Experimental Psychology: Human Learning and Memory, 2*, 509–522.

Potter, M. C. (1993). Very short-term conceptual memory. *Memory and Cognition, 21*, 156–161.

Pouget, A., Dayan, P., & Zemel, R. S. (2000). Inference and computation with population codes. *Annual Review of Neuroscience, 26*, 381–410.

Press, W. H., Teukolsky, S. A., Vetterling, W. T., & Flannery, B. P. (1992). *Numerical recipes in C: The art of scientific computing.* New York: Cambridge University Press.

Prestwich, W. V., Kenneth, T. J., & Pepper, G. T. (1986). Search for 1/f fluctuations in alpha decay. *Physical Review A, 34*, 5132–5134.

Prinz, W., & Hommel, B. (2002). *Common mechanisms in perception and action: Attention and Performance, XIX.* Oxford, England: Oxford University Press.

Rayner, K. (1998). Eye movements in reading and information processing: 20 years of research. *Psychological Bulletin, 124*, 372–422.

Rayner, K., Carlson, M., & Frazier, L. (1983). The interaction of syntax and semantics during sentence processing: Eye movements in the analysis of semantically biased sentences. *Journal of Verbal Learning and Verbal Behavior, 22*, 358–374.

Reynolds, J. H., & Desimone, R. (2001). Neural mechanisms of attentional selection. In J. Braun and C. Koch (Eds.), *Visual attention and cortical circuits* (pp. 121–135). Cambridge, MA: MIT Press.

Richardson, D. C., & Dale, R. (2004). Looking to understand: The coupling between speakers' and listeners' eye movements and its relationship to discourse comprehension. *Proceedings of the 26th Annual Meeting of the Cognitive Science Society.* Chicago: Cognitive Science Society.

Richardson, K. A., Imhoff, T. T., Grigg, P., & Collins, J. J. (1998). Using electrical noise to enhance the ability of humans to detect subthreshold mechanical cutaneous stimuli. *Chaos, 8*, 599–603.

Riley, M. A., Balasubramaniam, R., & Turvey, M. T. (1999). Recurrence quantification analysis of postural fluctuations. *Gait and Posture, 9*, 65–78.

Riley, M. A., & Clark, S. (2003). Recurrence analysis of human postural sway during the sensory organization test. *Neuroscience Letters, 342*, 45–48.

Rips, L. J., Shoben, E. J., & Smith, E. E. (1973). Semantic distance and the verification of semantic relations. *Journal of Verbal Learning and Verbal Behavior, 12*, 1–20.

Rolls, E. T., & Tovee, M. J. (1995). Sparseness of the neuronal representation of stimuli in the primate temporal visual cortex. *Journal of Neurophysiology, 73*, 713–726.

Rosch, E., & Mervis, C. B. (1975). Family resemblances: Studies in the internal structure of categories. *Cognitive Psychology, 7*, 573–605.

Rose, D. (1996). Some reflections on (or by?) grandmother cells. *Perception, 25*, 881–886.

Schall, J. D. (2000). Decision making: From sensory evidence to a motor command. *Current Biology, 10*, R404–R406.

Schmidt, R. C., Carello, C., & Turvey, M. T. (1990). Phase transitions and critical fluctuations in the visual coordination of rhythmic movements between people. *Journal of Experimental Psychology: Human Perception and Performance, 16*, 227–247.

Sebanz, N., Knoblich, G., & Prinz, W. (2003). Representing others' actions: Just like one's own? *Cognition, 88*, B11–B21.

Shepard, R. N., & Metzler, J. (1971). Mental rotation of three-dimensional objects. *Science, 171*, 701–703.

Shockley, K., Santana, M. V., & Fowler, C. A. (2003). Mutual interpersonal postural constraints are involved in cooperative conversation. *Journal of Experimental Psychology: Human Perception and Performance, 29*, 326–332.

Simonotto, E., Riani, M., Seife, C., Roberts, M., Twitty, J., & Moss, F. (1997). Visual perception of stochastic resonance. *Physical Review Letters, 78*, 1186–1189.

Simonotto, E., Spano, F., Riani, M., Ferrari, A., & Levrero, Pilot (1999). fMRI studies of visual cortical activity during noise stimulation. *Neurocomputing, 26–27*, 511–516.

Smith, E. E., Shoben, E. J., & Rips, L. J. (1974). Structure and process in semantic memory: A featural model for semantic decisions. *Psychological Review, 81*, 214–241.

Sparks, D. L., Holland, R., & Guthrie, B. L. (1976). Size and distribution of movement fields in the monkey superior colliculus. *Brain Research, 113*, 21–34.

Spencer, J. P., & Schöner, G. (2003). Bridging the representational gap in the dynamic systems approach to development. *Developmental Science, 6*, 392–412.

Spivey, M. J. (in preparation). *The continuity of mind.* Oxford, England: Oxford University Press.

Spivey, M., Fitneva, S., Tabor, W., & Ajmani, S. (2002a). The timecourse of information integration in sentence processing. In P. Merlo and S. Stevenson (Eds.), *The lexical basis of sentence processing: Formal, computational, and experimental issues* (pp. 207–232). Amsterdam: Benjamins.

Spivey, M., & Tanenhaus, M. (1998). Syntactic ambiguity resolution in discourse: Modeling the effects of referential context and lexical frequency. *Journal of Experimental Psychology: Learning, Memory, and Cognition, 24*, 1521–1543.

Spivey, M., Richardson, D., & Fitneva, S. (2004). Thinking outside the brain: Spatial indices to linguistic and visual information. In J. Henderson and F. Ferreira (Eds.), *The interaction of vision, language, and action.* San Diego, CA: Academic Press.

Spivey, M., Richardson, D., & Gonzalez Marquez, M. (in press). On the spatial and image schematic underpinnings of real-time language processing. In R. Zwaan & D. Pecher (Eds.), *The grounding of cognition: The role of perception and action in memory, language, and thinking* (pp. 161–189). Cambridge, MA: Cambridge University Press.

Spivey, M. J., & Marian, V. (1999). Cross talk between native and second languages: Partial activation of an irrelevant lexicon. *Psychological Science, 10*, 281–284.

Spivey, M., Tanenhaus, M., Eberhard, K., & Sedivy, J. (2002b). Eye movements and spoken language comprehension: Effects of visual context on syntactic ambiguity resolution. *Cognitive Psychology, 45*, 447–481.

Spivey, M., Tyler, M., Eberhard, K., & Tanenhaus, M. (2001). Linguistically mediated visual search. *Psychological Science, 12*, 282–286.

Spivey-Knowlton, M. J. (1996). *The integration of language and vision: Human data and model simulations.* Ph.D. Dissertation, University of Rochester.

Spivey-Knowlton, M. J., & Allopenna, P. D. (1997, August). A computational account of the integration of linguistic and visual information during spoken word recognition. Paper presented at the Computational Psycholinguistics Conference, Berkeley, CA.

Spivey-Knowlton, M., & Sedivy, J. (1995). Resolving attachment ambiguities with multiple constraints. *Cognition, 55*, 227–267.

Spivey-Knowlton, M., Sedivy, J., Eberhard, K., & Tanenhaus, M. (1994). Psycholinguistic study of the interaction between language and vision. *In AAAI-94 workshop proceedings on the integration of natural language and vision processing* (pp. 189–192). Menlo Park, CA: AAAI Press.

Stemmler, M., Usher, M., & Niebur, E. (1995). Lateral interactions in primary visual cortex: A model bridging physiology and psychophysics. *Science, 269*, 1877–1880.

Stevenson, S. (1994). Competition and recency in a hybrid network model of syntactic disambiguation. *Journal of Psycholinguistic Research, 23*, 295–322.

Tabor, W., & Tanenhaus, M. K. (1999). Dynamical models of sentence processing. *Cognitive Science, 23*, 491–515.

Takens, F. (1985). On the numerical determination of the dimension of an attractor. *Lecture Notes in Mathematics: Dynamical Systems and Bifurcations, 1125*, 99.

Talmy, L. (1983). How language structures space. In H. Pick and L. Acredolo (Eds.), *Spatial orientation: Theory, research and application*. New York: Plenum Press.

Tanaka, K. (1997). Mechanisms of visual object recognition: Monkey and human studies. *Current Opinion in Neurobiology, 7*, 523–529.

Tanenhaus, M., Spivey-Knowlton, M., Eberhard, K., & Sedivy, J. (1995). Integration of visual and linguistic information during spoken language comprehension. *Science, 268*, 1632–1634.

Tanenhaus, M., Spivey-Knowlton, M., & Hanna, J. (2000). Modeling the effects of discourse and thematic fit in syntactic ambiguity resolution. In M. Crocker, M. Pickering, and C. Clifton (Eds.), *Architectures and mechanisms for language processing* (pp. 90–118). Cambridge, England: Cambridge University Press.

Tanenhaus, M., & Trueswell, J. (1995). Sentence comprehension. In J. Miller and P. Eimas (Eds.), *Handbook of cognition and perception* (pp. 217–262). Academic Press.

Theeuwes, J., & Kooi, K. L. (1994). Parallel search for a conjunction of contrast polarity and shape. *Vision Research, 34*, 3013.

Thelen, E., & Smith, L. B. (1994). *A dynamic systems approach to the development of cognition and action*. Cambridge, MA: MIT Press.

Townsend, J. T., & Busemeyer, J. R. (1995). Dynamic representation of decision making. In R. F. Port and T. van Gelder (Eds.), *Mind as motion* (pp. 101–120). Cambridge, MA: MIT Press.

Treisman, A. (1988). Features and objects: The Fourteenth Bartlett Memorial Lecture. *Quarterly Journal of Experimental Psychology, 40A*, 201–237.

Treisman, A., & Gelade, G. (1980). A feature integration theory of attention. *Cognitive Psychology, 12*, 97–136.

Trueswell, J., & Kim, A. (1998). How to prune a garden path by nipping it in the bud: Fast priming of verb argument structure. *Journal of Memory and Language, 39*(1), 102–123, July.

Trueswell, J., Tanenhaus, M., & Garnsey, S. (1994). Semantic influences on parsing: Use of thematic role information in syntactic disambiguation. *Journal of Memory and Language, 33*, 285–318.

Tuller, B., Case, P., Ding, M., & Kelso, J. A. (1994). The nonlinear dynamics of speech categorization. *Journal of Experimental Psychology: Human Perception and Performance, 20*, 3–16.

Turvey, M. T., & Carello, C. (1981). Cognition: The view from ecological realism. *Cognition, 10*, 313–321.

Tyler, L. K., & Marslen-Wilson, W. D. (1977). The on-line effects of semantic context on syntactic processing. *Journal of Verbal Learning and Verbal Behavior, 16*, 683–692.

Usher, M., Stemmler, M., & Olami, Z. (1995). Dynamic pattern formation leads to 1/f noise in neural populations. *Physical Review Letters, 74*, 326–329.

Van Berkum, J. J. A., Brown, C. M., & Hagoort, P. (1999). Early referential context effects in sentence processing: Evidence from event-related brain potentials. *Journal of Memory and Language, 41*, 147–182.

Van Gompel, R. P. G., Pickering, M. J., & Traxler, M. J. (2001). Reanalysis in sentence processing: Evidence against current constraint-based and two-stage models. *Journal of Memory and Language, 45*, 225–258.

Van Orden, G. C., Holden, J. G., & Turvey, M. T. (2003). Self organization of cognitive performance. *Journal of Experimental Psychology: General, 132*, 331–350.

Van Rullen, R., & Thorpe, S. (2001). Is it a bird? Is it a plane? Ultra-rapid categorization of natural and artificial objects. *Perception, 30*, 655–668.

Von Neumann, J. (1958). *The computer and the brain.* Oxford, England: Yale University Press.

Voss, R. F., & Clarke, J. (1975). 1/f noise in music and speech. *Nature, 258*, 317–318.

Ward, L. (2002). *Dynamical cognitive science.* Cambridge, MA: MIT Press.

Ward, L., Moss, F., Desai, S., & Rootman, D. (2001). *Stochastic resonance in detection of auditory beats by humans.* Unpublished manuscript: University of British Columbia.

Webber, C. L., Jr., & Zbilut, J. P. (1994). Dynamical assessment of physiological systems and states using recurrence plot strategies. *Journal of Applied Physiology, 76*, 965–973.

Wickelgren, W. A. (1977). Concept neurons: A proposed developmental study. *Bulletin of the Psychonomic Society, 10*, 232–234.

Wolfe, J. M. (1994). Guided Search 2.0: A revised mode of visual search. *Psychonomic Bulletin & Review, 1*, 202–238.

Wolfe, J. M. (1998). What can 1 million trials tell us about visual search? *Psychological Science, 9*, 33–39.

Young, M. P., & Yamane, S. (1992). Sparse population coding of faces in the inferotemporal cortex. *Science, 256*, 1327–1331.

Zbilut, J. P., & Webber, C. L., Jr. (1992). Embeddings and delays as derived from quantification of recurrence plots. *Physics Letters A, 171*, 199–203.

Zeki, S. (1993). *A vision of the brain.* Oxford, England: Blackwell Scientific.

Zemel, R., Dayan, P., & Pouget, A. (1998). Probabilistic interpretation of population codes. *Neural Computation, 10*, 403–430.

Zemel, R., & Mozer, M. (2001). Localist attractor networks. *Neural Computation, 13*, 1045–1064.

Zeng, F. G., Fu, Q. J., & Morse, R. (2000). Human hearing enhanced by noise. *Brain Research, 869*, 251–255.

Zwitserlood, P. (1989). The locus of the effects of sentential-semantic context in spoken-word processing. *Cognition, 32*, 25–64.

ACTION AND MEMORY

Peter Dixon and Scott Glover

I. Introduction

In this chapter, we will advance a single principle as an explanation of a variety of effects in the control of action. Simply stated, that principle is that action is memory. More specifically, the selection and control of an action depends on what actions have been performed in similar situations in the past. In many ways, this is not a new idea, and the relationship between memory and action has a long history in motor control (cf. Kerr, 1983). The advance in the present work lies in three elaborations on this essential idea. First, we assume that a very large number of previous actions are effectively maintained in memory and that the use of that memory in the current context follows optimal (i.e., Bayesian) mechanics. Second, we extend the idea that memory determines action to the kinematics of actions rather than simply movement preparation or programming. Thus, memory determines movement dynamics as well as movement selection. Third, we apply this framework to a range of phenomena that are not typically conceived of in this way, including effects of repetition, perceptual and semantic context, and adaptation.

The chapter is organized as follows. First, in Section II, we present the core elements of our approach and summarize the critical variables that determine the interplay between action and memory. Second, in Section III, we review a variety of phenomena that bear on this analysis. These include repetition effects on posture choice and response time, effects of context-induced perceptual illusions on posture choice and movement

0079-7421/04 $35.00

trajectory, and effects of semantic context. In each case, we present some illustrative simulations to indicate how the model could be elaborated in order to apply to those results. Third, in Section IV, we discuss several other effects that would seem to provide compelling evidence for something like the hypothesized role of memory in action. These include effects of the predictiveness and reliability of contextual information, adaptation effects, and memory-contrast effects. Finally, in Section V, we discuss the common elements of and differences between our approach and a range of related theoretical ideas.

II. Basic Approach

The core assumption of this approach is that memory includes a vast repository of information about previous actions. In general terms, this assumption is consistent with instance-based models of memory such as those proposed by Hintzman (1976), Logan (1988), and Jacoby and Brooks (1984), among others. For the present purposes, it is not necessary to make any detailed assumptions about the format or content of those memories; we merely assume that portions of that information can be made available when it is relevant.

We assume that movements are specified by movement parameters and that these can be modeled as continuous real numbers. In any real movement, there are a large number of such parameters involved, and there are any number of complex dependencies among the parameter values. Further, we assume that movement parameters often have hierarchical relationships. For example, one parameter in a reaching movement may indicate whether a movement is to the left or right, a subordinate parameter may indicate whether the movement is near or far, and an even more detailed parameter may indicate whether the wrist is extended or flexed (cf. Rosenbaum, Kenny, & Derr, 1983). Alternatively, movement parameters may be conceived of as hierarchical constraints on movement dynamics (e.g., Saltzman & Kelso, 1983). Although we make no commitment to the content of such movement parameters at this point, we believe it is reasonable to assume that high-level parameters would specify a movement in relatively abstract terms, such as the egocentric location or direction of a goal or target, while lower-level parameters would be relevant to details of movement mechanics, such as the contraction of particular muscles or muscle groups. For the demonstrations in the present paper, we consider situations in which a single parameter can be used to model interesting aspects of behavior.

Given this background, the basis of our model is very simply that the task of movement selection amounts to estimating movement parameters based on previous actions and the current context. Formally, this is a straightforward problem in Bayesian estimation. The distribution of previous values of the movement parameter constitute the prior distribution, $f(m)$. For simplicity, we assume that the distribution is normal with mean μ_m. The current context, c, determines some subset of previous actions that are relevant to the current situation, and typically the posterior distribution, $f(m|c)$, is also a normal distribution that depends on the reliability of the contextual information and the variance of the prior. In particular, the mean of the posterior is a weighted sum of the expected value of the movement parameter based on the prior (i.e., μ_m) and the value of the movement parameter in similar contexts (m_c):

$$\mu_{m|c} = (1 - \rho_c)\mu_m + \rho_c m_c \tag{1}$$

where ρ_c is a correlation coefficient that indicates how diagnostic the context is of the appropriate movement parameter. This formulation is equivalent to predicting the movement parameter from memory using least-squares regression.

A central element of this framework concerns how actions are controlled. We assume that the current context c includes a mental representation of an actor's goals and intentional strategies, as well as a cognitive interpretation of the stimulus environment. Thus, the movement parameters that are retrieved from memory should only be those that are appropriate to those goals and interpretations, rather than simply responding to the immediate stimulus in a mechanical fashion. It is clear that such a mechanism suffices to control action in a general way. For example, eating actions will be retrieved for the food in front of you only if you are hungry. However, we envision a detailed hierarchy of such goals that are capable of controlling actions with much more precision. In particular, we assume that in general there will be a complex interplay between memory for previous actions, one's current goals and intentions, and the cognitive interpretation of the situation. In effect, one's intentions and interpretations determine how memory is used in the service of action (cf. Allport, 1980; Norman, 1981; Norman & Shallice, 1986; Schmidt, 1975). However, in the present development, we are primarily concerned with experimental tasks in which the subject's goals can be assumed to be fixed and the variation in movements can be analyzed in terms of the visual and experimental context.

III. Applications

The key to generating interesting results using this framework lies in analyzing the nature of the current context and what it indicates about the appropriate movement parameters. In this section, we consider several classes of effects and illustrate how those effects can be explained by a suitable analysis of the current context and its relationship to action memory. First, we consider repetition effects, both in posture choice and in response time measures. Our analysis is that these effects can be explained by simply assuming that the context includes the history of immediately preceding actions and that such history is generally predictive of future actions. Second, we consider dynamic effects in which a movement parameter varies over the course of an action. Our interpretation of such results is that the current context includes information derived from the current ongoing action as well as static information available prior to movement onset. Third, we consider semantic effects on action. In this case, the explanation lies in the assumption that context includes the current contents of consciousness and that movement selection will be affected by the range of concepts being attended and rehearsed. Finally, we turn to situations in which the informativeness of the preceding history of movements is deliberately manipulated. These results similarly follow from the view that the selection of movement parameters depends on memory for action and context.

A. Repetition Effects in Posture Choice

1. Evidence

The simplest evidence that action depends on memory consists of intertrial dependencies. There are many possible ways to demonstrate such dependencies. For example, Glover and Dixon (2001a) had righthanded subjects reach out and pick up a small bar on a tabletop; the orientation of the bar varied from 5–35° clockwise from the sagittal plane. Subjects grasped the bar with the thumb and forefinger of their right hand in either a wrist-abducted (thumb-right) posture or a wrist-adducted (thumb-left) posture. Not surprisingly, we found that the hand posture used to grasp the bar varied systematically with the orientation of the bar. For example, when the bar was oriented relatively far in the clockwise direction, subjects were much more likely to grasp the bar with the wrist abducted (that is, with the thumb on the right). However, in a post hoc analysis of these data, there was also a repetition effect: Subjects tended to use the same posture as they had on the previous trial, independent of the bar orientation. These data are shown in Fig. 1. As the orientation of the bar increases in a clockwise direction from sagittal, the probability of selecting the wrist-abducted posture increases. However, if one has just completed a wrist-abducted grasp on the previous trial, the entire function is shifted so that that posture is more likely to be repeated. We interpret this to mean that the recent use of a posture primes that action and increases the likelihood of that action on the subsequent trial.

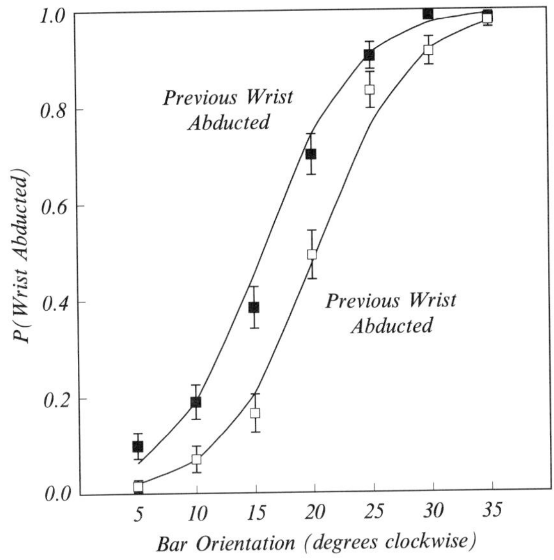

Fig. 1. Repetition effects on posture choice in the data of Glover and Dixon (2001a). Smooth curves depict the model simulation described in the text.

Comparable repetition effects were observed by Dixon (2002). In this case, subjects were asked to reach and touch a target location while avoiding an obstacle (a vertical rod) that interposed the initial position of the hand and the target location. The arrangements of the obstacle and the possible target locations are shown in Fig. 2. When the target was to the far right of the obstacle, subjects almost always moved around the right side of the obstacle; when the target was to the far left of the obstacle, subjects almost always moved around the left side. However, central target positions were more ambiguous, and subjects moved to either the left or right on different trials. The choice of posture for these central positions, though, depended on what action was performed on the previous trial, as shown in Fig. 3: Following a move to the right, for example, subjects were more likely to move to the right, even when the target position was relatively far to the left. Crucially, this result only occurred when the target on the previous trial was similar to the target on the present trial. As shown in Fig. 4, the choice of posture for central target trials was affected by the previous action only when the previous action was also to a central target.

Even more compelling evidence for the mediating role of similarity was obtained by Dixon (2003). The experimental task was the same as in Dixon (2002): Subjects reached around an obstacle to touch a target location. In

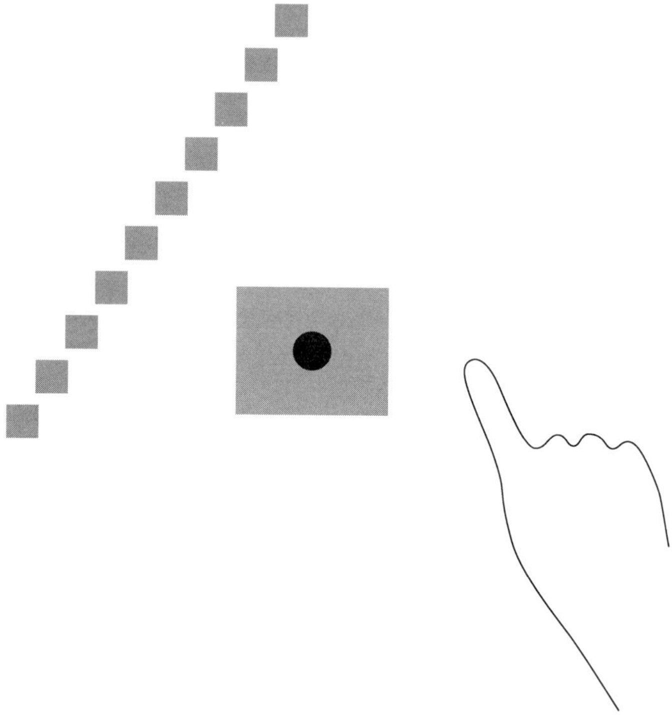

Fig. 2. Stimulus arrangement in Dixon (2002). Subjects reach around a vertical pole to touch a gray square target; the figure depicts the 10 possible locations for the target.

this case, though, two different types of backgrounds and targets were used: The target was either a gray square against a dark background or a blue cross against a red striped background. Even though this stimulus manipulation was completely independent of the required action, it still had an effect on posture choice: Movements to the central targets were likely to resemble the action on the preceding trial when either that action also involved a central target or the target and background were of the same form.

Comparable stereotypy in movements has also been observed in other contexts. For example, Diedrich, Thelen, Smith, and Corbetta (2000) found that infants who were likely to persevere in a reaching task also showed more consistency in movement trajectory across successive trials. Similarly, Jax and Rosenbaum (2003) found that movements designed to avoid an obstacle tended to be repeated on subsequent trials even when the obstacle was no longer present. These results seem to clearly implicate the role of memory for previous actions in the selection and control of current actions.

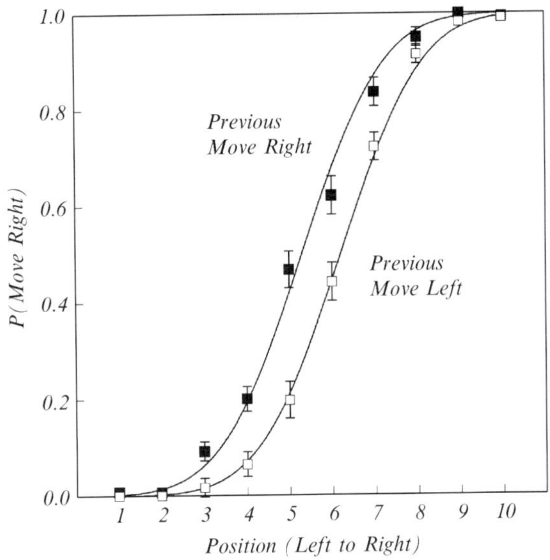

Fig. 3. Repetition effects on posture choice in Dixon (2002). Smooth curves depict the model simulation described in the text.

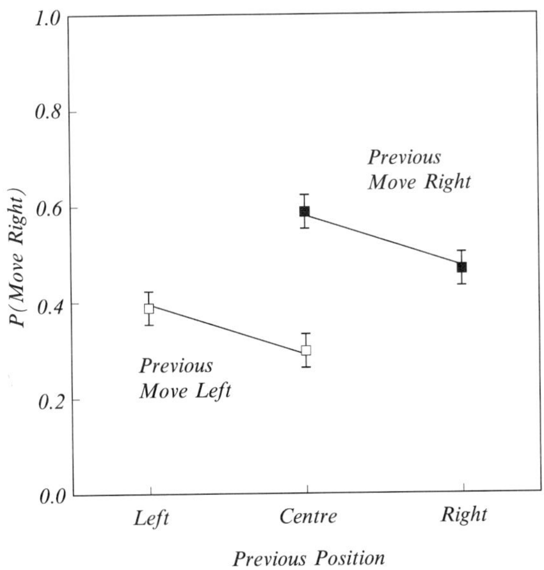

Fig. 4. Repetition effects for central targets in Dixon (2002) as a function of target position on the previous trial. Smooth curves depict the model simulation described in the text.

2. *Model*

The memory approach to repetition effects is based on the assumption that when the context remains the same, actions are often repeated. Life is filled with repetitive actions: When eating, for example, a series of very similar actions will take place, one after another. When typing, very similar movements are made in succession. When picking fruit, the general form of each reach is similar even if the specific target varies from one moment to the next. Thus, having just performed one action, it is a good bet that a similar action will follow. Any large repository of information about previous actions would reflect this contingency. Crucially, though, this repeated-action contingency is mediated by the similarity in the mental and situational context. Eating actions are only repeated as long as food remains and one is hungry; typing actions are performed only as long as the keyboard is available and one has a goal of finishing a paper; and so on. Thus, the more precise form of the contingency is that actions are likely to be repeated only when the context remains the same.

In order to model repetition effects, we thus elaborate the context c in Eq. (1) in several ways. First, we assume that there is a correlation in memory between the movement parameter used on one trial with the movement parameter used on the next. However, this correlation depends on the similarity in the context between the two trials. In particular, we assume that the movement parameters on successive trials have a bivariate normal distribution with correlation parameter s that depends on the contextual similarity. Second, we assume that current stimulus configuration also provides a constraint on the movement parameter. For example, in the configuration shown in Fig. 2, peripheral targets on the left are more likely to cue leftward movements, whereas peripheral targets on the right are more likely to cue rightward movements. However, in our analysis, this constraint is a product of one's movement history rather than a goal-directed computation done at the time of movement selection. Put another way, in an individual's movement history, targets to the left of an obstacle have typically been reached by moving around the obstacle to the left. Consequently, a stimulus configuration in which the target is on the left of the obstacle is more likely to lead to the selection of those previous actions of moving to the left.

Putting these elements together, one can derive expression for the posterior distribution of the movement parameter, given the current context, its similarity to the previous context, and the previous choice of movement parameter. In particular, this will be a normal distribution with mean

$$\mu_{m|p,c,s} = (1 - s - \rho_c)\mu_m + sp + \rho_c m_c \tag{2}$$

where ρ_c indexes the constraint provided by the current context, s depends on the similarity in context between the current and previous trial, and p is the movement parameter used previously.

As an illustration, this formulation was fit by eye to the data in Fig. 1 and 3. (Because the number of parameters is large relative to the degrees of freedom in the data, the graphs here and in subsequent simulations must be regarded as illustrations rather than "fits.") In both graphs, we assumed that negative movement parameters corresponded to leftward movements, that positive values indicated rightward movements, and that $\mu_m = 0$. Equation (2) was then used to calculate the probability of the best estimate of the movement parameter being larger than 0 (i.e., the probability of a rightward movement). As can be seen, it is straightforward to recover the same qualitative pattern of results. Based on the Bayesian estimation mechanics, the model predicts a repetition effect because past actions are predictive of future actions, and it predicts the role of similarity because such repetitions generally occur only with similar contexts.

B. Repetition Effects in Response Time

1. *Evidence*

There is an extensive history of research on repetition effects using response time as a dependent variable. It has long been known that in choice reaction tasks, repeated responses are faster than nonrepeated responses. An important problem in this area has been to disentangle effects of repeating the response from those of repeating the stimulus. For example, Bertelson (1965) had subjects perform tasks in which there were two possible stimuli for each response. The critical comparisons involved three kinds of trials: Those on which the stimuli differed but the response was the same; those on which both the stimulus and response were the same; and those on which both the stimulus and the response differed. He found that repeating the response produced a substantial benefit even when the stimuli were different. However, other researchers using the same type of manipulation have failed to replicate this result and have found substantial repetition effects only when the stimuli were the same (e.g., Smith, 1968; Smith, Chase, & Smith, 1973). Generally, repetition effects can occur across intervening trials; for example, responses will be faster when the stimulus and response matches that from two trials ago, regardless of the nature of the previous trial. Although repetition effects decline with increasing delay between trials, they are still found with an intertrial interval of 1 s and cannot readily be ascribed to a simple decay over time (e.g., Pashler & Baylis, 1991; Smith et al., 1973).

Pashler and Baylis (1991) argued that the similarity of the stimuli on repeated-response trials is a critical variable in determining whether the repeated responses are fast. In their results, different-stimulus/same-response trials were about as fast as same-stimulus trials when the stimuli on successive trials differed in a superficial and irrelevant manner (e.g., letter color when responses must be made on the basis of letter identity). But when the stimuli differed more significantly (e.g., upper and lower case letters), the advantage for different-stimulus/same-response trials was more modest, and when the stimuli mapped to the same response shared only stimulus category (letters vs. digits), the trials were almost as slow as different-response trials. Similar conclusions can be drawn from repetition effects observed in other paradigms. For example, Huettel and Lockhead (1999) found that in dimensional filtering tasks, responses were fast when both the irrelevant dimension and the correct response matched that on the previous trial. Gratton, Coles, and Donchin (1992) found comparable results in a letter-flanker task: Repetition effects on response time and error rates were specific to cases in which the irrelevant noise characters matched those on the previous trial.

Several authors have proposed what might be termed shortcut accounts of these repetition effects. In this form of explanation, there is an explicit or implicit comparison of the current stimulus with the stimulus presented on a previous trial. When the match is sufficiently close, the response from the previous trial can be produced; otherwise, a more time-consuming computation must be undertaken to identify the appropriate response. This general approach has been elaborated to incorporate a variety of different kinds of factors known to modulate repetition effects. For example, Schvaneveldt and Chase (1969) investigated the notion that the comparison process depends on a memory trace of the previous stimulus that decays over time. Huettel and Lockhead (1999) accounted for effects of stimulus similarity in terms of an explicit comparison process. Pashler and Baylis (1991) explained effects of alternating response hand by assuming that shortcut links could exist between relatively abstract descriptions of the required response. However, all of these mechanisms share the assumption that repetition effects arise because of the involvement of mechanisms that do not come into play with nonrepeated-response trials.

2. *Model*

Rather than assuming that repeated trials are somehow a special case, in our approach we assume that the responses for repeated stimuli are generated by the same process that generates responses on nonrepeated trials. The difference is that repeated stimuli provide a greater degree of constraint on the nature of the response to be performed and, by virtue of that constraint, produce more rapid responding. In order to model response time, we assume that the perceptual information that determines the nature of the current context is not available instantaneously but rather develops over time. In other words, the stimulus has to be recognized and interpreted in the context of the current goals and intentions—a time-consuming process. Without this stimulus information, both the similarity of the current context to the previous trial (i.e., s in Eq. [2]) as well as the relevance of the history of previous actions (i.e., ρ_c) would revert to a default value of 0. However, both should increase as the stimulus is processed. In particular, we assume that the mean of the posterior is:

$$\mu_{m|p,c,s}(t) = [1 - u(t)s - u(t)\rho_c]\mu_m + u(t)sp + u(t)\rho_c m_c \quad (3)$$

where $u(t)$ increases monotonically from 0–1 over time.

Clearly, when the context is similar to that on the previous trial, the best estimate of the movement parameter will change more quickly from the default based on the prior distribution, μ_m. An illustration is provided in Fig. 5. If we arbitrarily assume that in this simulation response time effects reflect the time to cross a threshold of 1, the figure suggests a repetition effect of about 70 ms (relative to a different stimulus and response). The dependence of the repetition effect in this formulation on stimulus similarity is also

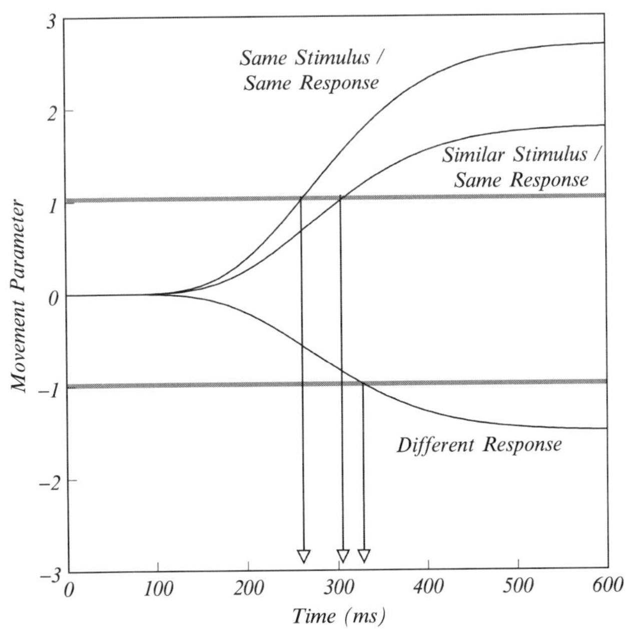

Fig. 5. Simulation of repetition effects on response time as a function of stimulus similarity across trials.

shown in Fig. 5. In this case, when the current stimulus is less similar to the previous (i.e., s is smaller), the repetition effect reduces to about 30 ms.

Related assumptions suffice to account for several other findings related to repetition effects. For example, it seems plausible to suppose not only that actions are likely to repeat immediately, but also with some frequency after a short delay. However, as the temporal gap increases, the likelihood that an action will be repeated becomes progressively less. For example, short pauses are common in the train of repeated actions involved in eating. However, after a significant delay it becomes much more likely that the meal is finished and that the associated actions will not reoccur for some time. As a consequence of this temporal relationship, the predictive value of a previous action for the upcoming trial can be expected to fall off with delay, and the parameter s in Eq. (3) would decline monotonically with the delay between actions. A similar analysis can also be used to explain the effects of intervening trials.

C. Visual Context Effects in Posture Choice

1. *Evidence*

An important problem in the control of movements concerns the role of vision. Milner and Goodale (1995) have argued that actions are controlled on the basis of a visual pathway that is distinct from that which informs conscious perceptual judgments. Among normal individuals, a crucial piece of evidence for this position concerns the effects of context-induced visual illusions such as the Ebbinghaus circles illusion. For example, Aglioti, De Souza, and Goodale (1995) found that when subjects reach out to grasp a disk surrounded by a context of smaller circles, the grip aperture was relatively unaffected by the visual illusion, even substantially prior to the end of the reach trajectory. This pattern of results and its interpretation have generated a great deal of debate (e.g., Bruno, 2001; Franz, 2001; Glover, 2002), and it is fair to say that both the circumstances under which illusions affect action and the magnitude of these effects remain largely unresolved issues.

One aspect of this debate concerns when during an action the effects of visual context are assessed. Generally, subjects gradually increase their grip aperture during most of the reach and then decrease the aperture as the hand nears the target. The maximum grip aperture may be achieved when the action is 65–80% complete. A number of studies that have found relatively little effect of visual context have measured grasping at this point of maximum grip aperture. However, more substantial effects of visual illusions can be found when grip aperture is measured somewhat earlier in the reach trajectory. For example, Glover and Dixon (2002a) examined the effect of the Ebbinghaus circles illusion. Subjects were asked to reach out and grasp a target disk lying on a tabletop, surrounded by drawings of either larger or smaller circles. In perceptual judgments, the larger surrounding circles cause the target to be judged as smaller, and the smaller surrounding circles cause the target to be judged as larger. An effect of context can also be found on grip aperture 50% through the reach, as shown in Fig. 6. Clearly, the grip aperture is affected by the size of the target, so that a larger grip is used for larger disks. However, grip is also affected by the context: Larger grip aperture is found with a small surrounding context than with a large surrounding context.

Clear effects of visual context can also be found when there is relatively little opportunity to correct the choice of posture in the course of the movement. In the task used by Glover and Dixon (2001a), subjects reached out and grasped a short wooden dowel with their thumb and forefinger with either a wrist-abducted (thumb-right) posture or a wrist-adducted (thumb-left) posture. An important aspect of the task was that it was awkward or costly in terms of time and effort to change grip posture after the movement was under way. In order to examine effects of visual context, the bar was placed on a background grating that was oriented either 10° clockwise or 10°

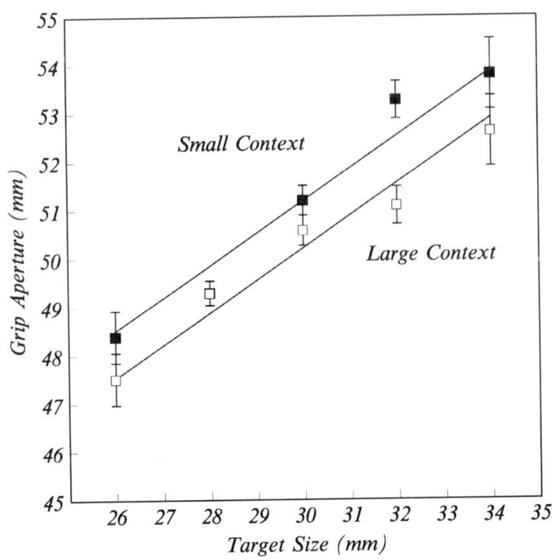

Fig. 6. Grip aperture at 50% of reach in the data of Glover and Dixon (2002a) as a function of object size and visual context. Smooth curves depict the model simulation described in the text.

counterclockwise from the sagittal plane. When the background was oriented counterclockwise from sagittal, the bar appeared slightly more clockwise than when the background was oriented clockwise from sagittal, and vice versa. That is, the orientation of the bar relative to the background had an effect on the perceived orientation of the bar. As shown in Fig. 7, this effect was also reflected in the choice of posture: Wrist-abducted postures were more likely with the counterclockwise background, and wrist-adducted postures were more likely with the clockwise background.

Other evidence that illusions can affect action planning was obtained by Glover and Dixon (2004). In this case, subjects were asked to jump from one end to the other of a Müller–Lyer illusion laid out on the floor. As in Glover and Dixon (2001a), it was difficult to adjust one's trajectory in the course of the movement, and, similarly, the visual context had an effect on performance: Subjects jumped farther for the "wings out" version of the illusion figure than for the "wings in" version.

2. *Model*

The role of many context-induced visual illusions in motor control is straightforward to explain in the present framework. Indeed, Bayesian accounts of perceptual phenomena have some precedent (e.g., Knill &

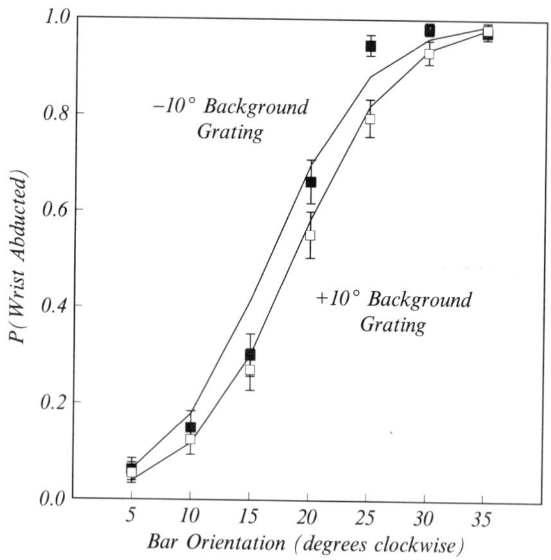

Fig. 7. Posture choice in Glover and Dixon (2001a) as a function of visual context and bar orientation. Smooth curves depict the model simulation described in the text.

Richards, 1996). For example, Richards, Jepson, and Feldman (1996) discussed the role of context in the interpretation of line drawing elements; Weiss, Siomcelli, and Adelson (2002) used Bayesian estimation to account for some visual motion illusions; and Mather (2000) suggested that some geometric illusions could be explained by Bayesian integration mechanisms. In the present application, we assume that, in the world, visual context is correlated with other aspects of the visual array. As a consequence, context is predictive of the posture required to grasp the target. Consider the Ebbinghaus circles illusion. In this effect, for example, adjacent larger circles make the central target circle appear smaller. However, from a Bayesian perspective, this is perfectly sensible because in the world, small objects are, on average, smaller than surrounding objects. Thus, the size of an object relative to its surround will be predictive of its absolute size. Moreover, there is some reason to suspect that under a range of circumstances, perceptual information about relative size will be more readily available than information about absolute size. For example, if the stimuli are viewed without head movements and without other surrounding visual context, the perceptual cues to distance may be minimal, and, consequently, estimates of absolute size based on the retinal image would have a degree of uncertainty. However, estimates of relative size would be unaffected by variation in distance: An object that is 10% larger than nearby objects will remain 10% larger regardless of the distance to those objects. The result is that, prior to the movement, the subject may know how much smaller or larger the target is relative to the surrounding circles but may not have accurate information about the absolute size of the stimuli. Under such conditions, it would not be surprising if relative-size information contributed to the estimation of the movement parameter.

To be more precise, we assume that the internal representation of size is logarithmically related to physical size. This would be consistent with the Weber–Fechner scaling of size magnitude and is likely to be at least approximately true under other formulations. A logarithmic representation of size implies that relative size (measured as the ratio of the size of the target to the size of the surrounding circles) would correspond to size difference in the internal representation. Suppose further that the represented size of graspable objects one encounters has a normal distribution and that the represented size of a second object in its immediate surround has a similar, independent distribution. In that case, relative size (i.e., the difference in the represented sizes) will also have a normal distribution and will have a correlation of .7 with the actual size of the target object. Thus, in principle, relative size should be predictive of the absolute size. The extent to which relative size should influence grip aperture will depend on how reliable the relative size and absolute size information is in the environment in which the grip aperture has to be selected. However, if the absolute size information is at least partially fallible, one would expect to see some effect of independent information concerning relative size. Indeed, as we previously argued, in many contexts relative-size information could be much more robust and precise than information about absolute size.

To apply these considerations to the choice of movement parameters, we assume that estimates of the movement parameter can be generated based on both relative size information, r, and absolute size information, a. In each case, a parameter value is selected based on prior movements associated with that information, namely, m_r and m_a. In general, the movement parameter based on absolute size and that based on relative size will be correlated. However, we may write the estimate of the movement by calculating the unique contribution of each:

$$\mu_{m|a,r} = (1 - \rho_{ma.r} - \rho_{mr.a})\mu_m + \rho_{ma.r}m_a + \rho_{mr.a}m_r \tag{4}$$

where $\rho_{ma.r}$ and $\rho_{mr.a}$ are partial correlations that index the unique contribution of a and r. This result is formally similar to that in Eq. (2), and it produces similar patterns of predictions. The match of this formulation to the grip aperture data of Glover and Dixon (2001a) is shown in Fig. 6. As can be seen, the approach readily accounts for the effect of visual context on grip aperture early in the reach.

The same approach suffices for the orientation illusion investigated by Glover and Dixon (2001a). In this case, we assume that the orientation of the bar relative to the background is mildly predictive of the absolute orientation of the bar. Consequently, if the absolute orientation of the bar is not immediately apparent, the relative orientation would provide some information about the appropriate movement parameter. As before, we argue that the predictive value of relative orientation accrues from an individual's history of actions in the world. For example, it seems plausible to suppose that there are commonly visual elements in one's work space that are aligned roughly with the sagittal plane. Such elements might include the edges of a desk or table, pieces of paper or tools, and so on. These elements in effect generate a frame of reference against which the orientation of other objects might be judged. As argued with respect to relative size, information concerning the orientation of objects relative to that frame of reference might be much more precise than information concerning egocentric orientation. Moreover, relative orientation will be predictive of egocentric orientation even when the frame of reference is not precisely aligned with sagittal. On average, for example, objects that are oriented somewhat clockwise from sagittal will also tend to be clockwise of other elements in the work space. Given this analysis, Eq. (4) applies just as readily to the use of relative orientation as it does to relative size. In Fig. 7, we assume that positive values of the movement parameter indicate a wrist-abducted posture, and Eq. (4) is used to predict the probability that the parameter is greater than 0. As with the size illusion, the approach provides a good account for the obtained results.

D. Dynamic Visual Context Effects

1. Evidence

A critical result for understanding effects of visual context is that those effects vary over the course of the reach trajectory. Early in the reach, the visual context has a fairly large effect on grip aperture, and this effect gradually declines as the hand approaches the target. This pattern of results has been obtained with the Ebbinghaus circles illusion (Glover & Dixon, 2002a), with the background-induced orientation illusion (Glover & Dixon, 2001a,b,c), with the Muller–Lyer illusion (Heath, Rival, & Binsted, 2004), with visual feedback (Glover & Dixon, 2001a,c, 2002a; Heath et al., 2004), and without visual feedback (Glover & Dixon, 2001a,c, 2002a; Heath et al., 2004).

A central consideration in evaluating such results is what counts as a "fairly large" effect. Glover and Dixon assessed the magnitude of the illusion effects by comparing them to the effects of the physical stimulus at the same point in the movement trajectory. For example, early in a reach, there is only a small effect of the physical size of a target disk on grip aperture, and consequently one would expect effects of visual illusion to be similarly small. As the reach progresses, the effect of disk size on grip aperture become more pronounced, and one would expect visual illusion effects to be more apparent as well. Thus, one technique used to assess the magnitude of the visual illusion is to scale those illusion effects by the size of the effect of the physical stimulus.

This pattern of results can be seen in the results of Dixon and Glover (2001). In these experiments, subjects grasped a target disk that was either 28, 30, or 32 mm in diameter; adjacent to the target was a context disk that was either smaller (26 mm) or larger (34 mm). The context disk generates a contrast effect comparable to that obtained with the Ebbinghaus circles illusion, so that in perceptual judgment tasks, the target is judged as smaller alongside a large context disk and larger alongside a small disk. Figure 8 shows the effects of the physical disk size and the visual illusion over the course of the reach. In the upper curve, the effect of disk size is expressed as the slope of the grip aperture $\times$ disk function; the lower curve indicates the size of the context effect (i.e., the difference in grip aperture between small and large contexts). Clearly, the effect of disk size increases over time; the

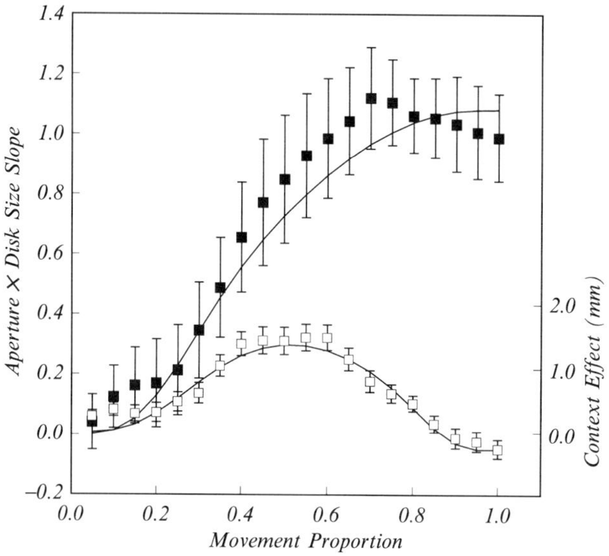

Fig. 8. Effect of context and disk size in Dixon and Glover (2001) as a function of movement proportion. Smooth curves depict the model simulation described in the text.

effect of context initially increases as well, but then it declines as the hand nears the target. Figure 9 shows the scaled context effect, that is, the effect of the context divided by the magnitude of the disk size effect. Based on the scaled context effect, our analysis is that the effect of the context is large initially and decreases monotonically over time. Concurrently, the effect of the represented disk size increases over time as the grip comes to be adapted to the size of the disk. These two trends combine to generate the nonmonotonic trend shown for the "raw" context effect shown in Fig. 8. The raw effect of the illusion is largest at about halfway through the reach. At this point, there are fairly substantial effects of disk size on grip aperture, but the hand is still far enough from the target that the effect of the illusion has not been reduced completely.

Glover (2002; see also Glover & Dixon, 2001a) interpreted these and similar results as supporting a distinction between action planning and action control, rather than a distinction between perception and action as argued by Milner and Goodale (1995). He suggested that the initial planning of the action depended heavily on contextual information in the stimulus environment and, as a consequence, was influenced by the context-induced visual illusions such as the Ebbinghaus circles display. Subsequently, though, different visual information is used in the course of the online

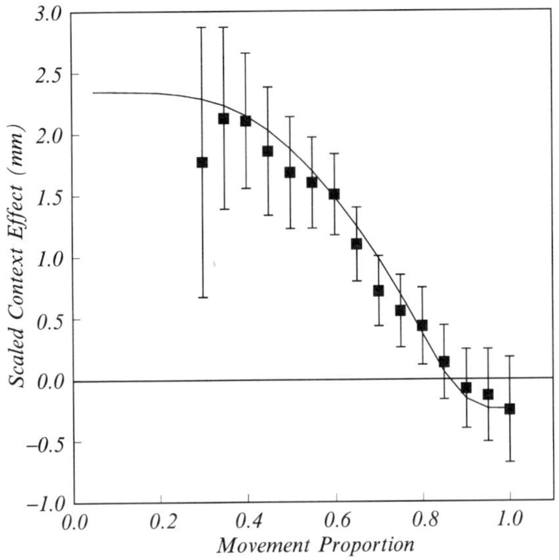

Fig. 9. Effect of context scaled by the effect of disk size in Dixon and Glover (2001) as a function of movement proportion. Smooth curves depict the model simulation described in the text.

control of the action. This control information is tuned to the discrepancy between the hand posture in the course of the reach and the final target contours. Consequently, the information used during the control of the action is much less affected by the visual illusions, and the magnitude of the illusion effects decreases as the movement trajectory unfolds.

2. *Model*

In order to explain dynamic effects, we build on the formulation of Eq. (4) to account for how movement parameters change over time rather than simply the choice of a movement parameter. However, we assume that the mechanism used to control action is mediated by memory in precisely the same way as the selection of movement parameters at the outset. We argue that there are two dynamic components: First, movements are not initiated instantaneously but rather develop over time as an internal representation of the intention to move is formed. Such an intention forms part of the context that allows suitable movement parameters to be retrieved from memory. Depending on the experimental paradigm, the intention to move may develop as a function of the stimulus onset (as was assumed, for example, in our discussion of repetition effects on response time), or as a function of a signal from the experimenter to initiate the movement. Second, we assume that new information becomes available as the movement unfolds. An obvious component of such new information is the discrepancy between the current movement parameter and the target. Because movements are usually not planned perfectly, such discrepancy will be associated with suitable corrections of movement parameters in an individual's history of movements. Discrepancy information can be critical because it is likely to be much more precise and reliable than other perceptual information as the movement progresses. One can readily see, for example, whether a grip aperture is smaller or larger than a target to be grasped as the hand nears the target. Even without visual feedback, proprioceptive information concerning hand posture is likely to become more precise as the hand moves (e.g., Pagano & Turvey, 1995). Consequently, the estimation of a movement parameter based on the relationship between the current state of the effector and the target is likely to be very precise and reliable late in a movement.

Prediction based on discrepancy is, of course, simply another way of saying that movement control uses feedback. The only point of putting it in these terms is to demonstrate that the use of feedback can be conceived as another way of estimating movement parameters based on memory. In particular, feedback can be included in the estimate of the movement parameter as follows:

$$\begin{aligned}\mu_{m|a,r,d} = {} & (1 - \rho_{ma.rd} - \rho_{mr.ad} - \rho_{md.ar})\mu_m + \rho_{ma.rd} m_a \\ & + \rho_{mr.ad} m_r + \rho_{md.ar} m_d\end{aligned} \tag{5}$$

As before, the ρ parameters are partial correlations that index the contributions of each source of information, independent of the others, and the *m*s indicate the corresponding movement parameter values. The dynamic effects of context arise in this approach because the availability of the discrepancy information follows a different time course than the relative and absolute size information. Thus, to be more precise, the formulation should be:

$$\begin{aligned}\mu_{m|a,r,d}(t) = {} & [1 - u(t)\rho_{ma.rd} - u(t)\rho_{mr.ad} - v(t)\rho_{md.ar}]\mu_m \\ & + u(t)\rho_{ma.rd} m_a + u(t)\rho_{mr.ad} m_r + v(t)\rho_{md.ar} m_d\end{aligned} \tag{6}$$

Here, $u(t)$ increases after the onset of the stimulus or movement signal, and $v(t)$ increases as the movement unfolds. Thus, although both u and v increase monotonically over time, u is assumed to increase relatively early in the movement trajectory as stimulus information is processed and the goal of moving to target is formed, whereas v increases more slowly as discrepancy information is acquired over the course of the movement. The predictions represented by Eq. (6) concern the estimated value of relatively high-level movement parameter, rather than the kinematics of the physical movements themselves, and in a more complete account these predictions would have to be filtered through a model of the actual movement mechanics. Nevertheless, as shown in Fig. 8 and 9, this simplistic formulation successfully captures the essential features of the dynamic effect observed by Dixon and Glover (2001). In Figure 8, the left axis shows the effect of the actual size of the object (represented as the slope of the grip aperture × disk size relation), represented in Eq. (6) by $u(t)\rho_{ma.rd}m_a + v(t)\rho_{md.ar}m_d$. The right axis shows the effect of context as predicted by $u(t)\rho_{mr.ad}m_r$. It increases at first because the movement takes time to be planned and executed; the effect decreases near the end of the reach as more reliable information becomes available. Figure 9 shows the predicted effect of the illusion when scaled by the predicted effect of actual target size.

E. Semantic Effects

1. *Evidence*

Several authors have demonstrated that effects of context on reaching are not limited to visual context but also include apparently irrelevant semantic information. For example, Gentilucci and Gangitano (1998) printed the words *long* and *short* on objects and observed movement kinematics comparable to that which would be expected if the objects were actually a long or short distance away. Specifically, higher peak velocities were observed when reaching to objects labeled "long" than to objects labeled "short," similar to that observed for objects that are actually farther away (Jeannerod, 1984). Similar observations were made for several other word pairs (Gentilucci, Benuzzi, Bertolani, Daprati, & Gangitano, 2000; see also Glover & Dixon, 2002b). Glover, Rosenbaum, Graham, and Dixon (2004) extended these findings to word pairs that were only implicitly related to object features. For example, reading the word *apple* led to larger grip apertures in a subsequent reaching and grasping movement than the word *grape*, even though the words were not predictive of actual object size.

In many ways, these semantic effects are similar to the effects of visual illusions. For example, they are found near the middle of the reach trajectory, and they tend to be minimal by the time the hand reaches the target. Figure 10 shows representative results from Glover et al. (2004). As with visual illusions, there is relatively little semantic effect either early in the reach or near the end, and the effect is clearest in the middle of the reach. Our interpretation of these dynamic effects is comparable to that proposed for effects of visual illusions: The effect increases initially as the system responds to the target and the signal to move, and then decreases as discrepancy information becomes available over the course of the movement.

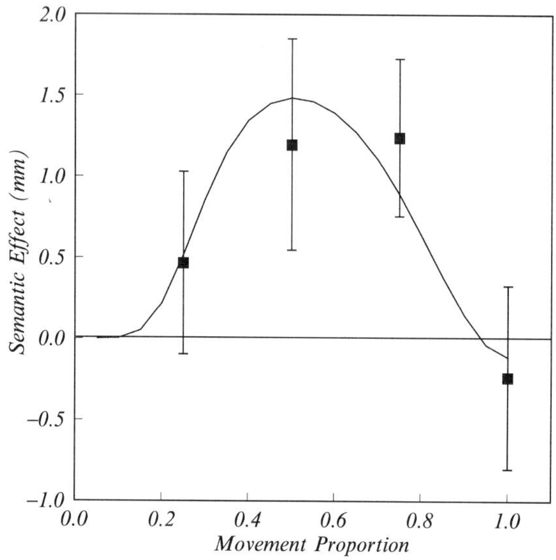

Fig. 10. Effect of semantic context in Glover et al. (2004) as a function of movement proportion. Smooth curves depict the model simulation described in the text.

Another, quite different source of evidence concerning semantic effects comes from experiments by Bargh (e.g., Bargh, Chen, & Burrows, 1996). When subjects were primed with the concept "elderly," they subsequently walked more slowly when leaving the lab. On our analysis, this result may occur because the activation of an "elderly" stereotype primes related actions, including slow walking, and these are more likely to be retrieved during the subsequent planning and control of actions. We suspect that this priming may be comparable to the priming of grasping posture observed by Glover et al. (2004; Glover & Dixon, 2002b) and Gentilucci and Gangitano (1998; Gentilucci et al., 2000).

2. *Model*

Because of the similarity to the visual illusion effects, it is not surprising that the same computational framework suffices for semantic effects as well. The critical step is to note that semantic context is predictive of motor actions just as the visual context is. For example, when picking up an apple, one is typically thinking about the concept of apple in one way or another; when picking up a grape, one is typically thinking about grapes, and so on. Thus, the activation of the apple concept is predictive of the posture needed to grasp an apple, and the activation of the grape concept is predictive of a grape-grasping posture. Of course, the predictive value of such activations is not very high since there are many circumstances in which the one may think about these concepts without grasping the objects. Nevertheless, as in the previous development, these weakly predictive effects can contribute to the estimation of the movement parameter when other sources of information are not perfectly reliable. Formally, the prediction is precisely the same as that for the effects of relative size context:

$$\begin{aligned}\mu_{m|a,e,d}(t) = {} & [1 - u(t)\rho_{ma.ed} - u(t)\rho_{me.ad} - v(t)\rho_{md.ae}]\mu_m \\ & + u(t)\rho_{ma.ed}m_a + u(t)\rho_{me.ad}m_e + v(t)\rho_{md.ae}m_d\end{aligned} \tag{7}$$

except that here, the prediction is based on the semantic context, e, rather than relative size. The model predicts the same form of dynamic effect, and, as can be seen in Fig. 9, it provides a reasonable match to the obtained results.

F. Summary

We have outlined a variety of results pertaining to the influences of visual, experiential, and experimental context on action and have demonstrated how each can be explained by assuming that movement parameters are estimated on the basis of previous experience. The core idea in this framework is simply that people have a great deal of available information about previous actions and that this information is used in an optimal (i.e., Bayesian) fashion to estimate movement parameters in the current context. Because it is reasonable to suppose that actions are often repeated, these assumptions predict repetition effects in posture choice and speeded response tasks; because a target's visual context is often predictive of the appropriate posture, we can predict effects of context-induced visual illusions on action; because feedback and other sources of information become available in the course of an action, we can explain the dynamic time course of illusion effects; and because semantic context is predictive of actions, we can account for semantic effects on movement trajectories as well. Thus, the approach integrates a wide range of different kinds of effects under a single conceptual and computational framework.

Alternative explanations have previously been proposed for some of these results. For example, repetition effects in response time have been explained by "shortcut" processes that curtail computation of a response when the stimuli on successive trials match, and the dynamic illusion effects have been explained on the assumption that different visual pathways subserve action planning and action control. Our argument, though, is that the memory and action framework is more general and parsimonious because it subsumes these other explanations. For example, the use of a distinct visual pathway during action control can be thought of as simply another source of information that can be used as a memory retrieval cue to make dynamic predictions of movement parameters. However, in Section IV we review several other results that would seem to implicate specifically the ability of the motor control system to make Bayesian-like predictions based on previous experience. These results provide evidence for something akin to the present approach over and above any gain in parsimony or comprehensiveness.

IV. Other Evidence on Memory and Action

A. Predictiveness of Relative Size

One result that seems to implicate the use of memory in action derives from the manipulation of the predictiveness of visual context in an experimental session. The usual manner in which one would vary visual context in an experiment would be to factorially manipulate the contextual information and the physical nature of the target. For example, in Dixon and Glover (2001), 28-, 30-, and 32-mm target disks were paired with either a 26-mm context disk or a 34-mm context disk. Although this design ensures that the size of the context disk does not predict the size of the target, *relative* size in fact does predict the target. For example, if relative size is defined as the size of the target divided by the size of the context, there is a modest correlation of .38 between relative and absolute size. Thus, irrespective of the movement history with large and small objects, one should expect an effect of relative size simply on the basis of the experience subjects have with the stimuli in the experiment.

A straightforward test of this interpretation is to alter the design of the stimuli so that relative size is no longer predictive of grip aperture. Dixon, Glover, and Schneider (2003) used context disks that were either a fixed percentage larger or a fixed percentage smaller than the target. The results of this manipulation are compared to the usual, orthogonal manipulation of context size in Fig. 11. The results demonstrate that in the crucial middle portion of the reach trajectory, the orthogonal manipulation of context produces a greater effect of context on grip aperture than when relative size is fixed and provides no information. This result strongly suggests that the dynamic effect of visual context depends on the predictive value of that context.

B. Reliability of Perceptual Information

Another manipulation that should produce related effects pertains to the reliability of perceptual information. In general, the magnitude of the context effect (i.e., $\rho_{mr.ad}$ in Eq. [6]) will depend in a complex way on the

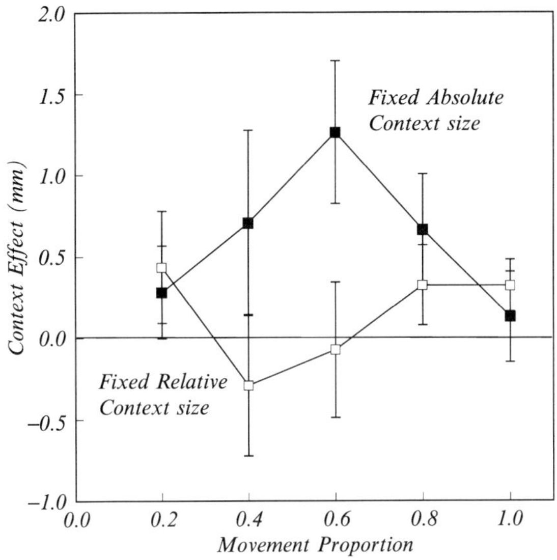

Fig. 11. Effect of context in Dixon et al. (2003) as a function of experimental context and movement proportion.

relationship among the different predictors. However, in a broad set of plausible circumstances, $\rho_{mr.ad}$ will decrease as ρ_{ma} increases. In other words, the unique contribution of relative size information will vary inversely with the reliability of the absolute size information. Relative size information will be most helpful if the absolute size information is noisy or unreliable, and, in the limit, relative size information will add nothing if absolute size information is perfect. The net implication then is that any manipulation that decreases the reliability of the perceptual absolute size information should increase the effect of relative size information.

Dixon and Glover (2001) found such a result when target contrast was manipulated. Subjects reached out and grasped a target disk in the presence of a context disk that was either larger or smaller than the target. The disks were white with a black edge and could be placed either on a black background or a white background. Absolute size information was difficult to discern when the disks were against a black background because the dark edge tended to blend in with the background; the contours of the disks were much easier to see when the disks were placed against a white background. Consistent with the prediction, the context effect was larger and longer lasting when the target was presented under low-contrast conditions (see Fig. 12). The predictions of the model were fit by eye to these results and

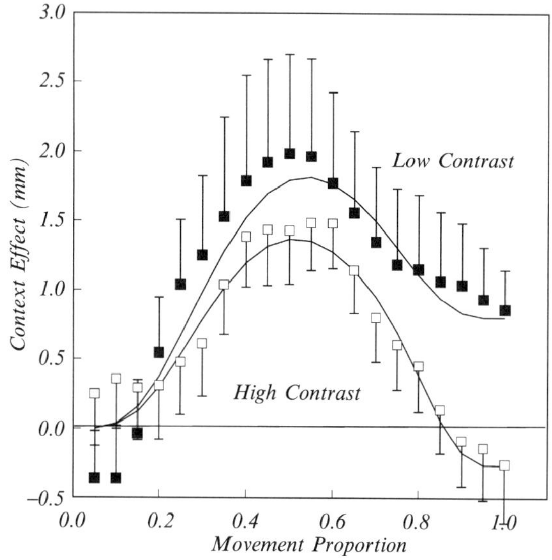

Fig. 12. Effect of context in Dixon and Glover (2001) as a function of stimulus contrast and movement proportion. Smooth curves depict the model simulation described in the text.

shown in the figure as well; the differing results for the two conditions was generated simply by varying the reliability of information about absolute size.

C. Adaptation to Experimental Context

A third source of evidence pertaining to the informativeness of the context comes from adaptation effects. Glover and Dixon (2001b) used the orientation illusion previously used by Glover and Dixon (2001a): Subjects reached out and picked up a bar resting on a grating oriented either 10° clockwise or 10° counterclockwise from sagittal. However, rather than changing randomly from trial to trial, the orientation of the background grating remained fixed for a block of 14 trials. While a clear effect of context was observed in the first half of each block, it disappeared by the second half. In a sense, subjects had become "adapted" to the illusory orientation of the bar. (We use the term *experimental context* to refer to such effects of the composition of blocks of trials, and reserve the term *visual context* for effects of the visual array on any given trial.)

These results are precisely what one would expect if the use of relative orientation information was mediated by memory for recent movements. As previously argued, the orientation of objects relative to other elements in the work space might be much more precise than egocentric orientation. However, because objects in the work space are unlikely to be perfectly aligned, corrections would need to be applied dynamically in grasping targets. The crucial observation is that, as long as the workspace is relatively stable, the corrections applied on one reach would be similar to those applied on subsequent reaches. Thus, because the correction applied on previous trials is likely applicable to subsequent trials, it can be used in estimating the movement parameters. In effect, the adaptation effect is a form of repetition effect, but pertaining to corrections. In this respect, the adaptation effect is a natural generalization of the results simulated so far. More formally, these ideas can be expressed as a variation of Eq. (4):

$$\mu_{m|a,r,k} = (1 - \rho_{ma.rk} - \rho_{mr.ak} - \rho_{mk})\mu_m + \rho_{ma.r}m_a + \rho_{mr.a}m_r + \rho_{mk}m_k \quad (8)$$

where k is the history of corrections, ρ_{mk} indexes how reliable those corrections are as an estimate of the movement parameter on the current trial, and m_k is the estimate of the movement parameter based on those previous corrections. We assume that m_k represents the pooled information from previous trials according to an exponential weighting function, so that the most recent trials are most likely to be predictive of the current trial and more distant trials less likely. This would seem to capture the notion that the elements of the workspace that comprise the frame of reference are only likely to be stable in the short term (cf. Scheidt, Dingwall, & Mussa-Ivaldi, 2001).

D. Memory-Contrast Effects

Another type of evidence for the role of memory in action comes from the work of Haffenden and Goodale (2002a,b). Haffenden and Goodale (2002a) used a surface texture as a cue to an object's size. For example, a texture of triangular shapes might be associated with large objects, and a texture of circular shapes with small objects. Subsequent reaches to a medium-sized object were influenced by the texture on its surface, so that, for example, grip aperture was smaller when the surface texture matched the previously viewed large objects. This result suggests a memory-based size-contrast effect. For example, experience with the large objects of a particular texture makes the medium-sized object with the same texture appear smaller by comparison, and this effect was evident in the grip trajectory. Haffenden and Goodale (2002b) examined the consequences of varying a target's position on such cue effects (using color in this case rather than surface texture). Cue effects were observed for movements made to targets presented in a single location but not for movements to targets whose location varied.

These results clearly implicate memory in the selection of movement parameters. On our analysis, the size of an object relative to previous encounters with similar objects can function as a relative-size cue just as does the size of an object relative to other objects in the work space. Thus, we can account for this result using a variant of Eq. (4), except that the information about relative size would be based on memory rather than comparisons to other, simultaneously visible objects. Consistent with our analysis of repetition effects, the use of memory in these circumstances is specific to the details of the action and the situation. Thus, varying target position reduces or eliminates the cue effects because movements of a different type (i.e., to a different location) are relevant to the estimation of the movement parameter.

V. Relation to Other Approaches

Although the present proposal is unique in at least some respects, it is closely allied with a variety of extant theories. Perhaps the most germane is the theory of motor control proposed by Rosenbaum, Loukopoulis, Meulenbroek, Vaughn, and Englebrecht (1995). They proposed that actions were accomplished by evaluating stored postures in terms of their match to a target. The stored postures in turn determine both final joint angles needed to arrive at the target and (implicitly) properties of the movement trajectory. What is different about the present proposal is that we assume that the use of the stored postures is based not on the intended target position but rather on task goals and the stimulus configuration. Further, much of the power in our framework derives from the more general use of context to constrain an extensive memory for previous actions.

Smith et al. (1973) proposed a conceptually related approach to account for repetition effects on response time. They argued that in order to identify a response, the stimulus must be compared to a set of possible stimulus-response pairs in short-term memory. To explain repetition effects, they assumed that the search of short-term memory was ordered by recency, so that the stimulus responded to on a recent trial is more likely to be encountered first. This is comparable to our framework in that contextually appropriate responses are selected from memory based on the match to the current stimulus configuration. Although we would not exclude the possible involvement of short-term memory in our approach, we assume that the selection of a response depends more generally on a long-term memory repository of previous actions. Moreover, the recency effect in our account follows in a straightforward fashion from the principles of optimal estimation rather than requiring ad hoc assumptions concerning the ordering of search.

The present conception is also similar in many respects to the instance theory of automaticity (Logan, 1988). In this account, memory traces of prior episodes with a stimulus and task race independently, and the winner determines the response on a given trial. Because the number of instances increases over time, the average speed of the winner will increase, in keeping with the pattern of speed increases observed with extended practice. The present proposal is related to Logan's analysis in that both depend on the availability of instances in memory. The mechanics of response selection are quite different, though: In Logan's model, a single instance is selected on the basis of a race process and is used to model the current response; in the present approach, we estimate movement parameters based on a posterior distribution of parameter values. However, there are a variety of conditions in which similar predictions could arise. For example, if the current context is sufficiently specific, the posterior distribution might be largely a function of a specific previous instance. Further, if the internal context develops over time (as was suggested in our discussion of repetition effects on response time), the selection of that previous instance might have some of the same properties as the independent race process envisioned by Logan.

Körding and Wolpert (2004) used precisely the same mechanics as described here to model the control of saccadic eye movements. In particular, they assumed that the selection of a movement parameter involves Bayesian estimation based on previous experience. Similarly, Vetter and Wolpert (2000) developed a related Bayesian account of some aspects of movement dynamics. However, the concern in these studies was with the integration of different sources of sensory information and the calibration of that information over trials; the potentially larger role of memory for action was not a primary focus. The present work builds on these ideas but accounts for a broader range of visual and semantic context effects by assuming that actions are based on a large repository of previous actions in memory.

The Bayesian approach to the use of memory is also related to the ideas of Anderson and Milson (1989). They proposed that the current context provides a set of memory cues, and that based on these cues, the memory system estimates a value termed a need probability for each item in memory. The most important difference between the present approach and that of Anderson and Milson is that we estimate properties of the entire posterior distribution rather than probabilities for individual items or instances. Nevertheless, the natural way in which Anderson and Milson's formulation accounts for various aspects of memory suggests that similar variables might be readily incorporated into the present framework. For example, Anderson and Milson explain effects of practice, spacing, and retention interval in terms of the Bayesian posterior probability calculations. However, related variables have effects on motor learning (e.g., Magill & Hall, 1990; Newell & Rosenbloom, 1981; Young, Cohen, & Husak, 1993), and it is tantalizing to suppose that a Bayesian account of these phenomena could be obtained using the estimation procedures developed here.

VI. Conclusion

We argue that the role of memory in action provides a collection of powerful explanatory principles for understanding a wide range of effects on action and action control. Moreover, the interpretation of action selection as the Bayesian estimation of movement parameters provides a variety of novel and perhaps surprising predictions. For example, as predicted by this approach, repetition effects on posture choice are mediated by contextual similarity; effects of visual illusions and visual context are expected to be larger when other visual information about the target is impoverished; and effects of relative size and orientation cues vary with the experimental context. In the present chapter, we have provided merely an outline for a more comprehensive application of these ideas and have only touched on a few aspects of the conceptual analysis that would ultimately be needed. Nevertheless, we believe that the present demonstrations provide clear evidence of the power of this approach.

References

Aglioti, S., De Souza, J., & Goodale, M. (1995). Size-contrast illusions deceive the eye but not the hand. *Current Biology, 5*, 679–685.

Allport, D. A. (1980). Attention and performance. In G. Claxton (Ed.) *Cognitive psychology: New directions*. London: Routledge & Kegan Paul.

Anderson, J. R., & Milson, R. (1989). Human memory: An adaptive perspective. *Psychological Review, 96*, 703–719.

Bargh, J. A., Chen, M., & Burrows, L. (1996). Automaticity of social behavior: Direct effects of trait construct and stereotype activation on action. *Journal of Personality and Social Psychology, 71*, 230–244.

Bertelson, P. (1965). Serial choice reaction-time as a function of response versus signal-and-response repetition. *Nature, 206*, 217–218.

Bruno, N. (2001). When does action resist visual illusions? *Trends in Cognitive Sciences, 5*, 379–382.

Diedrich, F. J., Thelen, E., Smith, L. B., & Corbetta, D. (2000). Motor memory is a factor in infant perseverative errors. *Developmental Science, 3*, 479–494.

Dixon, P. (2002, November). *Retrieving motor plans.* Poster presented at the meeting of the Psychonomic Society, Kansas City, KS.

Dixon, P. (2003, June). *Action and memory.* Paper presented at Canadian Society for Brain Behaviour, and Cognitive Science, Hamilton, Ontario, Canada.

Dixon, P., & Glover, S. R. (2001, November). *A rational analysis of illusion effects in reaching.* Paper presented at the meeting of Psychonomic Society, Orlando, FL.

Dixon, P., Glover, S., & Schneider, D. (2003, November). *Visual information, memory, and control of reaching.* Paper presented at the meeting of the Psychonomic Society, Vancouver, British Columbia, Canada.

Franz, V. H. (2001). Action does not resist visual illusions. *Trends in Cognitive Sciences, 5*, 457–459.

Gentilucci, M., Benuzzi, F., Bertolani, L., Daprati, E., & Gangitano, M. (2000). Language and motor control. *Experimental Brain Research, 133*, 468–490.

Gentilucci, M., & Gangitano, M. (1998). Influence of automatic word reading on motor control. *European Journal of Neuroscience, 10*, 752–756.

Glover, S. (2002). Visual illusions affect planning but not control. *Trends in Cognitive Sciences, 6*, 288–292.

Glover, S., & Dixon, P. (2001a). Dynamic illusion effects in a reaching task: Evidence for separate visual representations in the planning and control of reaching. *Journal of Experimental Psychology: Human Perception and Performance, 27*, 560–572.

Glover, S., & Dixon, P. (2001b). Motor adaptation to an optical illusion. *Experimental Brain Research, 137*, 254–258.

Glover, S., & Dixon, P. (2001c). The role of vision in the on-line correction of illusion effects on action. *Canadian Journal of Experimental Psychology, 55*, 96–103.

Glover, S., & Dixon, P. (2002a). Dynamic effects of the Ebbinghaus illusion in grasping: Support for a planning-control model of action. *Perception and Psychophysics, 64*, 266–278.

Glover, S., & Dixon, P. (2002b). Semantics affect the planning but not control of grasping. *Experimental Brain Research, 146*, 383–387.

Glover, S., & Dixon, P. (2004). A step and a hop on the Muller–Lyer illusion: Illusion effects on lower limb movements. *Experimental Brain Research, 154*, 504–512.

Glover, S., Rosenbaum, D. A., Graham, J. R., & Dixon, P. (2004). Grasping the meaning of words. *Experimental Brain Research, 158*, 103–108.

Gratton, G., Coles, M. G. H., & Donchin, E. (1992). Optimizing the use of information: Strategic control of activation of responses. *Journal of Experimental Psychology: General, 121*, 480–506.

Haffenden, A. M., & Goodale, M. A. (2002a). Learned perceptual associations influence visuomotor programming under limited conditions: Cues as surface patterns. *Experimental Brain Research, 147*, 473–484.

Haffenden, A. M., & Goodale, M. A. (2002b). Learned perceptual associations influence visuomotor programming under limited conditions: Kinematic consistency. *Experimental Brain Research, 147*, 485–493.

Heath, M., Rival, C., & Binsted, G. (2004). Can the motor system resolve a premovement bias in grip aperture? Online analysis of grasping the Muller–Lyer illusion. *Experimental Brain Research, 158*, 378–384.

Hintzman, D. L. (1976). Repetition and memory. In G. H. Bower (Ed.) *The psychology of learning and motivation* (pp. 47–91). New York: Academic Press.

Huettel, S. A., & Lockhead, G. R. (1999). Range effects of an irrelevant dimension on classification. *Perception & Psychophysics, 61*, 1624–1645.

Jacoby, L. L., & Brooks, L. R. (1984). Nonanalytic cognition: Memory, perception, and concept learning. In G. H. Bower (Ed.) *The psychology of learning and motivation* (pp. 1–47). New York: Academic Press.

Jax, S. A., & Rosenbaum, D. A. (2003). *Sequential effects in obstacle avoidance: The obstacle-perseveration effect*. Vancouver, British Columbia, Canada: Psychonomic Society.

Jeannerod, M. (1984). The timing of natural prehension movements. *Journal of Motor Behavior 16*, 235–254.

Kerr, B. (1983). Memory, action, and motor control. In R. A. Magill (Ed.) *Memory and control of action* (pp. 47–66). Amsterdam: North-Holland.

Knill, D., & Richards, W. (1996). *Perception as Bayesian inference*. Cambridge, England: Cambridge University Press.

Körding, K. P., & Wolpert, D. M. (2004). Bayesian integration in sensorimotor learning. *Nature, 427*, 244–247.

Logan, G. D. (1988). Toward an instance theory of automatization. *Psychological Review, 95*, 492–527.

Magill, R. A., & Hall, K. G. (1990). A review of the contextual interference effect in motor skill acquisition. *Human Movement Science, 9*, 241–289.

Mather, G. (2000). Integration biases in the Ouchi and other visual illusions. *Perception, 29*, 721–727.

Milner, A. D., & Goodale, M. A. (1995). *The visual brain in action*. Oxford, England: Oxford University Press.

Newell, A., & Rosenbloom, P. (1981). Mechanisms of skill acquisition and the law of practice. In J. R. Anderson (Ed.) *Cognitive skills and their acquisition* (pp. 1–55). Hillsdale, NJ: Erlbaum.

Norman, D. A. (1981). Categorization of action slips. *Psychological Review, 88*, 1–15.

Norman, D. A., & Shallice, T. (1986). Attention to action: Willed and automatic control of behavior. In R. J. Davison, G. E. Schwartz, and D. Shapiro (Eds.) *Consciousness and self regulation*. (Vol. 4, pp. 1–8). New York: Plenum Press.

Pagano, C. C., & Turvey, M. T. (1995). The inertia tensor as a basis for the perception of limb orientation. *Journal of Experimental Psychology: Human Perception and Performance, 21*, 1070–1087.

Pashler, H., & Baylis, G. (1991). Procedural learning: 2. Intertrial repetition effects in speeded choice tasks. *Journal of Experimental Psychology: Learning, Memory, and Cognition, 17*, 33–48.

Richards, W., Jepson, A., & Feldman, J. (1966). Priors, preferences, and categorical percepts. In D. C. Knill and W. Richards (Eds.) *Perception as Bayesian inference* (pp. 93–122). Cambridge, England: Cambridge University Press.

Rosenbaum, D. A., Kenny, S. B., & Derr, M. A. (1983). Hierarchical control of rapid movement sequences. *Journal of Experimental Psychology: Human Perception & Performance, 9*, 86–102.

Rosenbaum, D. A., Loukopoulis, L. D., Meulenbroek, R. G. J., Vaughn, J., & Englebrecht, S.E. (1995). Planning reaches by evaluating stored postures. *Psychological Review, 102*, 28–67.

Saltzman, E. L., & Kelso, J. A. S. (1983). Toward a dynamical account of motor memory and control. In R. A. Magill (Ed.) *Memory and control of action* (pp. 17–38). Amsterdam: North-Holland.

Scheidt, R. A., Dingwell, J. B., & Mussa-Ivaldi, F. A. (2001). Learning to move amid uncertainty. *Journal of Neurophysiology, 86*, 971–985.

Schvaneveldt, R. W., & Chase, W. G. (1969). Sequential effect in choice reaction time. *Journal of Experimental Psychology, 80*, 1–8.

Schmidt, R. A. (1975). A schema theory of discrete motor skill learning. *Psychological Review, 82*, 225–260.

Smith, M. C. (1968). The repetition effect and short-term memory. *Journal of Experimental Psychology, 77*, 435–439.

Smith, E. E., Chase, W. G., & Smith, P. G. (1973). Stimulus and response repetition effects in retrieval from short-term memory: Trace decay and memory search. *Journal of Experimental Psychology, 98*, 413–422.

Vetter, P., & Wolpert, D. M. (2000). Context estimation for sensorimotor control. *Journal of Neurophysiology, 84*, 1026–1034.

Weiss, Y., Simoncelli, E. P., & Adelson, E. H. (2002). Motion illusions as optimal percepts. *Nature Neuroscience, 5*, 598–604.

Young, D. E., Cohen, M. J., & Husak, W. S. (1993). Contextual interference and motor skill acquisition: On the processes that influence retention. *Human Movement Science, 12*, 577–600.

SELF-GENERATION AND MEMORY

Neil W. Mulligan and Jeffrey P. Lozito

I. Introduction

It is probably regarded as a truism that active or self-initiated encoding produces superior memory than does passive or perceptual encoding. There are any number of research areas that support such a view. In educational research, much is written on the superiority of active as opposed to passive learning strategies (e.g., Kalem & Fer, 2003; Michael & Modell, 2003). Research on persuasion typically shows that self-generated arguments are better remembered than arguments supplied by a speaker (e.g., Petty, Ostrom, & Brock, 1981). Memory research indicates that carrying out an action produces better memory for the act than merely viewing the action or hearing a verbal description of the action (*the enactment effect*; Engelkamp, 1998; Zimmer, Cohen, Guynn, Engelkamp, Kormi-Nouri, & Foley, 2001). Likewise, generating verbal materials leads to better memory than does reading the same materials (*the generation effect*; Slamecka & Graf, 1978). The effects of semantic elaboration may be encompassed in this generalization as well: greater semantic elaboration implies both greater active involvement with the materials and heavier reliance on self-initiated processing (e.g., Tailby & Haslam, 2003). This idea is also implied by theories of cognitive aging that focus on reduced cognitive control, with a concomitant reduction in self-initiated encoding (and retrieval) processes, as the locus of age-related declines in memory (e.g., Anderson & Craik, 2000). These and other findings are quite supportive of the traditional view "that material

0079-7421/04 $35.00

actively produced by the subject has a privileged place in retrieval, when compared to material passively received" (Greenwald, 1981, p. 218).

The present chapter explores some of the effects of self-generation on memory by reviewing recent research on the generation effect and a related phenomenon, the perceptual-interference effect. The generation effect has the virtue of isolating the effects of self-generation in a way that many other research procedures do not. Specifically, the typical generation manipulation is constrained so that the self-generated and passively processed materials are equivalent, eliminating the concern of item-selection confounds that haunt research using unconstrained generative or active-encoding procedures (Slamecka & Graf, 1978; see Greene, 1992, for discussion). A consideration of generation research affords an opportunity to determine the extent to which self-generation enhances memory. An accumulating body of research indicates that generation does not generally enhance memory but rather enhances only certain aspects of memory, and fails to enhance, or may even disrupt, other aspects of memory. We review research on this issue and review theoretical accounts suggesting that generation institutes a trade-off, enhancing some forms of memory but disrupting others.

II. The Generation Effect

A. Breadth of the Generation Effect

The generation effect has been demonstrated in a variety of ways. The most common generation manipulations use simple verbal materials. In one encoding condition, critical words are generated (e.g., from an antonym cue, *hot–c___*). In a second condition, critical words are simply read (typically accompanied by the same cue, e.g., *hot–cold*). The usual finding is that generated words are better recalled or recognized on a subsequent memory test (e.g., Mulligan, 2001; Slamecka & Graf, 1978). The generation effect has been found with a variety of generation tasks, including generation from antonyms or semantic associates (e.g., Jacoby, 1983; Mulligan, 2001; Slamecka & Graf, 1978), from sentence frames (Masson & MacLeod, 1992), from rhyme cues (e.g., *fold–c___*, for *cold*, Slamecka & Graf, 1978), from second-language translations (O'Neill, Roy, & Tremblay, 1993), from definitions (e.g., de Winstanley, 1995), and from fragments or anagrams (e.g., *c_ld* or *ocld* for *cold*; e.g., Kinoshita, 1989; Mulligan, 2002b; Nairne, Pusen, & Widner, 1985).

Generation effects occur with a variety of materials in addition to single words. For example, Gardiner and Hampton (1985) found generation effects with meaningful compounds and abbreviations. In these experiments, participants either read familiar compound words or abbreviations (e.g., *cheese cake, ET*) or generated them (by transposing the provided words or letters; e.g., *cake cheese*; see also, Mulligan, 2002b). In both cases, recall of the compounds or abbreviations was greater in the generate condition. Generation effects are likewise found at the level of sentences and coherent text. Memory for sentences is greater when the sentences are generated from words presented in a scrambled order (Graf, 1982). Similarly, better memory results when text is generated from randomly ordered sentences than when it is read in the correct sentence order (McDaniel, Einstein, Dunay, & Cobb, 1986).

The generation effect extends beyond verbal materials. Smith and Healy (1998) presented participants with arithmetic problems in which the answer was either supplied (the "read" condition, e.g., $5 \times 12 = 60$) or had to be generated (e.g., $5 \times 12 = ?$). Later recall of the problem answers was substantially higher for the "generated" than "read" answers (see also Gardiner & Rowley, 1984). Pictures can also produce a generation effect. In Kinjo and Snodgrass's (2000) study, participants named completed pictures or named fragmented pictures (the generate condition). Subsequent recall and recognition of picture names was higher in the generate than name condition. Similarly, Peynircioglu (1989) had participants draw objects from descriptions, copy objects from provided pictures, or simply look at pictures during encoding. Memory for the pictures was greatest when participants had previously generated the drawings from descriptions (Wills, Soraci, Chechile, & Taylor, 2000).

It is clear from this brief review that the generation effect generalizes over manipulations and materials. It also generalizes over memory tests. In the various studies previously cited, generation effects have been found on tests of free recall, cued recall, recognition, and comprehension.

The breadth of the generation effect is also exhibited in some of its applications. Foos, Mora, and Tkacz (1994) applied generation manipulations to students' study techniques. Students learned textual material under one of several study conditions. One group generated an outline for the text, another group generated study questions, and control groups read the text with outlines or study questions provided for them. When tested two days later, the groups that had generated their own study materials remembered more about the text. Tailby and Haslam (2003) investigated the errorless learning techniques used to improve memory performance in memory-impaired populations. The authors found that including a generation component enhanced the effectiveness of this procedure. A final application comes from advertising research, in which generative processing has been found to enhance memory for the content of ads. Sengupta and Gorn (2002) presented participants with print advertisements. In the generate condition, the graphics of the advertisement omitted a key detail. The detail was implied by the graphics of the ad (e.g., the missing element was outlined in such a way as to clearly indicate the identity of the missing component), or the detail was implied by participants' prior knowledge of the ad campaign (e.g., a print ad for Marlboro cigarettes from which the iconic Marlboro Man was missing). The generate conditions were contrasted with conditions in which the critical element appeared in the ad. Recall of both the critical element and the brand name were greater when the element was missing from (but implied by) the advertisement. Sengupta and Gorn attributed this effect to the covert generation of the missing detail.

B. Some Limiting Conditions of the Generation Effect

Despite the impressive generality of the generation effect, there are a number of important limiting conditions. Perhaps the most important for present purposes concerns the impact of experimental design. Research using the typical generation manipulation (with verbal materials, e.g., *hot–c___*) has found that when the generate and read conditions are manipulated between subjects, the generate condition often fails to produce superior recall (e.g., Grosofsky, Payne, & Campbell, 1994; Hirshman & Bjork, 1988; Slamecka & Katsaiti, 1987). Likewise, if the generate and read items are presented in separate sublists (a within-subjects, pure-list design), the generation effect is often not obtained in recall (Nairne, Reigler, & Serra, 1991; Serra & Nairne, 1993). Furthermore, as will be described in detail later, there are even conditions under which a between-subjects manipulation of generation produces a negative generation effect, in which the read condition produces superior recall than the generate condition (Schmidt & Cherry, 1989; Steffens & Erdfelder, 1998).

Another important determinant of the generation effect is the type of materials used. The generation effect is typically not obtained with unfamiliar materials, such as nonwords and unfamiliar word compounds (e.g., Gardiner, Gregg, & Hampton, 1988; Mulligan, 2002c; Payne, Neely, & Burns, 1986). For example, in Payne et al. (1986), participants generated nonwords that rhymed with cue words (e.g., *flop–tr___*, to generate the nonword *trop*) or read the nonwords in the same context. In Mulligan (2002c), participants generated pronounceable nonwords by transposing the first two letters (e.g., *alrt* for *lart*). In both studies, generating nonwords failed to enhance recognition or recall relative to the reading condition. Similar results were reported by Gardiner and Hampton (1985), who had participants generate or read word compounds that were familiar (e.g., *cheese cake*) or unfamiliar (e.g., *tomato cake*). On a recall test, a generation advantage was found for the familiar but not the unfamiliar compounds (a pattern that extends to recognition; Mulligan, 2002c). Gardiner and Hampton (1985) found the same result for familiar and unfamiliar abbreviations (e.g., *ET* and

ES, respectively). These results imply that generation effects are only obtained for stimuli with preexisting semantic and/or lexical representations (e.g., Gardiner & Hampton, 1985; Gardiner et al., 1988; Payne et al., 1986; cf. Johns & Swanson, 1988).

Finally, negative generation effects have been reported for tests of order memory. Although generation may enhance memory for the occurrence of a stimulus, it can disrupt memory for serial order information (e.g., Burns, 1996; Mulligan, 2002c; Nairne et al., 1991; Serra & Nairne, 1993).[1]

III. Trade-off Accounts of the Generation Effect

This initial review of generation research shows that self-generation does not always enhance memory, a conclusion that will be strengthened as additional results are considered in subsequent sections. Indeed, it appears that generation may impair memory for the certain aspects of the encoded event and can even impair recall for the central, generated stimulus under certain conditions. Next, we consider two theories designed to account for positive, null, and negative effects of generation. Although the two accounts differ in some particulars, they are similar in proposing that generation sometimes induces an encoding tradeoff, accentuating information about the individual item characteristics of the generated stimulus at the cost of disrupting associations between the stimulus and other aspects of the unfolding episodic context.

A. The Multifactor Account

Several theories have been advanced to accommodate the pattern of positive, null, and negative effects that generation can produce. Perhaps most successful is the multifactor account (e.g., Hunt & McDaniel, 1993; McDaniel, Wadill, & Einstein, 1988; Steffens & Erdfelder, 1998), rooted in the distinction between item-specific and relational information (Hunt & McDaniel, 1993). This view proposes that a complete account of the generation effect must take into consideration which sources of information are germane to the generation task and how the processed information transfers to the retrieval task (e.g., de Winstanley & Bjork, 1997; Hirshman & Bjork, 1988; Hunt & McDaniel, 1993; McDaniel et al., 1988; Mulligan, 2001; Steffens & Erdfelder, 1998).

[1] Negative generation effects have also been found on perceptual implicit tests, such as perceptual identification and word-fragment completion (see Roediger & McDermott, 1993, for review). Because the present chapter focuses on explicit memory, these results are not described in detail.

Consider a typical generation manipulation in which a cue word accompanies a fragment of the target item (e.g., *hot–c.—* or *stripes–z_br_*). According to the multifactor view, generation enhances the processing of item-specific features of the target item, those characteristics that differentiate the item from other items in the list and increase item distinctiveness (e.g., Begg, Snider, Foley, & Goddard, 1989; Gardiner & Hampton, 1988). Thus, whether implemented in between- or within-subjects designs, generation enhances performance on recognition memory, a test particularly sensitive to item-specific encoding (Begg et al., 1989; Hunt & McDaniel, 1993; Mulligan, 2002b). When a cue word accompanies the target item at encoding, the multifactor view proposes that generation also enhances the processing of the cue–target relation, a form of relational processing particularly important for later cued recall (e.g., Hirshman & Bjork, 1988).

A second type of relational information is intertarget relational information, which refers to the processing of relationships between target items of different study pairs (rather than between the cue and target within a study trial). For present purposes, this is the critical type of relational information (and is sometimes referred to simply as relational information). Free recall of targets relies heavily on this type of relational encoding (in addition to relying on item-specific encoding; e.g., Hirshman & Bjork, 1988; Hunt & McDaniel, 1993; Steffens & Erdfelder, 1998). Under the multifactor view, generation enhances item-specific and cue–target relational encoding but may disrupt intertarget relational encoding (e.g., Hirshman & Bjork, 1988; McDaniel et al., 1988; Nairne et al., 1991; Serra & Nairne, 1993). In particular, when the target items are nominally unrelated, processing resources focus on the target item and the cue–target relation, and are drawn away from forming associations between target items. In pure lists, generation will cause a listwide disruption of relational encoding, detracting from the usual generation effect in recall and causing it to disappear or reverse (e.g., Grosofsky et al., 1994; Hirshman & Bjork, 1988; Slamecka & Katsaiti, 1987; Steffens & Erdfelder, 1998). Despite this, the generation advantage persists in recognition, a test with little reliance on intertarget processing (e.g., Begg et al., 1989; Mulligan, 2002b). If generate and read items are intermixed, any disruption of relational processing caused by generation affects temporally adjacent read items as well. The equivalent relational encoding for read and generate items in a mixed list, in turn, permits the superior item-specific encoding in the generate condition to produce a recall advantage (Hunt & McDaniel, 1993).

Although generation is typically expected to impair relational encoding, there are conditions under which generation may enhance this type of processing. Specifically, the multifactor account conceives of generation as a problem-solving task (Jacoby, 1978) in which any relevant information is exploited (and its encoding enhanced, Hunt & McDaniel, 1993; McDaniel et al., 1988). Typically, information specific to the target (item-specific information) and information in the cue (the cue–target relation) are the only useful bases for generation and, as a result, these types of information are better encoded. However, if the study list is structured such that information from earlier targets is useful in the generation of subsequent targets, then intertarget relational processing will be enhanced. For instance, if the target items are all members of a common category, then processing their common characteristics would assist generation. Consequently, when structured lists are used, generation effects are obtained in free recall for between-subjects designs (e.g., de Winstanley et al., 1996; McDaniel et al., 1988; Mulligan, 2001). Also, under these conditions, generation leads to higher levels of category clustering than the read condition, providing additional evidence for enhanced intertarget processing (de Winstanley & Bjork, 1997; de Winstanley et al., 1996; McDaniel et al., 1988; Mulligan, 2001), a point to which we return shortly. With unrelated targets, intertarget processing is not useful and is neglected in favor of item-specific and cue–target relational processing. In summary, the multifactor view suggests that for unrelated target items, generation enhances item-specific and cue–target relational encoding but disrupts intertarget relational processing. For related target items, generation enhances all three types of information.

B. The Item-Order Account

Nairne et al. (1991; Serra & Nairne, 1993) found that although generation enhances memory for the occurrence of an item, it disrupts memory for the order in which the items were presented. Nairne et al. (1991) proposed that this decrement in order encoding is causally related to the moderating role of experimental design and that the effects of generation on item and order information are central to understanding the effects of generation on memory in general (Burns, 1996; DeLosh & McDaniel, 1996). Similar to the multifactor view, this account proposes that the generation condition institutes a trade-off in the encoding of item and order information, where order information is thought to be mediated by associations between items within an encoding context (e.g., Engelkamp & Dehn, 2000; Greene, Thapar, & Westerman, 1998; Hunt & McDaniel, 1993; McDaniel, DeLosh, & Merritt, 2000).

This view has been stated more generally by DeLosh and McDaniel (1996; Engelkamp & Dehn, 2000; McDaniel et al., 2000), who suggested that several memory effects (e.g., generation effect, bizarreness effects, the enactment effect, and the word-frequency effect) produce such a processing trade-off. The more unusual encoding condition (e.g., the generate condition, the bizarre condition, the enacted condition, low-frequency words) attracts greater processing of item features at the expense of encoding order and other forms of relational information. As stated by DeLosh and McDaniel (1996, p. 1137), ". . . resources are lured to processing and interpreting the unusual items, leaving fewer resources (or reducing attention) for the encoding of serial-order information. More generally, whenever items attract greater elaboration or processing of the individual features of the items, order encoding is expected to suffer."

Assuming that both item and order information are important determinants of free recall (Hunt & McDaniel, 1993; Nairne et al., 1991), this view accounts for the dependence of generation effects on experimental design in much the same way as the multifactor account. Specifically, when generate items are presented in a pure list, disruption of order and interitem encoding is listwide and detracts from the typical generation effect in recall (e.g., Hirshman & Bjork, 1988; Kinoshita, 1989; Slamecka & Katsaiti, 1987; Steffens & Erdfelder, 1998). In mixed lists, the disruption of order information affects read and generate items equally, permitting the superior item encoding in the generate condition to produce a recall advantage (Hunt & McDaniel, 1993; Nairne et al., 1991).

C. Other Trade-off Accounts

Jurica and Shimamura (1999) proposed a trade-off account similar to the foregoing. They adopted the common perspective that memory encoding requires limited-capacity processing resources and that these resources are allocated flexibly in encoding various aspects of an experience. Jurica and Shimamura argued that generation requires a focus on the item itself, increasing encoding of item-specific information but at a cost to the encoding of associations between the item and elements of the surrounding context. Thus, similar to the multifactor and item-order accounts, Jurica and Shimamura argue that generation induces a trade-off in the encoding of item and contextual information, or associative information more generally.

The processing account stems from research on implicit memory and, like the preceding accounts, claims that generation does not generally enhance memory (Jacoby, 1983; Roediger & McDermott, 1993). Rather, generation produces a difference in what is encoded, a difference that evinces itself in an important dissociation between implicit and explicit test performance. This dissociation was originally demonstrated in a study by Jacoby (1983), in which participants read words out of context (e.g., *xxx–cold*), read words in a meaningful context (e.g., *hot–cold*), or generated words from context (e.g., *hot–????*). Participants' memory for the words was then tested with either an explicit (recognition memory) or an implicit (perceptual identification) test. For recognition, the generated words produced the greatest accuracy, followed by words read in context and then words read out of context;

this is the traditional generation effect. On the perceptual-identification task, the opposite results obtained; reading words out of context produced the most priming, followed by reading words in context. The generate condition produced the least priming. Jacoby (1983) argued that generating a word from a meaningful associate necessitates substantial conceptual processing of the target. In contrast, reading a word out of context requires substantial perceptual processing of the target and less conceptual processing. Finally, reading a word in context produces intermediate levels of both conceptual and perceptual processing. This analysis was incorporated into the transfer-appropriate-processing account of implicit memory (Roediger & McDermott, 1993). Although we do not focus on implicit memory in the present chapter, this analysis is useful for some of the results discussed later.

IV. The Perceptual-Interference Effect

A. The Perceptual-Interference Effect and Similarities to the Generation Effect

The *perceptual interference effect* refers to the counterintuitive finding that interfering with perception during stimulus encoding can enhance later memory performance (Hirshman & Mulligan, 1991; Hirshman, Trembath, & Mulligan, 1994; Nairne, 1988). This phenomenon is typically investigated by presenting study words in one of two conditions. In the perceptual interference condition, each word is presented on a computer screen very briefly (e.g., 100 ms) and then backward masked by a row of *X*s. In the intact condition, words are presented on the screen for a longer duration (e.g., 2.5 s) with no backward mask. In both conditions, the participant's task is to identify the word. It should be noted that the perceptual-interference condition interferes with perception (as measured by naming reaction times; Hirshman et al., 1994) but does not prevent successful identification. The timing of the mask permits high levels of identification (usually higher than 95% correct for common words). The critical finding is that perceptual interference actually leads to superior memory performance on later tests such as recognition, free recall, and cued recall (Mulligan, 1996, 1999).

The perceptual-interference effect bears important similarities to the generation effect.[2] Most basically, perceptual interference and generation both enhance later item memory compared to the intact (or read) condition. Second, like the generation effect, the perceptual interference effect is

[2] Although we focus on the similarities, there are differences as well, indicating that the two effects are not completely equivalent. These differences lie primarily in the effects of generation and perceptual interference on implicit memory tests (see Mulligan, 2002a, for discussion).

moderated by design type (Mulligan, 1999, 2002c; Westerman & Greene, 1997). Perceptual interference consistently increases recall in mixed-list designs but not in between-subject designs (Mulligan, 1999; see Westerman & Greene, 1997, for a similar result). Third, both generation and perceptual interference can disrupt order memory (e.g., Burns, 1996; Mulligan, 1999, 2000a; Nairne et al., 1991). In addition, when order information is an important determinant of recall, both the generation and perceptual-interference effects can reverse, with the intact condition leading to better recall (Mulligan, 1999, 2000a, 2002c; Nairne et al., 1991). Both the generation and perceptual-interference effects are sensitive to the type of stimulus materials, occurring with words but typically not with nonwords (Mulligan, 2002c; Payne et al., 1986; Westerman & Greene, 1997). Finally, generation and perceptual interference produce similar patterns of item gains and losses across multiple recall tests (Mulligan, 2000b, 2001). Given the similarities between these two effects, it is not surprising that they can be accommodated within a common theoretical framework, based on the item-specific–relational distinction. However, we must first consider a specialized account of the perceptual-interference effect before we embed this account in the more general item-specific–relational framework.

B. Theoretical Analyses of the Perceptual-Interference Effect

1. *The Compensatory-Processing Account*

Mulligan (1996) and Hirshman et al. (1994) tested a number of accounts of the perceptual-interference effect (e.g., differential rehearsal, elaborative rehearsal, encoding effort, visual distinctiveness, and demand characteristics) and found that the compensatory processing hypothesis best accounted for the extant data (also see Mulligan, 1998, 1999, 2002a). This account is predicated on studies and models of word perception that indicate that phonological, lexical, and semantic information play a role in word perception (e.g., Balota, 1990; Brown, Roberts, & Besner, 2001; Pexman, Lupker, & Hino, 2002; Plaut, McClelland, Seidenberg, & Patterson, 1996). The account proposes that the presentation of a word's visual features activates not only low-level visual information but feeds activation to higher level, nonvisual representations (e.g., phonology, meaning, abstract lexical information). At some point in the processing of the perceptual-interference words, the backward mask renders visual information useless. This forces the perceptual system to rely on the partially activated higher-level information to finish the process of word identification. According to the compensatory-processing account, the differential processing of this higher-level information enhances later memory (see Mulligan, 1996, 1999, for more detail). In the intact condition, no extra processing of the higher-level information is necessary because the visual information is available over the entire course of word identification.

2. *Integrating the Compensatory-Processing Account into the Item-Specific–Relational Framework*

The higher-level information in the compensatory-processing account has been variously characterized as semantic, lexical, or phonological (the results of Mulligan, 1998, argue for a semantic basis). Regardless, for present purposes, the critical attribute of this information is that it is encoded during perception (Hirshman et al., 1994; Mulligan, 2000a). Evidence comes from experiments in which the backward mask is delayed so that it no longer interferes with word identification (e.g., 266 ms). A delayed mask no longer produces the perceptual-interference advantage in recognition (Mulligan, 2000a,b) or recall (Hirshman et al., 1994). Thus, the effect of perceptual interference, and the representations that underlie it, appear to arise at a very early stage (i.e., during word perception; see Mulligan, 1999, for more evidence on this point).

The representations underlying the perceptual-interference effect are encoded during initial word perception. In this sense, these are representations of the study item in isolation, as opposed to representations of the relations among ongoing events within the encoding context (e.g., associations between items on the list, associations between the item and spatiotemporal context, etc.). Consequently, the compensatory-processing hypothesis might be embedded within the broader item-specific–relational distinction, a framework that differentiates between encodings of items or events in isolation and encodings of relationships among items and events.

According to this analysis, the perceptual-interference effect is based on a type of item-specific information. Like generation, the item-specific–relational framework accounts for many of the observed effects of perceptual interference. First, perceptual interference enhances free recall and recognition, both of which are sensitive to item-specific information (Mulligan, 1999; Westerman & Greene, 1997). However, recognition tests are more sensitive to item-specific information than are free recall tests, which are sensitive to both item-specific and relational information. As a result, perceptual interference effects are more consistently observed on tests of recognition memory (cf. Hirshman & Mulligan, 1991; Mulligan, 1999; Nairne, 1988). Likewise, the dependence of the perceptual-interference effect on experimental design receives the same account as was applied to the generation effect (previously described).

More important, embedding the compensatory processing account within the item-specific–relational framework has generated a number of predictions, predictions that were not forthcoming from the compensatory processing account. These predictions stem quite naturally from the trade-off accounts implied by both the item-specific–relational framework and the item-order account. In the next section, we described this research.

V. The Effects of Generation and Perceptual Interference on Measures of Relational, Order, and Associative Information

The trade-off accounts suggest that generation and perceptual interference enhance the processing of item-specific features of the target item (and the cue-target relation in the case of generation from a cue). In contrast to item-specific and cue-target relational information is the arbitrarily large set of associations that might be formed between the target item and other stimuli in the encoding environment, including associations between target items of different study pairs (intertarget relational information), associations between a target and elements of spatiotemporal context (contextual associations), and associations that underlie serial order memory. According to the trade-off accounts, both generation and perceptual interference draw encoding resources to the target item (and cue–target relation), and away from the encoding of intertarget relational, contextual, or order associations. In this section, we review studies that have assessed the trade-off accounts using a variety of measures of relational, order, and associative information. These include studies that assess category clustering in recall, order memory, gains and losses across multiple recall tests, and context memory.

A. Category Clustering

One traditional measure of relational encoding is the amount of category clustering in recall (Hunt & McDaniel, 1993; Murphy, 1979). Experiments on clustering typically use study materials consisting of multiple examples from each of several taxonomic categories. The order in which the words are subsequently recalled is preserved, and the recall protocols are examined to determine the extent to which members from the same category are recalled contiguously (in category clusters or repetitions). Categorizable materials provide a basis for assessing interitem relational processing during encoding. The clustering in recall is thought to reflect the degree to which members of the same category were rehearsed together during the encoding session; that is, the clustering measure reflects the degree to which relational encoding has occurred along the dimension of shared categories (Hunt & McDaniel, 1993). Examples from category norms provide an a priori basis for assessing relational encoding, in contrast to the more idiosyncratic relational encoding that might occur with nominally unrelated items. A number of different measures of category clustering have been developed, applicable to different experimental designs (between-subjects, within-subject mixed lists, within-subjects pure lists), assessing repetition or clustering in somewhat different ways, and incorporating various corrections for chance level clustering (Murphy, 1979). Of these, the most commonly used is the adjusted-ratio-of-clustering (ARC) score (Roenker, Thompson, & Brown, 1971).

There are several demonstrations that clustering scores track the amount of relational encoding. First, when the study list is organized so that its categorical structure is obvious, overall recall and clustering scores increase. This is typically done with a blocked presentation, in which all the study words from a given category are presented in sequence. In the contrasting random condition, the study words are randomly intermixed, rendering list structure less obvious. The shared category relationship between items is a more important basis of encoding in the blocked than random condition, as reflected by enhanced category clustering (e.g., Cofer, Bruce, & Reicher, 1966; Horton & Cofer, 1975). Likewise, when the words are presented in a random order and participants are asked to sort the words by category (as opposed to performing a more individuating task such as rating each word for pleasantness), both recall and category clustering increase (Hunt & Einstein, 1981; Hunt & McDaniel, 1993).

1. *Effects of Generation on Category Clustering*

The multifactor account provides a detailed set of expectations about the relationship between generation and category clustering. Recall that the default expectation of the tradeoff account is that generation disrupts inter-item relational encoding in a between-subjects (or pure list) design but not in a mixed-list design. However, this expectation is for unrelated target items. Use of the category clustering measure entails the use of (categorically) related targets. For related items, the predictions differ. Related target items are assumed to encourage the processing of intertarget relations in the generate condition, as participants attempt to capitalize on information pertinent to the generation task. To the extent that the intertarget relations are apparent, the generate condition is expected to produce greater relational encoding than the read condition. Applied to category clustering, this analysis indicates that if the relationship between target words is both noticed and useful for generation, then the generate condition should enhance category clustering in recall. On the other hand, if the relationship is either not noticed or not useful for generation, then generation should produce less relational encoding and, thus, less clustering than the read condition. It should be noted that these predictions are made for between-subject (or pure-list) experiments, which encompass all the studies reviewed later.

Generally, the results are in accord with the expectations. First, in several experiments, the target items were members of common categories, and the targets were presented in blocks (all examples from a category presented in sequence), rendering the category structure of the list apparent. In these studies, generation leads to higher levels of category clustering than the read condition (de Winstanley & Bjork, 1997; de Winstanley et al., 1996; McDaniel et al., 1988; Mulligan, 2001). In contrast, when the structure of the list was not obvious or the categorical information was not relevant to generation, then the read condition produced greater clustering than the generate condition (Burns, 1990, 1992; de Winstanley et al., 1996). Perhaps the best example comes from de Winstanley et al. (1996), in which the same study materials were presented in blocked or nonblocked fashion (the latter case is not labeled "random" because target items from the same categories were purposely and maximally separated). For blocked presentation, category clustering was higher for generate than read. For the nonblocked presentation, the opposite pattern obtained.

Mulligan and Duke (2002, Experiment 2) examined the negative generation effect in recall and provided another assessment of generation's effect on category clustering. In a review of the negative generation effect, Steffens and Erdfelder (1998) argued that negative generation effects occur in between-subjects designs when the generation task conflicts with the intertarget relations. The study materials in Mulligan and Duke (2002) consisted of rhyming word pairs in which the second word of each pair (the targets) consisted of examples from each of a number of categories. The study list was organized so that targets from the same category appeared in sequential trials. In the generation group, the target word was generated from the rhyming cue; in the read group, both words were presented intact. For these materials, the intertarget relation is categorical-semantic, and the cue–target relation is phonological. Steffens and Erdfelder (1998) proposed that under these conditions, the generation task is especially disruptive of intertarget relational processing. Consequently, the generation condition should produce worse recall (which has a heavy reliance on intertarget relational information) and less category clustering.

The results of Mulligan and Duke (2002) were consistent with these expectations. The generate group produced lower recall and less category clustering than the read group, indicating disrupted relational encoding. In a second test condition, the same encoding materials and conditions were assessed with a recognition test, a test sensitive to item-specific encoding and relatively insensitive to interitem relational encoding. On this task, the typical generation effect was found: the generation group produced superior recognition. This pair of results conforms well with the multifactor account: generation disrupted interitem relational encoding while simultaneously enhancing item-specific information.

2. *Effects of Perceptual Interference on Category Clustering*

Mulligan (1999) examined the effects of perceptual interference in terms of the item-specific–relational account. According to this analysis, perceptual interference enhances item-specific processing but not interitem relational encoding. As is typical in assessments of category clustering, Mulligan used study lists composed of multiple examples from each of several categories. Mulligan contrasted the perceptual-interference manipulation, which is assumed to increase recall via enhanced item-specific processing, with the list organization manipulation, which enhances recall by increasing the amount of relational encoding. Specifically, these experiments varied list organization (blocked by category vs. random ordering) and encoding condition (perceptual-interference vs. intact). Blocking by category and perceptual interference both enhanced overall recall, but they had opposite effects on category clustering. Blocked presentation increased clustering (compared to the random condition), whereas perceptual interference significantly decreased clustering (relative to the intact condition). Thus, the item-specific–relational predictions were borne out: perceptual interference appears to enhance recall via item-specific processing without enhancing relational processing.

The effects of perceptual-interference on category clustering are generally but not completely consistent with those of generation. Specifically, perceptual interference disrupted clustering for both blocked and random list conditions. Generation disrupts clustering for random lists and also for block lists in some cases, as previously reviewed (Burns, 1990; Mulligan & Duke, 2002). However, if the generation task and the intertarget relations are congruent (e.g., both semantic–categorical), then generation enhances clustering for blocked lists (e.g., de Winstanley & Bjork, 1997; de Winstanley et al., 1996; Mulligan, 2001). The fact that perceptual interference fails to enhance clustering with blocked lists may indicate that category membership cannot be exploited in the course of word perception, whereas it can be used in generation tasks.

B. Order Memory

Nairne et al. (1991; Serra & Nairne, 1993) introduced a methodology that a number of researchers have since used to assess the effects of various encoding manipulations on item and order memory (e.g., DeLosh & McDaniel, 1996; Engelkamp & Dehn, 2000; Engelkamp, Jahn, & Seiler, 2003; Greene et al., 1998; Mulligan, 1999, 2000, 2002c; Olofsson, 1997). In this paradigm, participants are presented with multiple study–test trials. On each trial, a short study list is presented. Encoding conditions (e.g., generate vs. read) are either manipulated between lists (a pure-list design) or within lists (a mixed-list design). The study list is followed by a short period of distraction (e.g., categorizing digits as odd or even for 60 s). This is followed by either a free recall or an order reconstruction test. In the latter test, the study items are re-presented in a random order and the participant is asked to recreate the original order of presentation.[3]

In this paradigm, order information appears to be an important determinant of free recall (e.g., DeLosh & McDaniel, 1996; Nairne et al., 1991; Serra & Nairne, 1993). In the pure-list design, this paradigm affords two measures of order memory. The more straightforward assessment is the percent correct on the order reconstruction test. The second measure is the Asch–Ebenholtz (1962) index, which assesses the use of order information in free recall. This index measures the extent to which relative serial order at study is preserved in the order in which words are recalled. The index can be used to assess seriation strategies in free recall and whether the use of order memory differs across conditions.

1. Effects of Perceptual Interference and Generation on Order Memory

Recall that the item-order account predicts that generation and perceptual interference disrupt order memory in pure-list but not mixed-list designs. The account suggests that both manipulations attract attention to the item characteristics of the target and detract from the processing of associations supporting order memory. In pure lists, this will produce worse order memory in the generate or perceptual-interference condition than in the read or intact condition. In mixed lists, the order-disrupting effects of generation or perceptual-interference will affect (and degrade) the temporally contiguous read or intact items. Thus, the difference in order memory should be attenuated or eliminated in mixed-list designs.

Mulligan (1999, Experiment 4) examined the effects of perceptual interference on order memory using Nairne et al.'s (1991) paradigm. In each study-test block, the eight (unrelated) study words were presented in either the perceptual-interference or intact condition (a pure list design). The study list was followed by a brief period of distraction, which in turn was followed by either an order reconstruction test or a free recall test. The results are presented in Fig. 1a and 1b.

Figure 1a shows the results of the order reconstruction test, the proportion of study words allocated to their original position as a function of the

[3] In another variant of the experiment, half the study lists are followed by order reconstruction, and the other half are not immediately tested (a short rest period replaces the test phase of the study-test block). The words from these lists are tested with an end-of-session recognition test. The end-of-session test is used because immediately recognition tests for short study lists would likely yield ceiling-level performance.

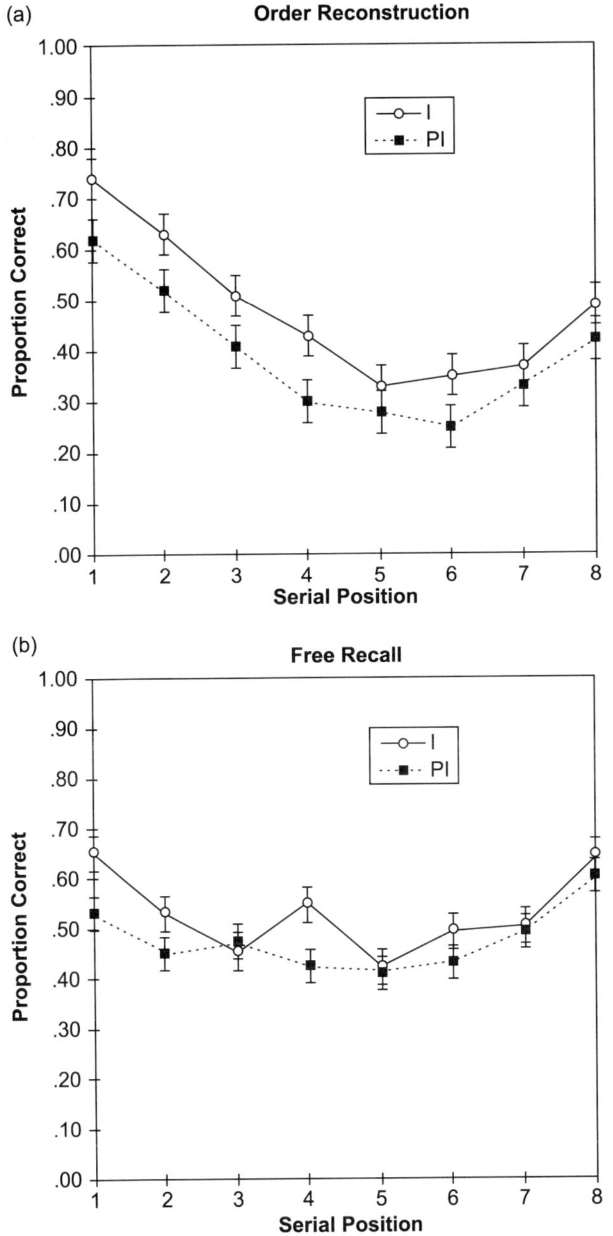

Fig. 1. (a) Mulligan (1999, p. 62) Experiment 4: Mean order reconstruction scores (±SE) for the Intact (I) and Perceptual-Interference (PI) conditions as a function of serial position. Copyright 1999 by the American Psychological Association. Used with permission. (b) Mulligan (1999, p. 62) Experiment 4: Mean recall performance (±SE) for the Intact (I) and Perceptual-Interference (PI) conditions as a function of serial position. Copyright 1999 by the American Psychological Association. Used with permission.

serial position in the study list. The results indicated significant effects of serial position and of encoding condition (with no interaction). The serial position effect reflects a strong primacy effect and an approximately bow-shaped form, typical of other studies using this paradigm (e.g., Nairne et al., 1991). More important, the effect of encoding condition indicates that perceptual interference disrupted order memory.

The results of the free recall test (Fig. 1b) also exhibit effects of serial position and encoding condition (with no significant interaction). The latter effect indicates that perceptual interference reduced recall. This negative perceptual-interference effect is in contrast to the typical positive effect in recall and recognition. More important, the obtained reversal of the perceptual-interference effect is just what is expected if free recall is especially reliant on order information in this paradigm, a result that comports well with the deficient order memory in the perceptual-interference condition. Likewise, the Asch–Ebenholtz index was significantly higher in the intact than perceptual-interference condition, with means of .69 and .60, respectively. This converges with the results of the order reconstruction test to indicate that perceptual interference disrupts order memory.

Mulligan (1999) also assessed order memory in mixed-list experiments. In these experiments, perceptual interference produced little or no disruption to order memory, in line with the item-order account. In addition, the recall trials either demonstrated no effect or a positive effect of perceptual interference.

With regard to generation, similar results are found. Nairne et al. (1991) demonstrated in a pure-list design that generation produced worse performance on order reconstruction and free recall than did the read condition (Mulligan, 2002c). In a mixed-list design, however, both effects were eliminated; generation affected neither order reconstruction nor free recall. These results were replicated by Serra and Nairne (1993), who also showed that the results generalize to incidental learning conditions. Burns (1996) demonstrated a similar set of results using a more traditional study-test design, which used a relatively long study list, a single study-test block, and a longer retention interval. Burns's study more closely matches the experimental procedures that form the bulk of the generation literature. Even under these conditions, generation disrupted order memory (Burns, 1996). The results of Serra and Nairne and of Burns are important in demonstrating the generality of the results of Nairne et al. (1991) and in indicating that the item-order tradeoff is not simply a by-product of specialized, intentional, encoding strategies applicable only to Nairne et al.'s (1991) paradigm.

Finally, a recent paper by Kelley and Nairne (2001) merits comment. This paper investigated the effects of isolation on order memory and found that isolates (items that differ from the rest of the study list) produce superior order reconstruction than nonisolates (or context items). In one version of this study, the isolate was a single generate item amidst a set of read items. In this case, the isolated generate item produced better order memory. This indicates that the positive effects of isolation can offset the negative effects of generation. However, it should be kept in mind that all other things (e.g., isolation status) being equal, generation produces worse order memory than reading.

2. *Tests of Relative Recency Versus Absolute Order*

In the order reconstruction test, an item must be assigned to its exact study position to be scored correct. In this sense, order reconstruction is a test of absolute order (Greene et al., 1998). Another traditional measure of order memory is the relative recency task, in which the participant must judge which of two stimuli occurred more recently. In this task, the exact position of each stimulus need not be recalled, just their relative positions. Greene et al. (1998) assessed whether the negative generation effect observed with order reconstruction would also obtain for a test of relative order. Greene et al. (1998) used an experimental design similar to that of Nairne et al. (1991; Mulligan, 1999) in which pure study lists of generate or read items were followed by tests of order memory. In some experiments, the order test was relative recency. In other experiments, participants had to recall the exact position of the studied words. Greene et al. found that generation produced worse performance on the latter (absolute) order tests but produced no effect on the test of relative recency.

Mulligan (2000) reported a similar result regarding perceptual-interference. In Experiment 1, encoding condition (perceptual-interference or intact) was manipulated between lists, and each eight-word study list was followed by a test of relative recency. The mean proportion correct on the relative recency test was .77 and .78 in the intact and perceptual-interference conditions, respectively. Performance was substantially above chance (.50) but did not differ across the encoding conditions. As with generation, perceptual interference disrupted order memory as assessed with order reconstruction (Mulligan, 1999) but not relative recency.

Greene et al. (1998) argued that the operative difference between the order reconstruction and relative recency tests is that the former but not the latter requires information about exact position. However, the tasks also differ in terms of the test cues provided. Mulligan (2000, Experiment 2) addressed this issue by pairing the test cues of the relative recency test with the requirement to retrieve exact position. In this experiment, each of the study lists was followed by an order recall test in which participants were required to recall the study positions of the two items. The mean proportion correct on the order recall test was significantly higher for the intact than perceptual-interference condition, .40 and .33, respectively (note that order recall has eight possible responses and relative recency two, accounting for the substantial difference in overall performance levels). An additional experiment (Mulligan, 2000, Experiment 3) directly contrasted relative recency and order recall within a single experiment, ruling out test-specific encoding strategies as an account of the difference.

These results indicate that generation and perceptual interference disrupt memory for absolute order, as measured by order reconstruction and order recall, but do not affect memory for relative order, as assessed by relative recency judgments. How then, does this relate to the trade-off accounts? Greene et al. (1998) argued that different types of order tasks rely on different types of memorial information (e.g., Engelkamp et al., 2003; Li & Lewandowsky, 1993, 1995). Under this view, one way to retrieve position information is to perform a serial recall of the list. Such a strategy relies heavily on interitem associations (e.g., Lewandowsky & Murdock, 1989; Li & Lewandowsky, 1993; Thomas, Milner, & Haberlandt, 2003; cf. Farrell & Lewandowsky, 2002). Greene et al. (1998) argue that this process underlies memory for absolute position. This idea is consistent with the item-order and multifactor hypotheses that propose that generation and perceptual interference direct attention away from interitem processing.

In contrast, Greene et al. (1998) suggested that relative recency judgments do not involve the retrieval of all items in the list, nor do they rely on interitem associations (as in serial recall) (Li & Lewandowsky, 1993). Rather, it is assumed that only the to-be-compared items are retrieved and the judgment is made on the basis of the strength of individual items, item-position associations, or total information retrieved (Greene et al., 1998). If relative recency judgments are not based on interitem associative information, then the failure of generation and perceptual interference to disrupt these judgments does not contradict the trade-off accounts.

C. Gains and Losses Across Multiple Recall Tests

1. *Gains and Losses as Measures of Item-Specific and Relational Encoding*

When people attempt to recall the same material multiple times, memory performance sometimes improves, an effect referred to as *hypermnesia* (see Payne, 1987, for a review). Across multiple recall tests, some items are recalled on later tests that were not recalled earlier (item gains) and other items recalled earlier are not recalled on later tests (item losses). If the number of item gains is greater than the number of item losses, hypermnesia results.

Although the phenomenon of hypermnesia is interesting in its own right, we are interested in the multiple-test paradigm as a methodological tool.

Specifically, Klein, Loftus, Kihlstrom, and Aseron (1989; Burns, 1993; Burns & Gold, 1999; Engelkamp & Seiler, 2003; McDaniel et al., 1998; Mulligan, 2000a; Olofsson, 1997) demonstrated that conditions fostering item-specific encoding increase the probability of item gains, whereas conditions fostering relational encoding protect against item losses. The item-specific–relational framework (e.g., Hunt & McDaniel, 1993; Klein et al., 1989; McDaniel et al., 1998) suggests an account of this empirical regularity. Under this view, relational information guides retrieval strategies and is used to generate potential responses. To the extent that targets are related to one another during encoding, it is expected that stable retrieval strategies will emerge and be applied consistently on successive recall trials (Hunt & McDaniel, 1993; McDaniel et al., 1998). Item-specific encoding is hypothesized to lead to richer, more extensive encoding of item attributes, leading to a more distinctive trace and facilitating discrimination among potential responses at retrieval. "Assuming that the recall of an item requires recovery of some minimal number of attributes, an item with many encoded attributes will, if not recalled on an initial trial, nevertheless have a better chance of some critical subset of those attributes being sampled on some subsequent trial (thereby producing item recovery) than would an item with fewer encoded attributes" (McDaniel et al., 1998, p. 175).

Theory aside, the critical point for present purposes is empirical: There is a positive relationship between gains and item-specific encoding, and a negative relationship between losses and relational encoding (Burns, 1993; Burns & Gold, 1999; Engelkamp & Seiler, 2003; Klein et al., 1989; McDaniel et al., 1998; Mulligan, 2000b; Olofsson, 1997). Thus, gains and losses provide a converging methodology for assessing the roles of item-specific and relational information in memory. This methodology is especially useful because it is not subject to potential limitations of category clustering scores and order reconstruction. The generality of clustering studies may be limited because they require the use of categorized materials (e.g., Burns, 1993; Olofsson, 1997). Order reconstruction may be likewise limited because this procedure (e.g., Mulligan, 1999; Nairne et al., 1991) differs from the standard study-test paradigms in a number of ways. For example, the order-reconstruction paradigm uses multiple study-test blocks with very short (e.g., eight-item) study lists. In addition, this paradigm may induce strategy differences such as increased attention to serial position at encoding or increased reliance on serial retrieval strategies during recall (Burns, 1996).

2. *The Gain–Loss Analysis Applied to the Generation Effect*

Mulligan (2001) examined the effects of generation on gains and losses across multiple recall tests. We have already seen that the multifactor account makes the following predictions. For unrelated targets and a between-subjects (or pure-list) design, generation should enhance item-specific processing and disrupt intertarget relational encoding. In a within-subjects design, generation still enhances item-specific encoding but no longer disrupts relational encoding (or, more accurately, disrupts relational encoding equally for generate and read items). Applied to the gain–loss analysis, the predictions are as follows. For unrelated materials and a between-subjects design, generation should produce more item gains and more item losses than the read condition. In the within-subject (mixed-list) design, generation should enhance gains but not affect losses.

Mulligan (2001, Experiment 1) used a between-subjects design in which participants either read word pairs (e.g., *hot–cold*) or generated the second word from its antonym (e.g., *hot–c___*). The target items across pairs were normatively unrelated. Following the encoding task, five successive recall tests (each of 5 min in length) were administered. The results are presented in Tables I and II. First, note that on the initial test there was no effect of generation on recall (Table I). This is the expected null effect of generation in a between-subjects design (Grosofsky et al., 1994; Hirshman & Bjork, 1988). Next, consider the critical gain–loss data (Table II). Item gains for test *i* were computed as the number of words recalled on test *i* but not on test *i–1*. Item losses for test *i* were computed as the number of words recalled on test *i–1* but not on test *i*. As can be seen in the table, the generate group produced more gains and more losses than the read group, consistent with the multi-factor prediction of greater item-specific encoding and worse intertarget relational encoding, respectively. As a final note, the number of gains significantly exceeded losses for the generate but not the read group. This is consistent with the finding of hypermnesia (increasing recall across tests) in the generate but not the read group (Table I). Thus, although there was no effect of generation on the initial test, the effect emerged over tests and was

TABLE I

MULLIGAN (2001) EXPERIMENT 1 (BETWEEN-SUBJECTS DESIGN): PROPORTION OF TARGET WORDS RECALLED AS A FUNCTION OF RECALL TEST AND ENCODING CONDITION

	Recall test				
Encoding condition	1	2	3	4	5
Generate	0.22	0.21	0.25	0.26	0.28
Read	0.21	0.20	0.19	0.21	0.21

Note: The study list contained 44 items.

TABLE II

MULLIGAN (2001) EXPERIMENT 1 (BETWEEN-SUBJECTS DESIGN): MEAN NUMBER OF ITEM GAINS AND LOSSES AS A FUNCTION OF RECALL TEST AND ENCODING CONDITION

	Between tests				
Encoding condition	1–2	2–3	3–4	4–5	Total
Gains					
Generate	2.26	3.47	2.59	2.76	11.09
Read	1.75	1.41	1.58	1.42	6.17
		Losses			
Generate	2.68	1.59	2.03	2.06	8.35
Read	1.89	1.36	1.47	1.23	6.00

significant on Tests 3–5. For more on the emergent generation effect in a between-subjects design, see Mulligan (2001, 2002b).

Next, Mulligan (2001) manipulated generation in a mixed-list design, finding that generation enhanced item gains but did not affect losses. This is also consistent with the multifactor account's prediction that in a within-subjects design, generation enhances item-specific processing but leaves relational encoding unaffected. Finally, Mulligan used a set of categorically related targets presented in a blocked list (this experiment used a between-subjects design). Recall that under these conditions, the multifactor account predicts that generation enhances both item-specific and intertarget relational information. The results were consistent with these expectations: the generate group produced more item gains and fewer item losses than the read group. The results of Mulligan (2001) were consistent in some detail with the predictions of the multifactor account, indicating that the gain–loss analysis converges nicely with the order and category-clustering assessments. Two additional studies using the multiple-test paradigm have produced generally consistent results (Mulligan, 2002b; Mulligan & Duke, 2002).

3. *Perceptual Interference and Multiple Recall Tests*

a. The Gain–Loss Analysis Applied to Perceptual Interference The multifactor account makes similar predictions regarding the effects of perceptual interference on gains and losses. In between-subjects designs (with unrelated study words), perceptual interference is expected to increase item-specific processing and disrupt relational encoding, which in turn predicts greater item gains and item losses in the perceptual interference condition. Mulligan (2002b) tested these predictions by examining the effects of perceptual interference across five consecutive recall tests. Relative to the intact group, the perceptual-interference group produced significantly more item gains and losses (see Mulligan, 2000b, for similar results).

b. Subjective Organization Across Multiple Recall Tests Multiple recall tests afford a second opportunity to assess relational encoding. We have already seen that relational encoding can be assessed by the amount of organization in recall protocols (i.e., category clustering). In the case of unrelated words and multiple tests, measures of subjective organization (rather than "objective" categorical organization) may be used (e.g., Hunt & McDaniel, 1993; Koriat, Pearlman-Avnion, & Ben-Zur, 1998). In Mulligan's (2002b) study, the bidirectional pair frequency (PF) measure was used (Sternberg & Tulving, 1977), a measure based on the number of word pairs recalled in adjacent positions on two successive tests, corrected for the expected number of chance pairings. Stable and consistent retrieval strategies are a by-product of higher levels of relational encoding and should be reflected in enhanced PF scores. To the extent that perceptual-interference disrupts relational encoding, PF scores should be lower. Mulligan (2002b) found that PF scores were significantly lower in the perceptual-interference group than in the intact group, providing further evidence that perceptual interference disrupts relational processing.

D. Context Memory

1. Jurica and Shimamura (1999): A Negative Generation Effect in Context Memory

Jurica and Shimamura (1999) reported a dissociation between item and context memory that appeared to fit quite well with the item-order and item-relational dissociations described. In the study portion of the experiments, the participant interacted with three computerized "individuals" who appeared as facial drawings on a computer screen. The faces took turns making statements (e.g., "I think dogs make great pets.") or posing questions (e.g., "What type of sports do you like to watch?"), to which the participant generated a response. Participants were instructed to remember the statements and questions, as well as the speaker of each. After the study phase, participants recalled the statements and questions, and then completed a context memory test in which the old questions and statements were intermixed with new distracters. Participants decided if each test item was old or new, and if old, identified the speaker. The studied questions served as the generate condition, and the statements served as the read condition.

The results indicated better recall for the topics presented as questions but better context (speaker) memory for the statements. Jurica and Shimamura (1999) concluded that their generation manipulation enhanced memory for the occurrence of the questions but degraded memory for contextual associations. As mentioned earlier, Jurica and Shimamura proposed an account of their results that is quite similar to the processing trade-off implied by the multifactor and item-order accounts. They adopted the common perspective that memory encoding requires limited-capacity processing resources and that these resources are allocated flexibly in encoding various aspects of an experience. Jurica and Shimamura argued that the task demands of generation induce the participant to focus on the item itself, increasing encoding of item-specific information but at a cost to the encoding of associations between the item and elements of the surrounding context (such as the speaker's identity). Thus, similar to the multifactor and item-order accounts, Jurica and Shimamura argue that generation induces a tradeoff in the encoding of item and contextual information, or associative information more generally.

2. *Mulligan: Generation and Context Memory*

Although intriguing, Jurica and Shimamura's (1999) study may not be an ideal test of the trade-off account for several reasons. First, as noted by Marsh, Edelman, and Bower (2001), there is a potential ambiguity in this experimental paradigm. The generation condition places the participant in the role of the respondent, who is later asked to recall the identity of a questioner. In the read condition, the participant is in the role of a passive bystander who is later asked to recall the identity of the respondent (i.e., the computerized "individual" who revealed the fact about himself). The pairing of the generation condition with recall of questioner identity and the read condition with recall of responder identity produces an ambiguity. Research on conversational source monitoring indicates that recall of questioner identity is more difficult than recall of respondent (Brown, Jones, & Davis, 1995). Thus, the results of Jurica and Shimamura might reflect a negative generation effect in context memory or worse recall of questioner identity in conversational source monitoring (see Marsh et al., 2001; Mulligan, 2004, for more detail).

Second, Jurica and Shimamura's experimental paradigm is quite different from traditional generation manipulations using simple verbal materials. It is reasonable to wonder if the negative generation effect observed by Jurica and Shimamura occurs with more typical generation manipulations and materials. Third, Jurica and Shimamura did not actually test context memory for the information that had been generated during encoding. In the question condition, participants generated an answer to a question but were later tested with the question rather than with the generated answer. In terms of the traditional generation manipulation, this is like examining context memory for the cue words rather than the generated target word.

a. Methods and Results Mulligan (2004) examined the effect of generation on memory for context, using traditional manipulations of generation and simple verbal materials. Across experiments, two types of contextual information were examined, color and location. In the study portion of the experiments, participants generated some target words (e.g., *open–c*_____) and read others (e.g., *open–close*). In some of the experiments, the study stimuli were presented in either red or green print; in others, the study stimuli were presented on either the left or right half of the computer screen. On the subsequent context-memory test, participants decided if the test word was old or new, and if old, its color or location in the study trial. Color and location were used because context memory for perceptual attributes of a stimulus sometimes produces different results than context memory for spatiotemporal information (e.g., Spencer & Raz, 1995; Troyer, Winocur, Craik, & Moscovitch, 1999). Consequently, an evaluation of the effects of generation on context memory is more complete if multiple types of contextual information are examined.[4]

The context test yields measures of both item and context memory. To measure item memory, responses of either context (e.g., "red" or "green") were scored as "old" and accuracy was assessed with corrected hit rates. Context memory was assessed with the identification-of-origin score (Johnson, Hashtroude, & Lindsay, 1993), defined as the proportion of items correctly recognized as old that were attributed to their correct context.[5]

[4] When the topic of research is context memory, it is natural to consider the relevance of research on the related topic of source memory. Johnson's model of source memory (Johnson et al., 1993; Mitchell & Johnson, 2000) indicates two bases for source judgments: (1) a rapid (heuristic) decision based on the qualitative characteristics of the memory trace, and (2) a relatively slow, more strategic process based on metamemorial knowledge about the sources. That is, according to this model, source may be inferred rather than directly retrieved. Studies on generation and source memory have produced variable results and are, from the present perspective, of limited utility in evaluating item-context trade-offs. This is because source judgments elicit the heuristic, inferential processes based on the participants' knowledge of the characteristics of generated versus perceived information. Accordingly, successful source memory does not unambiguously indicate which aspect of the original event was encoded. Indeed, source may be accurately inferred from the lack of certain characteristics (e.g., lack of perceptual information may signal an internally generated event; see Mitchell & Johnson, 2000). Consequently, an evaluation of the item-context tradeoff hypothesis is best approached by examining memory for contextual details directly (see Mulligan, 2004, for details on this argument).

[5] An alternative assessment of context memory, analyzed in the framework of Batchelder and Riefer's (1990) multinomial model of source memory, produced results consistent with the identification-of-origin scores.

Mulligan's (2004) Experiment 1 assessed memory for color. The results for item memory were expected: Generation produced greater accuracy. The results for context memory indicated the opposite: The identification-of-origin scores were significantly higher in the read than generate condition. Thus, using color as the context, generation dissociated item memory and context memory, enhancing the former but disrupting the latter. Experiment 2 assessed memory for spatial location. This experiment produced the same result for item memory (a positive generation effect) but different results regarding context memory: The identification-of-origin scores were unaffected by generation.

Across 11 experiments, consistent results were obtained. First, each experiment demonstrated a generation effect on item memory. Second, generation impaired context memory for color but produced no effect on context memory for location, a pattern obtained for the within-subjects (mixed-list) as well as between-subjects designs. Another experiment demonstrated that the negative generation effect for color memory did not depend on the amount of colored surface in the study stimulus; even when the generate trials presented a greater colored area than read trials, generation disrupted context memory for color. Still other experiments demonstrated the generality of the negative generation effect on color memory over changes in instructions (incidental vs. intentional context encoding), materials, and generation tasks. Finally, the negative generation effect on context memory was specific to the color of the target word. Generation produced no effect on context memory for background color or cue-word color.[6]

b. Theoretical Analysis A primary motivation for this study was the item-context trade-off hypothesis proposed by Jurica and Shimamura (1999), which can be viewed as a specific instantiation of the multifactor trade-off account. Although some of the results are consistent with this account (specifically, the negative generation effect on context memory for the target item's color), other results are inconsistent with a general encoding trade-off. In particular, generation did not affect context memory for location, background color, or cue color. The item-context trade-off account argues that generation draws attention away from item-context associative processing. If the present generation task is sufficiently distracting to draw attention from the encoding of target-color context, why is it not likewise sufficient for drawing attention away from encoding information about location, background color, or cue-word color? The specificity of the negative generation effect in context memory argues against a

[6] Some of these results conflict with those of Marsh et al. (2001), an issue that is investigated at length in Mulligan (2004).

general item–context trade-off. We return to this issue in our concluding discussion.

An alternative account is based on Jacoby's (1983) processing analysis. Jacoby argued that generating words does not necessarily produce better memory but rather produces a difference in what is encoded. Jacoby differentiated between data-driven (or perceptual) and conceptual-driven processing, arguing that reading and generating differ in the relative amounts of the two types of processing. Under this view, reading primarily consists of the analysis of perceptual features, whereas generating a word from a meaningful associate (e.g., an antonym) emphasizes conceptual processing. In the generate condition, there is little perceptual information (e.g., the first letter of the target item), so identifying the word is largely due to conceptual processing. Thus, according to this analysis, reading produces greater encoding of perceptual attributes of the target, whereas generation produces greater encoding of conceptual information and a concomitant reduction in the encoding of perceptual information. A number of results support Jacoby's analysis, particularly the contention that reading enhances the perceptual encoding. Generally, performance on memory tests that stress perceptual information (e.g., perceptual priming tests, graphemic-cued recall) is greater following reading than generation (see Roediger & McDermott, 1993, for a review).

In contrast to the multifactor account, however, the processing view does not imply a general item-context trade-off. More specifically, the processing account proposes that the read condition promotes greater perceptual processing of the target word than the generate condition, translating into better encoding of perceptual details about the target stimulus, such as its color. In contrast, this view proposes that the encoding of information external to the target stimulus is unaffected by the encoding conditions. Thus, the processing view proposes that the negative effects of generation on context memory are specific to perceptual attributes of the target stimulus itself. The results are in accord with this view. Generation disrupted context memory selectively for the target color, but not for location, background color, or cue color (see Mulligan, 2004, for additional discussion).

E. Summary

The multifactor and item-order accounts make detailed predictions about the effects of generation and perceptual interference on relational, order, and context information. One general implication of these accounts is that under a number of conditions, generation and perceptual interference institute an encoding trade-off, enhancing item-specific information but disrupting relational, order, and context information. The reviewed research is largely consistent with the predictions of these accounts, especially with regard to category clustering, measures of absolute order, and items gains and losses across multiple recall tests. In the case of context memory for details such as color and location, the results are not completely consistent with the accounts, a point to which we return after considering a final issuing regarding processing tradeoffs.

VI. Dissociating Enhanced Item Memory from Disrupted Order and Relational Information

Throughout this chapter, we have investigated the trade-off hypothesis embodied in the multifactor and item-order accounts. The term *trade-off* can be taken in two ways. In a theoretically neutral sense, the term simply summarizes a pattern of results in which an encoding manipulation has opposite effects on a measure of item memory and a measure of relational, order, or contextual information. Based on the preceding review, it is certainly the case that generation and perceptual interference can produce such trade-offs in observed performance.

A more theoretical interpretation implies a trade-off within a common encoding stage or via a common encoding mechanism. This interpretation seems consistent with the multifactor and item-order accounts. For example, the item-order hypothesis explicitly states that unusual encoding conditions (e.g., generate or perceptual-interference condition) draw resources to the processing of item characteristics, leaving fewer resources for the processing of serial-order information (e.g., DeLosh & McDaniel, 1996; Engelkamp & Dehn, 2000; Nairne et al., 1991). Under this view, disrupted memory for order arises from the same mechanism that produces enhanced item encoding and is causally related to the superior item memory (Greene et al., 1998). The multifactor account provides the same implication. According to this interpretation of "trade-off," the components of a manipulation that make it effective at enhancing item-specific processing are assumed to be the same as those that disrupt order and relational encoding.

Mulligan (2000a) argued that this might not be the case for perceptual interference. Recall that the compensatory-processing account (and the bulk of the evidence) argues that the positive mnemonic effects of perceptual interference arise during perception. But what of the negative effects? It seems unlikely that the associative processing thought to underlie relational and order memory arises during word perception. Rather, these forms of memory rely on postperceptual processing. That is, a representation of an item must be created (i.e., the item perceived) before it is associated with other items. This suggests that the positive effects of the backward mask may not arise at the same stage of processing as the negative effects. It may be possible, therefore, to develop versions of the perceptual-interference manipulation that dissociate its positive effects on item memory from its negative effects on order and relational information.

A. Order Memory

In this series of experiments, we contrasted the standard perceptual-interference and generation manipulations with versions of the manipulation that do not give rise to the normal item-memory advantage. We then determined whether these limiting conditions persist in disrupting order and relational information.

1. Perceptual Interference

The perceptual-interference effect in recall and recognition can be eliminated by delaying the mask until word perception is complete (Hirshman et al., 1994). Mulligan (2000a) contrasted this encoding condition with the standard perceptual-interference condition, using the order-memory paradigm described earlier. The study lists varied across three encoding conditions. The first was the standard perceptual-interference condition in which each study word was displayed for 100 ms prior to the mask (which was left on the screen for 2400 ms). The second condition also used backward masking, but the mask was delayed so that the word was presented for 266 ms (with the backward mask presented for 2234 ms). The final condition was the intact condition, in which the word was presented for the entire study duration (2.5 s) with no mask.

On a test of recognition memory, the 100 ms condition produced greater accuracy than either the 266 ms or the intact condition (the latter two conditions were equivalent). Thus, the standard (100 ms) perceptual-interference condition enhanced item memory (relative to the intact condition), but the delayed-mask condition did not. In contrast, on the order reconstruction task, the intact condition produced significantly better performance than either of the mask conditions (which did not differ). Comparison of the intact and 100-ms conditions replicates earlier research: perceptual-interference enhances item memory but disrupts order memory (Mulligan, 1999). In contrast, the 266 ms condition disrupted order memory without increasing item encoding. In sum, delaying the mask eliminated the positive effects of perceptual interference on item memory but preserved its negative effect on order memory. The item-enhancing effect of perceptual interference were dissociated from its order-disrupting effect.

2. Generation

Mulligan (2002c) reported a similar set of results with respect to the generation effect. As described earlier, an important determinant of the generation effect is the type of materials. The generation effect in item memory is not obtained with unfamiliar materials, such as nonwords and unfamiliar word compounds. In Mulligan's (2002c) Experiment 1, participants read or generated short lists of words or nonwords. In the generate condition, the items were generated by transposing the first two letters (e.g., *alrt* for *lart*). Half of the study lists were followed by tests of order reconstruction, and the other half were untested until the end-of-session recognition test (Nairne et al., 1991). Results for the words replicated earlier studies (e.g., Nairne et al., 1991; Serra & Nairne, 1993): Compared to reading, generation enhanced recognition memory but disrupted performance on order reconstruction. Likewise, the recognition results for the nonwords were expected: Generation produced no effect (e.g., Mulligan, 2002b; Payne et al., 1986). On the test of order reconstruction, however, nonwords produced a negative generation effect. Thus, generating words produces a positive effect on item memory and a negative effect on order memory, whereas generating nonwords produces no effect on item memory coupled with a negative effect on order memory. As was the case with perceptual interference, the item-enhancing effect of generation was dissociated from its order-disrupting effect.

As noted earlier, free recall in this paradigm relies heavily on order information, so much so that in a pure-list design, generation produces a negative generation effect on free recall. Mulligan (2002c, Experiment 2) demonstrated this negative generation effect for both words and nonwords. This experiment used the same study procedures as Experiment 1, but each study list was followed by either order reconstruction or free recall. The order reconstruction results were the same as Experiment 1, worse order memory for the generate condition, regardless of the stimulus class. Likewise, in free recall, a negative generation effect was obtained for both words and nonwords. When free recall is heavily reliant on order memory, generation disrupts recall and does so equally for words and nonwords.

In a final experiment (Mulligan, 2002c, Experiment 3), participants generated or read word compounds that were familiar (e.g., *cheese cake*) or unfamiliar (e.g., *tomato cake*). In the generate condition, the compounds were presented in reversed order (e.g., *cake cheese*) and participants generated the compound by transposition. In a study similar to Experiment 1, participants read or generated short lists of familiar or unfamiliar compounds (again, in a pure-list design). Half of the study lists were tested with order reconstruction, and the other half were tested with the end-of-session recognition test. The recognition results indicated a positive generation effect for familiar compounds but no effect for unfamiliar compounds. The results of order reconstruction showed an equivalent negative generation effect for both familiar and unfamiliar compounds. In sum, generating familiar compounds increases item memory and detracts from order memory, whereas generating unfamiliar compounds only detracts from order memory. This is another instance in which the item-enhancing and order-disrupting effects of generation are dissociated.

B. Gains–Losses Analysis and Subjective Organization

Similar dissociations have been uncovered with measures of item-specific and relational encoding. Mulligan (2002a) used the gain–loss analysis to examine the effects of perceptual interference on item and relational encoding. As in the order-memory study previously described, Mulligan (2002a) used two versions of the perceptual-interference manipulation, one that enhances item memory (100-ms mask onset) and one that does not (266-ms mask onset). Participants studied a list of 48 words in either the 100-ms, 266-ms, or intact condition (a between-subjects design). Following a 3-min distracter task, participants were given a series of five recall tests. Gains scores were significantly greater in the 100-ms condition than in either the 266-ms or intact conditions, and the latter two conditions did not differ. Loss scores were significantly lower in the intact condition than in either the 100-ms or 266-ms conditions, and the two masking conditions did not differ from one another. The logic of the gain–loss analysis indicates that the 100-ms condition produced greater item-specific encoding than either the 266-ms or intact condition. The loss data indicate that both masking conditions disrupted relational encoding to the same degree (relative to the intact condition). Delaying the mask (to 266 ms) eliminated the enhancement to item-specific encoding but not the disruption to relational encoding.

Mulligan (2002a) also computed PF scores in each of the encoding conditions to assess subjective organization. PF scores were significantly higher in the intact condition than in either the 100-ms or 266-ms masking conditions, and the latter conditions did not differ. This indicates greater subjective organization in the intact than in either of the masking conditions, a result that dovetails with the loss analysis in indicating that both the masking conditions disrupted relational encoding relative to the intact condition. Coupled with the gain–loss analysis, it appears that the item-enhancing effects of perceptual interference were dissociated from its relational-disrupting effects, as was the case with measures of order memory.

VII. Concluding Discussion

In this chapter, we have examined the effects of self-generation on memory as exemplified by the generation manipulation and the related perceptual-interference manipulation. We began by introducing the traditional view that self-generative encoding is advantageous. Although we have emphasized null and negative effects of generation because of their theoretical import, we should not neglect to mention the substantial evidence in favor of this traditional view. Indeed, the positive effects of generation and perceptual interference on tests of item memory (such as recognition) are pervasive, typically large and nearly uniform across studies. In this regard, generative encoding certainly enhances memory.

Of course, the present chapter focuses more on the limiting conditions of self-generation and the theoretical accounts that these limitations have shaped. Extant theoretical accounts of generation imply an encoding trade-off, in which generation enhances item-specific processing at a cost to the encoding of interitem relations, order memory, and contextual associations. As reviewed earlier, much of the relevant research is consistent with the trade-off hypothesis. Specifically, generation (and perceptual interference) generally produces positive effects on measures of item memory and negative (or null) effects on the various measures of relational, associative, and order information.

There are two aspects of the results, however, that merit additional comment. The first regards context memory. In our recent research (Mulligan, 2004), generation did not produce a general item-context trade-off. Generation consistently enhanced recognition (item) memory but disrupted context memory only for target color. Generation did not affect context memory for location, background color, or cue-word color. As noted, the specificity of this negative generation effect is not consistent with a general item–context trade-off but, rather, fits comfortably with a processing account. These results indicate that, to the extent that generation induces processing trade-offs, the trade-offs do not extend to all forms of contextual information. One speculation is that encoding trade-offs only occur for intertrial associative processing. For example, intertarget relational encoding requires associating information about targets from different study trials. In Mulligan's (2004) experiments, context memory relied on associations that were formed within trial: the identity of a word was associated with a location or a color that was available in the same study trial. This contrasts with intertarget relational encoding in which the study word from one trial is associated with information available in a later study trial (e.g., a later study word). It is possible that generation produces processing trade-offs, but only when the associative processing is cross trial, taxing working memory to a greater degree than within-trial associations.

A second challenge for the trade-off views is the dissociation between the item-enhancing effects and the order- or relational-disrupting effects of generation and perceptual interference. The trade-off accounts posit a trade-off within a common processing stage or via a shared encoding mechanism. Consequently, these models imply a necessary relationship between item enhancements and order or relational disruptions. Finding that the enhancements and disruptions can be independently obtained calls for some refinements to the trade-off accounts. For the perceptual-interference effect, the compensatory-processing account provides a well-articulated account that fits within the general item-specific–relational framework. According to this account, the higher-level perceptual representations that are the basis of the effect are a type of item-specific representation that arises during initial perception. The positive item effects are contrasted with the negative effects of perceptual-interference on relational and order memory, which are proposed to arise postperceptually. Thus, delaying the backward mask (to a point of time after word perception is complete) can dissociate the item-enhancing and relational-disrupting effects. The delayed mask is presented too late to affect perceptual processing (and enhance the encoding of higher-level perceptual information), but the mask still disrupts postperceptual processing of associative information.

What of the generation effect? Here, the use of nonwords and unfamiliar compounds dissociated item enhancement and order disruption (Mulligan, 2002c). There are at least two possibilities. First, these results may not be as problematic as they initially appear. Specifically, assume that generation induces an encoding trade-off between item and order information for both familiar and unfamiliar material, and further assume that in the case of unfamiliar stimuli, the item representations are not sufficient to render the stimulus distinctive. This view is consistent with the argument that a stimulus must possess a preexisting, unitized representations for generation to produce distinctiveness (Gardiner & Hampton, 1985; Gardiner et al., 1988; Nairne et al., 1985; Payne et al., 1986). This version of the item-order account argues that generating an item attracts attention to the item characteristics and away from representations of serial order, but that in the case of unfamiliar stimuli, the item representations are not sufficient to engender distinctiveness (and thus no generation effect ensues in item memory). Under this view, Mulligan's (2002c) dissociation implies different representational bases for item and order memory but does not necessarily imply different encoding mechanisms or processes. As an aside, it should be noted that this extension of the item-order view does not apply to the dissociations reported for perceptual interference, which occurred for familiar words.

A second possibility is based on Masson and MacLeod's (1992, 1997) distinction between initial interpretative encoding and later elaborative encoding. This distinction is similar to the distinction between perceptual and postperceptual encoding processes in the compensatory-processing account. Under Masson and MacLeod's view, when a stimulus is presented, an initial knowledge-based interpretation of the item is formed, strongly influenced by the context in which the item is presented. Masson and MacLeod conceived of the initial interpretative process as operating along the lines of an interactive-activation model (e.g., Plaut et al., 1996), much as is envisaged in the compensatory-processing account. Ensuing elaborative processing of the item may move beyond the constraints of prior knowledge and immediate context, allowing for a more flexible analysis of the stimulus and the formation of interitem associations. According to this view, both stages produce long-term memorial encodings.

According to both Masson and MacLeod's (1992, 1997) view and the compensatory-processing account, the positive effects of perceptual interference or generation can arise during the initial interpretive processing of the stimulus. What of the negative effects on order memory? To the extent that memory for serial order is based on interitem relational information (e.g., Greene et al., 1998; Li & Lewandowsky, 1993), it relies on processes occurring after initial word perception or interpretation. That is, a representation of the item must be created (i.e., the item perceived and interpreted) before it can be associated with other items in working memory (Masson & MacLeod, 1992). Under this view, elaborative, relational, and interitem associative processing are conceived of as postperceptual or postinterpretive. Consequently, the aspects of a manipulation that disrupt order encoding operate only at this later stage. In the case of perceptual interference, the backward mask may act as an interitem distracter, disrupting the formation of interitem associations (Li & Lewandowsky, 1993). Speculatively, typical generation tasks may likewise disrupt interitem associations. First, the generation task may simply take more time to complete, leaving less time for interitem associative processes. Second (and not necessarily exclusive of the first suggestion), a generation task might induce postresponse checking to verify the answer. This could cut into time for forming interitem associations (as suggested by the first point) and may act as an interitem distracter task, as was suggested in the case of perceptual interference.

In sum, the trade-off accounts are a useful corrective to the traditional belief that self-generative encoding necessarily or generally enhances memory. These accounts have provided theoretical reasons for observed limitations of the generation effect and pointed in the direction of new limitations. However, as previously detailed, the trade-off accounts themselves require additional clarification if we are to come to a more complete understanding of the role of self-generation in memory.

References

Anderson, N. D., & Craik, F. I. M. (2000). Memory in the aging brain. In E. Tulving and F. I. M. Craik (Eds.), *Oxford handbook of memory* (pp. 411–425). London: Oxford University Press.

Asch, S. E., & Ebenholtz, S. M. (1962). The process of free recall: Evidence for non-associative factors in acquisition and retention. *Journal of Psychology, 54*, 3–31.

Balota, D. A. (1990). The role of meaning in word recognition. In D. A. Balota, G. B. F. D. Arcais, and K. Rayner (Eds.), *Comprehension processes in reading* (pp. 9–32). Hillside, NJ: Erlbaum.

Batchelder, W. H., & Riefer, D. M. (1990). Multinomial processing models of source monitoring. *Psychological Review, 97*, 548–564.

Begg, I., Snider, A., Foley, F., & Goddard, R. (1989). The generation effect is no artifact: Generating makes words distinctive. *Journal of Experimental Psychology: Learning, Memory, and Cognition, 15*, 977–989.

Brown, A. S., Jones, E. M., & Davis, T. L. (1995). Age differences in conversational source monitoring. *Psychology and Aging, 10*, 111–122.

Brown, M. S., Roberts, M. A., & Besner, D. (2001). Semantic processing in visual word recognition: Activation blocking and domain specificity. *Psychonomic Bulletin & Review, 8*, 778–784.

Burns, D. J. (1990). The generation effect: A test between single- and multifactor theories. *Journal of Experimental Psychology: Learning, Memory, and Cognition, 16*, 1060–1067.

Burns, D. J. (1992). The consequences of generation. *Journal of Memory & Language, 31*, 615–633.

Burns, D. J. (1993). Item gains and losses during hypermnesic recall: Implications for the item-specific-relational information distinction. *Journal of Experimental Psychology: Learning, Memory, and Cognition, 19*, 163–173.

Burns, D. J. (1996). The item-order distinction and the generation effect: The importance of order information in long-term memory. *American Journal of Psychology, 109*, 567–580.

Burns, D. J., & Gold, D. E. (1999). An analysis of item gains and losses in retroactive interference. *Journal of Experimental Psychology: Learning, Memory, and Cognition, 25*, 978–985.

Cofer, C. N., Bruce, D. R., & Reicher, G. M. (1966). Clustering in free recall as a function of certain methodological variations. *Journal of Experimental Psychology, 71*, 858–866.

DeLosh, E. L., & McDaniel, M. A. (1996). The role of order information in free recall: Application to the word-frequency effect. *Journal of Experimental Psychology: Learning, Memory and Cognition, 22*, 1136–1146.

De Winstanley, P. A. (1995). A generation effect can be found during naturalistic learning. *Psychonomic Bulletin & Review, 2*, 538–541.

De Winstanley, P. A., & Bjork, E. L. (1997). Processing instructions and the generation effect: A test of the multifactor transfer-appropriate processing theory. *Memory, 5*, 401–421.

De Winstanley, P. A., Bjork, E. L., & Bjork, R. A. (1996). Generation effects and the lack thereof: The role of transfer-appropriate processing. *Memory, 4*, 31–48.

Engelkamp, J. (1998). *Memory for actions*. Hove, England: Psychology Press Ltd.

Engelkamp, J., & Dehn, D. A. (2000). Item and order information in subject-performed tasks and experimenter-performed tasks. *Journal of Experimental Psychology: Learning, Memory, and Cognition, 26*, 671–682.

Engelkamp, J., Jahn, P., & Seiler, K. H. (2003). The item-order hypothesis reconsidered: The role of order information in free recall. *Psychological Research, 67*, 280–290.

Engelkamp, J., & Seiler, K. H. (2003). Gains and losses in action memory. *Quarterly Journal of Experimental Psychology, 56A*, 829–848.

Farrell, S., & Lewandowsky, S. (2002). An endogenous distributed model of ordering in serial recall. *Psychonomic Bulletin & Review, 9*, 59–79.

Foos, P. W., Mora, J. J., & Tkacz, S. (1994). Student study techniques and the generation effect. *Journal of Educational Psychology, 86*, 567–576.

Gardiner, J. M., Gregg, V. H., & Hampton, J. A. (1988). Word frequency and generation effects. *Journal of Experimental Psychology: Learning, Memory, and Cognition, 14*, 687–693.

Gardiner, J. M., & Hampton, J. A. (1985). Semantic memory and the generation effect: Some tests of the lexical activation hypothesis. *Journal of Experimental Psychology: Learning, Memory and Cognition, 11*, 732–741.

Gardiner, J. M., & Hampton, J. A. (1988). Item-specific processing and the generation effect: Support for a distinctiveness account. *American Journal of Psychology, 101*, 495–504.

Gardiner, J. M., & Rowley, J. M. C. (1984). A generation effect with numbers rather than words. *Memory & Cognition, 12*, 443–445.

Graf, P. (1982). The memorial consequences of generation and transformation. *Journal of Verbal Learning and Verbal Behavior, 21*, 539–548.

Greene, R. L. (1992). *Human memory: Paradigms and paradoxes*. Hillside, NJ: Erlbaum.

Greene, R. L., Thapar, A., & Westerman, D. L. (1998). Effects of generation on memory for order. *Journal of Memory and Language, 38*, 255–264.

Greenwald, A. G. (1981). Self and memory. In G. H. Bower (Ed.), *The psychology of learning and motivation* (Vol. 15, pp. 201–236). New York: Academic Press.

Grosofsky, A., Payne, D. G., & Campbell, K. D. (1994). Does the generation effect depend upon selective displaced rehearsal. *American Journal of Psychology, 107*, 53–68.

Hirshman, E., & Bjork, R. A. (1988). The generation effect: Support for a two-factor theory. *Journal of Experimental Psychology: Learning, Memory and Cognition, 14*, 484–494.

Hirshman, E., & Mulligan, N. W. (1991). Perceptual interference improves explicit memory but does not enhance data-driven processing. *Journal of Experimental Psychology: Learning, Memory and Cognition, 17*, 507–513.

Hirshman, E., Trembath, D., & Mulligan, N. W. (1994). Theoretical implications of the mnemonic benefits of perceptual interference. *Journal of Experimental Psychology: Learning, Memory and Cognition, 20*, 608–620.

Horton, D. L., & Cofer, C. N. (1975). Free recall of categorically related list items over long retention intervals. *Bulletin of the Psychonomic Society, 5*, 127–129.

Hunt, R. R., & Einstein, G. O. (1981). Relational and item-specific information in memory. *Journal of Verbal Learning and Verbal Behavior, 19*, 497–514.

Hunt, R. R., & McDaniel, M. A. (1993). The enigma of organization and distinctiveness. *Journal of Memory & Language, 32*, 421–445.

Jacoby, L. L. (1978). On interpreting the effects of repetition: Solving a problem versus remembering a solution. *Journal of Verbal Learning and Verbal Behavior, 17*, 649–667.

Jacoby, L. L. (1983). Remembering the data: Analyzing interactive processes in reading. *Journal of Verbal Learning and Verbal Behavior, 22*, 485–508.

Johns, E. E., & Swanson, L. C. (1988). The generation effect with nonwords. *Journal of Experimental Psychology: Learning, Memory, and Cognition, 14*, 180–190.

Johnson, M. K., Hashtroudi, S., & Lindsay, D. S. (1993). Source monitoring. *Psychological Bulletin, 114*, 3–28.

Jurica, P. J., & Shimamura, A. P. (1999). Monitoring item and source information: Evidence for a negative generation effect in source memory. *Memory & Cognition, 27*, 648–656.

Kalem, S., & Fer, S. (2003). The effects of the active learning model on students' learning, teaching and communication. *Educational Sciences: Theory and Practice, 3*, 455–461.

Kelley, M. R., & Nairne, J. S. (2001). Von Restorff revisited: Isolation, generation, and memory for order. *Journal of Experimental Psychology: Learning, Memory, and Cognition, 27*, 54–66.

Kinjo, H., & Snodgrass, J. G. (2000). Does the generation effect occur for pictures? *American Journal of Psychology, 113*, 95–121.

Kinoshita, S. (1989). Generation enhances semantic processing? The role of distinctiveness in the generation effect. *Memory & Cognition, 17*, 563–571.

Klein, S. B., Loftus, J., Kihlstrom, J. F., & Aseron, R. (1989). Effects of item specific and relational information on hypermnesic recall. *Journal of Experimental Psychology: Learning, Memory and Cognition, 15*, 1192–1197.

Koriat, A., Pearlman-Avnion, S., & Ben-Zur, H. (1998). The subjective organization of input and output events in memory. *Psychological Research, 61*, 295–307.

Lewandowsky, S., & Murdock, B. B. (1989). Memory for serial order. *Psychological Review, 96*, 25–57.

Li, S. C., & Lewandowsky, S. (1993). Intralist distractors and recall direction: Constraints on models of memory for serial order. *Journal of Experimental Psychology: Learning, Memory, and Cognition, 19*, 895–908.

Li, S. C., & Lewandowsky, S. (1995). Forward and backward recall: Different retrieval processes. *Journal of Experimental psychology: Learning, Memory, and Cognition, 21*, 837–847.

Marsh, E. J., Edelman, G., & Bower, G. H. (2001). Demonstrations of a generation effect in context memory. *Memory & Cognition, 29*, 798–805.

Masson, M. E. J., & MacLeod, C. M. (1992). Reenacting the route to interpretation: Enhanced perceptual identification without prior perception. *Journal of Experimental Psychology: General, 121*, 145–176.

Masson, M. E. J. & MacLeod C. M. (1997). Episodic enhancement of processing fluency. In D. L. Medin (Ed.), *The psychology of learning and memory* (Vol. 37, pp. 155 –210). San Diego CA: Academic Press.

McDaniel, M. A., DeLosh, E. L., & Merritt, P. S. (2000). Order information and retrieval distinctiveness: Recall of common versus bizarre material. *Journal of Experimental Psychology: Learning, Memory, and Cognition, 26*, 1045–1056.

McDaniel, M. A., Einstein, G. O., Dunay, P. K., & Cobb, R. E. (1986). Encoding difficulty and memory: Toward a unifying theory. *Journal of Memory and Language, 25*, 645–656.

McDaniel, M. A., Moore, B. A., & Whiteman, H. L. (1998). Dynamic changes in hypermnesia across early and late tests: A relational/item-specific account. *Journal of Experimental Psychology: Learning, Memory, and Cognition, 24*, 173–185.

McDaniel, M. A., Wadill, P. J., & Einstein, G. O. (1988). A contextual account of the generation effect: A three-factor theory. *Journal of Memory and Language, 27*, 521–536.

Michael, J. A., & Modell, H. I. (2003). *Active learning in secondary and college science classrooms: A working model for helping the learner to learn.* Mahwah, NJ: Erlbaum.

Mitchell, K. J., & Johnson, M. K. (1997). Source monitoring: Attributing mental experiences. In F. I. M. Craik and E. Tulving (Eds.), *Oxford handbook of memory* (pp. 179–196). Oxford, England: Oxford University Press.

Mulligan, N. W. (1996). The effects of perceptual interference at encoding on implicit memory, explicit memory, and memory for source. *Journal of Experimental Psychology: Learning, Memory and Cognition, 22*, 1067–1087.

Mulligan, N. W. (1998). Perceptual interference at encoding enhances recall for high- but not low-image ability words. *Psychonomic Bulletin & Review, 5*, 464–469.

Mulligan, N. W. (1999). The effects of perceptual interference at encoding on organization and order: Investigating the roles of item-specific and relational information. *Journal of Experimental Psychology: Learning, Memory and Cognition, 25*, 54–69.

Mulligan, N. W. (2000a). Perceptual interference and memory for order. *Journal of Memory and Language, 43*, 680–697.

Mulligan, N. W. (2000b). Perceptual interference at encoding enhances item-specific encoding and disrupts relational encoding: Evidence from multiple recall tests. *Memory & Cognition, 28*, 539–546.

Mulligan, N. W. (2001). Generation and hypermnesia. *Journal of Experimental Psychology: Learning, Memory and Cognition, 27*, 436–450.

Mulligan, N. W. (2002a). The emergence of item-specific encoding effects in between-subjects designs: Perceptual interference and multiple recall tests. *Psychonomic Bulletin & Review, 9*, 375–382.

Mulligan, N. W. (2002b). The emergent generation effect and hypermnesia: Influences of semantic and non-semantic generation tasks. *Journal of Experimental Psychology: Learning, Memory and Cognition, 28*, 541–554.

Mulligan, N. W. (2002c). The generation effect: Dissociating enhanced item memory and disrupted order memory. *Memory & Cognition, 30*, 850–861.

Mulligan, N. W. (2004). Generation and memory for contextual details. *Journal of Experimental Psychology: Learning, Memory and Cognition, 30*, 838–855.

Mulligan, N. W., & Duke, M. (2002). Positive and negative generation effects, hypermnesia, and total recall time. *Memory & Cognition, 30*, 1044–1053.

Murphy, M. D. (1979). Measurement of category clustering in free recall. In C. R. Puff (Ed.), *Memory organization and structure* (pp. 51–83). New York: Academic Press.

Nairne, J. S. (1988). The mnemonic value of perceptual identification. *Journal of Experimental Psychology: Learning, Memory and Cognition, 14*, 244–255.

Nairne, J. S., Pusen, C. P., & Widner, R. L. (1985). Representation in the mental lexicon: Implications for theories of the generation effect. *Memory & Cognition, 13*, 183–191.

Nairne, J. S., Reigler, G. L., & Serra, M. (1991). Dissociative effects of generation on item and order retention. *Journal of Experimental Psychology: Learning, Memory and Cognition, 17*, 702–709.

Olofsson, U. (1997). Win some, lose some: Hypermnesia for actions reflects increased item-specific processing. *Memory & Cognition, 25*, 797–800.

O'Neill, W. A., Roy, L., & Tremblay, R. (1993). A translation-based generation effect in bilingual recall and recognition. *Memory & Cognition, 21*, 488–495.

Payne, D. G. (1987). Hypermnesia and reminiscence in recall: A historical and empirical review. *Psychological Bulletin, 101*, 5–27.

Payne, D. G., Neely, J. H., & Burns, D. J. (1986). The generation effect: Further tests of the lexical activation hypothesis. *Memory & Cognition, 14*, 246–252.

Petty, R. E., Ostrom T. M., Brock T. C. (Eds.) (1981). *Cognitive responses in persuasion.* Hillsdale, NJ: Erlbaum.

Pexman, P. M., Lupker, S. J., & Hino, Y. (2002). The impact of feedback semantics in visual word recognition: Number-of-feature effects in lexical decision and naming tasks. *Psychonomic Bulletin & Review, 9*, 542–549.

Peynircioglu, Z. F. (1989). The generation effect with pictures and nonsense figures. *Acta Psychologica, 70*, 153–160.

Plaut, D. C., McClelland, J. L., Seidenberg, M. S., & Patterson, K. (1996). Understanding normal and impaired word reading: Computational principles in quasi-regular domains. *Psychological Review, 103*, 56–115.

Roediger, H. L., & McDermott, K. B. (1993). Implicit memory in normal human subjects. In F. Boller and J. Grafman (Eds.), *Handbook of neuropsychology* (Vol. 8, pp. 63–131). Amsterdam: Elsevier.

Roenker, D. L., Thompson, C. P., & Brown, S. C. (1971). Comparison of measures for the estimation of clustering in free recall. *Psychological Bulletin, 76*, 45–48.

Schmidt, S. R., & Cherry, K. (1989). The negative generation effect: Delineation of a phenomenon. *Memory & Cognition, 17*, 359–369.

Sengupta, J., & Gorn, G. J. (2002). Absence makes the mind grow sharper: Effects of element omission on subsequent recall. *Journal of Marketing Research, 39*, 186–201.

Serra, M., & Nairne, J. S. (1993). Design controversies and the generation effect: Support for an item-order hypothesis. *Memory and Cognition, 21*, 34–40.

Slamecka, N. J., & Graf, P. (1978). The generation effect: Delineation of a phenomenon. *Journal of Experimental Psychology: Human Learning and Memory, 4*, 592–604.

Slamecka, N. J., & Katsaiti, L. T. (1987). The generation effect as an artifact of selective displaced rehearsal. *Journal of Memory & Language, 26*, 589–607.

Smith, R. W., & Healy, A. F. (1998). The time-course of the generation effect. *Memory & Cognition, 26*, 135–142.

Spencer, W. D., & Raz, N. (1995). Differential effects of aging on memory for content and context. *Psychology and Aging, 10*, 527–539.

Steffens, M. C., & Erdfelder, E. (1998). Determinants of positive and negative generation effects in free recall. *Quarterly Journal of Experimental Psychology, 51A*, 705–733.

Sternberg, R. J., & Tulving, E. (1977). The measurement of subjective organization in free recall. *Psychological Bulletin, 84*, 539–556.

Tailby, R., & Haslam, C. (2003). An investigation of errorless learning in memory-impaired patients: Improving the technique and clarifying theory. *Neuropsychologia, 41*, 1230–1240.

Thomas, J. G., Milner, H. R., & Haberlandt, K. F. (2003). Forward and backward recall: Different response time patterns, same retrieval order. *Psychological Science, 14*, 169–174.

Troyer, A. K., Winocur, G., Craik, F. I. M., & Moscovitch, M. (1999). Source memory and divided attention: Reciprocal costs to primary and secondary tasks. *Neuropsychology, 13*, 467–474.

Westerman, D. L., & Greene, R. L. (1997). The effects of visual masking on recognition: Similarities to the generation effect. *Journal of Memory and Language, 37*, 584–596.

Wills, T. W., Soraci, S. A., Chechile, R. A., & Taylor, H. A. (2000). "Aha" effects in the generation of pictures. *Memory & Cognition, 28*, 939–948.

Zimmer, H. D., Cohen, R. L., Guynn, M. J., Engelkamp, J., Kormi-Nouri, R., & Foley, M. A. (Eds.). (2001). *Memory for action: A distinct form of episodic memory?* New York: Oxford University Press.

AGING, METACOGNITION, AND COGNITIVE CONTROL

Christopher Hertzog and John Dunlosky

It has been known since before the turn of the century that the behavior of experimental subjects often includes efforts to cope with the requirements of the laboratory tasks they are presented with. They actively problem solve while learning. (W. Reitman 1971, p. 476)

I. Introduction

This passage by Walter Reitman (1971), published in the influential book *Models of Human Memory*, reminds would-be explorers of human memory that individuals may behave strategically so as to "cope with the requirements" of a memory task, which often includes effectively learning new materials as its primary goal. Well before scientists scrutinized the behavior of experimental subjects in the laboratory, people have known that strategies used to learn new materials can have a profound influence on memory and retention. The benefits of using strategies such as associating ideas, the method of loci, and imagery have been heralded since antiquity and—in part—comprise the art of memory (Yates, 1997), in which each individual can influence what is represented on memory's canvas. Indeed, there is ample experimental evidence that effective encoding strategies play a critical role in generating and

0079-7421/04 $35.00

remembering new associations (e.g., Bower, 1970; Richardson, 1998) and new information, in general (Craik, 2002; Hunt & Smith, 1996).

This chapter describes our ongoing research program on strategic behavior during learning, especially with reference to adult development and aging. The effects of aging on memory have been widely studied (see reviews by Light, 1996; Kausler, 1994; Zacks, Hasher, & Li, 2000). Older adults show substantial deficits in associative learning; memory for paired-associate materials has been shown to be impaired in both cross-sectional and longitudinal studies. These deficits occur in samples that are carefully screened for memory pathology (e.g., Alzheimer's disease) and hence cannot be attributed to age-correlated brain disease; instead, the associative learning deficit appears to be a feature of normal aging. The magnitude of observed age differences is affected to a degree by a number of experimental variables, including the pacing of study and test and the nature of the stimuli to be associated, but the evidence for an age-related associative learning deficit is overwhelming. It is also consistent with human and animal studies of age deficits in classical conditioning (Woodruff-Pak, 1999). Naveh-Benjamin (2000) has argued for an associative deficit hypothesis for aging and memory, claiming that "the extent to which a given memory task requires the creation or use of [associations] is a significant determinant of older people's memory performance" (p. 1170). Across several studies, Naveh-Benjamin and his colleagues garner critical support for this hypothesis (e.g., Naveh-Benjamin, 2000; Naveh-Benjamin, Hussain, Guez, & Bar-On, 2003), although they do not evaluate the specific processes at encoding and retrieval that contribute to this deficit.

A contribution of our own research to this area has been to evaluate the hypothesis that age differences in encoding strategies contribute to the associative deficit. Our chapter summarizes the key findings from our research program. We turn next to a definition of strategy use and to our conceptual framework of strategy and aging, which highlights the interplay between strategic behavior and other constructs central to both social and cognitive psychology. After presenting this framework and its relevance to research in this area, we review our major findings regarding strategy use and then discuss the future directions for our research program that we currently envision.

II. A Conceptual Framework of Strategic Behavior

A. Strategies

A strategy can be simply defined as "one of several alternative methods for performing a particular cognitive task" (p. 197, Salthouse, 1991). The actual implementation of a strategy is not necessarily so simple. Models of strategy use are typically predicated on the assumption that individuals engage in goal-directed behavior in task environments, such that selection of strategies for a task depends on the performance goals of the individual, and the affordances of the task context, and the individual's capabilities. Actual strategy use is embedded within and tailored to specific task contexts, requires employment of available cognitive resources (Craik & Byrd, 1982; Gopher & Koriat, 1999; Salthouse, 1991), and involves mechanisms of self-regulation (Schunn & Reder, 2001; Siegler & Lemaire, 1997) to optimize adaptation of a general strategic approach (e.g., use relational processing) to effective strategy use in context (e.g., find relations among to-be-remembered elements and bind them into a conceptual whole).

B. Metacognition and Strategies

Our approach on strategic behavior derives from a metacognitive perspective (e.g., Nelson, 1996). Metacognition can be conceptualized as a set of related cognitive constructs, including beliefs about cognition, knowledge about cognitive processes and mechanisms, and monitoring processes that are part of a larger architecture for achieving control over cognition and behavior (Dunlosky & Hertzog, 1998b; Hertzog & Dixon, 1994; Hertzog & Robinson, in press; Koriat, Goldsmith, & Pansky, 2000; Metcalfe & Kornell, 2003; Nelson & Narens, 1990). Metacognitive perspectives assume that adaptive control of behavior requires monitoring of that behavior, including the monitoring of internal cognitive states. Metacognitive monitoring plays a potentially important role in self-regulation of cognitive performance. For example, individuals can use judgments about ongoing learning or about test performance (e.g., recall successes and failures) as a basis for selecting items for restudy, for allocating more time and effort to learning items they have not yet mastered, or for spacing study to achieve optimal learning (Nelson, 1993; Nelson, Dunlosky, & Graf, 1994; Son, 2004). The process of selecting information for learning is apparently influenced by individuals' beliefs about what they are best prepared to master, as well as their performance goals for the task (Metcalfe & Kornell, 2003; Thiede & Dunlosky, 1999). Such findings underscore the argument that self-regulation is not routine, but instead relies on volitional behavior by individuals attempting to match actions to goals to achieve desired outcomes.

Studies showing that people can use monitoring to guide allocation of study time demonstrate the value of the monitoring and control framework that is at the heart of metacognitive approaches to cognition (Nelson & Narens, 1990). At the same time, they raise the important question of what people are doing with the time they allocate to learning new material.

We assume that they engage in adaptive selection and implementation of encoding strategies that they believe will lead to improved performance. Our research program has focused on understanding these encoding strategies and the monitoring processes that are involved in their use.

C. Strategies for Associative Learning

Our work on strategy use during learning and memory began by studying strategy use in relatively elementary experimental tasks, including paired-associate learning under standard list-learning conditions. The experimental constraints imposed by these tasks control a variety of relevant behaviors that could affect strategic behavior in a natural ecology that are certainly of theoretical interest. Nevertheless, a clear benefit of these tasks has been to enable us to develop reliable and valid methods to assess strategy use.

It is well-known that encoding strategies in list-learning tasks vary in their normative effectiveness. In associative learning, interactive imagery that links elements of a word pair leads to higher cued recall than does forming separate images of each element of the pair (Begg, 1978; Paivio, 1995; Richardson, 1998). In general, mediators like interactive imagery or sentence generation (linking both elements of a pair through forming a sentence about them) are far superior to using no strategy or to using an ineffective strategy like rote repetition. Research with incidental orienting tasks for lists of words (asking individuals to make different kinds of judgments about words, for example) has conclusively demonstrated that semantic or (conceptual) processing of the meaning of to-be-learned information leads to better memory for that information, relative to processing physical or phonological features of the words (see Craik, 2002, for a recent review). More generally, a critical factor concerns the match of processing at encoding to processing requirements required by the recall test. Finally, orienting tasks that ask individuals to focus on the ways in which words from taxonomic categories (e.g., fish and vegetables) are different from one another (orienting individuals to difference features of the exemplars from a category) lead to better memory for those words, relative to orienting individuals to think about characteristics of the words that define their membership in the category (Hunt & Smith, 1996). Focusing on differentiating characteristics improves memory above and beyond the benefit of knowing about category membership. Conversely, orienting individuals to think about relationships between inherently different items (relational processing) has substantial benefits for free recall of associatively unrelated items from a list.

The effects of different types of encoding processes are also observed when individuals intentionally apply encoding strategies under instructions to learn lists of items (Schneider & Pressley, 1997). For example, early work on free recall of word lists showed that subjective organization of to-be-remembered items into meaningful groups achieves higher levels of recall than item-specific encoding alone (e.g., Tulving, 1966). These experimental effects have analogs in spontaneous use of strategic behavior by individuals in memory tasks. People who retrospectively report using relational strategies for learning word lists recall more information from that list (e.g., Hertzog, McGuire, & Lineweaver, 1998).

The research we review in this paper is concerned with associative learning and memory in which relational processing across items is essentially irrelevant for learning. Instead, strategies are focused exclusively on learning a new association between a pair of words, in our case, English word pairs like *salt–mayor*. Individuals are presented a list of these items, one at a time, either with self-paced or experimenter-paced study time for each item. Our main question is, What kinds of strategies, if any, do they use to form new associations under different experimental conditions later described? After a brief delay, individuals are tested for associative learning by being cued with the first element (e.g., *salt*) of each item and asked to recall its associate from the list. Individuals may or may not be given multiple study-test trials with the same item list.

D. The Framework

Even this relatively simple and constrained learning task creates a host of interesting issues regarding strategic behavior. Our conceptual framework for strategy use during associative learning is captured in Fig. 1 (for an earlier version, compare Dunlosky & Hertzog, 1998b). This simple framework highlights the potential importance of several cognitive and metacognitive constructs for understanding strategy use: (a) task appraisal, (b) strategy knowledge, (c) beliefs about memory, (d) strategy selection, (e) strategy production, (f) monitoring encoding, (g) monitoring performance, and (h) learning about strategy effectiveness.

1. *General Assumptions*

The critical feature of the framework is that we assume that encoding strategies are chosen in the moment, and on the fly, so to speak, for different items at the time of item study. Hence, individuals will use different strategies for different items and may actually attempt to implement more than one strategy on any given item. The working assumption is therefore that, across a set of items, individuals will often use more than one strategy. More important, we assume that individuals will adaptively shift strategies for an item if they conclude that a strategy has been ineffective. Figure 1 does not

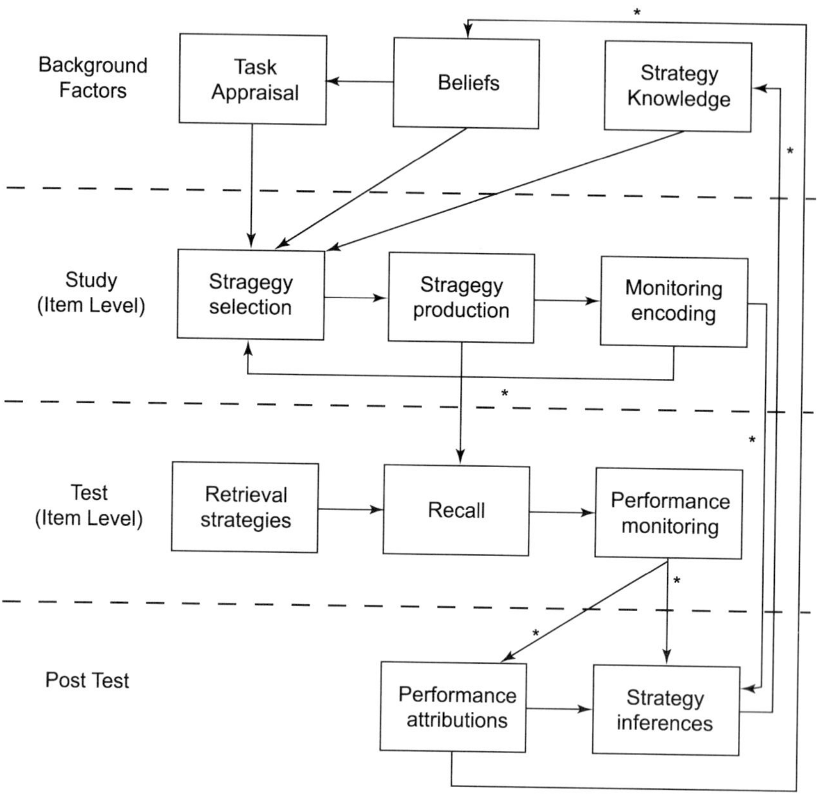

Fig. 1. Conceptual framework for understanding the strategic behavior in associative learning tasks. Paths that involve feedback loops from monitoring to control processes are denoted by an asterisk (*).

attempt to fully capture this dynamic because it does not directly represent the flow of processing that occurs within and between items or across multiple study trials, but the dynamics of adaptive self-regulation are embraced by our perspective.

The framework assumes that, for any target item to be learned, individuals choose a particular strategy on the basis of task appraisal, strategy knowledge, and beliefs. We shall say little more about task appraisal, other than to characterize it as a process in which the task characteristics, task performance demands, and personal performance goals of the individual are evaluated and aligned. Performance goals are, in all likelihood, generic to the task context and not to any specific item. Individuals can choose whether or not to study a given item at all, or with an effortful and time-consuming strategy, based on an appraisal of the item in the context of a performance goal (West, Thorn, & Bagwell, 2003). For instance, a goal to learn a few items from the list may generate different encoding behavior than a goal to learn all the items (Thiede & Dunlosky, 1999). Assessing both the general difficulty of the learning task and the differential difficulty of items within a list can influence study behavior as well (Metcalfe & Kornell, 2003).

2. Personal Beliefs

Beliefs refer to implicit theories about learning and memory (Dweck, 1999; Elliott & Lachman, 1989; Lineweaver & Hertzog, 1998) and beliefs about oneself as a performer in memory tasks (Cavanaugh, Feldman, & Hertzog, 1998; Miller & Lachman, 1999). An implicit theory that memory is a relatively immutable God-given ability, as opposed to a skill one can practice, sharpen, and develop, may have important consequences for whether an individual believes that strategies are an effective means for elevating learning. One relevant type of personal belief is memory self-efficacy (Bandura, 1997), which can be defined as a belief in one's ability to achieve a particular performance goal in a particular task (Berry, 1999; West et al., 2003). Another important type of personal belief involves personal control over memory, that is, the degree to which one believes that it is possible to control learning through action. To the extent that individuals believe that learning depends on skills and that they themselves possess the requisite skills, they may be more likely to attempt to use those skills, including, especially, effortful encoding strategies. For example, individuals who question their ability to use a difficult strategy, like interactive imagery, are unlikely to choose that strategy.

3. Strategy Knowledge and Selection

Strategy knowledge is declarative knowledge about possible strategies for learning and remembering, including their features and circumstances under which they are likely to be more or less effective in promoting learning. Such knowledge derives, presumably, from experience in sampling and using different strategies in actual life (Siegler, 1995) or from secondary sources (e.g., textbooks). Knowledge about strategy effectiveness is, according to our framework, necessary but not sufficient for strategy selection.

Strategy selection represents the process of choosing a strategy, akin to an intention. For example, one can intend to form an interactive image to associate two words. Strategy production, on the other hand, refers to the successful implementation of the chosen strategy (i.e., whether or not an interactive image was indeed formed, as intended). In practice, selection and production are conceptually distinct but difficult to measure empirically for any given item. The reason is that selection is, in our task environments, instantaneously followed by a production attempt. Conceptually, the distinction is useful because individuals may attempt to produce a mediator by using a particular strategy but fail, or they may make no attempt to use any strategy whatsoever.

4. *Metacognitive Monitoring*

Adaptive self-regulation of learning requires monitoring of processes and outcomes (Nelson, 1996). Our framework assumes that individuals do not merely choose to use a strategy and produce a mediator for a new association, they also are capable, in principle, of monitoring the encoding process itself and judging whether they have produced an effective mediator (Nelson & Narens, 1990). Generically, monitoring serves as a feedback loop for strategic self-regulation (Nelson, 1996). We do not claim that such monitoring is necessarily accurate; in fact, the literature suggests it is not (e.g., Koriat, 1997). Monitoring of encoding appears to be fallible and based on attributional processes that are subject to distortion. Nevertheless, an individual who becomes aware of a difficulty in producing interactive images may shift to using a different strategy. In Fig. 1, this type of feedback is shown by a recursive arrow from monitoring of encoding to strategy selection.

Individuals are also capable of monitoring their performance on a recall test for an item, and this type of monitoring may be relatively accurate (Hertzog & Dixon, 1994). Performance monitoring is critical for learning about the effectiveness of strategies, and as such is an important source of information regarding whether one should shift to a new strategy given another study opportunity. Figure 1 depicts several pathways that carry feedback from performance monitoring processes to control processes, such as the pathway from performance monitoring through strategy inferences to strategy knowledge.

5. *Knowledge and Belief Updating*

Updating strategy knowledge as a function of task experience requires that one monitors performance, attributes variation in performance outcomes to particular causes, and makes inferences about strategy effectiveness. Monitoring of encoding and performance monitoring both provide information that can be used to draw inferences about strategy effectiveness, which are then incorporated into the declarative knowledge base about strategies. Our framework assumes that monitoring performance is not, by itself, sufficient; instead, the additional steps of evaluating differential effectiveness and making appropriate inferences about differential effectiveness are also needed (see Dunlosky & Hertzog, 2000). Performance attributions about oneself, and about learning and memory in general, are the basis for shifts that may occur in the belief system (Elliott & Lachman, 1989).

III. Relevance of the Framework for Aging Effects on Memory

A. General Background

Kausler (1994), in reviewing the literature on strategy use and aging, suggested that there were age differences in the production of effective mediators, although these differences were not large enough to account for all age-related variance in associative memory. Salthouse (1991) and Light (1996) also reviewed the available evidence and concluded that age differences in strategy use, per se, were unlikely to explain age differences in memory. We agree with this conclusion, broadly speaking, and will review data that are relevant to it shortly. However, the framework we present here provides an opportunity for both (a) a more fine-grained analysis of these issues, in terms of refined conceptualization and measurement of underlying processes, and (b) an opportunity to evaluate boundary conditions under which older adults' encoding strategies will be deficient. Furthermore, our approach affords a concomitant evaluation of individual differences in strategic behavior, irrespective of individuals' chronological age. As we shall see, individual differences in strategic behavior are substantial and critical for understanding associative memory, even though they may not be important for explaining age differences in associative memory.

B. Aging and Metacognition

An important starting point for our work on aging and strategies, based on the framework in Fig. 1, is that our research has generated a considerable amount of evidence that older adults' elementary monitoring of encoding and performance in paired-associate tasks is largely spared by aging. In short, the available data suggests that older adults are capable, in principle, of accurate monitoring of learning that could generate accurate feedback serving strategic self-regulation. We cannot review this aspect of our work in detail here. Briefly, older adults show similar resolution (relative accuracy) of judgments of learning about paired-associate materials. That is, they can discriminate to an equal degree items they will recall from items they will not recall (Connor, Dunlosky, & Hertzog, 1997; Hertzog, Kidder, Powell-Moman, & Dunlosky, 2002). When asked to judge how well they have learned items studied under specific encoding instructions, both older and younger adults show very limited accuracy in their judgments, and both groups are similarly influenced by misleading cues, such as the fluency of generating an interactive image (Hertzog, Dunlosky, Robinson, & Kidder, 2003; Robinson, Hertzog, & Dunlosky, 2004). In contrast, both older and younger adults show highly accurate delayed judgments of learning (Connor et al., 1997; Dunlosky & Connor, 1997), suggesting that they can monitor paired-associate retrieval mechanisms with excellent accuracy. Earlier work on predictions and postdictions for free recall of words and texts (see Hertzog & Dixon, 1994), as well as our own collaborative research on associative learning (Dunlosky & Hertzog, 2000; Hertzog et al., 2002), indicates that older adults and younger adults are also equally accurate in monitoring recall performance on list-learning tasks, including paired-associate recall. From the point of view of our conceptual framework, we therefore have reason to believe that there are minimal age differences in the accuracy of monitoring either encoding or recall performance.

IV. Our Research on Strategies for Associative Learning

A. Strategy Knowledge and Aging

Consider the categories of relevant variables in Fig. 1. An important possible influence on age differences in strategy selection is differences in declarative knowledge about effective strategies for learning and remembering. Do older adults have deficient knowledge about effective strategies for remembering? Dixon and Hultsch (1983) developed a questionnaire that assessed both knowledge about memory and use of mnemonic strategies and external memory aids in everyday life. Older adults showed no deficits in knowledge about memory processes, were just as likely to report using mnemonic strategies in everyday life, and they were more likely to use external aids for memory (possibly to compensate for perceived age-related memory loss). These findings have been replicated in other studies (e.g., Loewen, Shaw, & Craik, 1990; see Hertzog & Hultsch, 2000).

However, such questionnaire measures use Likert ratings of items that are relatively impoverished samplings of the universe of possible strategic behaviors and may not capture individual differences in knowledge about the relative effectiveness of different encoding strategies in specific task contexts. Hence, Amy Powell-Moman and Christopher Hertzog developed a questionnaire designed explicitly to measure ratings of specific strategies that are possible in a standard paired-associate learning task. Appendix 1 reproduces the essential elements of that questionnaire. Respondents rate the effectiveness of mediational strategies that experimental research has shown to be effective for forming new associations (interactive imagery, semantic association, and sentence generation), along with strategies that are not as effective (e.g., generalized focused attention). Ratings are requested on a 1–10 Likert scale. One can evaluate effectiveness ratings for individual strategies and can also use a derived measure to capture respondents' strategy knowledge: The average difference between their ratings for normatively effective strategies and normatively less effective strategies.

We have used this questionnaire to measure strategy knowledge both before and after experience in a paired-associate learning task. Figure 2 shows unpublished data on strategy ratings of younger and older adults prior to actual paired-associate learning experience. All strategies tended to be rated as moderately effective (the midpoint of the scale is 5.5), although normatively effective strategies (the three strategies on the left) received reliably higher ratings than normatively ineffective strategies (the three strategies on the right) for both age groups. The mean difference was 1.63 Likert units (SE = .28) for younger adults and .97 units (SE = .28) for older adults. An interesting aspect of the data was that both age groups rated rote repetition as a relatively effective strategy (95% confidence intervals did not include the scale midpoint), even though it is not. Younger adults tended to have higher

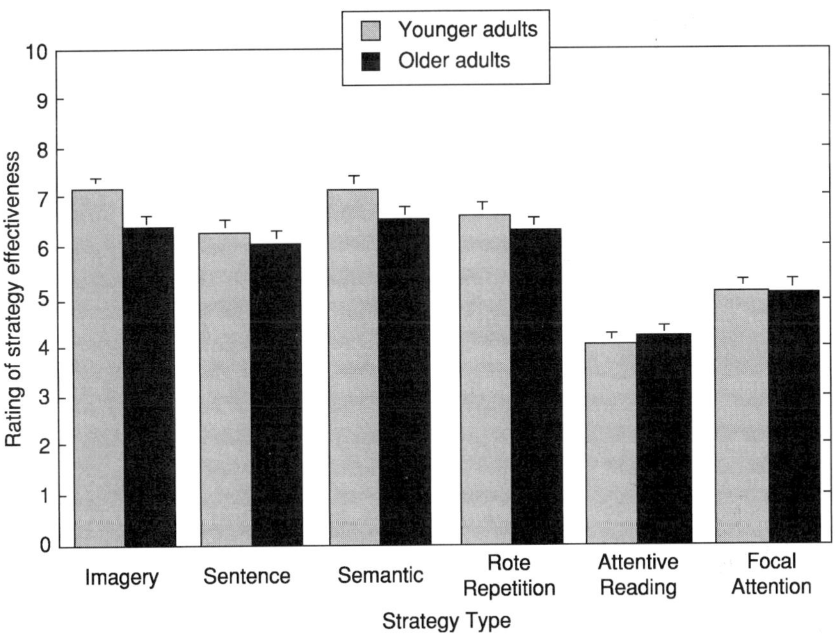

Fig. 2. Ratings of strategy effectiveness for six possible strategies in a paired-associate learning task by younger and older adults.

ratings for effective strategies overall ($p = .10$) and rated interactive imagery as more effective ($p < .01$). Both groups showed reasonably good declarative knowledge about effective strategies, although there were small age differences favoring young adults that could have an impact on spontaneous strategy selection. Age differences in declarative strategy knowledge, per se, do not appear to be a good explanation of any age differences in strategy use.

B. Strategy Production for Associative Learning

1. Hypotheses About Aging and Strategic Deficiencies

Historically, a prominent hypothesis for explaining age-related deficits in learning is the *production deficiency hypothesis*, which is that older adults are less likely to produce effective strategies during study (Kausler, 1994). According to this hypothesis, if older adults were given appropriate instructions and support about effective strategies, then age-related differences in memory performance would be eradicated.

A variety of other strategy-based deficiency hypotheses have been proposed. The *utilization deficiency hypothesis* posits that older and younger adults are equivalent in strategy production, yet older adults benefit less from their use, possibly due to the production of less effective mediators. The *retrieval deficiency hypothesis* states that even when strategic behavior is equivalent for both age groups, older adults are more likely to forget the mediator (e.g., the specific interactive image produced for a word pair) they generated, losing the potential benefit from having used a strategy.

2. Testing the Production Deficiency Hypothesis

A standard method to evaluate the production deficiency hypothesis has been to compare age differences in memory performance for uninstructed groups with groups who were instructed to use an effective strategy (e.g., interactive imagery). Based on his review of research conducted up to the mid-1990s, Kausler (1994) concluded that a production deficiency does account for some—but not all—of age-related memory impairments. Although this earlier research provided a solid beginning, it fell short of providing a definitive test of the production deficiency hypothesis. The difficulty is that participants do not universally comply with instructions to use a particular strategy (e.g., Eagle, 1967), and it is unknown whether there are age differences in compliance. Certainly, a more analytic method was needed, preferably one that could be used to describe the contribution of other strategy-based deficits as well.

Our approach was to use self-reports to measure strategy use for individual items (Yuille & Paivio, 1968). In our research, report options are obtained by having participants select, for each item, one of several strategies that are normatively used most often (e.g., imagery, sentence generation, and repetition). Participants can also report idiosyncratic strategies (i.e., a response option of "other") or not using any strategy whatsoever. To maximize the validity of these self-reports, individuals are informed of the nature of each type of strategy prior to the report. Strategy reports can be made concurrently (i.e., immediately after item study). In these cases, participants must be instructed about the nature of strategies prior to studying any items, and hence, concurrent reports prevent assessment of spontaneous strategy use. Spontaneous strategy use can be assessed by retrospective reports; after the standard study-test trial, individuals are serially presented with the items in the original order of study and asked to provide strategy reports for each item. Both kinds of item-by-item strategy reports provide a rich data set that offers a more analytic exploration of strategy-based deficiencies.

Of course, there are construct validity concerns for either method. Requiring a strategy report for each item may create a demand characteristic to claim having used an effective strategy even when one did not. Retrospective reports rely on represented items cueing retrieval of the mediator that had been produced, so memory deficits may make these reports less valid for older adults. Our research has addressed these issues.

3. *Empirical Results*

Our first study (Dunlosky & Hertzog, 1998a) used concurrent reports for associatively related (*salt–sugar*) and unrelated items (*salt–mayor*) in two separate experiments. Individuals were allowed to choose strategies (a self-chosen condition) or were instructed to use interactive imagery (an imagery condition). They were also informed of the existence of three strategies (imagery, sentence generation, and rote repetition), given a brief description of each one, and told that other strategies could be used as well. It was stressed that they should report the strategy, if any, they actually used, and not the strategy they were instructed to use. They received no information about the normative effectiveness of any strategy.

It is well-known that recall is better for related items than for unrelated items and that age differences are smaller for related items. One possible explanation is that older adults are better able to produce effective strategies for related items. Figure 3 shows the reported strategies for related and unrelated items under imagery instructions. Note that imagery use was similar for both age groups, even for unrelated items. Critically, compliance under imagery instructions was good but far from perfect—on average,

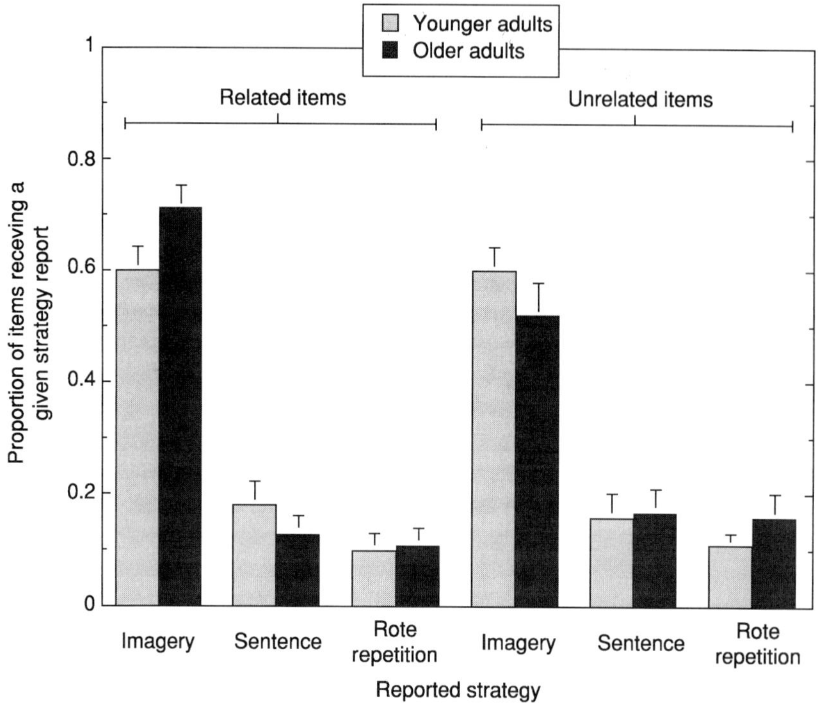

Fig. 3. Proportion of reported strategy (interactive imagery, rote repetition, and sentence generation) for related and unrelated items by young and older adults when instructed to use interactive imagery (adapted from Dunlosky & Hertzog, 1998a).

individuals successfully used interactive imagery for roughly 60% of the unrelated items. As expected, compliance was better for related items. Figure 4 shows the paired-associate recall for both types of items. Rote repetition was essentially as effective as interactive imagery and sentence generation for related items, but reports of using these normatively effective mediators were associated with reliably higher recall of unrelated items. This pattern is consistent with past literature and supports the validity of the concurrent strategy reports. Moreover, the large age differences in recall, even when effective mediators were produced, disconfirmed the production deficiency hypothesis. Finally, age differences in effective strategy production for related vs. unrelated items, shown in Fig. 3, apparently do not account for the patterns of recall results shown in Fig. 4.

In the self-chosen condition, both older adults and younger adults tended to choose effective strategies. For unrelated items, older adults chose interactive imagery for about 40% of the items, on average, and they chose

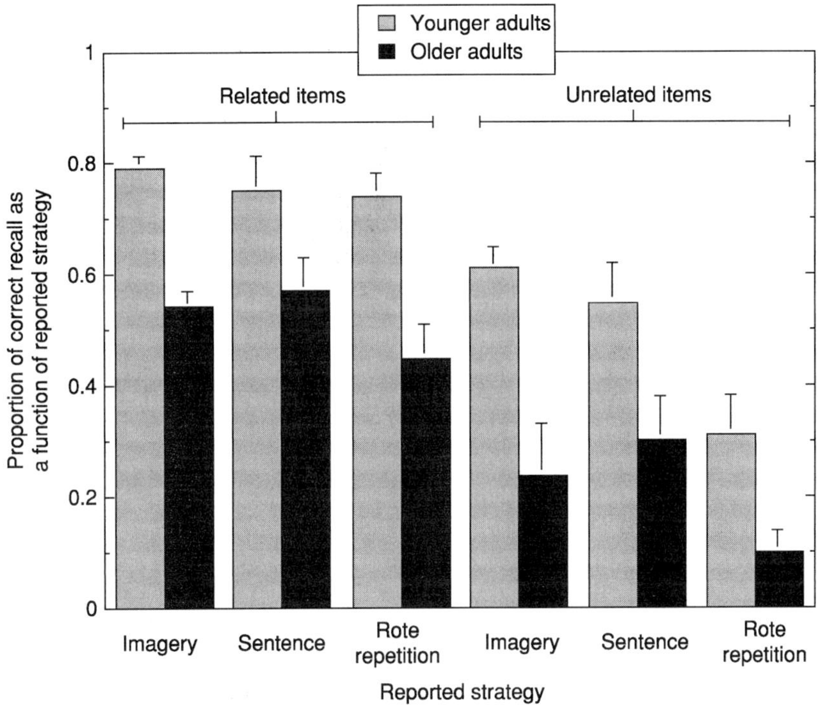

Fig. 4. Paired-associate recall for different reported strategies (interactive imagery, rote repetition, sentence generation) for related and unrelated items by young and older adults (adapted from Dunlosky & Hertzog, 1998a).

sentence generation for just under 30% of the items. We found no evidence that older adults were inherently averse to using imagery (see Kausler, 1994). Younger adults reported selecting both types of strategies about equally, on average, for just over 30% of the items. Of course, these selections were made after informing people about their existence and providing examples of each kind of strategy.

These data are therefore not relevant to spontaneous strategy use, and so a more definitive evaluation of production deficiencies as an explanation of age differences required retrospective strategy reports. Dunlosky and Hertzog (2001) combined instructional methods with retrospective item-by-item reports and added a concurrent report condition to evaluate the validity of the retrospective reports. Individuals studied a list of unrelated paired associates. Two instructional groups were compared. For the uninformed group, no mention of strategies was made prior to study and test, whereas the informed group received the same information about strategies provided in the Dunlosky and Hertzog (1998a) study. Whereas recall performance did not differ for the two groups of younger adults (.61 and .59, for informed and uninformed, respectively), performance for older adults was reliably less for the uninformed group (.17) than the informed group (.27).

When participants were informed of strategies they could use, production of normatively effective strategies (e.g., imagery and sentence generation, combined) was relatively high for both younger and older adults. For both groups, there was considerable variability in strategies used, and individuals typically used more than one strategy. However, when participants were not informed, use of effective strategies was substantially greater for younger adults. A reliable Age × Instruction interaction constituted evidence for an age-related production deficiency. These differences in strategy production also contributed to age deficits in recall performance, such that age differences in recall were larger between the uninformed age groups. Nevertheless, substantial age deficits in recall were still apparent for the informed groups, replicating Dunlosky and Hertzog (1998a). Thus, the age differences in strategy production could not account entirely for age differences in associative recall, contrary to the production deficiency hypothesis.

Two aspects of the results provided further evidence for the construct validity of the strategy reports. First, the retrospective reports showed good agreement with concurrent reports in the group giving both types of report, although agreement was slightly less for older adults. Second, both age groups generated similar patterns of superiority in recall when using effective strategies, relative to using rote repetition (as in Dunlosky & Hertzog, 1998a).

In sum, there appear to be reliable age differences in spontaneous strategy use for associative learning, and these differences contribute to age differences in associative learning. However, the age differences can be eliminated by merely informing participants about the existence of mediational strategies, and robust age differences in associative recall are found even when controlling on production of effective strategies. Hence, age differences in spontaneous strategy use are at best a small part of the explanation of age differences in associative learning.

C. Utilization and Retrieval Deficits

In a recent study (Dunlosky, Hertzog, & Powell-Moman, in press), we adopted a *mediator report-and-retrieval method* (see Yuille, 1973) to more closely scrutinize possible sources of mediator-related deficits. This method requires participants to describe the specific mediators that they generate at study (i.e., mediator report) and then recall these mediators at test (i.e., mediator retrieval), immediately after item recall. Older and younger adults were instructed to use either interactive imagery to associate word pairs or were instructed to use sentence generation. This approach allowed us to assess utilization deficits, because we could examine the qualities of mediators produced and determine whether older adults produce less effective mediators. For example, older adults' images could have been more characterized by poorly integrated images of both words, which would lead to lower recall (Richardson, 1998). It also allowed us to test whether older adults are less likely to retrieve mediators, even when their mediators are judged to be of similar quality as the mediators of younger adults.

Both older and younger adults complied with the instructions equally well in that they reported using the instructed strategy (either imagery or sentence generation) on about 80% of the study trials. The mediators reported at study were scored for multiple features, such as whether the word pairs interacted in each mediator, the number of content words, the syntactic role of the cue and target, and so forth. The nature of the mediators was essentially identical for older and younger adults, providing evidence against a utilization deficiency. This finding is consistent with other investigations that have examined mediator reports alone (Marshall, Elias, Webber, Gist, Winn, & King, 1978; Smith, Park, Earles, Shaw, & Whiting, 1998).

Mediator retrieval outcomes were also coded. We distinguished between no mediator retrieval, partial mediator retrieval (recall of some but not all critical features of the description), gist mediator retrieval (identical semantic content, but with different wording), and verbatim mediator retrieval. Figure 5 shows these data. Results for imagery instructions and sentence instructions were essentially identical. Even though age differences were negligible in mediator production and mediator features, substantial age-related declines occurred in the correct retrieval of mediators at test under imagery instructions (over 20% decline) and under sentence-generation instructions (over 30%). This difference was reflected primarily in omission errors—older individuals were more likely to fail to retrieve the mediators they had generated.

The conditional probability of recalling the correct response, given either gist or verbatim mediator retrieval, was high for both younger and older adults (>.85), although older adults were slightly less likely to correctly decode gist-accurate mediators to generate the correct response. Thus, age deficits in mediator retrieval appeared to be the critical source of the associative learning deficit. Indeed, a path analysis demonstrated that age deficits in mediator retrieval accounted for a substantial proportion of age-related variance in recall performance. One implication is that the associative deficit observed for concrete, unrelated noun pairs may not be a function of impaired encoding processes, because we detected similar success rates and

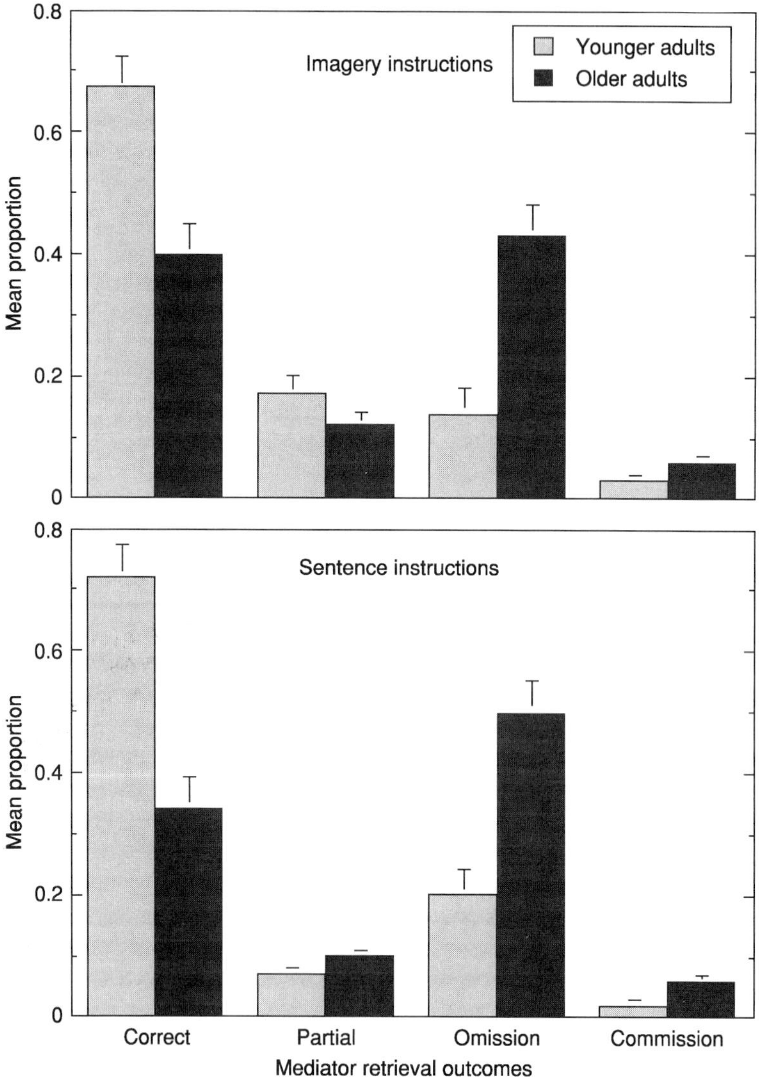

Fig. 5. Mediator retrieval outcomes for items studied under imagery or sentence instructions for young and older adults (from Dunlosky, Hertzog, & Powell-Moman, in press, Fig. 1, Copyright American Psychological Association, reprinted with permission).

could identify no qualitative differences in the mediators produced by older and younger adults. Instead, the deficit may be localized to binding, consolidation, or retrieval.

In sum, we find little evidence that older adults generate poor-quality mediators for concrete noun pairs. On the other hand, older adults are highly likely to fail to retrieve the high-quality mediators they generated at study. Given that we see little evidence of deficient quality of mediators between the age groups, it is difficult to see how a strategic encoding deficit can account for these results.

D. Individual Differences in Strategic Behavior

1. *Theoretical Background*

Resource theory (e.g., Gopher & Koriat, 1999) stipulates that individuals use relevant cognitive resources (e.g., attentional capacity, working memory capacity) to achieve effective solutions. Likewise, applications of resource theory to cognitive aging research (e.g., Salthouse, 1991) hypothesize that age changes in complex cognition, including memory and reasoning, can be attributed to age-related declines in resources like working memory. Given that individuals vary substantially in profiles of realized abilities and skills (i.e., resources), it stands to reason that different strategies may be optimal for different persons in different contexts. Moreover, individuals will vary in preferred modes or styles of cognition and decision making (Baron, 2000; Messick, 2001; Sternberg & Zhang, 2001), independently of whether their preferred mode of processing draws primarily on their strengths rather than their weaknesses.

One advantage of the strategy report methods we have developed is that they can be applied to analyses of individual differences in spontaneous strategic behavior. Theories of intelligence, such as Cattell and Horn's theory of fluid and crystallized intelligence (e.g., Horn, 1989), argue that fluid intelligence is characterized by flexible and effective analysis of information in novel situations and draw a link between fluid intelligence and the effective use of problem solving strategies, executive control, and self-regulation (see also Sternberg, 1985). However, only a few empirical studies support this link by directly measuring the relationship of intelligence to strategic behavior. For example, Schunn and Reder (2001) reported that adaptive shifts in strategies in a complex air traffic control simulation were correlated with general intelligence; as expected, high ability individuals were more likely to shift strategies to match changing task affordances. A number of studies have found a correlation between fluid intelligence and associative learning (e.g., Horn, 1980) but have not collected evidence about whether this relationship is mediated by greater spontaneous use of effective strategies by people with high fluid intelligence. Nor is this necessarily one of the correct explanations of the correlation. High fluid intelligence is associated with higher working memory capacity (Kyllonen &

Christal, 1990), which in turn is associated with greater resistance to proactive interference of information held in working memory (see Engle & Kane, 2004, for a review). Hence, the correlation could be mediated by better resistance to interitem interference during associative recall by persons high in fluid intelligence, among other mechanisms.

2. *Individual Differences in Spontaneous Encoding Behavior*

Newly collected data (Hertzog, Dunlosky, & Robinson, 2004) demonstrate a relationship between intellectual abilities and spontaneous use of effective encoding. We measured strategies for forming new associations among concrete, unrelated paired associates using the retrospective report methodology described earlier. A sample of over 300 adults, ages 25–79, participated in the study. This cross-sectional sample was drawn so we could get a better assessment of life span differences in strategic behavior and to avoid the typical extreme age-groups comparison of young adults (typically, university students) and older adults (see Hertzog, 1996). The design also involved a between-subjects manipulation of presentation rate; individuals were assigned at random to fast-paced study presentations (less than 4 s) or slow-paced presentations (greater than 10 s). Given what is known about the time course of forming new associations (e.g., Kliegl, Smith, & Baltes, 1989), we expected that fast pacing would suppress strategic behavior and alter correlations of intelligence with both strategic behavior and paired-associate recall.

Figure 6 shows the mean self-report strategies for persons in the fast-paced and slow-paced conditions. Again, the data provide support for the validity of the self-reports. In this community sample, spontaneous use of effective strategies was somewhat infrequent. Fast pacing caused reliably more instances of producing no strategy (not attempting to use a strategy or running out of time), which translated into reliably less use of interactive imagery and sentence generation. We summed the frequencies of imagery, sentence, or other strategies across items for each individual, under the assumption that these categories represent effective mediator use. There was a strong linkage of effective strategy use and paired-associate recall. Individuals differed in the proportion of items they reported spontaneously using effective strategies ($M = .31$, $SD = .33$), and these strategy reports correlated substantially with paired-associate recall ($r = .74$). Roughly half of the variance in associative recall was predicted by effective strategy use.

We also transferred participants to learning a new list in which all individuals received slow pacing. In this case, exposure to the strategy reports and task experience could have increased strategic behavior, and indeed it did so

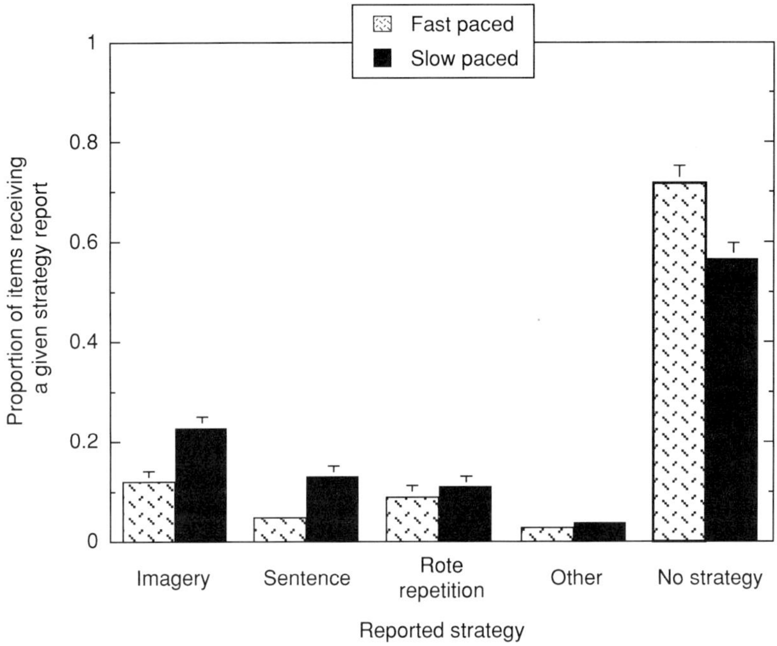

Fig. 6. Spontaneous use of strategies reflected in strategy report outcomes for fast-paced and slow-paced presentation rate conditions (from Hertzog, Dunlosky, & Robinson, 2004).

for persons who had already been in the slow-paced condition (from $M = .42$ to $M = .52$). Transfer from fast pacing to slow pacing had a far greater effect on increased strategy use, however. Overall, persons still manifested variability in effective strategy use on the transfer list ($M = .48$, $SD = .38$), and the correlation of effective strategy use and recall remained high ($r = .69$).

3. *Relationships of Ability to Strategy Use and Recall*

The study included multiple indicators of several intellectual abilities. These intellectual abilities were substantially correlated with effective strategy use, but the correlations shifted as a function of pacing (see Table I). In the fast-paced condition, all the intelligence measures correlated roughly .3 with effective strategy use. These correlations shifted upward in the slow-paced condition. Inductive reasoning (our best indicator of fluid intelligence), crystallized intelligence (world knowledge, including vocabulary) and associational fluency (rapid generation of associates or related ideas)—see Carroll (1993) for further information about these constructs—generated high correlations with strategy use in the slow-paced condition. The latter

TABLE I

CORRELATIONS OF PSYCHOMETRIC ABILITIES WITH EFFECTIVE STRATEGY USE IN FAST-PACED AND SLOW-PACED STUDY GROUPS

	Fast-paced	Slow-paced
Ability		
Perceptual speed	.32	.28
Spatial relations	.29	.32
Inductive reasoning	.29	.38
Associational fluency	.29	.49
Crystallized intelligence	.28	.47
Working memory	.25	.25

Data from Hertzog, Dunlosky, and Robinson (2004). All correlations were reliably greater than 0 ($p < .01$). *Note*: See Horn (1989) or Carroll (1993) for definitions and further discussion of these intellectual abilities.

two abilities can be considered alternative cognitive resources useful for producing mediators. High verbal knowledge and rapid access to associated concepts should increase the likelihood of successful mediator formation by enabling the individual to generate effective mediational concepts (e.g., for *salt–mayor*, "what are the properties of mayor I could associate with salt?"). We interpret the shift in correlations as evidence favoring a resource perspective. When encoding time is severely restricted, strategy use is suppressed because individuals cannot use their knowledge, skills, and abilities to generate effective mediators in an optimal fashion. However, when sufficient encoding time is provided, intelligent individuals generate more effective mediators, allowing a stronger relationship of individual differences in cognitive resources and strategy use to emerge.

Structural equation models showed that fluid intelligence and crystallized intelligence independently predicted effective strategy use. It is well known that these abilities also predict episodic memory performance (e.g., Hultsch, Hertzog, Dixon, & Small, 1998; Kyllonen, Tirre, & Christal, 1991). Hence, this new empirical evidence supports the claim that high-ability individuals are more likely to be strategic, although the relationship is not limited to general or fluid intelligence. However, strategy use did not fully mediate the intelligence-recall correlations. The analysis revealed that roughly one-third of the total effect of intellectual abilities on recall performance was mediated by effective strategy use; the remaining variance must be determined by other mechanisms.

Given that crystallized intelligence, including verbal knowledge, is an important resource for strategy production, is it simply because knowledgeable people, in general, have better strategy knowledge, in particular? Theoretically, the answer would seem to be no. Based on our framework, declarative knowledge about the existence of strategies is not isomorphic with the procedural skill of generating a mediator, and cognitive resources are needed to successfully implement the goal of generating a mediator. Our new data support this contention. Mediator strategy knowledge, as measured by the questionnaire described earlier (see Appendix 1), predicted strategy use independently of crystallized intelligence in our structural regression model. Apparently, knowing that certain strategies are effective is important but not sufficient for ensuring that effective mediators will indeed be produced.

5. *Effects of Aging on Strategy Use and Recall*

What about age differences in effective strategy production? Unlike Dunlosky and Hertzog (2001), we found little evidence of an age deficit in strategy production; the correlation of age with the production of effective mediators was less than −.10 in both conditions. This outcome suggests that university students (as in Dunlosky & Hertzog, 2001) may be superior to older adults in spontaneous strategy use for reasons other than aging, per se. However, there were small but reliable age differences in strategy production statistically controlling for intellectual abilities, particularly crystallized intelligence. Older adults typically show higher performance on recognition vocabulary tests than do younger adults, either due to the accumulation of knowledge over the life span (Ackerman & Rolfhus, 1999), or cohort differences in knowledge of word meanings (Schaie, 1996), or both. Given that older adults have higher crystallized intelligence, and given that crystallized intelligence is a potent predictor of strategy production, older adults are deficient in strategy production given their relative level of verbal knowledge. Nevertheless, any age differences in strategy production did not account for age differences in associative learning. Indeed, age differences in paired-associate recall were not reduced by controlling on strategy use and other ability measures, including fluid intelligence and perceptual speed (compare Salthouse, 1996).

6. *The Role of Personal Beliefs*

Finally, control beliefs also predicted spontaneous use of strategies in list-learning tasks, independent of the other predictors we have already reviewed. We collected questionnaire measures of memory self-efficacy and perceived control over memory (Hertzog, Lineweaver, & McGuire, 1999; Lachman, Bandura, Weaver, & Elliott, 1995). Composite measures of memory self-efficacy and perceived memory control correlated slightly less than .3 with effective strategy use. The structural regression model showed that perceptions of personal control over memory predicted strategy use. Believing that one can control memory apparently promotes spontaneous strategic behavior, independent of strategy knowledge and the cognitive resources available for generating mediators. This finding resonates with social psychological theories of efficacy and control (e.g., Bandura, 1997; Elliott & Lachman, 1989). One can know that a strategy is normatively effective (at least for others), but still (a) believe that the degree of control achieved is inconsequential and/or (b) lack confidence that one can use the strategy successfully in this context. Low personal control can inhibit action, whereas high personal control can facilitate it. The independent relationship of beliefs to strategic behavior reinforces the argument that we cannot fully understand strategic behavior without understanding (a) the implicit theory that individuals have about cognition and its causes (e.g., Dweck, 1999), and (b) how control and efficacy beliefs deriving from such implicit theories may affect individuals' behavior in the performance context (Elliott & Lachman, 1989; Hertzog et al., 1999).

7. *Summary*

The study of spontaneous individual differences in encoding behavior verifies that intellectual abilities are a reliable predictor of spontaneous use of effective mediators for new associations. Some of the relationship between abilities and recall can be attributed to the effects of abilities on strategy use. Furthermore, the pattern of ability–strategy correlations shifts as a function of the manipulation of presentation time, with more robust correlations emerging for long presentation times. Finally, personal control beliefs and self-efficacy beliefs are correlated with effective strategy use, and control beliefs predict strategy use independent of intellectual abilities. In general, these findings also reinforce the conclusion that age differences in spontaneous strategy use are not an important determinant of age differences in associative recall.

E. Learning About Strategy Effectiveness Through Task Performance

1. *Background*

The framework described in Fig. 1 captures one aspect of the dynamics of self-regulated learning we have not yet discussed—learning about strategy effectiveness through task experience. Investigations of age-related effects on knowledge updating have been implicitly or explicitly guided by metacognitive models (e.g., Bieman-Copland & Charness, 1994; Brigham & Pressley, 1988; Dunlosky & Hertzog, 1998b; Matvey, Dunlosky, Shaw, Parks, &

Hertzog, 2002). When using a given strategy to perform a memory task, a person may monitor ongoing learning of individual items, which can potentially provide personal insight into the relative effectiveness of that strategy. Accurate monitoring itself is presumably not sufficient, however, because one must also attribute any performance boosts to the effects of the strategy being used and then modify his or her own knowledge about that strategy (see Fig. 1). See Dunlosky and Hertzog (2000) for additional details concerning how different metacognitive judgments could, in principle, reflect monitoring and inferential mechanisms critical for knowledge updating.

In a typical empirical study of knowledge updating, the experimenter selects strategies (or manipulates a factor that influences memory performance) that are differentially effective and that participants do not initially have highly accurate knowledge about. Participants are then required to use these strategies to study new materials, followed by an initial test trial. During the test, each participant has the opportunity to monitor performance and potentially infer the effects of each strategy on memory. To assess knowledge updating, participant's knowledge about strategy effectiveness is assessed before and after the relevant task experience. Measures of knowledge have ranged from relatively implicit measures (e.g., choosing which of the strategies to use on a subsequent trial) to relatively explicit ones (e.g., judging which strategy would produce the best performance on a subsequent trial).

2. *Aging and Updating Knowledge About Associative Learning Strategies*

Conclusions in the literature are currently mixed as to whether age-related differences exist in knowledge updating. For instance, evidence from Bieman-Copland and Charness (1994) suggest that age deficits occur in knowledge updating after task experience (see also Brigham & Pressley, 1988), whereas Dunlosky and Hertzog (2000) arrived at the opposite conclusion. Because the latter study focused on associative learning, we describe outcomes from it here. Older and younger adults studied and were tested on two separate lists of paired associates. They were instructed to use rote repetition (normatively ineffective strategy) to study some paired associates on each list and to use interactive imagery (normatively effective) on the other items. The strategy instruction was randomly chosen for each item (with the constraint that half the items from each list were studied under each strategy instruction) and was displayed above the item (either "Imagery" or "Repetition") during study. Thus, participants had two consecutive study-test trials of different lists that involved using both strategies. The use of a mixed design gave participants experience in using both strategies, as well as recall performance relevant to their relative effectiveness. Updated knowledge about the differential effectiveness of these two strategies was measured by (a) performance postdictions (recall evaluations) immediately after the recall test for the first list, (b) performance predictions before studying the second list, and (c) judgments of learning (JOLs) collected during study of the first and second lists. Participants made separate performance predictions and postdictions for each type of strategy, and JOLs were collected for every item.

Older adults were given more time per item (10 s vs. 4 s) to reduce age differences in recall, given our focus on age differences in predictive accuracy and knowledge updating. As expected, recall performance was reliably higher for items studied under interactive imagery instructions for both age groups (see Table II). In fact, mean JOLs for the second list were sensitive to the recall differences between rote repetition and imagery, although performance postdictions and second-list predictions provided somewhat better differentiation. Note, however, that the absolute accuracy measures

TABLE II

RECALL, GLOBAL PREDICTIONS, MEAN JOLS, GLOBAL POSTDICTIONS, AND ABSOLUTE ACCURACY FOR TWO TRIALS OF PAIRED-ASSOCIATE LEARNING UNDER ROTE AND IMAGERY INSTRUCTIONS

	Trial 1		Trial 2	
	Imagery	Rote	Imagery	Rote
Young adults				
Recall	56	35	58	43
Predictions	43	42	42	30
Mean JOL	47	44	44	36
Postdictions	36	20	41	28
Pred accuracy	−13	7	−16	−13
JOL accuracy	−9	9	−14	−7
Post accuracy	−20	−13	−17	−15
Older adults				
Recall	50	31	53	35
Predictions	43	36	30	21
Mean JOL	38	31	33	25
Postdictions	31	19	35	20
Pred accuracy	−7	5	−23	−14
JOL accuracy	−12	0	−20	−10
Post accuracy	−19	−12	−18	−15

Note: Data adapted from Dunlosky and Hertzog (2000), Table I. All variables scaled in percentages. Accuracy scores = Judgment–Recall. Abbreviations: Pred—Prediction; JOL—judgment of learning; Post—Postdiction.

(scaled as judgments−recall) showed little sign of improvement across the two trials. In particular, postdiction accuracy was surprisingly low at both trials for both age groups. In contrast, between-person Pearson correlations of predictions with recall showed substantial increases between lists (Fig. 7). Participants were apparently learning quite a bit about their recall performance, but such learning did not necessarily translate into accurate calibration of the magnitude of performance predictions or JOLs with recall under the two strategies. Using absolute accuracy of these metacognitive judgments as the indicator of strategy knowledge may be problematic (see Connor et al., 1997; Hertzog et al., 2002, for discussions of this issue regarding metacognitive judgments and aging). Nevertheless, there was little indication of age differences in knowledge updating based on such measures, or on the correlations shown in Fig. 7.

Unpublished recent data from our lab suggests that the questionnaire measure of strategy knowledge described earlier shows a substantial increase in strategy knowledge after recall performance on the first list, reinforcing the argument that absolute accuracy (especially in JOLs) may be insensitive to knowledge updating. Nevertheless, some knowledge updating by this criterion did occur, and in the case of associative mediators for concrete nouns, it doesn't appear to be affected by aging. Given the larger literature, there may be age deficits in knowledge updating in other task environments. For further discussion and an attempt to resolve inconsistencies in this literature, see Matvey et al. (2002).

In summary, we find little evidence that older adults are impaired in their ability to learn about differential effectiveness of strategies for associative learning. Both older and younger adults show some evidence of knowledge updating, although this updating process is not finely calibrated and is not reflected in all relevant indirect measures (especially JOLs).

V. Future Directions

Our work on both (a) age differences in elementary monitoring processes and (b) age differences in generating mediators for associative learning (as reviewed here) indicates that there are minimal age differences in either kind of process, at least in optimal task contexts. Hence the interesting question becomes, to what extent are there age differences in the interplay between the two kinds of mechanisms, as in the use of monitoring to achieve control over memory in more complex learning tasks? There are several experiments indicating that older adults may be deficient in achieving optimal control over learning or recall in particular task contexts (e.g., Dunlosky & Connor, 1997; Kelley & Sahakyan, 2003; Murphy, Schmitt, Canuso, & Sanders,

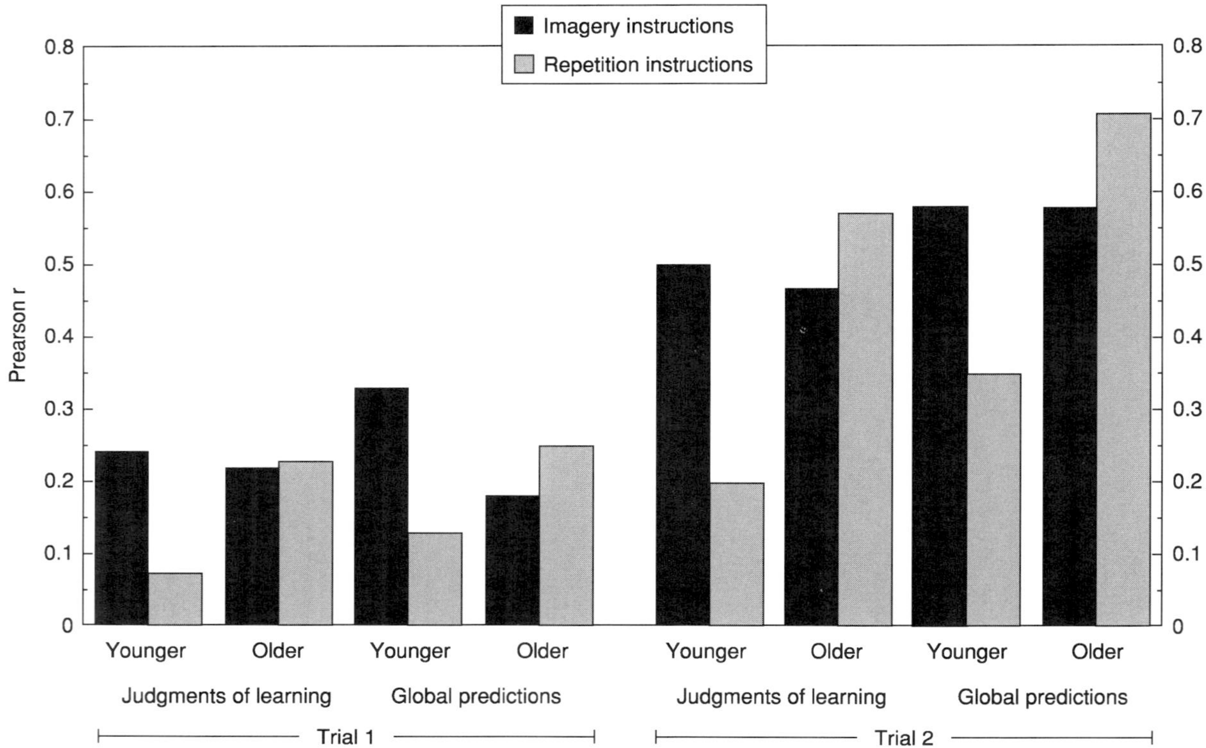

Fig. 7. Correlations of metacognitive judgments (predictions, JOLs, and postdictions) with recall over two different study-test trials (from Dunlosky & Hertzog, 2000, Fig. 2, Copyright American Psychological Association, reprinted with permission).

1987). Our working hypothesis is that age differences in effective cognitive self-regulation are most likely when optimal control requires (a) inferences about the current state of the cognitive system under informational uncertainty or (b) spontaneous use of complex control strategies for translating accurate monitoring into strategic behavior. Older adults may be more likely to show deficits in strategic behavior when complex tasks tax cognitive resources that are needed for executive self-regulation (Bieman-Copland & Charness, 1994). A number of possible avenues for further research on strategic self-regulation derive from our research program. We consider a few of them briefly.

A. Aging Effects on Encoding

The research we have reviewed indicates that aging does not have profound effects on associative encoding strategies for elementary materials such as concrete noun pairs. However, we believe there will be conditions under which age differences in effective encoding strategies will emerge. Hertzog et al. (2003) manipulated item concreteness as part of a study of encoding fluency, including concrete items (e.g., *salt–mayor*) and abstract items (e.g., *justice–loyalty*). Forming interactive images for abstract items is a more difficult endeavor, because one must identify concrete, imageable associates or properties of the abstract concepts and use them to produce mediators. An avid comic book reader, for example, might imagine key members of the League of Justice, Superman, Batman, and the Green Lantern, engaged in a one-for-all, all-for-one group hug. However, such interactive images are inherently more complex and difficult to conceive and generate, and retrieving the correct image at test is more at risk for errors of decoding the image due to the complex associative chain (e.g., generating "loyalty" after successfully retrieving the image of hugging superheroes; see Yuille, 1973). When we piloted abstract items with older adults, under conditions where we informed them of the possibility of strategies and instructed the use of interactive imagery, we found major deficits in interactive imagery production that resulted in low paired-associate recall (see also Rowe & Schnore, 1971). Further pilot work suggested that generating sentence mediators for abstract items also yielded an age difference in strategy production. We are currently conducting a mediator report-and-retrieval study to evaluate this phenomenon.

These pilot data suggest that the more complex and difficult the process of generating mediators, the more likely we will be to observe age differences in effective strategy production. It could also be the case, for example, given age changes in attentional resources, that concurrent attentional load or dual-task instructions would differentially impair older adults' production of effective mediators (see Anderson, 1999). One would not conclude from such results that production deficiencies account for age differences in memory, given the conditions under which strategy production is relatively unimpaired but memory itself is impaired. Instead, one would conclude that there are conditions under which older adults' encoding behaviors are more likely to fail (with additional negative consequences for memory performance) and hence would seek to predict and explain when such deficits would become manifest.

B. Complex Metacognitive Control

As noted earlier, studies of metacognitive control in more complex task environments suggest that the use of monitoring to achieve control may be impaired in older adults, even when monitoring itself is spared. For example, Dunlosky and Connor (1997) asked younger and older adults to learn paired associates over multiple study-test trials. Learning theory suggests that the optimal strategy for rapid learning of the entire list is to focus study at Trial N + 1 on those items not learned on Trial N that individuals are capable of learning (Atkinson, 1972; Fisher, 1996). In terms of study time allocation, one should allocate more time to the study of previously unlearned items. Hence, monitoring which items have and have not been learned can play a role in determining rates of learning (Nelson et al., 1994). Dunlosky and Connor (1997) showed that younger adults had a strong negative correlation between delayed JOLs for items at Trial N, with study time allocated to those same items at Trial N + 1 (indicating more study time allocated to unlearned material, as expected). Older adults also produced a negative correlation of these variables, but it was reliably lower than for younger adults, suggesting that their allocation of study time was less optimal for learning.

Such results suggest that investigating the dynamics of multiple-trial learning may reveal deficits in metacognitive control that are not apparent in the single study-test trial experiments we have reported here. Perhaps more important, studying multiple-trial tasks may be critical for revealing the dynamics of adaptive self-regulation that could differ as a function of age. For example, older adults may be less likely to change to a different mediational strategy or to change a specific mediator after an unsuccessful recall attempt. Exploration of such possibilities can be supported by the various self-report methods described earlier.

C. Generalization to Other Cognitive Tasks

We believe that the simple self-report method for measuring strategic behavior we have described in this chapter can be used in a wide range of cognitive tasks. Indeed, studies using retrospective self-reports of encoding strategies for free recall for word lists have also found that age differences in relational processing account for only a small proportion of age differences in free recall (Hertzog et al., 1998, 1999), suggesting that this inference is not limited to associative learning tasks. Evaluating methods of enhancing retrospective self-report validity should be a high priority in future research.

We have already conducted studies that use the self-report strategy method to evaluate the relationship of strategies to age differences in other cognitive tasks. Touron and Hertzog (2004a,b) examined older adults' delayed strategy shift from scanning to memory retrieval in a skill acquisition task based on associative learning, using item-by-item self-reports to track strategic behavior. The delayed strategy shift accounted for a substantial amount of age-related variance in skill acquisition. However, a simple associative learning deficit could not account for the delayed shift; older adults were reluctant to use a retrieval-based strategy even when a probe technique showed they can retrieve the correct answer from memory. Older adults are apparently less confident in their ability to use the memory retrieval strategy effectively.

Robinson and Hertzog (2003) imported strategy reports into a study of strategies in a relational spatial reasoning task (Byrne & Johnson-Laird, 1989). Consistent with the arguments of others (e.g., Roberts, 1993), they found that individuals do not always use spatial mental models on such tasks, but instead may use both spatial strategies and verbal-analytical strategies. Older adults reported greater use of spatial mental models for more complex items, consistent with the higher demands the verbal analytical strategy places on working memory for complex items, relative to the spatial strategy. This is evidence that older adults may engage in adaptive strategy shifts in complex cognitive tasks.

Dunlosky and Kane (2004) recently adapted retrospective strategy reports to the operation span task, which is a common measure of working memory (Engle & Kane, 2004). They found that self-reports of spontaneous application of effective strategies (e.g., grouping target words during presentation) accounted for variability in the operation span performance, demonstrating the influence of strategic behavior on tasks measuring working memory capacity. Such findings support the argument that working memory capacity is a dynamic construct influenced by executive regulation of task performance, rather than merely a passive form of memory storage.

An interesting question is whether individuals who appear to be spontaneously strategic in one task context are strategic in other contexts. Indeed, the study of associative mediators by Hertzog et al. (2004), described earlier, also included retrospective measurement of spontaneous relational processing in a free-recall task under fast-paced or slow-paced item presentations. We are currently analyzing these data to address whether there are age differences in effective encoding behaviors for this free-recall task, as well as whether there are correlations in effective strategy use between the two tasks.

VI. Conclusion

Our research has generated considerable evidence that older adults are capable of effective strategy use in at least some paired-associate tasks when they are given minimal information about these strategies. Our results therefore do not indicate that encoding deficits are a plausible general account of the age-related associative deficit (Naveh-Benjamin, 2000). These findings direct our attention to other explanations of the age-related associative deficit (see also Zacks et al., 2000). A major implication of this outcome is that older adults can, in principle, benefit from interventions that encourage a combination of effective strategy use and metacognitive control of strategy use through use of their intact monitoring skills (see Dunlosky, Kubat-Silman, & Hertzog, 2003, for details on a successful metacognitive intervention that trains self-testing behavior in older adults). Given the substantial individual differences in strategic behavior that our research has identified, training older individuals to be metacognitively aware and strategic could have substantial benefits for cognition in real life, not just in the laboratory.

Appendix 1

Personal Encoding Preference Questionnaire: Powell-Moman and Hertzog

The following material consists of instructions for the Personal Encoding Preference Questionnaire.

In the following experimental task you will be asked to learn a list of word pairs. An example of a word pair is *clown: paper*. In this task, you will need to make an association between the two words in the word pair so that when you are later given the first word you will be able to recall the second word in the pair. In this task, you will not be allowed to use any external aids, such as writing the words down. The learning of the pair has to be mental. There are many ways to learn pairs of words. Please read over the following choices and circle the number of the strategy that best describes your overall preference for learning pairs of words. Next, please rate how effective you think each strategy is for learning a word pair using the following scale in the line beside the strategy:

1	2	3	4	5	6	7	8	9	10
Least effective				Moderately effective					Most effective

1. *Rote repetition*. Say the word pair over and over. For example: *clown: paper, clown: paper, clown: paper*, etc.
2. *Attentive reading*. Reading over or saying the word pair once in your mind.
3. *Semantic reference*. Relate the word pair to something of meaning in your life. An example would be: My grandmother gave me a paper clown for my sixth birthday.
4. *Focal attention*. Focus on the word pair by looking or staring at it until you can see the word pair clearly in your mind.
5. *Imagery*. Imagine a scene using the two words as images in it. An example would be: imagining a scene where the tall clown jumped out of the paper car tearing the paper door off the hinges.
6. *Sentence generation*. Construct a sentence using both of the words. For example: "The clown wore a red and orange paper hat."
7. *Other Strategy*. (Please explain.)

References

Ackerman, P. L., & Rolfhus, E. L. (1999). The locus of adult intelligence: Knowledge, abilities, and nonability traits. *Psychology and Aging, 14*, 314–330.

Anderson, N. D. (1999). The attentional demands of encoding and retrieval in younger and older adults: 2. Evidence from secondary task reaction time distributions. *Psychology and Aging, 14*, 645–655.

Atkinson, R. C. (1972). Optimizing the learning of a second-language vocabulary. *Journal of Experimental Psychology, 96*, 124–129.

Bandura, A. (1997). *Self-efficacy: The exercise of control*. New York: W. H. Freeman.

Baron, J. (2000). *Thinking and deciding*. (3rd ed.) New York: Cambridge University Press.

Begg, I. (1978). Imagery and organization in memory: Instructional effects. *Memory & Cognition, 6*, 171–183.

Berry, J. M. (1999). Memory self-efficacy in its social cognitive context. In T. M. Hess and F. Blanchard-Fields (Eds.), *Social cognition and aging* (pp. 69–96). New York: Academic Press.

Bieman-Copland, S., & Charness, N. (1994). Memory knowledge and memory monitoring in adulthood. *Psychology and Aging, 9*, 287–302.

Bower, G. H. (1970). Imagery as a relational organizer in associative learning. *Journal of Verbal Learning and Verbal Behavior, 9*, 529–533.

Brigham, M. C., & Pressley, M. (1988). Cognitive monitoring and strategy choice in younger and older adults. *Psychology and Aging, 3*, 249–257.

Byrne, R., & Johnson-Laird, P. (1989). Spatial reasoning. *Journal of Memory and Language, 28*, 564–575.

Carroll, J. B. (1993). *Human cognitive abilities: A survey of factor-analytic studies*. Cambridge, England: Cambridge University Press.

Cavanaugh, J. C., Feldman, J., & Hertzog, C. (1998). Memory beliefs as social cognition: A reconceptualization of what memory questionnaires assess. *Review of General Psychology, 2*, 48–65.

Connor, L. T., Dunlosky, J., & Hertzog, C. (1997). Age-related differences in absolute but not relative metamemory accuracy. *Psychology and Aging, 12*, 50–71.

Craik, F. I. M. (2002). Levels of processing: Past, present, and future? *Memory, 10*, 305–318.

Craik, F. I. M., & Byrd, M. (1982). Aging and cognitive deficits: The role of attentional resources. In F. I. M. Craik and S. Trehub (Eds.), *Aging and cognitive processes* (pp. 191–211). New York: Plenum Press.

Dixon, R. A., & Hultsch, D. F. (1983). Structure and development of metamemory in adulthood. *Journal of Gerontology, 38*, 682–688.

Dunlosky, J., & Connor, L. T. (1997). Age differences in the allocation of study time account for age differences in memory performance. *Memory & Cognition, 25*, 691–700.

Dunlosky, J., & Hertzog, C. (1998a). Aging and deficits in associative memory: What is the role of strategy production? *Psychology and Aging, 13*, 597–607.

Dunlosky, J., & Hertzog, C. (1998b). Training programs to improve learning in later adulthood: Helping older adults educate themselves. In D. J. Hacker, J. Dunlosky, and A. C. Graesser (Eds.), *Metacognition in educational theory and practice* (pp. 249–275). Mahwah, NJ: Erlbaum.

Dunlosky, J., & Hertzog, C. (2000). Updating knowledge about strategy effectiveness: A componential analysis of learning about strategy effectiveness from task experience. *Psychology and Aging, 15*, 462–474.

Dunlosky, J., & Hertzog, C. (2001). Measuring strategy production during associative learning: The relative utility of concurrent versus retrospective reports. *Memory & Cognition, 29*, 247–253.

Dunlosky, J., Hertzog, C., & Powell-Moman, A. (in press). The contribution of mediator-based deficiencies to age-related differences in associative learning. *Developmental Psychology*.

Dunlosky, J., & Kane, M. J. (2004). *Evaluating the strategy-mediation hypothesis of working memory: Relations among operation span, strategy use, and higher-order cognition.* Manuscript in preparation.

Dunlosky, J., Kubat-Silman, A. K., & Hertzog, C. (2003). Training metacognitive skills improves older adults' associative learning. *Psychology and Aging, 18*, 340–345.

Dweck, C. S. (1999). *Self theories: Their role in motivation, personality and development.* Philadephia: Psychology Press.

Eagle, M. N. (1967). The effect of learning strategies upon free recall. *American Journal of Psychology, 80*, 421–425.

Elliott, E., & Lachman, M. E. (1989). Enhancing memory by modifying control beliefs, attributions, and performance goals in the elderly. In P. S. Fry (Ed.), *Psychological perspectives of helplessness and control in the elderly* (pp. 339–367). Oxford, England: North-Holland.

Engle, R. W., & Kane, M. J. (2004). Executive attention, working memory capacity, and a two-factor theory of cognitive control. In B. H. Ross (Ed.), *The psychology of learning and motivation.* (Vol. 44, pp. 145–199). New York: Academic Press.

Fisher, D. L. (1996). State models of paired associate learning: The general acquisition, decrement, and training hypotheses. In W. A. Rogers, A. D. Fisk, and N. Walker (Eds.), *Aging and skilled performance* (pp. 17–43). Mahwah, NJ: Erlbaum.

Gopher, D., & Koriat, A. (1999). *Attention and performance XVII: Cognitive regulation of performance: Interaction of theory and application.* Cambridge, MA: MIT Press.

Hertzog, C. (1996). Research design in studies of aging and cognition. In J. E. Birren and K. W. Schaie (Eds.), *Handbook of the psychology of aging* (4th ed., pp. 24–37). New York: Academic Press.

Hertzog, C., & Dixon, R. A. (1994). Metacognition and memory development in adulthood and old age. In J. Metcalfe and A. P. Shimamura (Eds.), *Metacognition* (pp. 225–251). Cambridge, MA: MIT Press.

Hertzog, C., Dunlosky, J., & Robinson, A. E. (2004). *Intellectual abilities and metacognitive beliefs influence spontaneous use of effective encoding strategies. Unpublished manuscript.*

Hertzog, C., Dunlosky, J., Robinson, E., & Kidder, D. (2003). Encoding fluency is a cue used for judgments about learning. *Journal of Experimental Psychology: Learning, Memory, & Cognition, 29*, 22–34.

Hertzog, C., & Hultsch, D. F. (2000). Metacognition in adulthood and old age. In F. I. M. Craik and T. A. Salthouse (Eds.), *The handbook of aging and cognition* (pp. 417–466). Mahwah, NJ: Erlbaum.

Hertzog, C., Kidder, D. P., Powell-Moman, A., & Dunlosky, J. (2002). Aging and monitoring associative learning: Is monitoring accuracy spared or impaired? *Psychology and Aging, 17*, 209–225.

Hertzog, C., Lineweaver, T. T., & McGuire, C. L. (1999). Beliefs about memory and aging. In F. Blanchard-Fields and T. M. Hess (Eds.), *Social cognition and aging* (pp. 43–68). New York: Academic Press.

Hertzog, C., McGuire, C. L., & Lineweaver, T. T. (1998). Aging, attributions, perceived control, and strategy use in a free recall task. *Aging, Neuropsychology, and Cognition, 15*, 85–106.

Hertzog, C., & Robinson, A. E., (in press). Metacognition and intelligence. In O. Wilhelm and R. W. Engle (Eds.), *Understanding and measuring intelligence.* London: Sage.

Horn, J. L. (1980). Concepts of intellect in relation to learning and adult development. *Intelligence, 4*, 285–317.

Horn, J. L. (1989). Models of intelligence. In R. L. Linn (Ed.), *Intelligence: Measurement, theory, and public policy* (pp. 29–73). Urbana: University of Illinois Press.

Hultsch, D. F., Hertzog, C., Dixon, R. A., & Small, B. J. (1998). *Memory change in the aged.* New York: Cambridge University Press.

Hunt, R. R., & Smith, R. E. (1996). Accessing the particular from the general: The power of distinctiveness in the context of organization. *Memory & Cognition, 24*, 217–225.

Kausler, D. H. (1994). *Learning and memory in normal aging.* New York: Academic Press.

Kelley, C. M., & Sahakyan, L. (2003). Memory, monitoring, and control in the attainment of memory accuracy. *Journal of Memory and Language, 48*, 704–721.

Kliegl, R., Smith, J., & Baltes, P. B. (1989). Testing-the-limits and the study of adult age differences in cognitive plasticity of a mnemonic skill. *Developmental Psychology, 4*, 217–221.

Koriat, A. (1997). Monitoring one's own knowledge during study: A cue-utilization approach to judgments of learning. *Journal of Experimental Psychology: General, 126*, 349–370.

Koriat, A., Goldsmith, M., & Pansky, A. (2000). Toward a psychology of memory accuracy. *Annual Review of Psychology, 51*, 481–537.

Kyllonen, P. C., & Christal, R. E. (1990). Reasoning ability is little more than working memory capacity? *Intelligence, 14*, 389–433.

Kyllonen, P. C., Tirre, W. C., & Christal, R. E. (1991). Knowledge and processing speed as determinants of associative learning. *Journal of Experimental Psychology: General, 120*, 57–79.

Lachman, M. E., Bandura, M., Weaver, S. L., & Elliott, E. (1995). Assessing memory control beliefs: The Memory Controllability Inventory. *Aging and Cognition, 2*, 67–84.

Light, L. (1996). Memory and aging. In E. L. Bjork and R. A. Bjork (Eds.), *Handbook of perception and cognition* (2nd ed., pp. 443–490). San Diego, CA: Academic-Press.

Lineweaver, T. T., & Hertzog, C. (1998). Adults' efficacy and control beliefs regarding memory and aging: Separating general from personal beliefs. *Aging Neuropsychology, and Cognition, 5*, 264–296.

Loewen, E. R., Shaw, R. J., & Craik, F. I. (1990). Age differences in components of metamemory. *Experimental Aging Research, 16*, 43–48.

Marshall, P. H., Elias, J. W., Webber, S. M., Gist, B. A., Winn, F. J., & King, P. (1978). Age differences in verbal mediation: A structural and functional analysis. *Experimental Aging Research, 4*, 175–193.

Matvey, G., Dunlosky, J., Shaw, R. J., Parks, C., & Hertzog, C. (2002). Age-related equivalence and deficit in knowledge updating of cue effectiveness. *Psychology and Aging, 17*, 589–597.

Messick, S. (2001). Style in the organization and defense of cognition. In J. M. Collis and S. Messick (Eds.), *Intelligence and personality: Bridging the gap in theory and measurement* (pp. 259–272). Mahwah, NJ: Erlbaum.

Metcalfe, J., & Kornell, N. (2003). The dynamics of learning and allocation of study time to a region of proximal learning. *Journal of Experimental Psychology: General, 132*, 530–542.

Miller, L. M. S., & Lachman, M. E. (1999). The sense of control and cognitive aging: Toward a model of mediational processes. In T. M. Hess and F. Blanchard-Fields (Eds.), *Social cognition and aging* (pp. 17–41). New York: Academic Press.

Murphy, M. D., Schmitt, F. A., Caruso, M. J., & Sanders, R. E. (1987). Metamemory in older adults: The role of monitoring in serial recall. *Psychology and Aging, 2*, 331–339.

Naveh-Benjamin, M. (2000). Adult age differences in memory performance: Tests of an associative deficit hypothesis. *Journal of Experimental Psychology: Learning, Memory, and Cognition, 26*, 1170–1187.

Naveh-Benjamin, M., Hussain, Z., Guez, J., & Bar-On, M. (2003). Adult age differences in episodic memory: Further support for an associative-deficit hypothesis. *Journal of Experimental Psychology: Learning, Memory, and Cognition, 29*, 826–837.

Nelson, T. O. (1993). Judgments of learning and the allocation of study time. *Experimental Psychology: General, 122*, 269–273.

Nelson, T. O. (1996). Consciousness and metacognition. *American Psychologist, 51*, 102–116.

Nelson, T. O., Dunlosky, J., & Graf, A. (1994). Utilization of metacognitive judgments in the allocation of study during multitrial learning. *Psychological Science, 5*, 207–213.

Nelson, T. O., & Narens, L. (1990). Metamemory: A theoretical framework and new findings. In G. H. Bower (Ed.), *The psychology of learning and motivation.* (Vol. 26, pp. 125–173). New York: Academic Press.

Paivio, A. (1995). Imagery and memory. In M. S. Gazzaniga (Ed.), *Cognitive neurosciences* (pp. 977–986). Cambridge, MA: MIT Press.

Reitman, W. (1971). What does it take to remember? In D. Norman (Ed.), *Models of human memory* (pp. 470–509). New York: Academic Press.

Richardson, J. T. E. (1998). The availability and effectiveness of reported mediators in associative learning: A historical review and an experimental investigation. *Psychonomic Bulletin & Review, 5*, 597–614.

Roberts, M. J. (1993). Human reasoning: Deduction rules or mental models, or both? *Quarterly Journal of Experimental Psychology: Human Experimental Psychology, 46A*, 569–589.

Robinson, A. E., & Hertzog, C. (2003). The role of strategies and instructions in relational deductive reasoning. *Proceedings of the 25th Annual Meeting of the Cognitive Science Society* (pp. 1000–1005). Mahwah, NJ: Erlbaum.

Robinson, A. E., Hertzog, C., & Dunlosky, J. (2004). *Aging, encoding fluency, and metacognitive monitoring.* Unpublished manuscript.

Rowe, E. J., & Schnore, M. M. (1971). Item concreteness and reported strategies in paired-associate learning as a function of age. *Journal of Gerontology, 26*, 470–475.

Salthouse, T. A. (1991). *Theoretical perspectives on cognitive aging.* Mahwah, NJ: Erlbaum.

Salthouse, T. A. (1996). The processing-speed theory of adult age differences in cognition. *Psychological Review, 103*, 403–428.

Schaie, K. W. (1996). *Intellectual development in adulthood: The Seattle Longitudinal Study*. New York: Cambridge University Press.

Schneider, W., & Pressley, M. (1997). *Memory development between two and twenty*. (2nd ed.). Mahwah, NJ: Erlbaum.

Schunn, C. D., & Reder, L. M. (2001). Another source of individual differences: Strategy adaptivity to changing rates of success. *Journal of Experimental Psychology, 130*, 59–76.

Siegler, R. S. (1995). Children's thinking: How does change occur? In F. E. Weinert and W. Schneider (Eds.), *Memory performance and competencies: Issues in growth and development* (pp. 405–430). Hillsdale, NJ: Erlbaum.

Siegler, R. S., & Lemaire, P. (1997). Older and younger adults' strategy choice in multiplication: Testing predictions of ASCM using the choice/no-choice method. *Journal of Experimental Psychology: General, 126*, 71–92.

Smith, A. D., Park, D. C., Earles, J. L., Shaw, R. J., & Whiting IV W. L., (1998). Age differences in context integration in memory. *Psychology and Aging, 13*, 21–28.

Sternberg, R. J. (1985). *Beyond IQ: A triarchic theory of human intelligence*. New York: Cambridge University Press.

Sternberg, R. J., & Zhang, L. (Eds.) (2001). *Perspectives on thinking, learning, and cognitive styles*. Mahwah, NJ: Erlbaum.

Son, L. K. (2004). Spacing one's study: Evidence for a metacognitive control strategy. *Journal of Experimental Psychology: Learning, Memory, and Cognition, 30*, 601–604.

Thiede, K. W., & Dunlosky, J. (1999). Toward a general model of self-regulated study: An analysis of selection of items for study and self-paced study time. *Journal of Experimental Psychology: Learning, Memory and Cognition, 25*, 1024–1037.

Touron, D. R., & Hertzog, C. (2004a). Age differences in knowledge, strategy use, and confidence during skill acquisition. *Psychology and Aging, 19*, 452–466.

Touron, D. R., & Hertzog, C. (2004b). Strategy shift affordance and strategy choice in young and older adults. *Memory & Cognition, 32*, 298–310.

Tulving, E. (1966). Subjective organization and effects of repetition in multi-trial free-recall learning. *Journal of Verbal Learning and Verbal Behavior, 5*, 193–197.

West, R. L., Thorn, R. M., & Bagwell, D. K. (2003). Memory performance and beliefs as a function of goal setting and aging. *Psychology and Aging, 18*, 111–125.

Woodruff-Pak, D. S. (1999). New directions for a classical paradigm: Human eyeblink conditioning. *Psychological Science, 10*, 1–3.

Yates, F. A. (1997). *The art of memory*. London: Pimlico.

Yuille, J. C. (1973). A detailed examination of mediation in PA learning. *Memory and Cognition, 1*, 333–342.

Yuille, J. C., & Pavio, A. (1968). Imagery and verbal mediation instructions in paired-associate learning. *Journal of Experimental Psychology, 78*, 436–441.

Zacks, R. T., Hasher, L., & Li, K. Z. H. (2000). Human memory. In F. I. M. Craik and Salthouse (Eds.), *The handbook of aging and cognition* (2nd ed., pp. 293–357). Hillsdale, NJ: Erlbaum.

THE PSYCHOPHARMACOLOGY OF MEMORY AND COGNITION: PROMISES, PITFALLS, AND A METHODOLOGICAL FRAMEWORK

Elliot Hirshman

I. Introduction

Over the last two decades, dramatic methodological developments have spurred empirical research and theory construction in cognitive neuroscience (Rugg, 1997). Procedures for imaging brain functions, a renewed emphasis on neuropsychological studies, as well as developments in the mathematical modeling of neural and cognitive systems, have all contributed to rapid developments in cognitive neuroscience. In contrast to these dramatic developments, the experimental manipulation of human brain functioning has not yet emerged as a widespread tool for examining theories of cognition. This omission is ironic in that researchers in cognitive psychology and the neurobiology of animal behavior traditionally conceptualize experimental methods as the cornerstone of their methodological arsenal.

The purpose of this article is to consider the role of psychopharmacology (e.g., Duka, Curran, Rusted, & Weingarten, 1996) in the study of cognition. Procedures in cognitive psychopharmacology involve the experimental administration (or withholding) of a drug and the examination of the effects of this manipulation on cognitive performance and processes. These paradigms involve a broad array of possibilities including, but not limited to: the acute administration of exogenous substances, as in the case of anesthesia and

0079-7421/04 $35.00

alcohol intoxication (Ghoneim & Mewaldt, 1975); the chronic administration of replacement dosages of endogenous substances, as in hormone replacement therapy (Hogervorst, Williams, Budge, Riedel, & Jolles, 2000), and the withholding of exogenous substances that were previously (self-) administered chronically, as in tobacco or alcohol abstinence (Bell, Taylor, Singleton, Henningfield, & Heishman, 1999). These procedures are often assumed to influence cognition through direct effects on neural functioning.

These procedures can be used to ask a broad range of questions about: the effects of drugs on cognitive performance, the theoretical bases of cognition, and the relations between brain and cognitive processes. These can include straightforward empirical questions, such as "Does tobacco abstinence affect recognition memory performance?" and "Does estrogen replacement therapy affect perceptual identification performance?" as well as more theoretically oriented questions, such as "Does midazolam amnesia impair encoding processes in episodic memory?" and "Are the negative effects of testosterone replacement therapy on recognition memory performance mediated by effects on sustained attention processes?"

The specific logic underlying inferences from the results of cognitive psychopharmacology experiments to theories of cognitive and brain processes is identical to that used in traditional studies of cognition. Administering a drug is simply another experimental manipulation, albeit a much more powerful one, that can be added to traditional manipulations (e.g., study time) used in the study of cognition. For example, drugs can be used to produce dissociations on various tasks (e.g., Hirshman, Pasannante, & Arndt, 2001), allowing one to test hypotheses about the cognitive and brain processes mediating performance on the tasks. An important case arises when one can demonstrate that a drug has selective effects on specific cognitive and brain processes. These selective effects are especially powerful for testing theories (see the later section, "Cognitive Specificity").

II. Methodological Advantages of Cognitive Psychopharmacology

Given these potential uses of pharmacological methods, it is important to emphasize that these methods enjoy important advantages over extant methods. In comparing pharmacological methods to neuropsychological methods, one notes three important differences. First, experimental control of drug administration allows participants to act as their own controls. This approach contrasts to the painstaking matching of participant groups that is necessary in neuropsychological studies. In this latter case, one cannot be sure that some unidentified participant characteristic does not differ between the neuropsychological and control participants. Second, pharmacological experiments allow researchers control over the timing of drug effects. For example, investigators can induce pharmacological amnesia prior to the study and/or test periods in memory experiments (Polster, McCarthy, O'Sullivan, Gray, & Park, 1993). This procedure allows researchers to isolate the effects of impairing learning during the study period from the effects of impairing learning during the memory test. This contrasts sharply to neuropsychological approaches in which lesions are permanent and irreversible. Third, given that many drugs can be administered safely and easily, pharmacological methods permit the testing of many more participants than do neuropsychological studies in which only a relatively small set of participants have suffered a specified type of lesion.

Pharmacological methods also have three significant advantages over traditional methods used in cognitive psychology. First, pharmacological variables can be much more powerful than variables traditionally used in cognitive psychology. For example, administering the benzodiazepine midazolam prior to the study period in a memory experiment can decrease later memory performance to floor levels. Hirshman et al. (2001) demonstrated that even though participants recalled an average of 12 items in a placebo-control condition, they recalled an average of less than one item in a midazolam condition. These powerful methods permit the exploration of a range of questions that cannot be explored with traditional methods. For example, in the case of midazolam amnesia, one can explore the effect that conscious memory processes normally have on a range of cognitive tasks by using amnesia to determine how performance on these tasks is affected when conscious memory processes are diminished dramatically.

Second, pharmacological manipulations often have much greater intrinsic or practical importance than do manipulations traditionally used in cognitive psychology. Drugs are a mainstay of clinical practice in medicine (Lister, 1985), and are frequently implicated in quality-of-life issues (Morales, Haubricht, Hwangt, Asakura, & Yen, 1998). Similarly, drug abstinence plays a critical role in preventive medicine (Hughes & Hatsukami, 1986). To give one example, understanding the effects of tobacco abstinence on cognition (Hirshman, Rhodes, Zinser, & Merritt, 2004) is of great practical importance because informing patients of these effects, and their transitory nature, may help patients maintain abstinence.

Third, in contrast to many of the traditional manipulations used in cognitive psychology, drug effects can be examined across cognitive tasks. Many traditional manipulations are designed to affect the processes underlying specific cognitive tasks and, as such, are often only applicable to these tasks. Examples of such task-specific manipulations (Solso, 1995) include the manipulations of study time, study instructions (intentional vs. incidental), length of retention interval, and test list composition commonly used in studies of episodic memory. Whereas theories focusing on task-specific manipulations (e.g., Gillund & Shiffrin, 1984) have been extremely productive, the abundance of task-specific manipulations in cognitive psychology has focused studies on individual tasks. By introducing numerous manipulations that can be applied across tasks, cognitive psychopharmacology may help promote theories focusing on general principles and processes of cognition (see Shepherd [2004] for comments regarding the importance of identifying general principles of cognition).

III. Illustrative Examples

Although the focus of this paper is on methodological issues, I mention two illustrative examples from our laboratory to indicate the usefulness of cognitive psychopharmacology methods. The first example concerns the use of midazolam amnesia for exploring the bases of implicit memory (Hirshman, Pasannante, & Arndt, 1999; Hirshman et al., 2001). Specifically, midazolam amnesia is used to explore the role conscious memory processes play on implicit memory tests. As noted above, midazolam dramatically impairs conscious memory. By comparing performance in a midazolam and a saline control condition, we can determine whether specific experimental effects found on implicit memory tests are due to conscious memory processes. If midazolam removes an experimental effect on an implicit memory test, this is consistent with the perspective that conscious memory processes contribute to the effect. On the other hand, if midazolam amnesia does not influence an effect on an implicit memory test, this suggests that conscious memory processes do not contribute to the effect.

Using this approach, Hirshman et al. (1999, 2001) have demonstrated some counterintuitive findings that challenge traditional conceptions of implicit memory. Hirshman et al. (1999) examined the effect of midazolam amnesia on the modality-match effect in single-item perceptual identification, an effect hypothesized to arise from sensory–perceptual processing (Weldon, Roediger, Beitel, & Johnston, 1995). Hirshman et al. (2001) examined the effect of midazolam amnesia on the generation effect in cued perceptual identification, an effect hypothesized to arise from semantic–conceptual processing (Toth & Hunt, 1990).

Given that semantic processing enhances performance on conscious memory tests more than does sensory processing (Craik & Tulving, 1975), one might intuit that conscious memory processes mediate the generation effect in cued perceptual identification (i.e., the effect hypothesized to arise from semantic processing), but not the modality-match effect in single-item perceptual identification (i.e., the effect hypothesized to arise from sensory processing). In this perspective, one would expect midazolam amnesia to remove the generation effect, but not the modality-match effect. Empirically, the opposite result held. Midazolam amnesia removed the modality-match effect in single-item perceptual identification (Hirshman et al., 1999) but had no effect on the generation effect in cued perceptual identification (Hirshman et al., 2001).

These findings suggest that while conscious memory processes may contribute to the modality-match effect in single-item perceptual identification, they do not contribute to the generation effect in cued perceptual identification. The first implication undercuts traditional interpretations of the modality-match effect as an implicit memory effect (Weldon et al., 1995). The second implication reinforces the hypothesis (Hirshman et al., 2001) that semantic processing may play a larger role in implicit memory than is traditionally acknowledged. This example illustrates how the powerful methods of cognitive psychopharmacology can generate empirical results that challenge our standard conceptions.

A second example demonstrates how the methods of cognitive psychopharmacology can facilitate cross-task comparisons and integrative theorizing. Hirshman, Rhodes, Zinzer, and Merritt (2004) examined the effect of tobacco abstinence on recognition memory, digit span memory, and visual attentional vigilance. Hirshman et al. (2004) examined the effects of androgens, estrogens, and obesity on these same tasks. The results demonstrated that: (1) tobacco abstinence impaired recognition memory and visual vigilance but had no effect on digit span; (2) estrogens enhanced recognition memory but had no effect on visual vigilance or digit span; (3) androgens impaired recognition and visual vigilance but had no effect on digit span; and (4) obesity had no effect on recognition memory or visual vigilance but did impair digit span.

Making comparisons across tasks, we see that some pharmacological manipulations (i.e., tobacco abstinence and androgens) produce negative effects on both recognition memory and visual vigilance, whereas others (i.e., estrogens) only influence recognition memory. These results suggest that changes in visual vigilance might influence recognition memory (or that a common process might influence both tasks) and that estrogen's influence on recognition memory is not mediated by effects on vigilance processes. Similarly, they suggest that the underlying physiological mechanism of estrogen's effect on recognition memory is distinct from the nicotinic mechanisms influenced by tobacco abstinence.

In a second across-task comparison, we see that even though estrogens, androgens, and tobacco abstinence affect recognition memory and/or visual vigilance, they do not affect digit span. Thus, changes in the processes influencing digit span are not mediating the effects of estrogens, androgens, and tobacco abstinence on recognition memory or visual vigilance. Moreover, even though the three aforementioned manipulations do not affect digit span, obesity does impair digit span, suggesting that the physiological mechanism of obesity's effect on digit span is independent of the physiological effects of estrogens, androgens, and tobacco abstinence. This latter suggestion is particularly dramatic given the extensive physiological effects of obesity.

Although space constraints do not permit a full exposition of the implications of the results of Hirshman, Rhodes et al. (2004) and Hirshman, Merritt et al. (2004), the preceding description demonstrates how cognitive psychopharmacology methods can generate useful cross-task comparisons and facilitate the generation of novel hypotheses.

In the context of these examples and the methodological advantages cited above, it is important to note that studies in cognitive psychopharmacology raise a large number of issues that do not arise in traditional studies of cognition. The remainder of this paper provides a primer on these issues and discusses some of the approaches we, and others, have used to address them. In presenting this methodological framework, I hope to encourage other researchers in cognition to consider how pharmacological methods might advance their own research programs.

IV. Challenges of Cognitive Psychopharmacology

A. Dosage Issues: Accommodating Dose-Response Curves

The administration of drugs differs qualitatively from most experimental manipulations used in the study of cognition because the effect of a drug can be a nonmonotonic function of the amount administered (Stoelting, 1991). For example, variables like study time or exposure duration used in traditional studies of cognition have monotonic effects on cognition. In contrast, the nonmonotonic effects of drugs can manifest themselves in inverted U-shaped dose-response functions (e.g., Parsons & Gold, 1992) in which cognitive performance increases with the administration of a drug at lower doses but decreases with further increases in dosage.

This phenomenon presents complex challenges for studies examining human cognition. The most appropriate response to understanding dose-response functions is to map out the function using multiple dosage conditions. This is, of course, a common practice in the literature studying nonhuman animals. Unfortunately, cost and safety considerations mitigate against the use of multiple doses in human studies. Adding additional between-participant conditions to a hormone replacement experiment dramatically increases the cost of the experiment because of the costs of medical prescreening and assays. Similarly, while the safety of a single dose of an amnesiac drug may be well established, the safety of the multiple doses necessary to establish the dose response function may not be documented.

Although there is no simple way to handle this problem, we have addressed it by conducting small pilot studies to identify a dose that produces experimental effects of interest (e.g., amnesia) and satisfies safety concerns. A larger study can then be conducted using the identified dose. When this approach is used, researchers must bear in mind that the effect of a drug on cognition may differ at other doses.

Setting doses appropriately is a pressing concern even when the dose-response function can be assumed to be monotonic. This is because, in many circumstances, dosages must be set not only to enhance (or impair) a cognitive process of interest, but also to have limited effects on other ancillary cognitive processes. For example, in the study of pharmacological amnesia, a broad range of doses will produce substantial amnesia. However, at higher doses, perception and attention processes will be substantially impaired (Boucart, de Visme, & Wagemans, 2000), making memory impairments difficult to interpret. Thus, in most cognitive psychopharmacology experiments, the dose must be set to have desired effects on a range of cognitive processes and tasks. As mentioned earlier, extensive pilot testing is necessary to accomplish this aim.

Other considerations relevant to dosing concern whether the dose is supraphysiological (e.g., Baethge et al., 2002) or physiological and whether the dose is given as part of an acute (e.g., Mintzer & Griffiths, 2001) or chronic regimen. Although supraphysiological doses, raising levels of hormones above their natural endogenous levels are common in animal research, they raise significant safety concerns in human research, as well as questions regarding the generalizability of results. Similarly, although acute effects can be of great theoretical interest, adaptation to drug effects is common (Zack & Vogel-Sprott, 1995), so the demonstration of effects in a chronic regime is often necessary.

B. Pharmacokinetics and Metabolism: Challenges of Setting Temporal Parameters

Understanding the pharmacokinetics and metabolism of a drug (e.g., Martin et al., 2003) is critical to its use in cognitive psychopharmacology experiments. This is because these factors can produce dramatic changes in a drug's effect at different times. For example, a drug that is administered intravenously will reach its peak effect more rapidly than a drug administered orally, and a drug that is eliminated and metabolized rapidly will have only a brief period of efficacy. These factors must be accommodated in designing cognitive psychopharmacology experiments, with particular attention given to the timing of drug administration and cognitive tasks. In our own studies of pharmacological amnesia (e.g., Arndt, Passannante, & Hirshman, 2004), intravenous administration of the benzodiazepine midazolam, produces dense amnesia when the study period is 5 min after drug administration. However, due to midazolam's rapid elimination, its cognitive effects are largely eliminated approximately 1 hr after drug administration. By presenting the study period 5 min after drug administration and the test period 1 hr after drug administration, we have been able to ensure that a range of cognitive processes are similar in the midazolam and placebo control conditions during the test period (e.g., Hirshman et al., 2001), even though these processes may differ dramatically during the study period.

Determining the appropriate interval between drug administration and cognitive tasks becomes more difficult when drugs have metabolites that produce cognitive effects (e.g., Bitran, Purdy, & Kellogg, 1993). In this case, the observed effect of drug administration can vary with time not only because of the metabolism and elimination of the administered substance, but because its metabolites can affect cognition. This problem can be exacerbated by the tendency of metabolites to produce contrasting cognitive and physiological effects. For example, when androgens (e.g., testosterone) are administered, these androgens can metabolize into estrogens (e.g., estradiol; Mortola & Yen, 1990), whose cognitive effects differ from those of androgens (Hirshman, Merritt et al., 2004).

Understanding these complex dynamics requires the simultaneous measurement of the administered substance and its metabolites across multiple time periods. This measurement allows the exploration of the relations between these substances and cognitive performance. For example, in our studies of the relationship between sex steroids and cognition (Hirshman, Merritt et al., 2004), we administered dehydroepiandrosterone (DHEA, an adrenal androgen) and measured serum levels of DHEA and its metabolites, testosterone and estradiol, as well as cognitive performance. We conducted these measurements four times over the course of a day to permit analysis of the relations between the different sex steroids and cognition. (See the later section, "Statistical Issues" for a description of relevant measurement issues.)

C. Incorporating Individual and Group Differences

The study of individual and group differences has played a limited role in traditional studies of cognition. Theoretical models (e.g., Hintzman, 2001) have focused on modal information processing systems, whereas empirical studies have generally treated differences between individuals or groups as components of error variance. In contrast, consideration of individual and group differences is intrinsically important in cognitive psychopharmacology because the cognitive effects of drugs are very likely to differ across individual and groups. One important reason for these differences is differences in baseline levels of critical biological functions (e.g., levels of neurotransmitters) across individuals and groups (e.g., Fournet, Moreaud, Roulin, Naegele, & Pellat, 2000). Specifically, in the context of the inverted U-shaped dose-response functions discussed earlier, these baseline differences can produce different effects of drug administration.

Examples of individual factors that might affect baseline biological functions and, hence, merit attention in cognitive psychopharmacology experiments include: the use of medications or other substances (e.g., benzodiazepines, nicotine, alcohol, and caffeine) that could affect cognition, psycho-social variables (e.g., education level and socioeconomic status) that may influence brain functioning, and medical conditions (e.g., Parkinson's disease) that might affect cognition. Examples of group factors include gender, an especially important factor in studies examining the effects of sex steroids and hormone replacement therapy, and race/ethnicity. In each case, the factor cited might alter the effect of a drug and must be accommodated in the research design in some way.

Potential approaches include: (1) controlling the factor (e.g., having participants abstain from caffeine on the day of testing); (2) measuring the factor and incorporating it in statistical analyses (e.g., comparing effects for participants with different education levels); and (3) excluding participants (e.g., participants who are currently taking benzodiazepines are excluded from studies on midazolam amnesia).

Safety considerations further highlight the importance of individual and group differences in cognitive psychopharmacology because drugs may only be safe for a selected set of participants. For example, we have focused our studies of DHEA administration on women, rather than men, because DHEA administration produces hypertrophy of the prostate in men (Jones, Nguyen, Straub, Leidich, Veech, & Wolf, 1997). Similarly, many drugs may have increased risks for participants who have psychiatric disorders (e.g., schizophrenia), neurological disorders (e.g., Parkinson's disease), or significant physical illnesses (e.g., heart disease). These safety considerations mandate the measurement of relevant individual difference variables in an initial screening phase of the experiment, as well as the use of these measures in exclusion criteria.

Other individual difference variables assume great importance in cognitive psychopharmacology for logistical or practical reasons. A prominent example for researchers to be aware of is participant's weight. While a participant's weight has played almost no role in traditional studies of cognition, it can be a critical variable in cognitive psychopharmacology because a participant's weight can influence drug metabolism and its effects (Davidson,

Harris, & Rosenberg, 1987). For example, if one administers a constant dose of a drug, it is likely to constitute a larger functional dose in lighter participants. Thus, for reasons related to the dose-response functions described earlier, a constant dose could produce different drug effects in participants of varying weights.

Researchers have responded to this issue by setting doses proportional to a participant's weight or by using a preexperimental titration procedure that sets doses based on the participant's behavioral response to various doses. One important caution concerning the former approach is that increasing doses proportional to weight does not necessarily produce proportional and identical effects in all cognitive and physiological processes. Given this complication, experiments that set doses proportional to weight will often only test participants whose weight falls within a circumscribed range. Although titration procedures address the above concerns by setting doses based on behavioral criteria, they can produce safety concerns associated with multiple doses, as well as practical concerns due to the increased cost and participant attrition associated with additional testing.

As the foregoing considerations indicate, the ubiquity of individual and group differences presents researchers in cognitive psychopharmacology with difficult dilemmas. The risk of ignoring these differences is that they can make the results of an overall analysis misleading. If researchers acknowledge these differences, they can focus on a subset of participants or subgroups (excluding others) or measure the relevant characteristics and include them as a factor in data analyses. The limitation of the former approach is that, barring compelling theoretical, practical, or safety considerations, the choice of the individual characteristic or subgroup to study may be arbitrary (or based on prevailing social norms). The limitation of the latter approach is that the size of any study is limited, permitting sufficient power to analyze only a limited set of variables.

Although there are no panaceas for these issues, selection of individuals and subgroups for study can sometimes be guided by theoretical, practical, and safety considerations. For example, the safety considerations discussed earlier indicate why studies of DHEA administration focus on women. In the absence of such considerations, a commonsense principle is that the incidence or prevalence of the individual difference or subgroup should influence the researcher's approach. For a low-incidence individual difference or subgroup, it may be best to measure this factor in a prescreening phase and exclude relevant participants. The rationale for this approach is that with low-incidence conditions, it is unlikely that even a very large study would produce sufficient observations to allow analysis of the effects of this variable. (Of course, this strategy does not argue against separate studies focusing solely on the low-incidence condition.) In contrast, for a high-incidence individual difference or subgroup, it is much more likely that the study will produce sufficient observations to allow a meaningful analysis of the variable's effects. Moreover, excluding a large subgroup raises the risk that the study's results will not be general.

Although the preceding section outlines the complications that individual and group differences present to the cognitive psychopharmacology researcher, it is also important to note that cognitive psychopharmacology may represent a critical method for elucidating individual and group differences. Thus, differential effects of drugs on cognition across individuals and groups may enhance our understanding of the cognitive and physiological bases of individual and group differences.

D. Clinical Trials and Medical Logistics

Cognitive psychopharmacology experiments are often clinical trials (e.g., Wolf, Naumann, Hellhammer, & Kirschbaum, 1998). Thus, researchers must be thoroughly versed in the issues of safety, compliance, placebo blinding, and attrition that are central to conducting clinical trials. The necessity and importance of clinical trials in cognitive psychopharmacology is especially pronounced because sensitization and tolerance effects (Zack & Vogel-Sprott, 1995), routinely demonstrated in empirical studies, mandate the use of long-term drug administration regimes to ensure the generalizability of findings.

Considering safety issues, studies must include procedures for monitoring side effects and adverse events. These procedures can be simple ones in which participants keep diaries recording side effects, as well as more complex ones in which participants receive regular medical check-ups and results are forwarded to safety monitoring boards consisting of outside experts for review. These safety procedures may also include follow-up monitoring of participants. In the context of safety concerns, studies must include procedures for responding to reports of adverse events and side effects. Communication between the participants, physicians, safety monitoring board, and experimenters must be structured so that any reports of adverse events can be responded to rapidly for the safety of the patients affected, as well as other participants in the study. As previously mentioned, safety considerations also mandate a prescreening phase in experiments. In this phase, relevant individual characteristics are measured and participants for whom the procedures are unsafe are excluded from the study.

Adherence and compliance issues (e.g., manipulation checks) are common in traditional studies of cognition. For example, in a typical memory experiment, participants might be asked to respond to semantic or phonological processing questions during the study period to verify that they, in fact, have carried out the requisite encoding processes. Issues of adherence and compliance differ somewhat in clinical trials because participants may have (or may perceive themselves to have) larger incentives to be noncompliant and it may be much more difficult for experimenters to verify compliance. For example, participants are often paid relatively large sums of money (e.g., $300; Hirshman, Merritt et al., 2004) to participate in clinical trials and they may perceive that there is significant risk associated with the study procedures. Thus, they have incentives to participate in the experiment but not comply fully with the procedures. Similarly, many procedures for verifying compliance can be evaded. For example, pill-counting techniques, in which additional pills are provided to the participant at the study's outset to allow retrospective verification of compliance, can be evaded by disposing of the appropriate number of pills. Given that noncompliant participants can easily mimic the behavior of compliant participants, pill-counting techniques may be of limited benefit in some studies.

Because of these complications, the construction of strategies for ensuring compliance is a critical component of research design in cognitive psychopharmacology. Examples of particularly effective strategies include being physically present during drug administration and using manipulation checks that are based on physiological measures that cannot easily by altered by participants. For example, studies of tobacco abstinence (Hirshman, Rhodes et al., 2004) regularly monitor carbon monoxide in expired air to verify tobacco abstinence.

Other aspects of clinical trials that merit discussion include placebos and blinding procedures. Experimental control conditions are, as a rule, used in traditional studies of cognition, and the use of a placebo-control condition is consistent with these approaches. The difference between traditional studies of cognition and studies in cognitive psychopharmacology concerns the importance of blinding both the experimenter and the participant to the identity of the drug and placebo. Double-blind designs are generally not possible with the experimental manipulations used in the traditional study of cognition because the manipulations are readily apparent (e.g., manipulations of presentation duration). Moreover, blinding is implicitly assumed to be unnecessary in these studies. In contrast, blinding is clearly essential in clinical trials because of the potential impact of placebo effects (Stewart-Williams & Podd, 2004).

Placebo-controlled double-blind designs do not, unfortunately, ensure blinding in cognitive psychopharmacology because the active drug may have a range of correlated effects that allow participants and experimenters to identify it. For example, women who receive estradiol as a component of hormone replacement therapy may be able to identify it because of the hormone's correlated effects on physical appearance (Niiyama, Happle,

& Hoffmann, 2001). In this context, experimenters must include procedures to verify the success of the blinding procedures in clinical trials and should identify the implications of failures of blinding procedures prior to examining the success of the blinding procedure.

Last, study attrition, and the possibility of differential attrition across conditions, require special attention in clinical trials. Given a lengthy clinical trial, it is possible that participants who drop out of the trial will have different characteristics from those who complete it. For example, participants who do not (perhaps, by chance) derive a benefit from the administered drug may drop out of the trial, leading to an overestimate of the drug's beneficial effects. To respond to this issue, researchers should build low-cost procedures into the research design to prevent attrition. Examples include explicitly verifying participant's availability for the dates of later testing sessions at study onset and using experimenter-initiated reminder calls to ensure that participants remember testing sessions. In the event that significant attrition occurs, analyses should be conducted to test whether the participants who have left the trial differ in a material way from those who have completed it. The incisiveness of these analyses depends on the collection of extensive data on individuals during the preenrollment screening.

Implicit in the preceding discussion of clinical trials is one of cognitive psychopharmacology's most challenging aspects. Research in cognitive psychopharmacology requires an interdisciplinary team consisting of cognitive psychologists and medical personnel. Moreover, the preenrollment screening, administration of drugs, manipulation checks (e.g., blood draws for verifying effects of an administered drug), and safety monitoring will require the use of medical facilities. Specific challenges associated with these procedures include the substantial clinical responsibilities of academic physicians, as well as the significant costs associated with the use of medical facilities.

Although the problems associated with "medical logistics" should not be underestimated, our experience has been that academic physicians are eager to collaborate on projects in cognitive psychopharmacology and that they bring an important intellectual perspective, as well as critical technical and practical skills, to the research project. Moreover, in the context of a successful collaboration, cost issues can be resolved reasonably. Having noted these sanguine possibilities, it is important to emphasize that research in cognitive psychopharmacology is substantially more expensive than traditional studies of cognition. Thus, as in any burgeoning subfield (e.g., neuroimaging), cognitive psychopharmacology must become an important component of the portfolios of relevant grant funding agencies to develop and flourish.

E. Experimental Design and Statistical Issues

Studies in cognitive psychopharmacology present important experimental design and statistical analysis issues. A critical design issue concerns whether the variable of type of drug administered (active drug vs. placebo) should be manipulated between participants or within participants. Manipulating this variable between participants has the advantage that experience in one condition (active or placebo) cannot have any effects on performance in the other condition. The weakness of the between-participant design is that it has less power to detect differences between conditions. This weakness is especially problematic in studies of cognition because of large individual differences in cognitive performance. In traditional studies of cognition, experimenters remedy this power problem by testing additional participants. This tactic is less useful in cognitive psychopharmacology because of the large costs associated with participant testing. Thus, the use of between-participant designs faces greater practical constraints in cognitive psychopharmacology studies than in traditional studies of cognition.

Although manipulating the drug administered within-participants helps enhance a study's power, this approach confronts other complications. Carryover (e.g., practice) effects from one condition to the other, always a concern in within-participant designs, are more likely to manifest themselves in cognitive psychopharmacology studies than in traditional studies of cognition. This is because the drug in the active drug condition may not be fully metabolized when the placebo is administered. Similarly, the administration of a drug may have long-term effects on brain processes. Thus, performance in the placebo condition may reflect the effects of the drug when a within-participant design is used.

A strategy for dealing with the problem of insufficient metabolism is to ensure that an appropriate washout period occurs between the administration of the active drug and placebo (e.g., 1 week). Turning to the latter problem, and those of the within-participant design more generally, it is important to recognize that the effect of a drug is inherently confounded with the effects of practice and drug order for each participant in this design. To accommodate this confounding, experimenters can use a crossover design in which the participant receives one treatment followed by the other (placebo followed by active drug or active drug followed by placebo), with the drug order counterbalanced across participants. This crossover design allows investigators to examine the effects of practice (Session 1 vs. Session 2) and drug order (placebo first vs. active drug first), and the interaction of these effects with those of the administered drug.

Although this approach does not prevent long-term effects of a drug on brain processes or practice effects, it allows researchers to identify these effects, facilitating the interpretation of the effects of drug administration. For example, if the administration of a drug had a long-term effect on brain processes, we would expect performance in the placebo condition, as well as the difference in performance between the placebo and drug condition, to differ when participants received the active drug first. Thus, examining the interaction of the effects of drug order (placebo first vs. active drug first) and type of drug (active drug vs. placebo) can provide evidence on whether an administered drug has had a long-term effect on brain processes.

The statistical analyses used in cognitive psychopharmacology studies (e.g., Hirshman, Merritt et al., 2004) also differ significantly from those used in the traditional study of cognition. Although the latter approach primarily uses analyses of variance that examine the effects of, and interactions between, experimental variables, correlational approaches (e.g., multiple regression analyses; Azen & Budescu, 2003) play a critical role in cognitive psychopharmacology. This is because drugs influence a range of underlying factors that might themselves influence cognitive performance. This situation requires correlational analyses to identify which of these underlying factors might be related to performance.

Determining appropriate predictor variables in correlational approaches raises a number of measurement issues that do not generally arise in traditional studies of cognition. These include the importance of demonstrating substantial variability in each predictor variable, as well as the necessity of verifying independent variance among the predictor variables (Morrison, 2003). Substantial variability in individual predictor variables is necessary to observe relations between the predictors and cognitive performance. Substantial independent variance among the predictor variables is necessary to identify the unique relations between individual predictors and cognitive performance. Identifying predictor variables with substantial independent variance may require a multistep process in which one first examines the correlational structure among the potential predictor variables and then derives a set of predictors that have substantial independence variance.

Our studies of DHEA administration, sex steroids and cognition (Hirshman Merritt, Wang et al., 2004) illustrate some of these measurement issues. Examining the effect of DHEA administration on cognition is complex because DHEA administration increases serum levels of androgens and estrogens (Hirshman, Merritt et al., 2004; Mortola & Yen, 1990). Moreover, these androgens and estrogens are highly correlated, making it difficult to identify the unique relations associated with a particular steroid or set of steroids. To derive appropriate predictor variables, we examined the correlations between serum levels of two gonadal androgens (total and free testosterone), two adrenal androgens (DHEA and DHEA-S) and two estrogens (Estradiol and Estrone). The four androgens were highly correlated with each other, as were the two estrogens. The correlations between individual androgens and estrogens were positive, but lower. Thus, we used two derived predictors, one representing a standardized average of the values of the four androgens and the other representing a standardized average of values of the two estrogens, in our analyses. These derived predictors had substantial independent variance and our regression analyses demonstrated unique variance in cognitive performance associated with both estrogens and androgens.

The importance of correlational approaches in cognitive psychopharmacology increases the importance of participant (i.e., individual difference) variables in statistical analyses. Participant characteristics may be correlated with other predictor variables, so it is critical to determine if the effects of predictor variables are independent of these participant characteristics. For example, in analyzing the effects of estradiol on cognition, we know that a participant's body mass index (BMI) may be correlated with estradiol levels (Rodin, Mancuso, Granger, & Nelbach, 1991). Thus, observed relations between sex steroids and cognition may reflect the effect of BMI, rather than sex steroids. Demonstrating that the effects of sex steroids on cognition are independent of those of BMI by including measures of BMI in regression analyses allays such concerns.

The potential importance of between-participant differences also emphasizes an additional benefit of using a within-participant design in cognitive psychopharmacology research. In this design, one may be able to gather sufficient data to determine that the relations between predictors and cognitive performance hold within individual participants.

F. Cognitive Specificity

Establishing the cognitive specificity of a drug is one of the most important challenges in cognitive psychopharmacology. If a drug has effects on a broad range of cognitive processes, its usefulness for exploring theories of cognition and the relations between cognitive and brain processes is limited. This challenge is formidable because the diffuse neuro-anatomical architecture of neurotransmitter systems (e.g., Kehoe, Shoemaker, Arons, Triano, & Suresh, 1998) make it very unlikely that a drug will affect only one brain region or cognitive processes. Thus, the cognitive specificity of a drug should be considered a relative, rather than an absolute, attribute with more specific drugs producing effects that are differential across cognitive processes and tasks.

Our perspective is to approach the problem of cognitive specificity in two steps. The first step is to examine the effect of a drug across a range of tasks hypothesized to reflect different cognitive processes. For example (Hirshman, Rhodes et al., 2004), one could examine the effect of a drug on: (1) the perceptual identification task hypothesized to reflect basic processes in visual perception; (2) the visual vigilance task hypothesized to reflect the process of sustained attention; (3) the digit span task hypothesized to reflect short-term memory processes; and (4) the recognition memory task hypothesized to reflect episodic memory processes. Demonstrating that a drug has different effects across these tasks provides initial evidence for cognitive specificity and constrains hypotheses regarding the cognitive and brain processes influenced by the drug. Conversely, failing to demonstrate such effects suggests that the drug in question may not be appropriate for use in cognitive psychopharmacology research.

The second step is to test specific hypotheses regarding the cognitive and physiological effects of the drug by examining the interaction of the effects of the drug with the effects of other theoretically motivated variables. For example, if the initial studies suggested that the drug had a negative effect on sustained attention processes, one might examine the effect of the drug on the episodic test of recognition memory when the study list contained many items (presumably, placing strong demands on sustained attention) or when the study list contained fewer items (presumably, placing fewers demands on sustained attention). If the drug had a negative effect on sustained attention processes, we would expect, all other things being equal, that it would have a larger negative effect on memory performance when the study list was longer.

Examining the effects of a drug in this two-step process has two advantages. The initial step helps identify theoretical hypotheses to be investigated. Moreover, failures to demonstrate cognitive specificity in the initial step deter investigators from further exploration of the drug, conserving scarce resources.

In considering the problem of cognitive specificity, it is important to note that this problem is not unique to cognitive psychopharmacology; it applies to a range of research endeavors. For example, aging affects a diffuse range of cognitive and brain functions (Schmiedek & Li, 2004). Similarly, brain damage resulting from neuro-degenerative diseases or various forms of traumatic brain insult may also reflect many mechanisms. Thus, demonstrating cognitive specificity should be seen as a standard challenge to research purporting to use changes in brain processes to explore theories of cognition.

Our recent studies of midazolam amnesia (Hirshman, Fisher, Henthorn, Arndt, & Passannante, 2002, in press; Hirshman et al., 1999), present an example of the two-step process described here. Pharmacological (anterograde) amnesia occurs when material presented subsequent to drug administration is poorly remembered on a later episodic memory test (e.g., free recall). One common interpretation of pharmacological amnesia (Veselis, Reinsel, Feschenko, & Wronski, 1997) is that it represents a general effect of the sedation that accompanies drug administration. To demonstrate evidence for cognitive specificity, we examined the effect of midazolam amnesia on episodic memory tasks (e.g., free recall), implicit memory tasks (e.g., perceptual identification), short-term memory tasks (e.g., digit span), and semantic memory tasks (e.g., category retrieval).

Our results demonstrated that midazolam produces differential impairment across cognitive tasks. Impairments are (1) large and dramatic on episodic memory tasks; (2) demonstrable, but relatively smaller on implicit memory tasks; (3) very small and detectable only under very limited circumstances on short-term memory tasks; and (4) to date, not detectable on retrieval in semantic memory tasks. For example, in comparing midazolam's effect on episodic memory and semantic memory tasks (Hirshman et al., 2003), we asked participants to retrieve items from semantic categories, and then we tested their later ability to recall the items they had retrieved from semantic categories. Our results demonstrated that even though midazolam had no detectable effect on the number of items participants retrieved from semantic categories (i.e., no effect on semantic memory), the participants were substantially impaired in their ability to recall these items later (i.e., dramatic effect on episodic memory). Similarly, in comparing the effects of midazolam on episodic and short-term memory, we demonstrated that even though midazolam impaired episodic recall of a list of words, as well as performance on a digit span task, the former effects were dramatically larger (η^2, a standard measure of effect size [Hays, 1981], was four times as large on the recall test).

This pattern of specific cognitive effects suggests that midazolam amnesia can not be attributed to sedation and that midazolam impairs cognitive and brain processes that have a dominant influence on episodic memory. Moreover, since midazolam only produces its effects when it is administered prior to the study period (Polster, McCarthy, O'Sullivan, Gray, & Park, 1993), it is reasonable to hypothesize that it impairs the encoding of information in episodic memory.

To test the hypothesis that midazolam impairs encoding in episodic memory per se (Step 2), Hirshman et al. (2001) compared the effect of midazolam on episodic and implicit memory tasks. In our experiment, word pairs were presented to participants during the study period and all aspects of the study period were identical in the episodic and implicit tests. Moreover, both tests presented participants with a stimulus word and asked them to output an associated word. The only difference was that in the episodic memory test, participants were asked to recall a word that accompanied the stimulus word during study, whereas in the implicit memory test, participants were simply asked to output the first word that came to mind (i.e., free association). Stimulus words from pairs that had not been presented in the study were also presented during each test, so a measure of memory (words outputted to old stimuli–words outputted to new stimuli) could be computed for both tasks. Our results demonstrated that midazolam had a dramatic effect on memory in the episodic memory task but had minimal effects on memory in the implicit memory task. These results provide converging evidence for the hypothesis that midazolam's effect are specific to episodic memory processes.

V. Concluding Remarks

Studies in cognitive psychopharmacology hold the promise of permitting experimental manipulations of brain processes. Engaging in these studies requires investigators to consider a range of technical issues regarding the dose, pharmacokinetics, and metabolism of the study drug. Similarly, a number of safety, compliance, design, and statistical issues arise in pharmacological studies that do not arise in traditional studies of cognition. Although these issues present challenges, pharmacological manipulations can produce provocative and theoretically incisive results, as well as provide new perspectives on neglected issues in the study of cognition (e.g., individual and group differences). Given these benefits, further studies exploring the role cognitive psychopharmacology can play in the study of cognition are merited.

References

Arndt, J., Passannante, A., & Hirshman, E. (2004). The effect of midazolam on implicit and explicit memory in category exemplar production and category cued recall. *Memory, 12*, 158–173.

Azen, R., & Budescu, D. (2003). The dominance analysis approach for comparing predictors in multiple regression. *Psychological Methods, 8*, 129–148.

Baethge, C., Reischies, F., Berghoefer, A., Buar, H., Schlattman, P., Whybrow, P. C., *et al.* (2002). Effects of *supraphysiological* doses of L-thyroxine on cognitive function in healthy individuals. *Psychiatry Research, 110*, 117–123.

Bell, S. L., Taylor, R. C., Singleton, E. G., Henningfield, J. E., & Heishman, S. J. (1999). Smoking after nicotine deprivation enhances cognitive performance and decreases tobacco craving in abstinent users. *Nicotine & Tobacco Research, 1*, 45–52.

Bitran, D., Purdy, R., & Kellogg, C. (1993). Anxiolytic effect of progesterone is associated with increases in cortical allopregnanolone and GABA-sub(A) receptor function. *Pharmacology, Biochemistry & Behavior, 45*, 423–428.

Boucart, M., de Visme, P., & Wagemans, J. (2000). Effect of benzodiazepine on temporal integration in object perception. *Psychopharmacology, 152*, 249–255.

Craik, F. I. M., & Tulving, E. (1975). Depth of processing and the retention of words in episodic memory. *Journal of Experimental Psychology: General, 104*, 268–294.

Davidson, M., Harris, M., & Rosenberg, C. (1987). Inverse relationship of metabolic clearance rate of insulin to body mass index. *Metabolism: Clinical and Experimental, 36*, 219–222.

Duka, T., Curran, H. V., Rusted, J. M., & Weingartner, H. J. (1996). Perspectives on cognitive psychopharmacology research. *Behavioural Pharmacology, 5*, 401–410.

Fournet, N., Moreaud, O., Roulin, J., Naegele, B., & Pellat, J. (2000). Working memory functioning in medicated Parkinson's disease patients and the effect of withdrawal of dopaminergic medication. *Neuropsychology, 14*, 247–253.

Ghoneim, M. M., & Mewaldt, S. (1975). Effects of diazepam and scopolamine on storage, retrieval and organizational processes in memory. *Psychopharmacologia, 44*, 257–262.

Gillund, G., & Shiffrin, R. (1984). A retrieval model for both recognition and recall. *Psychological Review, 91*(1), 1–67.

Hays, W. (1981). *Statistics*. 3rd ed. New York: Holt, Rinehart and Winston.

Hintzman, D. (2001). Similarity, global matching and judgments of frequency. *Memory & Cognition, 29*, 547–556.

Hirshman, E., Fisher, J., Henthorn, T., Arndt, J., & Passannante, A. (2002). Midazolam amnesia and dual-process models of the Word-Frequency Mirror Effect. *Journal of Memory and Language, 47*, 499–516.

Hirshman, E., Fisher, J., Henthorn, T., Arndt, J., & Passannante, A. (2003). Midazolam amnesia and retrieval from semantic memory. *Brain & Cognition, 53*, 427–432.

Hirshman, E., Merritt, P., Wang, C., Wierman, M., Budescu, D., Kohrt, W., *et al.* (2004). Androgenic and estrogenic metabolites influence the effects of dehydroepiandrosterone (DHEA) on cognition in post-menopausal women. *Hormones & Behavior, 45*, 144–155.

Hirshman, E., Passannante, A., & Arndt, J. (1999). The effect of midazolam on the modality-match effect in implicit memory. *Cognitive Brain Research, 7*, 473–479.

Hirshman, E., Passannante, A., & Arndt, J. (2001). Midazolam amnesia and conceptual processing in implicit memory. *Journal of Experimental Psychology: General, 130*, 453–465.

Hirshman, E., Rhodes, D., Zinser, M., & Merritt, P. (2004). The effect of tobacco abstinence on recognition memory, digit span recall and attentional vigilance. *Experimental and Clinical Psychopharmacology, 12*, 76–83.

Hogervorst, E., Williams, J., Budge, M., Riedel, W., & Jolles, J. (2000). The nature of the effect of female gonadal hormone replacement therapy on cognitive function in post-menopausal women. *Neuroscience, 101*, 485–512.

Hughes, J., & Hatsukami, D. (1986). Signs and symptoms of tobacco withdrawal. *Archives of General Psychiatry, 43*, 289–294.

Jones, J., Nguyen, A., Straub, M., Leidich, R., Veech, R., & Wolf, S. (1997). Use of DHEA in a patient with advanced prostate cancer: A case report and review. *Urology, 50*, 784–788.

Kehoe, P., Shoemaker, W., Arons, C., Triano, L., & Suresh, G. (1998). Repeated isolation stress in the neonatal rat: Relation to brain dopamine systems in the 10-day-old rat. *Behavioral Neuroscience, 112*, 1466–1474.

Lister, R. (1985). The amnesic action of benzodiazepines in man. *Neuroscience and Biobehavioral Reviews, 9*, 87–94.

Martin, P., Warwick, M., Dane, A., Hill, S., Giles, P., Phillips, P. J., *et al.* (2003). Metabolism, excretion and pharmacokinetics of rosuvastatin in healthy adult male volunteers. *Clinical Therapeutics, 25*, 2822–2835.

Mintzer, M., & Griffiths, R. (2001). Acute dose-effects of scopolamine on false recognition. *Psychopharmacology, 153*, 425–433.

Morales, A. J., Haubricht, R. H., Hwangt, J. Y., Asakura, H., & Yen, S. S. C. (1998). The effect of six months treatment with a 100 mg daily dose of dehydroepiandrosterone (DHEA) on circulating sex steroids, body composition and muscle strength in age-advanced men and women. *Clinical Endocrinology, 49*, 421–432.

Morrison, C. M. (2003). Interpret with caution: Multicollinearity in multiple regression of cognitive data. *Perceptual & Motor Skills, 97*, 80–82.

Mortola, J. F., & Yen, S. S. C. (1990). The effects of oral dehydroepiandrosterone on endocrine-metabolic parameters in postmenopausal women. *Journal of Clinical Endocrinology and Metabolism, 71*, 57–62.

Niiyama, S., Happle, R., & Hoffmann, R. (2001). Influence of estrogens on the androgen metabolism in different subunits of human hair follicles. *European Journal of Dermatology, 11*, 195–198.

Parsons, M., & Gold, P. (1992). Glucose enhancement of memory in elderly humans: An inverted-U dose-response curve. *Neurobiology of Aging, 13*, 401–404.

Polster, M., McCarthy, R., O'Sullivan, G., Gray, P., & Park, G. (1993). Midazolam-induced amnesia: Implications for the implicit/explicit memory distinction. *Brain & Cognition, 22*, 244–265.

Rodin, J., Mancuso, J., Granger, J., & Nelbach, E. (1991). Food cravings in relation to body mass index, restraint and estradiol levels: A repeated measures study in healthy women. *Appetite, 17*, 177–185.

Rugg, M. (Ed.). (1997). *Cognitive neuroscience.* Cambridge, MA: MIT Press.

Schmiedek, F., & Li, S. (2004). Toward an alternative representation for disentangling age-associated differences in general and specific cognitive abilities. *Psychology & Aging, 19*, 40–56.

Shepherd, R. (2004). How a cognitive psychologist came to seek universal laws. *Psychonomic Bulletin & Review, 11*, 1–23.

Solso, R. (1995). *Cognitive psychology.* (4th ed.). Boston: Allyn & Bacon.

Stewart-Williams, S., & Podd, J. (2004). The placebo effect: Dissolving the expectancy versus conditioning debate. *Psychological Bulletin, 130*, 324–340.

Stoelting, R. K. (1991). *Pharmacology and physiology in anesthetic practice.* Philadelphia: Lippincott.

Toth, J., & Hunt, R. (1990). Effect of generation on a word identification task. *Journal of Experimental Psychology: Learning Memory and Cognition, 16*, 993–1003.

Veselis, R., Reinsel, R., Feschenko, V., & Wronski, M. (1997). The comparative amnestic effects of midazolam, propofol, thiopental, and fentanyl at equisedative concentrations. *Anesthesiology, 87*, 749–764.

Weldon, M., Roediger, H., Beitel, D., & Johnston, T. (1995). Perceptual and conceptual processes in implicit and explicit tests with picture fragment and word fragment cues. *Journal of Memory & Language, 34*, 268–285.

Wolf, O. T., Naumann, O., Hellhammer, D., & Kirschbaum, C. (1998). Effects of dehyroepiandrosterone replacement in elderly men on event-related potential, memory and well being. *Journal of Gerontology: Medical Sciences, 53A*, M385–M390.

Zack, M., & Vogel-Sprott, M. (1995). Behavioral tolerance and sensitization to alocohol in humans: The contribution of learning. *Experimental and Clinical Psychopharmacology, 3*, 396–401.

INDEX

B

C

E

F

J

K

L

M

R

S

T

CONTENTS OF RECENT VOLUMES

Volume 33

Volume 34

Volume 35

Volume 36

Volume 37

Volume 38

Volume 39

Volume 40

Volume 41

Volume 42

Volume 43

Volume 44